SUBSIDIA BIBLICA

25

subsidia biblica – 25

ROBERT F. O'TOOLE, S.J.

Luke's Presentation of Jesus: A Christology

EDITRICE PONTIFICIO ISTITUTO BIBLICO – ROMA 2004

ISBN 88-7653-625-6
© E.P.I.B. – Roma – 2004
Iura editionis et versionis reservantur

EDITRICE PONTIFICIO ISTITUTO BIBLICO

Piazza della Pilotta, 35 - 00187 Roma, Italia

In memory of three women whom I deeply admired and respected –

Mrs. Peggy McGuire, my sister

Ms. Helen Earner, my aunt

Mrs. Maureen McCarthy, my dear friend

Preface

The present volume represents the results of research and reflections on a topic that has fascinated me since my earliest days of teaching, namely, Luke's Christology. I have tried to remain faithful to Luke and to summarize his thoughts about Jesus. Scholars and students of Luke will have to decide whether I have done this accurately or not.

This book would have been impossible without the help of a number of institutions and individuals. After my term as Rector of the Pontifical Biblical Institute, the new Rector, the Rev. Stephen F. Pisano, S.J., was kind enough to grant me a sabbatical to write this book. The Missouri Province of the Society of Jesus generously agreed to pay my living expenses during the sabbatical, and I benefited considerably from the liberal use of the Pius XII Library of Saint Louis University and from the kind hospitality of the Jesuit Hall Community there.

Many individuals encouraged me during the writing of this book, and I wish to thank all of them. Two of my colleagues from the Pontifical Biblical Institute proved particularly helpful. The Rev. John J. Kilgallen, S.J., carefully read over the entire manuscript and made many helpful corrections and suggestions. The Rev. James H. Swetnam, S.J., the Editor of the series "Subsidia Biblica," accepted my manuscript into his series and has been exceptionally accommodating both in readying my book for publication and in doing the indices. The Rev. John J. Mueller, S.J., Chairman of the Department of Theological Studies at Saint Louis University, also looked over several chapters and made a number of beneficial observations. Whatever errors this book contains are, I fear, mine.

Finally, the McCarthy Family Foundation has generously paid for the publication expenses.

To all of these friends and benefactors I express my grateful thanks with the hope that the quality of this volume matches the generosity of their goodness.

I am grateful above all to Almighty God.

Rev. Robert F. O'Toole, S.J.
Pontifical Biblical Institute
Rome, April 22, Feast of the Mother of the Society of Jesus, 2004

Table of Contents

Introduction

A study of Luke's Christology corresponds very well with his own desire to tell his readers about Jesus and his meaning for human history. Luke has a theme of seeking to see Jesus (Luke 2:28-49; 9:9bc; 11:29?; 19:3-4.10; 23:8; 24:5; cf. Acts 17:27) and a number of times has someone ask who Jesus is (Luke 5:21; 7:20.49; 8:25; 9:9bc.18; 22:67.70; 23:3). There is no denying that, since Luke wrote after Jesus' resurrection, he could and did read back into Jesus' earthly life his own faith about Jesus which properly belongs to his risen life, and the present study must take this into account. Also, any attempt to describe Luke's Christology without including Jesus' earthly existence is misguided, for Luke insists that the earthly Jesus and the risen Jesus are the same([1]). Our general approach to Luke's Christology will be to attempt to gather everything that he says about Jesus and to organize this information in an intelligible, summary fashion. However, since that data have been considered elsewhere([2]), we will not consider how the disciples say and do the same things as Jesus or how Luke thus establishes continuity among the OT, Jesus and the Christian community and also challenges Christians to imitate Christ. To present all of the other data, we will naturally use the titles predicated of Jesus; for although many scholars correctly point out that a consideration of the titles for Jesus does not constitute a thorough methodology for studying

---

[1] Keck, "New Testament Christology," 337, makes the general observation, "Even the current emphasis on the identity of the earthly Jesus and the exalted Christ is not really appropriate to texts which never separated them to begin with."

[2] See O'Toole, *The Unity*, 62-94.

Luke's Christology([3]), in fact, any consideration that does not include the titles will be definitely flawed. On the other hand, there is some truth to the statement that Luke mingles the meanings of titles with one another, but he does not do this to such an extent that each title loses all of its individual meaning and thus can be reduced to the others. Rather the titles are similar in that they all refer to the same person, Jesus, and so are naturally associated with one another. However, each time a title occurs, it needs to be studied in its context to determine its meaning and thus how Luke may have employed it to develop his Christology. So, the titles have their importance.

Most scholars now hold that Luke wrote both his Gospel and the Acts of the Apostles and wanted to tell both the story of Jesus and of the early Christian community; and so, his two volumes constitute a unity([4]). Hence, the present study must address the contents of both Luke's volumes. It is common knowledge that the Septuagint (LXX) had a considerable influence on Luke's composition([5]), and that most scholars now accept the two-source theory that Luke copies from the Gospel of Mark and from another source that he had in common with Matthew. Obviously, there is also "L," Luke's own sources. However, even if Luke often depends on his sources for the expression of his Christology, the meaning he attributes to the various aspects of these sources may well indicate his own personal understanding. Luke can and does give different meanings or nuances to Christological concepts. Moreover, even if Luke does not appear to change the meaning of a given expression or title found in his sources, still that expression or title becomes part of his overall

---

[3] For instance, Conzelmann, *The Theology of Luke*, 170, 172, 179, claims that Luke is no longer aware of the original peculiarities of titles and so Jesus the prophet, the holy one, the righteous one and the servant ($\pi\alpha\hat{\iota}\varsigma$) have become traditional and in Luke's view have the same meaning as the other titles, Christ and Lord. He also maintains that in the use of titles, Luke makes no distinction between the historical and the exalted Christ.

[4] J. Verheyden, "The Unity of Luke-Acts," 3-56, esp. 3 and 56. See also Baarlink, "Die Bedeutung der Prophetenzitate," 491 and Neirynck, "Luke 4,16-30 and the Unity of Luke-Acts," 357-395.

[5] However, in the conclusion to his fine book, *Proclamation from Prophecy*, 278, Bock contends, "The conceptual arguments presented in Luke-Acts from the OT for Christology are just as possible from the Hebrew text as they are from the LXX."

presentation and world-view (*Weltanschauung*) and so normally changes meaning or nuance. When someone writes, he unites information that he has gathered from others as well as his own thoughts; he provides a whole picture, which, if studied only in part, is distorted and misrepresented. Consequently, the aim in this book is to provide a total picture of Luke's Christology.

This study does not depend on establishing the precise literary form of Luke-Acts or of either volume, should they be different in this regard. Nonetheless, Luke-Acts do bear a striking resemblance to the portrayal of persons found in the historical books of the Old Testament.

Methodology

This is not a historical-critical study of NT Christology, although data from these studies that bear on Luke's Christology will be considered. Rather, we will be using composition criticism, a specification of redaction criticism. This methodology grew out of the fruitless search in Acts of the Apostles for sources([6]). To be sure, there are sources in Acts; but Luke has apparently rewritten much of the material, and so there is not always the possibility of delineating with much precision these sources or of demonstrating how Luke changed them. The solution was composition criticism. When sources can be delineated, as in the case of Mark's Gospel or "Q," then we will show how Luke has used them. However, in other situations we will study the present text as we have it and assume that there was a final editor, whom we will name Luke, who composed Luke-Acts. We shall also assume that we can study this editor's final composition([7]). Consequently, the main aim of composition criticism is to determine what the final author (editor) wanted to say to his readers or, if one wishes, what the present text tells us. Obviously, we are not thinking of an editor who has made only a few editorial changes. The general rule in composition criticism is that one can use any argument that helps him or her gain a deeper understanding of the author's or text's meaning. One can likewise use insights or techniques from other methodologies, but the

---

[6] Minear, "Luke's Use of the Birth Stories," 111-118, reflects on this same problem in the Gospel.

[7] The weakness of Resseguie's ("The Lukan Portrait of Christ," 5-6) reflections is that he fails to see that an author determines everything he writes and so makes the whole presentation his own.

main purpose must always be kept in mind: what does the author want to say? The basic rule and control are that the argument used should prove convincing or at least probable.

Naturally, composition criticism becomes more complicated when applied to a topic like Luke's Christology; for such a study must cover both volumes and every passage in which a particular theme is found. We will need to consider these passages as well as the word-pattern that a given theme normally embraces and then to summarize the results.

Many other authors have studied Luke's Christology([8]), and H.D. Buckwalter provides a good survey of the Christologies which, scholars have argued, principally determine what Luke says about Jesus in Luke-Acts([9]). Our main scope is not to determine which aspect of Christology Luke emphasizes, although the evidence supports the conclusion that the dominant characteristic is Jesus as savior, but rather to present the whole of this Christology. After all, Luke has a multifaceted description of Jesus; surely he emphasizes certain aspects; but he wants to present a complete portrait. On the other hand, we accept Meeks' caution about the study of the real Jesus, "Of course, there is more, there is an ineffable center we cannot grasp"([10]).

It is important to appreciate the extremely difficult task Luke and the other NT authors faced in portraying Jesus. Jesus' family and his early followers only slowly came to an understanding of who he was, and this reality was coupled with the later problem faced by the NT authors of how personally to express the belief of the early Christians with whom they were associated. These factors naturally led to unevenness in Luke's portrait of Jesus, for sometimes he is bringing out this gradual perception; at others, the later, deeper understanding of who Jesus is. Haenchen rightly

---

[8] The bibliography provided in this book testifies to this fact. See also Radl, *Das Lukas-Evangelium*, 81-83, for further bibliographical information.

[9] *The Character and Purpose*, 6-24. Buckwalter himself (30; cf. 281-284) aims at detecting a *most probable scenario* from the Lucan material, which makes good sense of Luke's reason for writing, his literary affinities with the synoptic tradition and Paul, and the part his Christology plays in this. Buckwalter wants to determine how Christology is central to Luke's purpose and in all probability governs what he has chosen to say Christologically. Our task is not an easy one since some authors like Schweizer, *The Good News according to Luke*, 381-385, claim that Luke does not offer a clear Christology.

[10] Meeks, "Asking Back to Jesus' Identity," 50.

wrote that Luke was not a systematic theologian but did have his own theology[11]. Certainly, Luke was not a systematic theologian and very likely would have had many fewer readers than he has actually had, should that have been his style of presentation. Luke is rather a believer who wants to assure others of the reliability of the instruction they have received (Luke 1:4). His two volumes, although not as systematic as an academic presentation, have a definite message about the activity of God and Christ in human history; and this message has been studied through the centuries. So, although Luke's presentation of Jesus is not systematic, he provides his reader with an overall picture of who Jesus is. The present volume attempts to discover this Lucan portrait.

In his two volumes, Luke faced still other challenges. If for the sake of argument we grant that he thought Jesus was divine, Luke stood before the daunting task of writing about the God-man. Is it possible to do this without at times giving the impression that Jesus was subordinate to the Father or to the Spirit, or that Luke held for a certain adoptionism[12]? In addition, if the Jewish doctrine of there being only one God be accepted, as in fact the early Christians believed, how could Luke write of Jesus as divine? He could not call Jesus, "God," for no one would have claimed that Jesus is the same person as God (the Father). Luke had to find other ways to express the Christians' faith in Jesus.

The study of Luke's Christology calls for a methodology that can remain open to what Luke, the author of Luke-Acts, wishes to say. Although we all have our theories and, at times, even preconceived notions, it is obvious that, if these are not in tune with how Luke composes his two volumes and with his way of thinking, we will end up concluding to our own ideas, not to his. Luke did write for Christians. The meaning that Luke attaches to anything that he says about Jesus derives primarily from the Jesus story itself, and not from the meaning given that concept in

---

[11] *The Acts*, 91. It is in this theological context that Ernst, *Lukas: Ein theologisches Portrait*, 105-111, offers his thoughtful reflections on Luke's Christology.

[12] Radl, *Das Lukas-Evangelium*, 83, comments on the difficulty that authors face, "Das Hauptproblem ist die einmalige Stellung der Person Jesu zwischen Gott und Menschen . . . . Lukas deutet für Jesus weder eine himmlische Präexistenz noch eine Adoption durch Gott an."

Jewish or other traditions([13]). If one reflects on it, this makes perfect sense, for Luke is a Christian and so centers on Jesus and on Christian faith. He rightly subordinated his titles and sources to what he knows about Jesus and about the Christian understanding of who Jesus is([14]).

---

[13] On these points, Tuckett, "The Christology of Luke-Acts," 133-164, esp., 161-164 is surely correct. However, Tuckett's approach to the question of Luke's Christology hinders him from viewing all the data in Luke-Acts on this topic.

[14] According to Coleridge, *The Birth of the Lucan Narrative*, 219, the Lucan narrator uses various techniques "to subvert an old world in order that it may appear in the narrative that both a new world and a new mode of recognition come to birth in Jesus."

CHAPTER I
Jesus, a Human Being

How does Luke portray Jesus as a human being[15]? At his birth Jesus is wrapped in swaddling clothes and has a manger for his crib; these, along with the presence of the shepherds, underline his humble beginnings. His parents were pious Jews. Of interest is the question of Jesus' father. His supposed father's name was Joseph (Luke 3:23; cf. 1:27; 2:4.16; 4:22); and his mother's name was Mary[16]. Almost all of these passages are unique to Luke, who needed this clarity to establish the identity of Jesus' true father and to justify statements like that of the child Jesus, who knows that he has to be in his Father's house (2:49). Of course, everyone not involved in God's actions in Jesus' life views him as a normal human being. In Acts 1:14, Luke speaks of "brothers" but does not clarify their exact relationship to Jesus (cf. Luke 8:19-21)[17], although at Jesus' conception he definitely identifies Mary as a virgin (1:27.34; cf. 3:23). In accord with Jewish customs, Jesus is presented in the temple; and at twelve years of age, he participates in the annual pilgrimage to Jerusalem for the Passover. He remains there after his parents' departure and in his Father's house amazes everyone in his interaction with teachers of the Law. Nonetheless, he returns to Galilee with his parents and is obedient to them. By way of summary, Luke states that the infant Jesus, with God's grace, matures in

---

[15] See Bouttier, "L'humanité de Jésus," 33-43; Fletcher-Louis, *Luke-Acts: Angels*, 20.

[16] Luke 1:27.30.34.38; 2:5.16.19; Acts 1:14; cf. Luke 1:39.41.46.56; 2:34.

[17] See Blinzler, *Die Brüder*, 73-82; Bock, *Luke 1:1 – 9:50*, 752-753 and Fitzmyer, *The Gospel According to Luke I–IX*, 723-724. Nolland, *Luke 1 – 9:21*, 394, summarizes the situation, "The matter is of no importance to Luke." Luke tones down the negative aspects of Mark 3:31-35. Jesus' relatives do not call him and are prevented from approaching him because of the large crowd. In Luke, family ties are viewed more positively to describe Jesus' followers.

his awareness of God and his providence and is popular with the people (cf. 2:40.52), but reports nothing more about the long subsequent period of Jesus' life until we encounter him after the baptism. Consequently, in the Infancy Narrative Luke leaves no doubt about Jesus' humanity; but as we will likewise see below, he also portrays his uniqueness. Certainly, Mary's memory of all these events serves as a model for the readers (vv. 19.51).

In the rest of this chapter, in accord with our methodology, composition criticism, we will consider those moments and aspects of Jesus' life which Luke reports. However, we will not consider Jesus' passion since it will be considered in various other chapters.

Jesus of Nazareth

A number of times Luke offers summaries of Jesus' active ministry[18]. His living conditions were not ideal; at times, he had nowhere to lay his head (Luke 9:58). Apparently, he did not always sleep indoors, for he spent some nights on the Mount of Olives (21:37). Also, more than any other NT writer, Luke writes of Jesus' being from Nazareth[19]; and most of the passages in the present paragraph are unique to Luke-Acts. Jesus grew up in Nazareth, and people later use the name of this town to identify him. The annunciation to Mary occurred in Nazareth (1:26); and since Jesus was from the house of David, Joseph and Mary leave from there to go to Bethlehem (2:4), but they return with Jesus to Nazareth (2:39; cf. v. 51) to live. Jesus begins his public life in the synagogues of Galilee; he enters the one in Nazareth and there interprets the Sacred Scripture in relationship to himself (4:14-21). Even evil spirits address him as "Jesus of Nazareth" (4:34), and by the time of Acts 24:5 the Christians are described as the sect of the Nazarenes. The ordinary Jewish people (Luke 18:37) and the disciples refer to Jesus "of Nazareth" (24:19). Luke himself summarizes Jesus' earthly ministry as follows: "How God anointed Jesus of Nazareth with the Holy Spirit and power; how he went about doing

---

[18] Luke 2:30-32.34; 4:18-19; 5:32; 19:10; Acts 1:21-22; 2:22-23; 10:37-39; 13:23-29.

[19] Bruce, *The Acts*, 122, discusses the meaning of Ναζαραῖος. Obviously, Ναζαρυη-νός (Luke 4:34; 24:19), Ναζαρέθ (1:26; 2:4.39.51; Acts 10:38) and Ναζαρά (Luke 4:16) are also relevant to this consideration. See also Cadbury, "The Titles of Jesus in Acts," 356-357.

good and healing all who were oppressed by the devil, for God was with him" (Acts 10:38). Through this same designation for the risen Jesus, Luke draws a radical connection between the earthly and risen Jesus and so is naturally opposed to any interpretation which proposes a separation between these two periods of Jesus' existence. Jesus of Nazareth was confirmed by God with miracles and signs (Acts 2:22), and in his name the paralytic at the Beautiful Gate is healed and can walk around (Acts 3:6; 4:10). Stephen is accused of saying that Jesus the Nazarene will destroy the temple and will change the customs of Moses (Acts 6:14). Paul himself was convinced that he had to do many things against Jesus the Nazarene (Acts 26:9), and under this same designation, the risen Jesus identifies himself with the Christians who are being persecuted (Acts 22:8; cf. 9:4; 26:15). By way of summary, Jesus grew up in Nazareth and was active in the whole of Galilee. During his earthly life and after his resurrection, both friend and foe knew him as Jesus of Nazareth. Thus, Luke does not allow us to lose sight of Jesus as a person who actually existed nor to separate the risen Jesus from his earthly existence.

Jesus' Baptism

Luke, in an apocalyptic scene, expresses Jesus' act of baptism and praying by using a genitive absolute. He thus emphasizes the opening of the heavens, the descent of the Spirit "in bodily form" and the words of the voice from heaven[20], "You are my beloved Son. On you my favor rests" (Luke 3:22)[21]. In fact, these three aspects of the experience are arranged in climactic order, the words of the heavenly voice being the most important. Moreover, Luke has completely eliminated from this scene John the Baptist, so there is no need to explain further, as must Matthew, that John is not superior to Jesus. The following observations relate to our discussion. According to the present participle, προσευχομένου, Jesus is praying after his baptism; and during the course of this prayer, he has a profound spiritual experience. Luke portrays this experience as a vision since he alone writes of "in visible form like a dove"; on the other hand, he provides no clear indication as to who saw it. Logically, at least, Jesus did. Luke 4:18-19, "The Spirit of the Lord is upon me; therefore he has

---

[20] J.B. Green, *The Gospel of Luke*, 185; A. Plummer, *Gospel according to S. Luke*, 98-99.

[21] Cf. v. 38; 1:35; 9:35; 22:70; Gn 22:2.12.16; Ps 2:7; Is 42:1.

anointed me" (cf. Acts 10:38), makes clear that Jesus' baptism looks to his mission. Jesus does begin his ministry, "full of the Spirit" (Luke 4:1; cf. v.14); and in the latter verse, only Luke inserts, "in the power of the Spirit." In later chapters we will see the significance of Jesus being called son and the one on whom God's favor rests.

Genealogy of Jesus

Jesus' baptism is followed by his genealogy[22], and Luke again reflects on Jesus' humanity. Obviously, a genealogy conveys the importance of the person. Luke's genealogy of Jesus is more complicated than at first appears, for right after the baptism, at the very beginning of the genealogy, we are informed that Joseph was the supposed father of Jesus (Luke 3:23). The genealogy itself ends with the words, "son of Adam, son of God" (v. 38). Through the mention of Adam, Luke relates Jesus to all humanity; and according to a number of scholars, Luke is presenting Jesus as a second Adam[23]. This claim would be much stronger if the genealogy ended with "of Adam." It would seem rather than Luke views Jesus primarily as God's son. At the baptism, the voice from heaven identifies Jesus as "my son." Further, at the beginning of the genealogy, Joseph is Jesus' *supposed* father. Finally, immediately after the genealogy, "son of God" will twice (4:3.9) appear in the temptation scene[24]. Probably by ending the genealogy with "son of God" (although grammatically this phrase primarily refers to Adam), Luke wants his reader to recall these earlier instances and particularly 1:34-35, which first clarified that Joseph was not Jesus' father. This interpretation that Luke regards Jesus as God's son will be discussed in more detail in a later chapter.

---

[22] For the possible Greco-Roman influence on this genealogy, cf. Kurz, "Luke 3:23-38," 169-172. See also Hood, "The Genealogies of Jesus," 1-15.

[23] Lagrange, *Évangile selon Saint Luc*, 126

[24] Fitzmyer, *The Gospel According to Luke I –IX*, 504; cf. 498; Nolland, *Luke 1 – 9:20*, 174; although he sees Jesus as the second Adam; Rigaux, *Témoignage*, 144, writes of a reference in the passage to Jesus as Son of God, "Il n'est pas certain que cette spéculation soit voulue par Lc. Elle correspond en tout cas à sa manière de penser." Without denying the universal significance of Adam, Bock, *Luke 1:1 – 9:50*, 360, concludes, "So Jesus' sonship in its narrow and broad senses links 3:21-22 to 3:23-38."

Jesus' Temptation

Temptation is a common human experience, and so again Jesus demonstrates his humanity (Luke 4:1-12)[25]. In the temptation story, Luke contrasts Jesus' answers with Israel's actions in the desert. J.B. Green has listed a number of similarities between Jesus' temptation and Israel in the desert[26]. We are particularly interested in Israel's being afflicted with hunger and then being fed with manna (Dt 8:3). Also, they are instructed that there was only one God and no others (Dt 6:4-15; cf. 9:15-21; Acts 7:39-43) and that they were not to put the Lord God to the test (Dt 6:16; cf. 9:22-24; Ex 17:1-7). Israel failed these temptations, but Jesus does not; through his temptation in the desert Jesus shows himself loyal to God and faithful to his will.

Doing His Father's Will

Doing the Father's will is at the heart of Jesus' existence. As noted above, Jesus must be in his Father's house or about his business (2:49); the "must" of this verse indicates that this is God's will[27]. The scripture passages which function as the heart of the programmatic passage (vv. 14[16]-[30]44) really constitute a statement of the ministry that God has given Jesus. In this context, there is not the least hint that Jesus is not in total agreement with what God asks of him. This attitude explains his conversation with Moses and Elijah about the "exodus" which he was destined to fulfill ($\tau\grave{\eta}\nu$ ἔξοδον αὐτοῦ, ἣν ἤμελλεν πληροῦν) in Jerusalem (9:31) and his subsequent action of setting his face firmly to go up to Jerusalem (9:51). Jesus again reveals his complete acceptance and joy because the Father has selected the disciples, the "simple," as the recipients of his salvation and has shared everything, including mutual knowledge and the right to reveal it, with Jesus (10:21-22). Later, despite the frightening possibility of his passion, Jesus is willing to endure it, if that is what the Father wants (22:39-46)[28]. Jesus is tempted and, under the shadow of

---

[25] E. Schweizer, *The Good News according to Luke*, 84.

[26] J.B. Green, *The Gospel of Luke*, 192-193.

[27] O'Toole, *The Unity*, 27-28.

[28] Feldkämper, *Der betende Jesus*, 224-250, esp, 249-250.

the passion, truly challenged; but he always wills to do what the Father asks of him and does it.

Prayer[29]

Jesus knows that one is to worship only God (Luke 4:7-8); and, of course, prayer is the natural response to God's saving activity. More than the other Synoptics, Luke has stressed Jesus' prayer and developed this topic. Jesus is devoted to prayer (5:16), can spend the night in prayer (6:12) and regularly prays before important events (3:21; 6:12; 9:18a.28-29; 11:1; 22:39-46)[30]. The Our Father (11:1-4) provides an example of how Jesus praised and petitioned the Father. Jesus likewise prays that Peter's faith may not fail (22:32)[31] and, if the verse be genuine, asks forgiveness for those who are crucifying him (23:34a). His Last Supper is a prayer of thanksgiving which contains the Greek word εὐχαριστήσας which the Lucan account, in contrast to Matthew and Mark, mentions twice (22:17.19-20; cf. 9:17). His final prayer in the Gospel is one of confidence in the Father to whom he entrusts his spirit (23:46). Twice, once at his baptism (3:21-22) and again at the Transfiguration (9:28-36; cf. 10:21-24)[32], Jesus' prayer is followed by an intense religious experience. Finally, Jesus taught his disciples to pray with confidence: God is more generous than any earthly father is, and will give his Holy Spirit to anyone who asks him (11:5-13)—they are to pray always and not to lose heart. Thus, Jesus was radically aware of the significance of God for human existence, and realized the importance of prayer. Often Jesus prayed alone, and this fact suggests the unique and incommunicable aspects of these encounters with his Father[33]. Jesus' prayers often occur before important

---

[29] Cf. Trites, "The Prayer Motif in Luke-Acts," 168-186

[30] There is the question about whether Luke 22:43-44 are genuine. Metzger, *A Textual Commentary*, 151; for a recent summary of the various scholarly opinions, see Bock, *Luke 9:51 – 24:53*, 1763-1764, who favors their inclusion.

[31] Crump, *Jesus the Intercessor*, 175, rightly claims that prayer is a chief means for resisting temptation and that Luke presents Jesus as a model in so doing.

[32] We would have another example, if Luke 22:43-44 is genuine.

[33] George, *Études sur l'œuvre de Luc*, 415-417.

events and so are of petition, confidence and thanksgiving and sometimes lead to mystical experiences([34]).

Jesus frequents the synagogues([35]), and Luke associates him from his youth with the temple([36]) and with Jerusalem([37]). Consequently, Jesus is linked with the places most important to Jewish religious life; he is a pious Jew who does what pious Jews do. These centers provided Jesus with an audience and a platform for his activity.

Jesus, the Teacher([38])

Jesus' disciples and contemporaries viewed him as a "teacher"([39]), but neither ῥαββι nor ραββουνι (Aramaic) appears in Luke-Acts. Since Luke's intended readers included non-Jews, he chose to use "teacher" (διδάσκαλος)([40]), which he predicates once of John the Baptist (3:12) and frequently of Jesus. Luke was interested in the title, for he not only took it over from Mark, but has often introduced the terms for "teacher" (διδάσκαλός—7:40; 11:45; 12:13; 19:39; 20:39; 21:7) and "to teach" (διδάσκειν—6:6; 13:22.26; 23:5)([41]) where they are not found in his sources, Matthew and "Q." Jesus teaches in synagogues (Luke 4:15.31-33; 6:6; 13:10) and in the temple (19:47; 20:1; 21:37; cf 22:53). Once (20:21), Luke even introduces a second "to teach" into a verse which

---

[34] For an extended treatment of Jesus' prayer, see Crump, *Jesus the Intercessor*, esp., 152-153, 201-203, 237-241 and Feldkämper, *Der betende Jesus*. However, "prayer" for Crump includes more than seems justified and, as he himself recognizes, must be viewed in relationship to Luke's whole Christology.

[35] Luke 4:15-30.33.38.44; 6:6; 13:10.

[36] Luke 2:22-38.46-50; 4:9; 19:45 – 21:38; 22:52-53.

[37] Luke 2:22-38.41-50; 4:9; 9:3.5.53; 13:22.32-33.34; 17:11; 18:31; 19:11.28; 24:51.

[38] Normann, *Christos Didaskalos*, 45-54; see also Rieser, *Jesus als Lehrer* and Rengstorf, διδάσκαλος, 152-157.

[39] Luke 7:40; 8:49; 9:38; 10:25; 11:45; 12:13; 18:18; 19:39; 20:21.28.39; 21:7; 22:11.

[40] Cf. Mt 12x; Mk 12x; Lk 17x; Jn 8x; Acts 1x.

[41] In the NT διδάσκειν occurs 14 times in Matthew, 17 times in Mark, 17 times in Luke, 9 times in John, and 16 times in Acts.

already contains the word "teacher." Like the rabbis, Jesus sat while he taught (5:3; cf. 4:20; 10:39); and Luke passes on the "Q" wisdom saying, "A disciple is not above the teacher, but everyone who is fully qualified will be like the teacher" (6:40), but makes no mention of the relationship between a slave and his master (Mt 10:24-25; cf. Jn 13:16; 15:20). Apparently, Luke does not want to put the relationship between a slave and his master on the same level as that between a disciple and Jesus. The appearance of the verb "to teach" in Acts is in part explained by Luke's portrayal of the disciples as imitating Jesus.

"Jesus as teacher" should not be isolated from related Lucan concepts and so it is a more inclusive topic than at first may appear. For instance, below we will see that in the programmatic passage Luke 4:14-44 διδάσκειν can embrace both "preach the good news" (εὐαγγε-λίζεσθαι; vv. 18, 43) and "proclaim" (κηρύσσειν; vv. 18-19, 44); also the same needs to be applied to "say" (λέγειν, vv. 21, 24, 25) and "said" (εἰπεῖν vv. 23-24). Actually, Luke does not often predicate "preach the good news" (vv. 18, 43; 7:22 [passive], 8:1; 16:16 [passive]; 20:1) or "proclaim" (8:1; 24:47 [passive]) of Jesus. In two summary statements, Luke employs one of his favorite stylistic devices, double expressions. In 8:1 Luke ascribes to Jesus both "preach the good news" and "proclaim"; in 20:1 both "preach the good news" and "teach." It would seem that Luke views these three expressions as closely related. If one considers "to say or tell" and "to speak," the Synoptic parallel can indicate that the given verb in Luke contains the nuance of "teaching"; for instead of "to speak" in 9:11 or "to say" in 9:22, the Marcan parallels have "to teach"; for the expression "to say" in Luke 6:20, the Matthean parallel has "to teach." More importantly, we not infrequently find "to say"(42), "to tell"(43) and "to speak"(44) in contexts where Luke also speaks of Jesus as teacher or teaching; and so these passages relate to teaching. Surely, each of these words keeps its denotation, but at times Luke has also attributed to them the nuance of teaching since that is Jesus' main activity in the given passage. Moreover, Luke in many other passages has used these same three

---

[42] Luke 4:21.24.25.31; 11:1; 12:16; 19:40; and all the instances in 19:47 – 21:38.

[43] Luke 4:23-24; 7:40; 10:30; 11:2.5.46; 12:15-16.42; 13:15-16.23.32; 18:19.22.24.27.29; 19:40; all instances of this verb in 19:47 – 21:38.

[44] Luke 5:4.21; 8:49; 11:37.

verbs to report Jesus' teachings, but this can only be established by studying the nature of what is said in each passage. This book is not the forum in which to address this question in detail; but below, both under how and what Jesus teaches, reference will be made to those passages judged to fit into this category and relevant to our discussion. Certainly, Jesus' teaching covers a considerable portion of Luke's Gospel.

Some passages where Jesus is portrayed as a "teacher" carry much more weight than do others. In the Infancy Narrative, Jesus' parents find him in the temple, sitting among the teachers, listening to them and asking them questions; and everyone was amazed at his understanding and answers (Luke 2:46-47). F. O'Fearghail([45]), following Fitzmyer and Kilgallen, interprets the scene as foreshadowing Jesus' future role as teacher, and such foreshadowing of future greatness in an infancy story is a common theme of ancient bibliographical writing. Moreover, by means of the audience's amazement Luke implies that Jesus will be outstanding as a teacher. We will study Luke 2:41-51a in more detail in the consideration of Jesus as "Son of God"; suffice it here to say that, even though a variety of structures has been proposed for Luke's Infancy Narrative, some observations are definitely true. In reality, Luke 2:41-51a is not an infancy account, since Jesus is twelve years old; rather it is a high point of Luke 1–2 and a transition to the body of the Gospel([46]). This is the only time in the Infancy Narrative Jesus speaks; he answers his mother's concerned question with the words, "Why did you search for me? Did you not know that I had to be in my Father's house" (2:49). Whether one translates ἐν τοῖς τοῦ πατρός μου as "my Father's house"([47]) or "my Father's affairs," the phrase must include Jesus' teaching; for that is what he was doing in the temple. Such activity befits the temple. Consequently, Jesus at an important moment in the narrative speaks for the first time; and his

---

[45] O'Fearghail, *The Introduction to Luke-Acts*, 139. See also Kilgallen, "Luke 2,41-50: Foreshadowing," 553-559.

[46] Bock, *Luke 1:1 – 9:50*, 259; see also Fitzmyer, *The Gospel According to Luke I–IX*, 434-435, but I cannot agree with his statement, "The story of the finding in the Temple is in reality an independent unit . . . which could be dropped without any great loss to the narrative."

[47] Plummer, *St. Luke*, 77-78; see also Nolland, *Luke 1:1 – 9:20*, 131-132.

summary statement about being in his Father's house embraces his remark-
ably intelligent interaction with the teachers in the temple.

Later, as Jesus goes through one town or village after another and
makes his way to Jerusalem, Luke, in passages unique to him, recapitulates
Jesus' activity as "teaching." "He went through cities and towns teaching"
(Luke 13:22), "You taught in our streets" (13:26), "He stirs up the people
by his teaching throughout the whole of Judea, from Galilee, where he
began to this very place" (23:5; cf. Acts 10:37)([48]). The last passage covers Jesus' ministry from its beginning up to that moment. When the scribes
and chief priests send spies to trap Jesus, they begin their question to him
with the words, "Teacher, we know that you are right in what you say and
teach, and you show deference to no one, but teach the way of God in
accordance with the truth" (Luke 20:21). Despite the hypocrisy of these
opponents and given the irony of the passage, Luke wants his readers to
accept this statement as an accurate evaluation of Jesus' teaching. Even
his opponents admit that he was not intimidated by anybody but truthfully
taught the way of God. Also, only according to Luke, during the period
portrayed from 19:47 ("Each day he was teaching in the temple") to 21:38
(cf. v. 37: "He would teach in the temple by day"), Jesus was teaching
daily in the temple.

At the very beginning of Acts, Luke describes his Gospel, "In the
first book, Theophilus, I wrote about all that Jesus did and taught from the
beginning . . ." (Acts 1:1: Τὸν μὲν πρῶτον λόγον ἐποιησάμην περὶ
πάντων, ὦ Θεόφιλε, ὧν ἤρξατο ὁ ᾽Ιησοῦς ποιεῖν καὶ διδάσκειν . .
.). This passage calls for a number of observations. First, Luke feels that
he can summarize his whole Gospel as "all that Jesus did and taught."
Secondly, since "did" in this phrasing refers to all of Jesus' deeds, it is only
reasonable to assume that "taught" embraces all that Jesus said in the
Gospel. So, Luke is willing to summarize everything Jesus said, preached
and proclaimed in the Gospel as "teaching." This helps us appreciate the
weight Luke gives to this term. Likewise, "all that Jesus did and taught"
may not only summarize the Gospel, but, depending on how one
understands and translates ἤρξατο, may look to the book of Acts as well;

---

[48] Lagrange, *Évangile selon Saint Luc*, 578, notes the slight exaggeration in this verse
but defends its phrasing.

for a possible rendering of the verse would be, "about all that Jesus *began*
to do and to teach."(^{49}).

Luke's programmatic passage (4:14[16]-[30]44)(^{50}) should be considered along with Acts 1:1; for after Jesus disappears from the synagogue
of Nazareth, he goes to Capernaum and in that synagogue on the Sabbath
teaches the people who are astounded by what he says (Luke 4:31-32).
According to Luke, Jesus immediately begins to carry out the mission he
received in vv. 18-19. His teaching with authority, freeing the man from
the unclean spirit and curing Peter's mother-in-law and all of the other sick
correspond to the prophetic statements, "bring the good news to the poor"
and "proclaim release to the captives . . . to proclaim the year of the
Lord's favor." Luke's readers were already aware that the pericope was
about teaching because v.15 reads, "He (Jesus) was teaching in their
synagogues and was praised by everyone"; and the scene in Nazareth
begins with the words, "he went to the synagogue on the Sabbath day, as

---

^{49} In my book, *The Unity*, 62-63, I argued that the risen Jesus, the prophet like Moses (Acts
3:22-23), can be heard because he speaks through his witness Peter, and can proclaim light
to the people and to the Gentiles (Acts 26:23) through his witness Paul, who actually
accomplished this task (cf. vv. 17-18, 22). However, in Acts Luke predicates, "doing"
(ποιεῖν) only indirectly of the risen Jesus. In Acts 4:7 the rulers, elders and scribes ask Peter
and John about the healing of the crippled beggar, "By what power or by what name did you
do (ἐποιήσατε) this?" Peter solemnly answers that the man is standing before them in
good health by the name of Jesus Christ of Nazareth, for there is no other name under heaven
given among mortals by which they must be saved (vv. 10,·12; cf. 9-12; 3:12-13). Earlier, in
Acts 3:16, Peter had already affirmed that it was through trust in Jesus' name that the man's
limbs were strengthened. Of course, Acts 4:12 deals with universal salvation.

^{50} Vv. 15, 17-21, 23, 25-30 are unique to Luke. There is a unity to Luke 4:16-30. Nonetheless, Luke has stressed the larger unit 4:14-44 as can be seen from the fact that we
find summaries of Jesus' teaching and preaching at both the beginning and end of the
pericope (vv. 14-15: καὶ αὐτὸς ἐδίδασκεν ἐν ταῖς συναγωγαῖς αὐτῶν and v. 44:
Καὶ ἦν κηρύσσων εἰς τὰς συναγωγὰς τῆς Ἰουδαίας). We find as well the following thematic vocabulary grouped together in the larger unit: ἐξῆλθεν (v. 14),
ἦλθεν and εἰσῆλθεν (v. 16), ἐξελθὼν (v. 42), ἡμέρα (vv. 16, 42), and συναγωγή (vv.
15-16, 44; cf. vv. 20, 28, 33, 38). Further, the scripture citation in vv. 18-19 corresponds to the divine will expressed at the end of the section in δεῖ (v. 43). In addition,
the expressions εὐαγγελίσασθαι (vv. 18, 43), ἀποστέλλω (vv. 18[2x], 43), and κηρύσσω (vv. 18-19, 44) are found at the beginning and end of the section. Finally, the
τοῦ πνεύματος of v. 14 is reflected in the πνεῦμα of v. 18. Luke presents the programmatic passage, and then Jesus begins to actualize it.

was his custom." So, although there is no mention of teaching in vv. 16-30, in the larger pericope, Luke clarifies Jesus' actions as "teaching."

Healings occur in the context of Jesus' teaching (Luke 5:17; 6:6) and of his being designated, "teacher." In 9:38, "Just then a man from the crowd shouted, 'Teacher, I beg you to look at my son; he is my only child,'" Luke associates Jesus the teacher with his ability to heal. Moreover, after he is described as teaching in the synagogue, Jesus on his own initiative heals the crippled woman on the Sabbath (13:10-17).

As noted above, Jesus' teaching with authority actualizes the mission that he received in the synagogue in Nazareth (cf. Luke 4:31-32). Sometimes, no information is given about the contents of Jesus' teaching; but elsewhere it includes the good news (4:18, cf. v. 43; 8:1; 20:1), release to captives, the acceptable year of the Lord and the kingdom of God (4:18-19.43; 8:1; 9:11; 13:18-21; 16:16). Jesus can forgive sins (5:22), and there is tremendous joy in heaven over the repentance of one sinner (ch. 15). Jesus' disciples are to imitate the Father who is kind to the ungrateful and the wicked; they are challenged to be merciful as God is (6:35-36; cf. vv. 27-36)([51]). Even though evil individuals tend to be more worldly wise (16:1-8), Christians are to be diligent servants who accept Jesus (cf. 17:7-10; 19:11-27). Jesus teaches about fasting (5:33-39), the neighbor (10:29-37), prayer (11:1-4.5-13; 18:1-8), divorce (16:18), forgiveness of the neighbor (17:3b), concern for the disadvantaged (14:12-14; 16:19-31) and prudent humility (14:7-11). Those who have been forgiven more should love more (7:41-43) and no one should be self-righteous and look down on others (18:9-14). Jesus attacks hypocrisy (12:1-3), scandal (17:1-3a) and the vanity and dishonesty of the scribes (20:45-47). He manifests considerable skill in handling or in addressing difficult situations. When asked to settle a family financial dispute (12:13), he answers that such is not his task; and his observations about the teachers of the law come too close to home for their comfort (11:45; cf. vv. 45-52). Jesus' cleverness easily allows him to escape the charge of being an agent of Beelzebub (11:17-23) and the trick question about paying taxes to Caesar (20:20-26); it also permits him to pose the riddle about David's son (20:41-44). Individuals should be trustworthy with

---

[51] Topel, *Children of a Compassionate God*, provides an exhaustive study of this passage. For a more general consideration of the topic in Luke-Acts, see Owczarek, *Sons of the Most High*.

money (16:9-13); and it is important to be rich toward God (12:16-21) and to have treasure in heaven (12:33-34). On the other hand, although it is difficult for a rich man to enter the kingdom of God, what is impossible for human beings is possible for God (18:24-30). Jesus is approached on such serious questions as healing on the Sabbath (6:8-9), how many will be saved (13:20), eternal life (10:25; 18:18-19) and when the end will come (21:7-11). His teaching about the resurrection of the dead pleased the scribes of the Pharisees (20:27-40). Jesus' audience should fear the person who not only can kill them but cast them into Gehenna (12:4-5). However, the risen Christ is with his persecuted followers (21:12-19); and they all are always under the protective providence of God (12:6-7.22-32). Jesus is the cornerstone and the rock of judgment (20:17-18); if the disciples are silenced in their joyous proclamation of his kingly arrival in Jerusalem, the very stones will acclaim him (19:39-40). Consequently, since the then leaders of Israel do not accept him, others who will run the vineyard properly will take their place (20:9-16).

Often no indications are given about how Jesus teaches. However, a review of the passages, which relate to teaching, reveals that he uses parables(52) and responds to questions(53) and to what others are thinking (5:22; 6:8; 11:17). Jesus himself can ask a question (20:41-44). On other occasions, someone makes a request of him (11:1; 12:13-15; 19:39-40) or asks about an interpretation of the law (20:21-22.28; cf. 16:16-18). Jesus warns (12:1-3; 17:1-3a; 20:45-47), exhorts (12:4-7; 14:12-14; 17:3b), encourages (12:22-32; 21:12-19) and uses wisdom sayings (12:33-34; 16:9-13; 20:17-18). Also, while Jesus is teaching, situations arise to which he reacts(54) or he comments on what someone else says (11:45; 18:24-30). So, Jesus taught in a manner like that of contemporary rabbis; but his teaching was exceptional and at times amazing, and he always spoke the truth and taught with confident authority.

'Επιστάτης ("Master")(55) is unique to Luke. Some interpreters

---

52 E.g., Luke 5:33-39; 7:40-43; 10:29-37; 11:17-22; 12:16-21; 13:18-21; 14:7-11; 15:3-7.8-32; 16:1-8.19-31; 17:7-10; 18:1-14.25; 19:11-27; 20:9-16.

53 E.g., 10:29; 13:22-23; 18:18-19; 20:20-38; 21:7-11.

54 E.g., 13:10-17; cf. 14:1-6; 18:16-17; 19:45-46; 21:1-4.

55 Luke 5:5; 8:24[2x].45; 9:33.49; 17:13.

associate it with Luke's use of "teacher." This understanding is based on the fact that "master" is almost exclusively addressed by the disciples to Jesus, and on that fact that the Marcan parallels (4:38 and 9:39, respectively) to Luke 8:24 and 9:49 both have "teacher" and the parallel (Mark 9:5) to Luke 9:33 has ῥαββι. To be sure, twice the relationship between Jesus and a given disciple is particularly obvious (8:45; 9:49). However, in none of the Lucan occurrences does "master" relate to teaching, but rather to Jesus' authority([56]), power over the material world and the working of miracles. Peter employs the title of Jesus when the latter tells him to put out into the deep water and to let down his nets for a catch (5:5). It is likewise the address Jesus' disciples use when they encounter the storm at sea and ask for help (8:24); their question in the following verse, "What sort of man can be this who commands even the winds and the sea and they obey him," points to the nuance of exceptional ability of the "Master." Luke describes Peter, who employs this title, as "not knowing what he said," when he tells Jesus at the Transfiguration that it is good to be there and suggests their building three dwellings: one for Jesus, one for Moses and one for Elijah (9:33). The last example is the ten lepers who call out, "Jesus, Master, have mercy on us" (17:13)! So, since it deals mostly with Jesus' authority and with his power over the material world, one may well wonder if it is best to associate ἐπιστάτης with Luke's view of Jesus as teacher. Perhaps, more correctly it should be associated with Jesus as "Lord"; for shortly after the miraculous draught of fish and his calling Jesus "Master," Peter addresses him as "Lord" (5:8: κύριε). If one decides that "master" is to be associated with "teacher," this latter term must then involve more than teaching and authority; it must also relates to miracles; and above we saw that to be true. Still, why would Luke who was not opposed to the term, "teacher," have chosen to use a different term? Variety, or did he feel the context of power over the material world called for a different expression than "teacher"?

By way of conclusion, one might doubt, as does Fitzmyer([57]), whether "teacher" makes any contribution to Lucan Christology. Naturally, in part, that depends on how one defines Christology; but if the term refers to what we can learn about Jesus, then, "teacher" does make a

---

[56] Nolland, *Luke 1 – 9:20*, 222.

[57] Fitzmyer, *The Gospel According to Luke I–IX*, 218.

contribution. Obviously, the earthly Jesus behaved as a teacher (a rabbi) and so held a certain social rank, and only Luke a number of times bothers to summarize all of Jesus' speaking activity as "teaching." In fact, Jesus' teaching constitutes a considerable portion of Luke's Gospel. People recognize Jesus' authority and wisdom; and according to Luke, Jesus outshines all contemporaries and is an extraordinary teacher, the like of whom does not exist. Jesus respected synagogues and the temple, but manifested exceptional integrity and independence in his teaching. Without human respect, he authoritatively and truthfully taught God's stance on things. At times, Jesus the teacher is associated with healings. "Teacher" and "master" imply disciples or followers, and we now turn to that consideration.

Jesus Calls Others to Follow Him([58])

The Lucan Jesus sees discipleship as denial of self, a taking up of one's cross and following Jesus. For one cannot be saved apart from Jesus. To follow Jesus one must give oneself totally to him; but in contrast to the other Synoptics, Luke makes it clear that this holds for everyone and that the cross is to be taken up daily (Luke 9:23). Luke has developed the call of the first followers and highlighted Peter (Luke 5:1-11; cf. Mt 4:18-22; Mk 1:16-20; Jn 21:1-11). Soon afterwards, Jesus calls Levi, whom Luke, alone among the Synoptics, specifies as leaving everything in following this call (5:27-28). The call of Jesus could be phrased in a challenging manner. The rich young man is told that one thing was yet lacking: he was to sell all that he had and give it to the poor so as to have treasure in heaven and then to follow Jesus (18:22). Following Jesus is more important than burying one's father. Only Luke expands this thought and indicates that it is likewise more important than saying "goodbye" to one's family and that to be worthy of the kingdom of God, once one has started following Jesus, one is not to look back (9:57-62). Jesus in a special manner chose twelve of his followers whom he named apostles (6:12-16; Acts 4:13); and with them (22:14) he celebrated the Last Supper (vv. 14-22). Jesus was also assisted by several women among whom are numbered Mary (called Magdalene), Joanna, the wife of Herod's steward Chuza, and Susanna([59]); only Luke names these last two women. Con-

---

[58] Luke 5:10-11.27-28; 9:23.57-62; 18:22; cf. 8:38-39; 9:49-50; 10:1; 11:23; 18:28.43.

sequently, unlike the rabbis, Jesus did invite others to follow him and some of these were to follow him in a closer manner. In 14:25-33 (cf. vv. 34-35) Luke writes of the demands of discipleship: one's relatives should not be of greater value to him than the following of Jesus, and the disciples are to carry the cross behind him and be willing to give up everything. They are to be like good salt, which still has flavor. So, the call to follow Jesus is challenging. Women were also included among Jesus' followers, but their exact relationship is not spelled out. However, there are different ways of following Jesus; for instance, the women remained very loyal and were the first to witness the empty tomb and to hear of Jesus' resurrection (cf. Luke 8:2-3; 23:49.55-24:11.22-24; cf. Acts 1:14).

Faith in Jesus

Luke's concept of "faith" in Jesus is not a univocal term; rather as his Gospel and Acts unfold, the meaning of faith develops. Ultimately, belief in Jesus will find a more complete expression in the confessional statement: "we believe that we will be saved through the grace of the Lord Jesus, just as they (the Gentiles), will be" (Acts 15:11)([60]). Of course, faith is God's gift (Acts 14:27). John the Baptist tells the people that they should believe in the one who is to come after him (Acts 19:4; cf. Luke 3:15-17); and in a sense, one is either with Christ or against him, gathering with him or scattering (Luke 11:23; cf. Acts 26:18). Thus, belief in Jesus can cause division (12:49-53). For Luke it is necessary to discern the time (12:54-59) and to repent and respond correctly to Jesus (13:1-17; cf. Acts 20:21; 24:24). Faith in Jesus leads to cures (7:1-10; 8:50; cf. Acts 14:9); and several times, according to Luke, Jesus says, "Your faith has saved you" (7:50; 8:48; 17:19; 18:42). In addition, one's faith or that of someone else can lead to Jesus' forgiving of sins (Luke 5:20; 7:46-50; cf. Acts 10:43; 26:18). Faith is so efficacious that, should one have faith the size of only a mustard seed, he could say to a sycamore tree, "Be uprooted and transplanted into the sea," and it would obey him (Luke 17:5-6). Nonetheless, the response of the disciples at times is such that Jesus can say to

---

[59] Luke 8:2-3; cf. 23:49.55-56; 24:1-10.22-24.

[60] A few passages so speak of faith that it must be identified with Christian living (Acts 13:8; 14:22; 16:5), and a designation for the early Christians is "believers" (e.g., Acts 2:44; 4:32; 5:14; 11:17; 22:19). "To believe" is just another way of saying that someone became a Christian (cf. Acts 4:4; 9:42; 11:21; 13:12; 14:1; 15:7).

them, "You faithless and perverse generation, how much longer must I be with you and bear with you" (9:41; cf. 8:13.25); and Jesus prays that Peter's faith will not leave him (22:32). After the resurrection, he chides two of the disciples for being slow of heart to believe all that the prophets said, that the Christ must suffer and so enter his glory (24:25-27). When the disciples are arguing about who is the greater, Jesus stands a child next to himself and says, "Whoever receives this child in my name receives me and whoever receives me receives him who sent me" (9:48; cf. 22:24-27). Faith is not an excuse for vanity: the disciples should see Jesus in those whom they may judge to be less significant. Since the disciples are having this disagreement among themselves, Jesus' instruction is probably to be interpreted as bearing on one's attitude toward one's fellow Christians. Also, Jesus himself is not rigid, as can be seen from his answer to John's question about the exorcist who, though not a disciple, is casting out demons in Jesus' name: "Do not stop him; for whoever is not against you is for you" (9:50). For Luke, "blasphemy" refers to the actions of opponents who do not accept or speak respectfully of Jesus (Luke 22:65; cf. 23:39; cf. Acts 18:6; 26:11). Faith, then, is a gift and grows with time. Jesus' disciples should not be slow to believe or to appreciate the power of their belief. Faith in Jesus is the correct response; one is either with him or against him. Faith in him leads to cures, salvation, forgiveness of sins, and calls us to humble belief and to the openness of Jesus himself.

Listening to and Hearing Jesus
Faith in Jesus involves hearing him. The most solemn expression of these directives is probably to be found in the Transfiguration when the voice from the cloud proclaims, "This is my Son, my Chosen One. Listen to him" (9:35; cf. Acts 3:22-23). We will see that this passage is part of the parallel that Luke draws between Jesus and Moses. It suffices here to remark that shortly after this heavenly instruction there follows the second passion prediction, preceded by the words, "Pay close attention to what I tell you"; but Luke in this second passion prediction makes no mention of a resurrection (v. 44), and so the disciples hear only of Jesus' suffering. Jesus' visit to Martha and Mary (Luke 10:38-42) is a forceful expression of the importance of listening to Jesus. Part of the difficulty in understanding this story comes from the Jewish language and tradition, where contrasts are not made as smoothly or as precisely as we do in some modern languages. In the story, there is no belittling or looking down on the no-

bility of what Martha is doing. Still, when her actions are compared to Mary's, there is no way in which preference can be given to them. Mary is portrayed as the ideal disciple who realizes that the most important aspect of human living is listening to Jesus; she has chosen the better part.

In Luke (14:35c) Jesus concludes his words about the cost of discipleship and the tasteless salt with the words, "Let him who hears this, heed it." It is not enough to hear or be willing to call on Jesus as "Lord"; no, one must also do what Jesus says. The one who so acts is like a man who builds his house on a solid foundation, for even if the floods come, his house stands. On the other hand, whoever fails to put Jesus' words into action is like a man who did not build on a solid foundation. When the floods came, that house fell (6:46-49; cf. 8:19-21; 11:27-28). Yet not everyone listens. We probably have an explanation of this failure to listen at the end of parable of the rich man and Lazarus: "If they do not listen to Moses and the prophets, they will not be convinced even if one should rise from the dead" (16:31; cf. vv. 29-30). Here Jesus is clearly the person who is not being listened to. At other times, people are fickle and change the reasons for their belief. For example, they do not accept the Son of Man because he came eating and drinking (7:34). Hearing Jesus includes listening to the disciples; and to refuse to hear Jesus amounts to refusal to hear God: "He who hears you, hears me. He who rejects you, rejects me. And he who rejects me, rejects him who sent me" (10:16). Only Luke among the Synoptics introduces into this verse "hearing" and "rejecting" (cf. Mt 10:40). Consequently, we are to listen to Jesus; this listening characterizes his disciples and must lead to action. Listening to Jesus includes listening to his disciples; failure to listen, for whatever reason, is to build without a solid foundation.

Jesus' Popularity

In Luke, Jesus is very popular with the ordinary Jewish people. In 8:40 Luke makes the observation that a crowd welcomes Jesus. And in v. 42 Luke intensifies Mark's text by writing: "The crowds almost crushed him." Again, in 12:1, Luke expands on his source and uses a hyperbole to report that Jesus' audience is so numerous that the people are trampling on one another. Also only Luke reports that the people were getting up early in the morning to hear Jesus in the temple (21:38; cf. John 8:1). The chief priest, scribes and leaders can do nothing against him, for all the people are spellbound by what they hear him saying (cf. 19:48; 20:19; 22:2).

Jesus likewise receives sinners and publicans and eats with them (15:1-2)([61]); and both this passage and 19:1-10, the story of Zacchaeus, are unique to Luke. To appreciate this last activity, we need only ask ourselves when we last ate with a modern social outcast. Moreover, Jesus' meals with others play a significant part in Luke's Gospel([62]). Jesus, then, is popular with the ordinary people and draws huge crowds; this popularity proves a natural defense against his enemies. He was so open to people that he received and ate with the outcasts of his day.

Jesus' Expressions of Emotions
Luke has modified some Marcan passages which express Jesus' emotions or seem negative. For example, he does not report that Jesus' relatives think him to be crazy (Mk 3:21), or that Jesus is ignorant of the time of the day of the Lord (Mk 13:32). According to Luke, Jesus is not moved with pity and gives no stern warning to the man cured of leprosy (Mk 1:41.43; cf. 6:34), or get angry (Mk 3:5; 10:14), or take the children into his arms (cf. Mk 9:36; 10:16), or look on the young man with love (Mk 10:21). Nor is mention made of Jesus' anguish in the garden of Gethsemane (Mk 14:34-36; cf. Luke 22:43-44), or of his cry on the cross (Mk 15:34)([63]). On the other hand, in these very passages, Luke, in contrast to Mark, inserts Jesus' healing of those in need (Luke 9:11), his call for the children (18:16) and his standing the child next to himself (9:47)([64]). Moreover, Luke has by no means eliminated all expressions of human emotions on Jesus' part; a number of these passages are unique to him. In the story of the raising of the widow's son at Nain, Jesus is moved with pity upon seeing her and tells her, "Do not cry." He then raises her son from the dead and gives him back to her (7:13-15; cf. 8:52)([65]). Jesus

---

[61] Luke 5:27-32; 15:1-2; 19:1-10; cf. 7:34.

[62] For a listing of these meals, see Heil, *The Meal Scenes in Luke-Acts*, 1-233, 307-311; Talbert, *Reading Luke*, 229.

[63] See Fitzmyer, *The Gospel According to Luke I–IX*, 94-95.

[64] Bovon, *Luke 1*, 392, claims that Luke is not rejecting Jesus' expression of emotion but rather describing a child who can stand on his own, not as Mark an infant who must be carried. In Luke 2:28, Simeon does take the infant Jesus into his arms.

takes action on his own initiative in the story of the woman badly stooped and unable to stand straight (13:11-17). He calls her to himself and says, "Woman, you are free of your infirmity". He then lays his hand on her and immediately she stands up straight([66]). Both for this woman and the man with dropsy (14:5), Jesus points out that on the Sabbath his audiences take better care of a son and even of their animals than of these two needy individuals. Luke keeps the "Q" tradition that Jesus often wanted to gather the inhabitants of Jerusalem just as a hen gathers her brood under her wings, but they were unwilling (13:34). Both the ten lepers and a blind man ask Jesus to have pity on them, and he grants their cures (17:11-19; 18:35-43). Only Luke writes that Jesus weeps over the fate of Jerusalem whose inhabitants did not recognize the things which made for peace, or the time of her visitation from God (19:41-44). In the cleansing of the temple, as the prophets of old, Jesus acts in righteous anger and pious zeal, but Luke has toned down Mark's account since he leaves out the buyers, the overturning of the tables and chairs and the preventing of anyone carrying things through the temple area (19:45-46; cf. Mark 11:15-18). Jesus is not interested in violence. He will not call down fire from heaven on the Samaritan village, which will not receive him and the apostles because they are headed toward Jerusalem (Luke 9:51-56), and he heals the right ear of the slave of the High Priest who was with those who came out against Jesus on the Mount of Olives (22:50-51). During the journey to Calvary, he does not concentrate on his own sufferings but on those of the women of Jerusalem (23:27-31). Although the text is disputed([67]), Jesus while on the cross forgives those who have so mistreated him: "Father, forgive them; for they do not know what they are doing" (23:34; cf. 6:27-36; Acts 7:60). Nonetheless, despite these passages, all the healing miracles and his extensive theme of Jesus, the savior of the needy([68]), Luke has dropped certain Marcan passages, which speak of

---

[65] See Bock, *Luke 1:1 – 9:50*, 654-655; Fitzmyer, *The Gospel According to Luke I–IX*, 658-659; Rigaux, *Témoignage*, 174-175.

[66] Kilgallen, "The Obligation to Heal," 409, comments, "The cure of the bent woman illustrates not what is allowed on the sabbath, but what work should be done—that one might love one's neighbor fully as God commands."

[67] Metzger, *A Textual Commentary*, 154.

Jesus' emotions or seem negative. Surely, Luke does not want to deny Jesus' humanity but rather to portray it at a different level. For, as this book hopes to make clear, Luke has preferred to reflect on the supernatural and divine aspects of Jesus.

Jesus Sends His Followers on Mission

Jesus' act of missioning is prefigured in Jesus' words to Peter, "Do not be afraid. From now on you will be catching men" (Luke 5:9). Jesus sends out the Twelve to proclaim the kingdom of God and to heal the sick (9:1-2; cf. 22:35-36). However, it is the risen Jesus who most missions the disciples. Only Luke writes of Jesus' sending out the Seventy(-two; 10:1); however, in this passage Jesus is designated as "Lord" (κύριος), and so it is clear that Luke is thinking of the risen Jesus. Obviously, the same is true when the risen Jesus tells the Eleven that they are witnesses and in his name repentance for the forgiveness of sins is to be proclaimed to everyone (24:47-48; Acts 1:18). The risen Jesus also missions his witness Paul (Acts 26:16-18; cf. 9:15-16; 22:14-15).

Conclusion

Luke leaves his readers with no doubt that Jesus is a human being and acts as such. Still, Jesus is unique, some of his actions are truly marvelous, and he teaches with authority. Luke never permits his reader to lose sight of the fact that Jesus of Nazareth was the same person his followers proclaimed as raised from the dead; so the earthly Jesus constitutes an essential part of Luke's Christology. Jesus' baptism looks to his mission and to the Spirit's part in it as well as to his relationship with the Father. "Adam" in the genealogy marks Jesus' mission to all humankind, and the phrase "of God" (Luke 3:38) calls to mind "Son of God" (1:35; cf. 3:22). This latter phrase also prepares the reader for Jesus' temptation. Israel failed its temptations; Jesus does not. In fact, Jesus always wants to do the Father's will. This stance explains his frequenting of the Jewish religious places and his prayer, especially before important events; he is grateful and confident of the Father's activity in his life and prays for this in the lives of his followers. Jesus lives as a teacher and so enjoys a certain social status, and a number of times Luke inserts statements about Jesus as a teacher and so summaries his activity. Luke associates "preaching the

---

[68] See O'Toole, The Unity, 109-148.

good news," "proclaiming" and even words for "saying" with Jesus'
teaching. He is an extraordinary teacher who with wisdom, authority and
integrity speaks about God's activity in this world. Obviously, some passages (Luke 2:49; 4:14-44; 13:22.26; 23:5; Acts 1:1), which report Jesus'
teaching are more important than others. His teaching embraces the good
news, the kingdom of God, information about himself, discipleship and
numerous instructions about Christian living; sometimes, his teaching is
associated with healings. On the other hand, "master" (ἐπιστάτης), with
its emphasis on power over this material world, might more correctly be
associated with Jesus as "Lord." He teaches through parables, questions
and answers, and his knowledge of what others are thinking; he exhorts,
warns and makes use of opportunities as they arise to communicate his
ideas. Jesus calls others to follow and to imitate him, and these disciples
are living testimony to Jesus, the teacher and master. Following Jesus is
radically important and variously challenges those called. Among Jesus'
followers we find apostles and other disciples who include women. Discipleship means taking up one's cross and following Jesus and can even
demand that one give up everything. One is either for or against Jesus, but
faith in him is a gift and grows with time. Believers should appreciate the
power of their faith in Jesus: it leads to cures, forgiveness of sins and a
caring attitude toward one's weaker brothers and sisters. In short, it leads
to salvation. So, we are to listen to Jesus; and this listening should lead to
action. Failure to listen to Jesus is equivalent to building without a solid
foundation. Jesus himself was very popular with the ordinary people.
True, Luke does drop a number of Marcan passages that speaks of Jesus
expressing affection or emotion; however, Luke has so many other passages that do portray Jesus in this light that the more reasonable
conclusion is that Luke just wishes to do this a little differently. As in the
other Synoptics, Jesus sends his followers to proclaim the gospel message,
but he does this mostly as the risen Jesus.

Other aspects of the earthly Jesus' life, including his passion and
death, will be amply treated in other chapters of this book. Surely, these
aspects, particularly his passion that many scholars view as also embracing
his death, constitute a very significant part of his earthly existence.

CHAPTER TWO
Jesus As Prophet[69]

Our consideration of Luke's presentation of Jesus as a prophet falls into four parts: 1) the programmatic passage and closely related pericopes; 2) passages which speak of Jesus as being similar to other prophets; 3) Jesus acts as a prophet; 4) others identify Jesus as a prophet.

The Programmatic Passage and Closely Related Pericopes
It is generally granted that Luke 4:[14]16-30[44][70] (cf. 7:18-23) is programmatic for Luke's Gospel[71], and some scholars would contend that this also holds true for the Acts of the Apostles. Certainly, the programmatic passage is one of mission[72]. According to Luke, what Isaiah said about himself Jesus applies to himself; and so we have a comparison between the prophet Isaiah and Jesus. Thus, Jesus presents himself as a prophet. There is likewise an implied self-identification in Jesus words, "Amen, I say to you, no prophet is accepted in his own native place"; and

---

[69] For general considerations of this topic, see Bock, *Luke 1:1 – 9:50*, 29-31. Bock holds that Luke's editorial notes in the Gospel demonstrate that central to his Christology is Jesus as "leader-prophet" who is "more than Messiah." Cf. also: Cadbury, "The Title of Jesus in Acts," 371-372; Fitzmyer, *The Gospel According to Luke I–IX*, 213-215; Foakes Jackson and Lake, "Christology," *The Beginning of Christianity*, I, 403-408; Friedrich, προφήτης, 841-848; Hastings, *Prophet and Witness in Jerusalem*; Kingsbury, "Jesus as the 'Prophet Messiah,'" 29-42; Minear, *To Heal and to Reveal*; Nebe, *Prophetische Züge im Bilde Jesu*; Rigaux, *Témoignage*, 364-382; Voss, *Die Christologie*, 155-170.

[70] Schürmann, "Zur Traditionsgeschichte," 187-205, provides a history of the tradition for Luke 4:16-30; and Schreck, "The Nazareth Pericope," 399-471, a summary of recent research on this pericope.

[71] See Tiede, *Prophecy and History*, 55-63. Confer Busse, *Das Nazareth-Manifest*.

[72] Catchpole, "The Anointed One in Nazareth," 251.

as the programmatic passage progresses, Jesus, is sent to the disadvantaged and non-Jews as were Elijah and Elisha. The Holy Spirit has come upon Jesus, has anointed him "to bring glad tidings to the poor," and has sent him "to proclaim liberty to captives and recovery of sight to the blind, to let the oppressed go free and to proclaim a year acceptable to the Lord." These words occur in a context of the accomplishment of God's salvific will, whether this be expressed by reading of the Scriptures or the formal assertion, "Today this scripture passage is fulfilled in your hearing."

Furthermore, the programmatic passage brings out another aspect typical of the prophets, namely, rejection (cf. 11:47-51; 13:34; Acts 7:52)([73]). Initially, the audience at Nazareth describes what Jesus says as "words of grace" and reacts positively. However, their wondering about Jesus' origins and his reply to this wondering with the skeptical proverb, "Physician, cure yourself," and with the statement of their implied challenge, "Do here in your native place the things that we heard were done in Capernaum," all this shows that they will soon move in a negative direction. Jesus reacts to this when he observes that no prophet is accepted in his native place. This is even more true at the end of the scene; for Jesus' audience is enraged, drives him out of their midst and tries to throw him off a cliff. We will see that we can make a good case for Jesus' identification in this programmatic passage as "Christ" and "Servant of Yahweh." Nonetheless, he identifies himself here as a prophet and compares his ministry to that of Isaiah, Elijah and Elisha([74]). Finally, since "a year acceptable to the Lord" (v. 19) should be understood eschatologically, we are in the end-times, which according to Luke begin with the birth of Jesus([75]).

Luke 7:18-23 is a pronouncement story([76]), and so the emphasis is on

---

[73] See Hill, "The Rejection of Jesus," 161-180 and Karris, *Luke: Artist and Theologian*, 18-20, 93-95; cf. Squires, *The Plan of God*, 138.

[74] Bock, *Luke 1:1 – 9:50*, 416-420 and Rigaux, *Témoignage*, 375-376. See also Voss, *Die Christologie*, 156-160.

[75] O'Toole, *The Unity*, 149-159. Ernst, *Herr der Geschichte*, 112, observes, "Die Eschatologie ist für Lukas in diesem Sinne ein—freilich durchaus zentraler und wesentlicher—Aspekt der Christologie."

[76] Fitzmyer, *The Gospel According to Luke I–IX*, 663.

vv. 22-23. Vv. 21-23 constitute a parallel to the programmatic passage, especially to 4:18.24-27 (cf. vv. 33-37, 41). The reason for this is that in vv. 22-23
the following data likewise appear about Jesus: "he cured many of their
diseases, sufferings, and evil spirits . . . granted sight to many who were blind .
. . the blind regain their sight . . . lepers are cleansed . . . the dead are raised,
the poor have the good news proclaimed to them." Therefore, what Jesus said
about himself in the programmatic passage is seen as now being actualized.
We have here an example of what a number of scholars have explained as the
promise/fulfillment pattern or, if one prefer in this case, Jesus the prophet, who
accurately predicts what he will do. As Jesus in the programmatic passage is
identified implicitly as a prophet, Luke so portrays him in 7:18-23. This
interpretation agrees with the context. At the end of the previous scene, the
raising of the widow's son at Nain—unique to Luke and resembling but far
exceeding Elijah's raising of the son of the widow of Sarepta (4:25-26; cf. 1
Kgs 17:17-24)—the people exclaim, "A great prophet has arisen in our midst"
(Luke 7:16). "The dead are raised" (7:22) looks back to this event and confirms the contention that Luke views Jesus as a prophet in 7:18-23. On the
other hand, Jesus' words, "And blessed is the one who takes no offense at me"
(v. 23) stands in contrast to the Jewish audience, which in 4:16-30 did take
offense and tried to do Jesus violence. The statement in its present context
creates the impression that surely John the Baptist and his disciples take no
offense at Jesus, and that the blessing has universal application because it is
intended for anyone who responds appropriately to Jesus (cf. v. 35).

The explanation of the twice-repeated question placed by John the
Baptist and two of his disciples, "Are you the one who is to come, or
should we look for another" (vv. 19-20: σὺ εἶ ὁ ἐρχόμενος ἢ ἄλλον
προσδοκῶμεν) proves more difficult(77). "Are you the one who is to
come" may well look to Jesus as Messiah (19:38 [cf. 13:35]: "Blessed is
the king who comes in the name of the Lord"), although Luke in this
pericope may be beginning to use this expression also of the Son of Man
who is to come (9:26; 12:40; 18:8; 21:27; cf. 19:10). Therefore, this
phrasing will be considered in the chapters which study Jesus as the Christ
and the Son of Man. Of course, Luke 7:18-35 shows John the Baptist's
respect for Jesus, who is recognized as the more important personage.
The passage also suggests that Jesus is more than "a great prophet"
(7:16). Jesus' greatness is underlined by the significance that 7:18-35

---

77 See Nolland, *Luke 1 – 9:20*, 328-329.

attributes to John the Baptist, who himself is more than a prophet and the messenger who prepares the way, than whom no one born of women is greater, except for the least in the kingdom of heaven (vv. 26-28).

Jesus again implicitly identifies himself as a prophet([78]): he speaks of his activity and the journey that God wants him to make, "for it is impossible that a prophet should be killed outside Jerusalem" (Luke 13:31-35)([79]). In v. 33 Jesus' passion and death are seen as the martyrdom of a prophet, and Jesus as the persecuted prophets of the OT([80]). Luke 13:31-35, then, are similar both to the programmatic passage and to 7:18-35; for miracles are associated with Jesus, who is being rejected but should be accepted. This rejection explains Jesus' lament in 13:32-35. Moreover, in both the programmatic passage and in 13:31-35 we find two additional similarities. Jesus implicitly identifies himself as a prophet who is doing God's will, inasmuch as 4:17-21 speaks of the fulfillment of a prophecy, and in 13:32-33 we find the words "it is necessary" accompanied by the words "my purpose is accomplished" and "it is impossible" and Jesus' rejection and suffering reach the point of his being threatened with death. On the other hand, we find "blessed is he who comes (ὁ ἐρχόμενος) in the name of the Lord" (13:35) which recalls "are you 'he who is to come' (ὁ ἐρχόμενος) or do we look for someone else" (7:19-20) and reminds us that Jesus is more than a prophet and prepares us for his entrance into Jerusalem (19:38).

Some other aspects of Luke 13:34-35 relate to the theme of Jesus as prophet. Jerusalem appears as the city that kills the prophets and stones those sent to her. Jesus prophesizes that this city will not see him until she says, "Blessed is the one who comes in the name of the Lord," which is fulfilled in "Blessed is the king who comes (ὁ ἐρχόμενος) in the name of the Lord" (19:38) at Jesus' entrance into Jerusalem([81]). Moreover, even

---

[78] Prete, *L'opera di Luca*, 256-257 and Schweizer, *The Good News according to Luke*, 230-232.

[79] Rese, "Einige Überlegungen zu Lukas XIII, 31-33," 201-225, discusses various interpretations of vv. 31-33.

[80] Friedrich, προφήτης, 843.

[81] Christ, *Jesus Sophia*, 150-152, contends that the reference is to the Parousia and that in the background of Luke 13:34 is an identification of Jesus with wisdom.

though the attitude of Jerusalem is one of rejection, Jesus shows his loving concern by comparing himself to a hen that gathers her brood under her wings.

Jesus' Similarity to Other Prophets
Luke is less interested in limiting his presentation of Jesus by any parallel with a given prophet of the Old Testament. However, these parallels do help to identify Jesus and support Luke's theme of continuity; for all the prophets of the Old Testament, Jesus and, then, the latter's disciples, are all agents of God's salvation.

Jesus' contemporaries thought him to be John the Baptist or Elijah returned from the dead or still some other prophet (Luke 1:7-8.19). In the programmatic passage, Jesus applies to himself Isaiah's reflections about his mission and compares himself to both Elijah and Elisha (4:18-19.25-27; cf. Is 61:1-2; 58:6). Actually, Elijah plays a double role in Luke's Gospel. Luke has clearly associated Elijah with John the Baptist, who will bring many of the sons of Israel back to God and, "in the spirit and power of Elijah," will turn the hearts of fathers to their children . . . (Luke 1:16-17; cf. Sir 48:10). Later, we again find this association of Elijah with John, who is a prophet and something more; for Scripture says of him, "I send my messenger ahead of you to prepare the way before you" (Luke 7:27; cf. Mi 3:1.23-34; Ex 23:20). Also, Jesus refuses to act like Elijah since he does not acquiesce to the request of James and John that he call down fire on the Samaritan town which will not receive them (Luke 9:52-55; cf. 2 Kgs 1:9-15).

Nevertheless, Luke has drawn some parallels between Elijah and Jesus([82]). Elijah's raising of the widow's son is reflected in Jesus' raising of the son of the widow of Nain (Luke 4:25-26; 7:11-17; cf. 7:22; 1 Kgs 17:1 – 18:1). Motifs from 1 Kgs 17:8-24 are probable in Luke 8:42.55; 9:38.42; and more definitely between 1 Kgs 19:19-21 and Luke 9:61-62([83]). Ahab's charge that Elijah was subverting Israel (1 Kgs 18:17: ὁ διαστρέφων τὸν Ισραηλ—cf. v. 18) employs the same verb as that in

---

[82] Confer Hinnebusch, "Jesus, the New Elijah," 2175-2182, 2237-2244; Miller, "Elijah, John and Jesus," 611-612. However, not everyone will be convinced by J.A.T. Robinson's ("Elijah, John and Jesus," 276-281) understanding of Luke's presentation of Jesus as Elijah.

[83] See Nolland, *Luke 1:1 – 9:50*, 322.

the Sanhedrin's accusation against Jesus (Luke 23:2)([84]). Elijah appears (along with Moses) at the transfiguration and is speaking with Jesus. These two might well be the men who appear to the women at the empty tomb (24:4-7) and at Jesus' ascension (Acts 1:10-11)([85]).

At first the reader gets the impression that the parallel in the Transfiguration story is mostly with Moses([86]). However, the additional parallel between the exodus that Jesus is to fulfill in Jerusalem (9:31) and the words of v. 51 ("when the days for his [Jesus'] being taken up [τῆς ἀναλήμψεως αὐτοῦ] were fulfilled, he resolutely determined to journey to Jerusalem") leave little doubt that Luke intends a comparison between Elijah's being taken up to heaven and Jesus' ascension. (Compare 2 Kgs 2:9-11; cf. Sir 48:9; 1 Mc 2:58: "before I am taken from you" [ἀναλημφ-θῆναι μὲ ἀπὸ σοῦ], "still, if you see me taken [ἀναλαμβανόμενον] up from you", along with "and Elijah was taken up [ἀνελήμφθη] to heaven in a whirlwind" and Acts 1:11: "this Jesus who has been taken [ὁ ἀνα-λημφθείς] up from you into heaven; cf. vv. 9-11; Luke 24:51; Mk 16:19)([87]). In Acts 1:2, Jesus' ascension is referred to with the words, "until the day that he was taken up" [ἀνελήμφθη]). Finally, A.W. Zwiep is correct in maintaining that the words "Whom heaven must receive until the times of universal restoration" (Acts 3:21) are another reference to Jesus' ascension and have been influenced by terminology traditionally applied to Elijah (Mal 3:23; Sir 48:10; cf. Mk 9:12; Mt 17:11). Moreover, Mal 3:22 speak of Elijah "being sent" and so Acts 3:20 also reflects this terminology. In fact, Acts 1:11 and 3:20-21 speak of Jesus being received

---

[84] Plummer, St. Luke, 520.

[85] See L.T. Johnson, The Acts, 27

[86] For some redactional links of the Transfiguration with the rest of Luke-Acts, see Trites, "The Transfiguration in the Theology of Luke," 71-81.

[87] For a thorough study of the ascension and extensive bibliographical information, see Zwiep, The Ascension of the Messiah, although his contentions that Luke sharply distinguished between Jesus' ascension and his resurrection-exaltation, and that the ascension reflects a "subordinationist" concern (197), are mistaken. Cf. Lohfink, Die Himmelfahrt Jesu, and O'Toole, "Luke's Understanding of Jesus' Resurrection-Ascension-Exaltation."

into heaven but returning and so connect Jesus' ascension with his parusia([88]).

The comparison of Jesus with Elisha in Luke 4:27 (cf. 2 Kgs 5:1-19) is expanded on in "Lepers are cured" (7:22) and in the stories of the cleansing of the leper (5:12-16) and of the ten lepers (17:10-19). Below, I will argue that the feeding of the five thousand (Luke 9:10-17) characterizes Jesus as Moses; but there is a definite parallel between this pericope and Elisha's multiplication of loaves (2 Kgs 4:42-44). Certainly, Luke's text (at 9:17: "They all ate [ἔφαγον] and were satisfied. And when the leftover fragments were picked up, they filled twelve wicker baskets") reflects 2 Kgs 4:44, "And when they had eaten (ἔφαγον), there was some left over, as the Lord had said." Elisha's instruction to Gehazi to greet no one along the way (2 Kgs 4:29) probably influenced the phrasing of Luke 10:4.

In the demand for a sign Jesus is compared to Jonah in Luke 11:29-32; and vocabulary links justify the claim that Jonah 1:4-16 has influenced the composition of Luke 8:22-25, "the calming of the storm"([89]).

Jesus a Prophet like Moses([90])
Both Jesus and Moses have the Spirit (Luke 4:1-2.14; Num 11:17.25)([91]), and the contexts of these passages support a parallel between Jesus and Moses. Luke 4:1-2 report the forty days in the wilderness and thus recall Acts 7:36, a pericope which, as we shall see, stands in an extended comparison between Moses and Jesus. Moreover, Num 11:16-17 report the selection of the seventy elders, an idea which Luke apparently has

---

[88] Zwiep, *The Ascension of the Messiah*, 109-115, 196; see also Barbi, *Il Cristo celeste*, 45-97 and Dubois, "La figure d'Elie," 155-176.

[89] Nolland, *Luke 1 – 9:28*, 398.

[90] For this presentation I will be using my article, "The Parallels between Jesus and Moses," 22-29; however, a number of changes have been made. See also Hooker, "'Beginning from Moses,'" 228-230; Lampe, "The Lucan Portrait of Christ," 168-169; Voss, *Die Christologie*, 160-170.

[91] See Franklin, *Christ the Lord*, 68; G.R. Greene, "The Portrayal of Jesus as Prophet," 37-38.

taken up in his gospel (10:1; cf. v. 17). Probably the feeding of the five thousand (Luke 9:10-17) implies that Jesus is to be viewed as Moses. In Luke's text the feeding of the five thousand occurs between the questions about Jesus and the two initial answers that he is a prophet (cf. vv. 7-9, 18-20). The suggestion that Jesus is a prophet points to two possible models in the LXX for the feeding of the five thousand: Elisha's multiplication of loaves (2 Kgs 4:42-44) or Moses and the manna in the desert. Above, we noted the parallel between Luke 9:17 and the story of Elisha (2 Kgs 4:44); however, Luke (4:27) is the only author in the NT who explicitly mentions Elisha; yet he does not demonstrate much interest in this prophet. More probably, a comparison with Moses was what Luke had in mind; for the feeding of the five thousand occurs "in a desert place" (9:12), which suggests Moses (Luke is the only one of the Synoptics who has changed the position of this phrase). Besides, Luke develops a comparison between Jesus and Moses in the Transfiguration story, which follows almost immediately in his text.

Finally, the Greek wording of the feeding of the five thousand (Luke 9:16: "Then taking the five loaves and the two fish, and looking up to heaven, he said the blessing over them, broke them, and gave them to the disciples to set before the crowd"; cf. 22:17.19), reflects the words of the Institution Narrative. In the Last Supper scene (22:14-38), Luke compares Jesus to Moses, for only Luke inserts at the beginning of the actual scene the notice that the celebration is that of the Passover, which in the Old Testament is particularly associated with Moses (cf. Ex 12:1-27; Dt 16:1-8). In addition, at this paschal celebration Jesus speaks of a "new" covenant in his blood. Paul and Luke mention a "new" covenant (1 Cor 11:25; Luke 22:20; cf. Jer 31:31-34), and they both also write "in my blood" and so tie the covenant to the one that the Lord through Moses made with the people of Israel (Ex 24:6-8).

At the Transfiguration([92]) Jesus, like Moses, ascends a mountain with three close companions (Luke 9:28; Ex 24:1.9); and his countenance is changed (Luke 9:29; cf. Ex 34:29-35). Ex 24:16 (cf. vv. 17-18; 19:9; Dt 5:24), "The glory of the Lord settled on Mount Sinai. The cloud covered it for six days, and on the seventh day he called to Moses from the midst of the cloud," surely resembles the divine glory and the end of the

---

[92] See Gils, *Jésus Prophète*, 35-36 and Teeple, *The Mosaic Eschatological Prophet*, 84, 116.

Transfiguration story where God speaks from the cloud. In contrast to the other synoptics, at the Transfiguration Luke mentions a cloud three times instead of two (Luke 9:34-35), and only he twice speaks of "glory" (vv. 31-32). These additions, especially the latter, increase the similarity with the Sinai event. At the Transfiguration only Luke of the Synoptics follows the Greek word order of Moses' prophecy in Dt 18:15, "Hear him" (Luke 9:35: αὐτοῦ ἀκούετε), and expands on the idea in Acts 3:22-23 where he makes definite reference to Moses.

Exodus motifs play a part in Jesus' life, and according to the Transfiguration story, he has an exodus to fulfill in Jerusalem (9,31)([93]); and a parallel to this verse notes his determination to journey there (cf. 9:51), a journey which contains many instructions for his disciples([94]). This journey is an example for them, a way to follow. C.F. Evans and D.P. Moessner([95]) claim that Luke draws an extended parallel between Jesus' journey and that of Moses in the wilderness, but their claim is exaggerated. Nonetheless, Luke does name the Christians' faith in Jesus, "the Way" (9:57); and in the story of Emmaus (Luke 24:32.35) and the episode of the Ethiopian eunuch (Acts 8:26.36.39), "way" portrays a correct understanding and response to Jesus([96]). Moreover, Jesus' "exodus" does not point to the purely negative experience of his death but looks also to his resurrection([97]). The resurrection aspects of the Transfiguration support such an interpretation, for Luke there speaks of "glory" (9:31-32; cf. vv. 26, 51) and later has Jesus ask the disciples on the road to Emmaus, "Was it not necessary that the Messiah should suffer these things

---

[93] Carruth, *The Jesus-As-Prophet Motif*, 160-161; Tiede, *Prophecy and History*, 46; Bock, *Proclamation from Prophecy*, 116-117.

[94] Resseguie, "The Lukan Portrait of Christ," 16-20; J. Schneider, "Zur Analyze des lukanischen Reiseberichtes," 219-225.

[95] Confer Evans, "The Central Section," 37-53 and Moessner, "Luke's Preview of the Journey," 575-605. On the other hand, Brodie, "The Departure for Jerusalem (Lk 9,51-56)," 96-109, wants to see in Jesus' journey an imitation of Elijah's departure for the Jordan.

[96] O'Toole, "Philip and the Ethiopian Eunuch," 31-33.

[97] Mánek, "The New Exodus," 8-23. Cf. also Garrett, "Exodus from Bondage."

and then enter his glory" (Luke 24:26)? Of course, the Jewish tradition of
the exodus ends with positive experiences of freedom from slavery and
possession of the land.

An event, which follows on the Transfiguration, probably continues the parallel between Jesus and Moses. Luke 9:41, "Jesus said in
reply, 'O faithless and perverse (διεστραμμένη) generation , how long
will I be with you and endure you,'" looks quite similar to Moses' laments,
"a perverse and crooked (διεστραμμένη) race" (Dt 32:5), "What a fickle
(ἐξεστραμμένη) race they are, sons with no loyalty in them (Dt. 32:20)
and "But how can I alone bear the crushing burden that you are, along
with your bickering" (Dt 1:12).

God's activity in others finds no resistance in Jesus, who refuses to
forbid the exorcism of demons in his name by a man who was not his
follower (Luke 9:49-50). This action corresponds to Moses' endorsement
of the prophesying of Eldad and Medad (Num 11:26-30)([98]). Also, in
view of everything which has been said up to this point, there is good
reason to compare the words of the risen Jesus, "He said to them, 'These
are my words that I spoke to you (οὗτοι οἱ λόγοι μου οὓς ἐλάλησα
πρὸς ὑμᾶς) while I was still with you'" (Luke 24:44) with the LXX
summary statement, "These are the words which Moses spoke (οὗτοι οἱ
λόγοι οὓς ἐλάλησεν Μωυσῆς) to all Israel beyond the Jordan" (Dt 1:1).

The whole of Jesus' ministry can be described in words very
similar to those used of Moses: "a prophet mighty in deed and word"
(24:19; cf. Acts 7:22)([99]). Jesus, too, performed wonders and signs (Acts
2:22; 4:30; 7:36); and "the finger of God"([100]) was with him in a conflict-
situation between good and evil, between those who are for God and those
against (Luke 11:20; cf. Ex 8:15; cf. 31:18; Dt 9:10). For the charge of
the Jewish high priest, elders and scribes against Jesus, "We found this
man perverting (διαστρέφοντα) our nation, opposing the payment of
taxes to Caesar" (Luke 23:2), the closest parallel in the LXX is an
accusation of the Pharaoh, "What do you mean, Moses and Aaron, by

---

[98] Teeple, *The Mosaic Eschatological Prophet*, 116

[99] Dupont, "La Mission du Paul", 452.

[100] Luke has "the finger of God"; Matthew (12:18), "in the spirit of God." For a
general discussion of this phrase, see George, *Études sur l'œuvre de Luc*, 127-132.

taking the people away (διαστρέφετε τὸν λαόν) from their work?" (Ex 5:4; cf. 1 Kgs 18:17-18)([101]).

J.J. Kilgallen correctly observes that both Acts 3:22 and 7:35 are set in a framework of covenants with Abraham, of Moses as a predecessor of Christ, and of an audience who should hear the prophets (Acts 3:25; 7:51-52)([102]). The context of Acts 3:22-23 allows us to determine that Luke holds that Jesus, the "prophet like Moses," was likewise the suffering servant (vv. 13, 26) and the Christ (vv. 18, 20). Luke, through the use of the word "raise" (Acts 3:22.26), has connected the "prophet like Moses" and the "servant" who blesses Peter's audience by turning them from their wickedness. Since for Luke, the messianic age is the eschatological age (cf. v. 24: "these days"; Acts 2:17, "in these last days")([103]), Acts 3:22-23 informs us that Jesus is the eschatological prophet like Moses([104]), who fulfills the promises of the prophets; and so this pericope reminds the reader of Luke 4:16-30. Furthermore, according to Acts 3:22-23, there is now a new criterion for belonging to the people of God: one must either listen to Jesus, the prophet like Moses, or be cut off from the people.([105]) Jesus' message replaces that of Moses (cf. 13:38-39; 15:10-11). This is as close as Luke gets to the claim that Jesus' proclamation constitutes a "new" Torah."

Many scholars have written about the extensive comparison or parallel between Jesus and Moses in Acts 7:17-44([106]). As noted above,

---

[101] Schmidt, "Luke's 'Innocent' Jesus," 119.

[102] Kilgallen, *The Stephen Speech*, 82. *Pace* Saito, *Die Mosevorstellungen*, 77-79.

[103] See my *The Unity*, 149-159.

[104] Greene, "The Portrayal of Jesus as Prophet," 51, 61-62; Teeple, *The Mosaic Eschatological Prophet*, 86, 92, 120.

[105] Dupont, "La conclusion des Actes," 393-394; Seccombe, *Possessions and the Poor*, 217-218.

[106] See Carruth, *The Jesus-As-Prophet Motif*, 282-283, Casalegno, *Gesù e il tempio*, 177-178; Colomenero Atienza, "Hechos 7,13-43," 49-50; Greene, "The Portrayal of Jesus as Prophet," 51-52; L.T. Johnson, *The Literary Function*, 70-78; Kilgallen, *The Stephen Speech*, 66-67, 73, 78-87, 92; Kurz, "Luke 3:23-28," 174-175 and Schütz, *Der leidende Christus*, 83-84.

both Jesus (Luke 1:68-75; Acts 3:25-26) and Moses (Acts 7:17) touch on the promise made to Abraham. Both grow in wisdom, are powerful in word and work (Luke 2:40.52; 24:19; Acts 7:22) and are associated with "visits" to the people of Israel (Luke 1:68-69.78-79; 7:16; 19:44; Acts 7:23). Surprisingly, Luke predicates "redeemer" (λυτρωτής) of Moses even though in the Jewish Scriptures God is the one who redeems (e.g., Ex 6:6; Mi 6:4). Very likely Luke has done this because he pictures Moses as a prototype of Jesus who is truly "redeemer." On the road to Emmaus the two disciples explain that they had hoped Jesus was the one to redeem Israel (Luke 24:21). Luke certainly holds that their hope is actually well founded; for earlier, the prophetess, Anna, speaks of Jesus to all who were looking for the redemption of Jerusalem (Luke 2:38; cf. 1:68-69).

Both Moses and Jesus are related to the bringing of peace[107]. Moses tries to bring peace to two fellow Jews quarreling among themselves (Acts 7:26), and Jesus as the dawn will guide the feet of his followers on the way of peace (Luke 1:79). At Jesus' birth the angels sing, "Glory to God in the highest, and on earth peace to those on whom his favors rests" (2:14). Later, Peter proclaims, "You know the word (that) he sent to the Israelites as he proclaimed peace though Jesus Christ, who is Lord of all" (Acts 10:36). Moses' Jewish opponents question him, "Who appointed you ruler and judge over us" (Acts 7:27; cf. v. 35); however, Luke does not use these same Greek words of Jesus. He does predicate "leader" (Acts 3:15; 5:31), "just one" (Luke 23:47; Acts 3:14; 7:52; 22:14) and "judge" (Acts 10:42; cf. 17:31) of Jesus. Acts 3:14-15 and 7:52 relate to Luke's portrait of Moses in Acts 7; and Acts 5:31, "God exalted him at his right hand as leader and savior to grant Israel repentance and forgiveness of sins," resembles 7:35-36: "This Moses, whom they had rejected with the words, 'Who appointed you ruler and judge?' God sent as (both) ruler and deliverer, through the angel who appeared to him in the bush. This man led them out, performing wonders and signs in the land of Egypt, at the Red Sea, and in the desert for forty years."

God sends Jesus (Luke 10:16; Acts 3:20.26; cf. Luke 4:18.43) and Moses (Acts 7:34-35). Each of them performs wonders and signs (Acts 2:22; 4:30; 7:36), and each of them is connected with the wilderness (desert; Luke 4:1-2; Acts 7:36.38). To be sure, Moses' words, "God will raise up for you, from among your own kinsfolk, a prophet like me" (Acts

---

107 Comblin, "La paix," 447-449.

7:37) parallel their application to Jesus in Acts 3:22-23 (cf. Dt 18:15-16). Another possible comparison would be in Acts 7:38 where Moses is said to receive "living utterances" to give to the Jews. The reference is doubtless to the Torah. The parallel to Jesus would be found in his being designated "the leader of life" (Acts 3:15; cf. 2:28; 5:20; 13:46.48). Moses' utterances produce life, and Jesus leads to life.

In Acts 7, Moses particularly prefigures Jesus who is misunderstood, denied and rejected[108]. Moses thought that his fellow Israelites would realize that God was acting through him, but they did not understand (Acts 7:25). An important parallel of a misunderstanding concerning the significance of Jesus for salvation comes at the end of Acts where Paul testifies to the kingdom of God, trying to convince the Jewish leaders in Rome about Jesus from both the Law of Moses and the prophets. When the response is ambivalent, Paul claims that the words of Isaiah have been fulfilled: "Go to this people and say: 'You shall indeed hear but not understand . . . so that they may not see with their eyes and hear with their ears and understand with their hearts and be converted, and I heal them" (Acts 28:26-27; cf. Is 6:9-10)[109]. The ancestors of the Jews denied (Acts 7:35; cf. vv. 26-27, 39) that God sent Moses as ruler and judge: just as their rulers denied Jesus before Pilate, they denied the holy and just one (Acts 3:13-14; cf. 7:51-53).

Only a few interpreters of the Stephen speech have noted that the rejections of both Moses and Jesus have the same result, namely, false worship[110]. The Jews asked Aaron to make them gods to worship, and God turns them over to the worship of the hosts of heaven (Acts 7:39-42). The same follows on the rejection of Jesus; for in doing this the Jewish opponents resist the Holy Spirit and prophets, and the significance of the

---

[108] Schütz, Der leidende Christus, 34-35; Teeple, The Mosaic Eschatological Prophet, 86-87, 92; Tiede, Prophecy and History, 124-125.

[109] Elsewhere, Luke explains that the Jews rejected Jesus out of ignorance (Acts 3:17; 13:27-28).

[110] Kilgallen, The Stephen Speech, 83-93, who also maintains (37-44, 62-63) that "worship" unifies the speech of Stephen and Tiede, Prophecy and History, 42. See also Giblin, Destruction of Jerusalem, 111 and Via, "Moses and Meaning," 124.

temple is, therefore, perverted (vv. 48-53)([111]).

This consideration of the Lukan parallels between Jesus and Moses leads to a final question: does Luke in the programmatic passage (Luke 4:14[16]-[30]44) intend such a parallel([112])? After all, in the programmatic passage Luke writes of Jesus, things that are predicated of Moses elsewhere in Luke-Acts: God sends both of them, and each has the spirit. Luke speaks of Jesus' miracles and "appealing discourse" in the programmatic passage, and both Jesus and Moses work wonders and signs and are prophets powerful in word and deed. "A year of favor from the Lord" is an eschatological phrase([113]), and we recall that Jesus is the eschatological prophet like Moses; yet both are misunderstood and ultimately rejected. So, although Luke does not explicitly state any parallel between Jesus and Moses in the programmatic passage, the evidence supports there being one in the background.

Jesus Acts As a Prophet

We have seen that in the programmatic passage Jesus is indirectly identified as a prophet, and that the hope expressed about Jesus the prophet by the two disciples on the road to Emmaus in Luke 24:19 ("The things that happened to Jesus the Nazarene, who was a prophet mighty in deed and word before God and all the people . . . .") was valid. And so we conclude that this verse functions as a true summary of Jesus' life. We have also pointed out that Luke through the mouth of Peter maintains that Jesus was the prophet about whom Moses spoke, who would be like him and to whom one must listen if one does not want to be cut off from the people (Acts 3:22-23)([114]). A natural conclusion from these verses, especially, from Luke 24:19, would be that all of Jesus' words in the Gospel

---

[111] Casalegno, *Gesù e il tempio*, 183-191; O'Toole, "Luke's Notion of Worship," 185-197.

[112] Marshall, *Luke: Historian and Theologian*, 127-128 and Tiede, *Prophecy and History*, 46-47, 53 and 124-125.

[113] Grundmann, *Das Evangelium nach Lukas*, 121, Harrington, *The Gospel according to Luke*, 87-88, Schweizer, *The Good News according to Luke*, 88-89.

[114] Haenchen, *The Acts*, 209 and Polhill, *Acts*, 135-136.

are prophetic([115]). Acts 3:22-23 would reinforce this understanding since, in addition to what Peter is saying in this speech, the most obvious reference to everything that Jesus said would be what he says in the Gospel.

However, Luke's identification of Jesus as a prophet is not so exclusive that we are obliged in each case to demonstrate why we claim that Jesus is speaking or acting as a prophet. To be sure, some few activities are so characteristic of prophets that we are on solid ground when we claim that these passages justify our viewing Jesus as a prophet. For instance, prophets are associated with knowledge not possessed by others, with miracles and with suffering; and although for some time there was a scholarly movement to deny that prophets, in accord with the Greek word (προφήτης) used most often to designate them, could foretell the future, now most scholars grant that this activity was also characteristic of prophets. Actually, foretelling the future plays an important part in Luke-Acts. Finally, although we pointed out above that Luke 24:19 and Acts 3:22-23 function as summaries of Jesus' life, they do occur late in the narrative; and more importantly these summaries describe Jesus from only one point of view, his being a prophet. However, this book should clarify that for Luke Jesus is much more than prophet.

For the sake of clarity let us take two examples. In the programmatic passage Jesus indirectly identifies himself as a prophet; so in this passage we could conclude the following about how Jesus the prophet acts: he reads and interprets Scriptures (vv. 16-20); his words bring grace and at times are well received, but at other times are rejected; he challenges the thinking of his audience (vv. 22, 23, 28-29); cites proverbs (v. 24) and makes use of comparisons (vv. 25-27); he can miraculously escape from opponents (v. 30). However, should each of these activities be attributed to Jesus because he is a prophet? Below, we will contend that Luke in Luke 7:36-50 portrays Jesus as a prophet who knows the persons he is dealing with and what they are thinking. However, in the same pericope, Jesus also uses a parable (vv. 41-42), challenges the behavior of Simon (vv. 41-46), twice proclaims that the woman's sins are forgiven (vv. 47-48) and commends the quality of her love and employs the proverb, "But the one to whom little is forgiven, loves little" (v. 47).

---

[115] On the other hand, the reader will recall that earlier we showed that Luke was likewise able to refer to everything that Jesus said as "teaching" (cf. Acts 1:1).

Of all of these words and actions, the one which surely seems inappropriate to apply to Jesus as prophet is the forgiveness of sins because the question, "Who is this who even forgives sins" (v. 49) suggests to the reader that this action points to Jesus as being more than just a prophet. One might want to conclude the same about "Your faith has saved you; go in peace" (v. 50) since it depends on the forgiveness of sins. Consequently, in the final analysis, one realizes that not everything Jesus says and does can automatically be claimed as a proof that he is a prophet, even if he implies that he is a prophet in the programmatic passage or is so identified in any given passage or generalization about his activity.

Keeping the above reflections in mind, there are still actions Jesus performs which point to him as a prophet. Jesus works cures, knows with whom and with what kind of person he is dealing, and predicts the future. In a sense, the programmatic passage associates all of the miracles worked by Jesus with his being a prophet, and Luke foreshadows these miracles with his references to those of Elijah and Elisha (Luke 4:25-27). Also, the disciples' description of Jesus' life as, "a prophet mighty in deed and word before God and all the people" (24:19; cf. 7:16; Acts 7:22), surely regard his miracles as part of his prophetic activity[116].

Jesus, like the prophets of old, knows people for who they are and what kind of a character they have. We see this in the story of "A Sinful Woman" (Luke 7:36-50), which for all practical purposes is unique to Luke. The woman stands at Jesus' feet weeping and begins to bathe his feet with her tears and to dry them with her hair and continues to kiss his feet and to anoint them with the ointment. Jesus' host, the Pharisee, says to himself, "If this man were a prophet, he would know who and what sort of woman this is who is touching him, that she is a sinner" (v. 39)[117]. However, in v. 47, Jesus recognizes that the woman was a sinner, but proclaims that her sins have been forgiven because of her great love. Even more striking is Jesus' awareness of what kind of a person the Pharisee is. He knows that the Pharisee is prejudiced against him and notes that the woman has acted as his host should have. Clearly, although the Pharisee did not want to recognize Jesus as a prophet and lacks the woman's love, Luke wants his readers to regard Jesus in the pericope as a prophet and

---

[116] Squires, *The Plan of God*, 23-24 and n. 34.

[117] Bock, *Luke 1:1 – 9:50*, 697 and his note 11.

gives them all the evidence they need to draw such a conclusion. A prophet knows people for who and what they are (cf. John 4:16-19).

Jesus knows what others are thinking. Here, "discussing" or "wondering" and its cognate are of some assistance for our study. When Jesus tells the paralytic that his sins are forgiven, the scribes and Pharisees wonder whether his claim to forgive sins is blasphemous. Jesus perceives their thoughts and asks, "Which is easier, to say, 'Your sins are forgiven,' or to say, 'Rise and walk'" (Luke 5:23)? Of course, the subsequent cure demonstrates Jesus' authority to forgive sins; but our interest here lies in his prophetic ability to know what others were thinking. Jesus likewise knows what the scribes and Pharisee are thinking about the possibility of his curing the man with the withered hand on the Sabbath (6:7-8b). His subsequent question and cure, however, do not succeed in getting them to rethink their position. Luke 9:46-48 (cf. 22:24-27), too, provide an example of Jesus' prophetic knowledge of what others are thinking([118]). The disciples are arguing about which of them is the greatest; and Jesus, aware of their thoughts, takes a little child and stands him by his side and says, "Whoever receives this child in my name receives me, and whoever receives me receives the one who sent me. For the one who is least among all of you is the one who is the greatest."

Jesus likewise knows what some of the crowds are thinking when they ask for a sign from heaven to show that he is not casting out demons in the name of Beelzebub (11:17; cf. vv. 14-16). At the Last Supper, Jesus likewise knows that the one who will betray him is also there (22:22). When, after his resurrection, Jesus appears to his disciples, he knows that they are fearful and think that he might be a ghost (24:38); so he shows them his hands and feet and invites them to touch him and see that he is not a ghost. He further reassures them by eating part of a broiled fish. Finally, when the risen Jesus joins Cleopas and the other disciple on the way to Emmaus, Luke's implication is that Jesus knows what they have been discussing. To be sure, these last two passages speak of the risen Jesus; but his actions are like those of a prophet. In the last passage the earthly Jesus is described as a prophet, mighty in deed and word (24:19).

Luke regards Jesus and all that he does, and what happens to him, as the fulfillment of God's design for salvation announced through the prophets. A number of scholars have identified this pattern as proph-

---

[118] G. Schneider, *Evangelium nach Lukas*, 134.

ecy/promise and fulfillment. To a certain extent, they are correct; however, Luke also has other ways of showing that God continues to bring his salvation to Israel who are now the Christians([119]). More to the point of our present discussion is the evidence that in first-century Judaism OT prophecy was seen primarily as predictions of the age-to-come or of events leading up to it. Naturally, our interest falls on any predictions Jesus may have made and what they may reveal about him. In part, we will be following the lead of B.C. Frein([120]).

All three Synoptics report Jesus' three predictions of his suffering, death and resurrection (Luke 9:22.43b-44; 18:31-34; par.); but Luke reports three other predictions of Jesus' death and resurrection each of which contains "it is necessary" and so connects Jesus' prophetic ability with his knowledge of God's will (13:33; 17:25; 24:7; cf. 22:37). As noted above, Jesus in 13:33 predicts that his death in Jerusalem will be the death of a prophet; his prophetic identity necessitates his death, and this passage likewise connects Jesus' journey to Jerusalem with his identity as a prophet. Moreover, in v. 35 he assures his audience that they will not see him until the time comes when they say, "Blessed is he who comes in the name of the Lord." Most scholars grant that this is a prophecy that is fulfilled in what is generally described as Jesus' triumphal entry into Jerusalem when the whole multitude of disciples praise God for all that they have seen and say, "Blessed is the king who comes in the name of the Lord!" (19:38a). According to 17:25, the Son of Man must first "suffer greatly and be rejected by this generation." Jesus predicts that before the day of the Son of Man comes he must suffer much.

We find a more complicated situation in the scene of Jesus before the Sanhedrin during which he predicts, "But from this time on the Son of Man will be seated at the right hand of the power of God" (22:69). This prediction calls for a number of observations. It occurs immediately after the scene of the mocking and beating of Jesus during which the soldiers blindfold him and keep asking, "Prophesy! Who is it that struck you" (22:64)? Of course, by this time Luke's readers have no doubt that Jesus is a prophet and can prophesy, or that this prophetic capability includes his

---

[119] See my *The Unity*, 23-32.

[120] "Narrative Predictions," 23-37.

next prophecy, a few verses later, in v. 69([121]). Moreover, this prophecy is realized in Acts 2:33-35, where Jesus is portrayed as being exalted at the right hand of God, and in Acts 7:55-56, where Stephen sees Jesus so exalted([122]). Also, Jesus predicts that his suffering as a criminal will fulfill Is 53:12 (Luke 23:37; cf. Acts 8:30-35)([123]). Moreover, in the third passion prediction only the Lucan Jesus predicts that his suffering, death and resurrection will fulfill what was written in the prophets about the Son of Man (Luke 18:31; cf. vv. 32-34). Jesus states in 24:44-46 that this prediction has been fulfilled. Two other passages in Acts report this fulfillment of the prophecies about Jesus' sufferings (3:18; 13:27-29). Earlier, the two men in dazzling clothes speak of the realization of the predictions about Jesus' passion; for they say to the women, "'Remember what he said to you while he was still in Galilee, that the Son of Man must be handed over to sinners and be crucified, and rise on the third day.' And they remembered his words" (24:6-8).

The disciples are the subjects of several prophecies which are fulfilled soon after they are made. Jesus tells the disciples how they will find the colt, which he is to ride into Jerusalem, and the events narrated afterwards match Jesus' prediction (Luke 19:30-34). Only Luke writes that they "found it as he had told them" (v. 32b)([124]). Later, when Jesus tells the disciples how they will find a place for the celebration of the Passover Meal, we read in both Mark and Luke that, "They found it as he had told them" (22:13; cf. Mk 14:16). Luke's account of Jesus' prediction of Peter's denial specifies that he will deny that he "knows" Jesus three times (22:34); and in 22:57 (cf. vv. 58, 60), Peter says, "Woman, I do not know him."

Several other predictions look to the disciples' future activity. Jesus tells Peter that he will be catching people (Luke 5:10), which is realized in the response to Peter's preaching in Acts (e.g., 2:41; 4:4; cf.

---

[121] Although he does not refer to v. 64, Bock, *Luke 9:51 – 24:53*, 1790, holds that this mockery of Jesus' prophetic ability recalls his prediction (Luke 18:32-33) which is realized in 22:63; 23:11.36 and in the fulfillment of the prediction of Peter's denial.

[122] Polhill, *Acts*, 207.

[123] Fitzmyer, *The Gospel According to Luke X–XXIV*, 1432, reminds us that this is the only time that Is 53:12 is quoted in the gospel tradition.

[124] Lenski, *St. Luke's Gospel*, 962.

5:14). In Luke 22:32, Jesus foretells that Peter, after being tested by Satan, will turn and strengthen the other Christians. Apparently, Luke regarded Peter's leadership in the first part of Acts as the actualization of this prophecy. Jesus in 12:11-12 and 21:12-19 foretells the hardships that the disciples will have to endure. These predictions are fulfilled in various parts of Acts([125]). Luke 12:12, "For the Holy Spirit will teach you at that moment what you should say" finds fulfillment in Peter who, filled with the Spirit, answers the temple authorities in Acts 4:8 (cf. v. 31) and in Stephen (Acts 6:10; cf. 7:55; 13:9-11).

"They will lay hands on you and persecute you" (Luke 21:12a) is fulfilled when the opponents "lay hands on" the apostles in Acts 4:3; 5:18; 12:1; 21:27; and a great persecution occurs after Stephen's death (Acts 8:1b) and against Paul and Barnabas (Acts 13:50). Paul likewise persecutes the Christians (Acts 9:4-5; 22:4-8; 26:11-15). Christians (Acts 8:3; 22:4,19; 26:11), Peter (12:4) and Paul (21:11; 28:17) are all "handed over to synagogues or prison" (cf. Luke 21:12b.16), in which passage only Luke writes of prisons. Luke has introduced "governor" into Jesus' prediction in Luke 21:12 to prepare for his comparison between Jesus (Luke 23:1-25; cf. vv. 1, 7) and Paul (Acts 25:23 – 26:32) who are both led before a governor and a king([126]). Finally, the prediction that some of the disciples will be put to death (Luke 21:16) finds fulfillment in the stoning of Stephen (Acts 7:54-60) and the execution of James (Acts 12:2).

The risen Jesus acts like a prophet. In Luke 24:44-47, Jesus not only contends that the Scriptures are fulfilled in his (the Christ's) suffering and resurrection but claims that the same is true of the forthcoming preaching in his name of repentance and of the forgiveness of sins for all peoples. Jesus' prediction in Acts 1:8 again refers to this mission and looks back to his earlier one that he would send the promise of the Father (Luke 24:49: the Holy Spirit and power). Of course, these predictions are actualized in the coming of the Holy Spirit (Acts 2:1-4) and in the preaching activity of the apostles in Acts. For instance, Peter speaks of the gift of the Spirit, repentance and the forgiveness of sins in Jesus' name (Acts 2:38-39; cf. 3:19; 10:42-43). In Acts 1:4-5, the risen Jesus takes up the prophecy of John the Baptist (Luke 3:16b)

---

[125] Schweizer, *The Good News according to Luke*, 315-316, provides the references for many of these passages in Acts.

[126] O'Toole, *Acts 26*, 22-25.

and the contrast between John's baptism with water and Jesus' with the Holy Spirit. Probably, the tongues of fire at Pentecost (Acts 2:3) realize John's original prophecy that "He will baptize you with the Holy Spirit and fire" (Luke 3:16).

Jesus also prophesies about the mission and imprisonment of Paul. In each of the accounts of his conversions, the risen Jesus (Acts 9:15; 22:21; 26:16) speaks of Paul's mission to the Gentiles, and in 9:16 he tells Ananias how much Paul must suffer for his name([127]). At the end of one of these accounts (Acts 22:17-21), Luke records a vision of Jesus to Paul in the temple in which he informs him that the Jews of Jerusalem will not accept Paul's witness about him. These predictions are realized in Paul's missionary journeys among the Gentiles, in his imprisonments and mistreatment and in the general failure of the Jews to accept his witness. In Acts 18:10-12 the risen Lord encourages Paul and promises that no harm will come to him, the realization of which we should probably see in Gallio's refusal to prosecute Paul (18:12-17; cf. Luke 21:15). The risen Christ appears to Paul again in Jerusalem and foretells that he will bear witness to Jesus in Rome as he has there (Acts 23:11), which prophecy finds fulfillment in the final scenes of Acts.

Other predictions made by Jesus need to be considered. They are those left unfulfilled, most of which deal with eschatological events. The fact that these predictions occur in the same context as prophecies that are fulfilled reassures Luke's reader that they, too, will be accomplished. For instance, immediately after his first passion prediction, Jesus speaks of the reversals of fortunes in the age to come and of whom the Son of Man will be ashamed when he comes (Luke 9:24.26-27). In Luke 13:22-30, Jesus predicts who will and will not enter the kingdom of heaven. He likewise speaks of the coming of the Son of Man (17:22-37) along with another passion prediction, unique to him (17:25). Jesus' eschatological warnings (12:8-10; 21:8-11.25-28) occur in the same context as the prophecies about the persecutions that the disciples will have to endure (cf. 12:11-12; 21:12-19). Jesus' promise that the apostles will eat and drink at his table in his kingdom and sit on thrones and judge the twelve tribes of Israel (22:29-30) occurs just before his words about how Satan has sought to sift the apostles like wheat and how Jesus prays for

---

[127] Haenchen, *The Acts*, 325, observes, "Ananias had averred that Saul would make those suffer who call on the Name of Christ. Quite the reverse! Christ will show him how much he must suffer for the Name!"

Peter's faith so that, repentant, he can strengthen his brothers. These words occur just before Jesus' prediction of Peter's denial (vv. 31-34).

Jesus' predictions about the fall of Jerusalem (19:41-44; 21:6.20-24) need to be addressed. One might be tempted to hold that Luke does not show that these predictions about the fall of Jerusalem were later realized. Yet there are a number of details, which may not have been in the original prophecies themselves, that suggest Luke knew about the fall of Jerusalem and may have assumed that his reader did, too: "When your enemies encircle you with a rampart, hem you in, and press you hard from every side. They will wipe you out, you and your children within your walls, and leave not a stone upon a stone within you" (19:43-44; cf. 21:6) and "When you see Jerusalem encircled by soldiers, know that its devastation is near . . . . The people will fall before the sword; they will be led captive in the midst of the Gentiles. Jerusalem will be trampled by the Gentiles" (21:20.24). J.H. Neyrey holds for a prophetic judgment oracle in Jesus' address to the women of Jerusalem (23:27-31)[128], which most likely looks to the above fall of Jerusalem.

Jesus performs symbolic prophetic actions. Above we noted that when he sends out the seventy(-two) (Luke 10:1), Jesus is compared to Moses who selected seventy elders to help him with the leadership of the people (Num 11:16-25). Only Luke speaks of these seventy(-two), and the scope of Jesus' prophetic action looks to the later expanding church and her need for a more multifaceted leadership. In the cleansing of the temple (Luke 19:45-46) Jesus again acts as a prophet. As it stands in Luke's Gospel today, the cleansing of the temple is a pronouncement story since the emphasis falls on Jesus' statements in v. 46. As he enters Jerusalem Jesus, like the prophets of old, concerns himself with the sacred character of the temple. The strongest argument that Jesus acts as a prophet in this pericope is the OT citations of two prophets who were speaking about the temple: "My house shall be a house of prayer" (v. 46a; cf. Is 56:7) and "But you have made it a den of thieves" (Luke 19:46b; cf. Jer 7:11). The first of these citations occurs in a context of returning the temple to its true purpose; the second in a prophetical criticism of how some Jews of the time were using the temple. So, Jesus performs a prophetic symbolic action[129], which challenges those who are misusing

---

128 Neyrey, "Jesus' Address to the Women," 79.

129 Green, *The Gospel of Luke*, 692; Nolland, *Luke 18:35 – 24:53*, 933-938.

the temple to remember its true purpose. Since Jesus immediately afterwards begins teaching in the temple, Luke is suggesting that Jesus has cleansed the temple and with his teaching is returning it to its true purpose.

At the Last Supper, during which Luke compares Jesus to Moses and Jeremiah, and, as we shall see, to the Servant of Yahweh, we should probably see prophetic symbolism in Jesus' actions which establish the Christian Passover. Of course, "symbolic" does not mean "unreal." Rather Jesus' prophetic symbolic actions with the bread and wine and his words give the meal its theological significance and determine a liturgical celebration, which is to be repeated and looks to the messianic banquet.

Jesus Is Identified As a Prophet
At the end of the story of Jesus' marvelous raising of the widow's son at Nain (Luke 7:11-17), everyone glorifies God and exclaims, "A great prophet has risen in our midst" and "God has visited his people" (v. 16). This exclamation comes at the end of the story and so stands as the conclusion that the people have drawn from the experience. The two statements of the people seem to be an instance of Hebrew parallelism, that is, the fact that a great prophet has arisen among them can also be expressed as God's visitation of his people. So, the people of Nain recognize that Jesus is a great prophet and that his compassionate miracle means God's presence among them. However, Luke generalizes the people's exclamations; Jesus' being a great prophet and God's presence among his people embrace all Jews and not just the townsfolk of Nain.

Above, we noted that in Luke 9:7-8.18-19 the ordinary people have various opinions about who Jesus is, all of which see him as a prophet[130]. Some view him as John the Baptist, others as Elijah returned from the dead and still others regard him as one of the prophets of old. We will see in our consideration of Jesus as Son of God that Luke is not content with these identifications and in 9:1-50 highlights two other designations of Jesus. Aside from how Luke wishes his readers to interpret it, the explanation of the disciples on the road to Emmaus, "The things that happened to Jesus the Nazarene, who was a prophet mighty in deed and word before God and all the people," reveals how up to the crucifixion these two disciples and others had viewed Jesus and his activity. We have

[130] Ravens, "Luke 9,7-62 and the Prophetic Role of Jesus," 119-129.

already studied Peter's proclamation of Jesus as the prophet like Moses (Acts 3:22-23).

Summary of Luke's Portrayal of Jesus As a Prophet
The programmatic passage (Luke 4:[14]16-30[44]) and related pericopes (7:18-23; 13:31-35) reveal that according to Luke Jesus implies an identification of himself as prophet([131]). God sends the prophet Jesus to the disadvantaged and both Jews and Gentiles, yet his own people will reject him. Jesus interprets the Sacred Scriptures and works miracles, and his words are occasions of grace. Although, just like other prophets, he will be killed in Jerusalem, Jesus' loving concern for that city and the Jewish people remains a constant.

Luke draws parallels between Jesus and various OT prophets, and these form part of the continuous story of God's saving activity. However, these parallels do not limit his presentation of Jesus to any given OT prophet. The most numerous parallels are between Jesus and Moses, and the most important of these are found in the Transfiguration story, Luke 24:19, Acts 3:22-23; 7:17-44. The following aspects are stressed: Jesus is an eschatological prophet, mighty in deed and word, whose Transfiguration recalls the Sinai event and whom, like Moses, God sends. Jesus, too, has an exodus to achieve which includes the journey to Jerusalem and explains the designation of Christianity as the "Way." This exodus not only embraces his being misunderstood, denied and rejected in all of which he is compared to Moses, but also his resurrection. One must listen to Jesus, the promised prophet like Moses; and whoever does not now listen to him will be cut off from the people. Jesus is one who leads to life and to peace, who remains open to God's activity in others and whose teachings are summarized, as were those of Moses. Rejection of either Moses or of Jesus has the same result, false worship.

Luke compares Jesus with Moses in a number of other ways. Both grow in wisdom and are filled with the Spirit and associated with "forty" and with the selection of seventy(-two?). Probably the feeding of the five thousand mirrors the manna in the desert, and the Passover celebration and

---

[131] L.T. Johnson, in *Living Jesus*, 159-175, and in his *The Gospel of Luke* and *The Acts of the Apostles* has provided abundant information about Luke's portrayal of Jesus as a prophet; but in the opinion of the present writer, Johnson has overstated the role that Jesus as prophet plays in Luke-Acts.

the covenant in Jesus' blood looks to further comparison with Moses. Both accuse others of being perverse and unbelieving, yet are accused themselves of perverting the people. Luke writes of Moses as "Redeemer" mainly because he functions as a prototype of Jesus, the Redeemer.

Luke compares Jesus to Isaiah and to the Servant of Yahweh in Luke 4:18-19. There is also a parallel to Elijah in the programmatic passage and in the raising of the son of the widow of Nain. Luke has another parallel to Elijah in Jesus' ascension, and, like Elijah, Jesus is accused of subverting the people. When rejected by a Samaritan village, Jesus refuses to imitate the fiery violence of Elijah. Elisha in the programmatic passage and in Jesus' cure of lepers in the Gospel serves as a model; and this is true also of Jonah, who is the sign to the Ninevites and whose story has influenced that of the calming of the storm. Finally, at the Last Supper, Luke has Jesus speak of the "new covenant" of Jeremiah.

Ultimately, these parallels or comparisons form part of Luke's portrayal of the continuity of God's plan of salvation, convey the importance of the event in question, and give Luke's readers assurance about what they have been instructed (Luke 1:4). All of these data witness to Luke's presentation of Jesus as a prophet, though he is unique among the prophets.

Jesus acts like a prophet, works cures, knows what others are thinking and with what kind of persons he is dealing, and predicts the future. Nonetheless, he has to suffer. His predictions flow from the Jewish prophetic tradition, which finds its main fulfillment in Jesus, and belong to what some scholars have called prophecy/promise–fulfillment. Furthermore, these predictions are important plot devices and serve to carry the narrative forward. They build suspense because the reader is not exactly sure when and how they will be realized. Ultimately, these predictions fall under Luke's major theme: God continues to bring his salvation to Israel, now embodied in the Christians, particularly, through Jesus. At times, Jesus fulfills the prophecies of the OT and at others his predictions about his own ministry. Likewise, Jesus predicts things of the disciples which are fulfilled soon afterwards or which look to their future activity. Some predictions made by Jesus remain unfulfilled; however, since they appear in contexts where his other prophecies are realized, Luke's reader feels assured that they also will be accomplished.

Jesus performs symbolic prophetic acts. His actions that can be so qualified are the selection of the seventy(-two), the cleansing of the temple and the Passover celebration. Each of these events has a particular message for Jesus' audience and for Luke's readers.

Others view Jesus as a prophet. The crowd that witnesses the raising of the son of the widow of Nain so identifies Jesus (Luke 7:16), as do the ordinary people (9:18-19; cf. v. 7b-8) and Peter (Acts 3:22-23). The doubt that the Pharisee has about Jesus being a prophet in Luke 7:39 in the course of the pericope is shown to be superficial; and in the Emmaus story, Luke intends his reader to regard the hope of the disciples in Jesus the prophet as sound, even if at the time the disciples do not (24:19). Nonetheless, "prophet" is not Luke's dominant title for Jesus; for instance, we will see that in 9:1-50 Luke definitely subordinates "prophet" to "the Christ" and "my Son."

CHAPTER THREE
Jesus As Savior

When we speak of "salvation" in this section, we cannot refer only to σῴζω ("I save")([132]) and its cognates, but must include any wording that Luke uses to express Jesus' liberation of human beings from physical or moral evil([133]). Since Luke is so strongly influenced by the LXX, we have every reason to assume that his concept of "salvation" was definitely influenced by the Jewish notion of "salvation" which strongly relates to what happens in this world, i.e., during this earthly life. Of course, human beings are not able to save themselves; God makes this possible (Luke 8:26-27). So, God is the savior (1:47) and so saves (Acts 2:47; 7:25), yet for Luke Jesus also saves.

---

[132] Confer van Unnik "L'usage de σῴζειν," 16-34. See also Fohrer, σωτήρ, 1012-1013; Foerster, σωτήρ, 1015-1016.

[133] The topic of this chapter has interested a number of scholars, e.g., Bovon, "Le salut," 296-307; Cadbury, "The Titles of Jesus in Acts," 370-371; Crump, *Jesus the Intercessor*; Danker, *Benefactor*; Doble, *The Paradox of Salvation*; Dömer, *Das Heil Gottes*; Donfried, "Attempts at Understanding the Purpose," 112-122; Feldkämper, *Der betende Jesus als Heilsmittler*; Fitzmyer, *The Gospel According to Luke I–IX*, 219-227, 262-266; Flender, *St. Luke: Theologian of Redemptive History*, 146-162, 166-167; Fletcher-Louis, *Luke-Acts*; Glöckner, *Die Verkündigung des Heils*; Jacquier, *Les Actes des Apôtres*, cciv-ccv; Kränkl, *Jesus der Knecht Gottes*; Lohse, "Lukas als Theologe der Heilsgeschichte"; Prete, *L'opera di Luca*, 13-15; O'Toole, "Activity of the Risen Christ," 491-496; Rigaux, *Témoignage*, 383-404; Summers, *Jesus. The Universal Savior*; Voss, *Die Christologie*, 45-60; Wilcock, *The Savior of the World: The Message of Luke*; Tannehill, "The Mission of Jesus," 51-75, discusses the mission contained in these verses. See also Reicke, "Jesus in Nazareth — Lk 4,14-30," 47-55.

σώζω ("I Save") and Its Cognates

The programmatic passage (Luke 4:14-44[134]; cf. 7:21-22) provides an excellent example that Luke does not limit himself to a specific Greek word to express his theme of Jesus as savior. In the synagogue scene itself the following phrasings relating to Jesus express "salvation" (4:18-19; cf. 7:21-22): "to bring good news to the poor," "to proclaim release to the captives and recovery of sight to the blind," "to let the oppressed go free," "to proclaim the year of the Lord's favor" and "words of grace which came out of his mouth (v. 22)." The import of most of these phrasings about salvation is immediately obvious. Of course, the "good news" is a message about the reign of God (v. 43) and so of salvation, and "the year of the Lord's favor," which Jesus will actualize([135]). Below we will see that grace is also involved with salvation (cf. Acts 15:10). To these expressions should be joined the implied comparison between Jesus and Elijah and Elisha respectively, both of whom were sent to help ("save") disadvantaged non-Jews (vv. 25-27).

In Luke 4:31-44 Jesus immediately begins his mission described in the synagogue scene. He teaches in the synagogue of Capernaum and in those of Judea. He liberates the man possessed by an evil spirit and cures Simon's mother-in-law's fever. He lays his hands on those with various illnesses and cures them; demons leave some of them.

Luke's strongest and most embracing statement about Jesus as savior occurs in Acts 4:11-12; (cf. v. 9): "He is 'the stone rejected by you, the builders, which has become the cornerstone.' There is no salvation through anyone else, nor is there any other name under heaven given to the human race by which we are to be saved"([136]). These verses are an

---

[134] For the programmatic function of these verses or of 4:16-30, see Bock, *Luke 1:1 – 9:50*, 394, 420; Glöckner, *Die Verkündigung des Heils*, 124-134; Nolland, *Luke 1 – 9:20*, 195; Prior, *Jesus: The Liberator*, 161-162; and Talbert, *Reading Luke*, 54-57. Tuckett, "The Christology of Luke-Acts," 143, contends that the ideas expressed in Luke 4:18-19 little reflect or influence the story that follows. To an extent, he is correct, but his conclusion is based on a preconceived notion of how Luke should develop his themes. Luke employs an extensive word pattern to express salvation and leaves his reader to perceive the whole picture. A rigid approach toward Luke's thought only distorts it.

[135] See O'Toole, "Il Giubileo."

example of Luke's literary ability, for almost without being detected he moves his readers from one level of thought to another. From the one physical cure of a paralytic at the Beautiful Gate and from the speech which follows upon it, Luke in less than a chapter and a half brings his readers to the proclamation that Jesus is the only savior—on all levels. Another expression of this thought occurs in Acts 15:11: "On the contrary, we believe that we are saved through the grace of the Lord Jesus, in the same way as they." Yet another general statement about Jesus as savior appears in the story about Zacchaeus (19:1-10), which concludes with the assertion, "For the Son of Man has come to seek and to save what was lost." Again Luke moves from an action of Jesus, the saving of Zacchaeus, to a general statement. In the story Jesus tells Zacchaeus that he must stay in his house (v. 5) and rephrases this in v. 9, "Today salvation (σωτηρία) has come to this house because this man too is a descendant of Abraham"; but is it not Jesus who has come to his house?

Luke portrays Jesus even before his birth as an instrument of God's salvation. Salvation terminology abounds in the *Benedictus* (Luke 1:68-79). Zechariah prophesies that God has raised up a mighty savior (κέρας σωτηρίας) for us in the house of his servant David (v. 69); but Luke's readers already know that God will give Jesus the throne of his ancestor David and that he will reign over the house of Jacob forever and of his kingdom there would be no end (1:32-33). So the "mighty savior" in the house of David must be Jesus. The Benedictus continues and assures us that we will be saved from our enemies and from those who hate us (v. 71). A few verses later John the Baptist is called the prophet of the Most High who will go before the Lord (cf. 7:26), who must be Jesus[137], to prepare his ways and to give knowledge of salvation to his people by

---

[136] See Haenchen, *The Acts*, 217-218, 223 and Polhill, *Acts*, 144-145.

[137] Fitzmyer, *The Gospel According to Luke I–IX*, 385-386, and Schweizer, *The Good News according to Luke*, 41. Luke writes of John the Baptist going before Jesus (cf. Luke 3:3-6.16; Acts 13:24-25). One perceives the difficulty of claiming a reference to God by what some authors write. Bock, *Luke 1:1 – 9:50*, 189, contends, "In the Messiah, God's plan and design are found, so that when the Messiah comes, God comes"; Lenski, *St. Luke's Gospel*, 109, explains, "The idea is that Yahweh himself comes to his people in the person of Jesus"; and Nolland, *Luke 1 – 9:20*, 89, "And there may, therefore, be a happy ambiguity about the reference of "Lord" (Κύριος) here (see further at 1:17 and 3:4)."

the forgiveness of their sins (1:76-77). Below we will see that "forgive-ness of sins" is another Lucan expression for salvation. In order not to miss the full force of the message of salvation contained in the *Benedictus*, let us note the other expressions of "salvation" that appear there and that relate to the Christ-event: God has redeemed his people (v. 68), he (God) has shown mercy (v. 72) and remembered his holy covenant, the oath that God swore to Abraham, that we being rescued (vv. 73-74) from the hand of our enemies . . . , through the loving kindness of God, the dawn from on high (Jesus) will break upon us to give light to those who sit in darkness and in the shadow of death, to guide our feet on the way of peace" (v. 79). In brief, the *Benedictus* is a hymn of thanksgiving to God for the salvation he brings us in Jesus, which Luke describes in various traditional Jewish ways.

At his birth (Luke 2:8-20), the angel tells the shepherds, who represent the disadvantaged, "For today in the city of David a savior has been born for you who is Christ and Lord" (v. 11; cf. Acts 13:22-23.26). Only Luke uses the phrasing, "Christ (and) Lord," in this verse. The angel also identifies Jesus as "savior" and associates him with David (cf. Luke 1:69). We have a solemn proclamation of an angel about who Jesus is, but the immediate context does not supply us with much information about this savior. However, at his birth Jesus is associated with the disadvan-taged; and in their brief hymn of praise, the angels speak of "peace on earth to those on whom his (God's) good pleasure rests." We will see that "peace" belongs to Luke's word pattern of salvation, and "good pleas-ure"([138]) refers to God's grace or favor toward the individuals who will benefit from the saving activity of the child just born.

While holding the infant Jesus in his arms, Simeon in his canticle (Luke 2:29-32) exclaims, "For my eyes have seen your salvation, which you prepared in the sight of all the peoples (cf. 3:6; Acts 28:28; Is 40:5; 52:10), a light to be revealed to the Gentiles (cf. Acts 13:47; 26:18; Is 49:6), and the glory for your people Israel" (Luke 2:30-32; cf. Acts 26:23). Obviously, Jesus in this prayer is identified as God's salvation, and in apposition to this "salvation" is "light" (cf. Is 42:16; 51:4-5; Ps 43:1-9) which we have already seen can stand for salvation (Luke 1:78-79; cf. 4:18). This light is said to be for the ἀποκάλυψις of the Gentiles, which

---

[138] Fitzmyer, *The Gospel According to Luke I–IX*, 411-412, provides reasons for the translation, "good pleasure."

Greek word should probably be translated "unveiling." However, should "glory" be taken in apposition to "light"? A parallel between "light" and "glory" accords more with Luke's usage of these two words (2:9; 9:31-32; Acts 22:11) and with his openness to both Gentiles and Jews and is supported by the parallel between Luke 2:30-32 and Acts 26:23 (cf. Is 58:8; 60:19)([139]): "That the Messiah must suffer and that, as the first to rise from the dead, he would proclaim light both to our people and to the Gentiles." From the risen Jesus' mission to Paul, part of which appears in Acts 26:18 ("to open their eyes that they may turn from darkness to light and from the power of Satan to God, so that they may obtain forgiveness of sins and an inheritance among those who have been consecrated by faith in me") we know that "light" refers to salvation; and in v. 23 this is what Christ proclaims to both the people (Jews) and the Gentiles. So, in both Luke 2:30-32 and Acts 26:23 we find "light" as an image of salvation and associated with universality. In the latter passage we do not find "glory" but we do find "light" in reference to both the Jews and the Gentiles. So, it is more probable that in Luke 2:32 "glory" is parallel to "light." Another important passage for understanding Luke 2:30-32 is Is 60:1-3 (cf. 40:5; 42:6-7): "Shine, Shine, O Jerusalem. Your light has come, the glory of the Lord shines upon you. See, darkness covers the earth, and thick clouds cover the people; but upon you the Lord shines, and over you appears his glory. Nations shall walk by your light, and kings by your shining radiance." This passage treats of God's salvation, and "light" and "glory" are paralleled yet contrasted with darkness and thick clouds. Moreover, there is universality, since kings and Gentiles will benefit from Jerusalem's light. This passage likewise supports the interpretation of ἀποοκάλυψις in Luke 2:32, as "unveiling," i.e., unveiling of the darkness over the Gentiles([140]).

After Peter has identified him as "the Christ of God," Jesus predicts his passion for the first time and speaks about discipleship: if anyone wants to follow him, he must deny himself, take up his cross each day and follow him. Jesus continues: "For whoever wishes to save his life will lose it, but whoever loses his life for my sake will save it. What profit is there for one to gain the whole world yet lose or forfeit himself? Whoever is ashamed of me and of my words, the Son of Man will be

---

[139] Cf. Lagrange, *Évangile selon Saint Luc*, 86-87.

[140] See Evans, *Saint Luke,* 217-218.

ashamed of when he comes in his glory and in the glory of the Father and of the holy angels" (Luke 9:24-26; cf. 12:8-12). This passage contends that no one can save himself; that being saved depends on following Jesus and even being willing to lose one's life for him. V. 25 develops the idea of trying to save oneself by pointing out that remarkable material gain does not guarantee one's salvation. In v. 26 we find a heavenly judgment scene whose wording recalls the thought that some will not be willing to lose their lives for Jesus and so will not gain them. Worthy of note is that this passage attributes salvation to Jesus, without any reference to God.

Luke makes telling use of irony during Jesus' passion. Jesus on the cross is mocked as "savior," yet Luke's readers know Jesus remains the savior and can still save. The leaders of the people scoff and say, "He saved others; let him save himself if he is the chosen one, the Christ of God" (23:35b); the soldiers, too, made fun of him, "If you are the king of the Jews, save yourself" (v. 37), and finally, the so-called "bad thief" derides him, "Are you not the Christ? Save yourself" (v. 39). The leaders of the people, who admit that Jesus has saved others and theoretically should most be able to appreciate who he is, fail to do so. The soldiers' inability to recognize who Jesus is proves less surprising since their very profession hardens their sensibilities. Moreover, they often imitate individuals whom they view as superior; and so they entertain themselves by using the inscription over Jesus' head to jeer him. Unfortunately for himself, the "bad thief" likewise fails to recognize in Jesus the savior of the disadvantaged, precisely the one he needs in his present predicament; but Jesus' words to the good thief belie this failure to believe in him as savior, "Amen, I say to you, today you will be with me in Paradise" (v. 43). Of course, Luke's readers are well aware that Jesus saves, and that those who mock Jesus do not perceive that their very mockeries constitute true identifications of who Jesus is([141]).

Luke connects salvation with baptism in the name of Jesus. The evidence indicates that in the Pauline churches baptism was in the name of the Lord Jesus (1 Cor 1:2; 6:11; Rom 10:9-13; Gal 3:26-28); and, given

---

[141] We have already established that Jesus is the savior. However, Jesus has also been identified as the Christ (Luke 2:11; 9:20; 22:70-71). The voice from heaven called him, "My Chosen" (9:35; cf. 3:22) and Luke has designated him the king of the Jews (1:32-33.69; 2:11).

the amount of space dedicated to Paul in Acts, we have every reason to believe that Luke was from a Pauline church. After the Pentecost speech, the Jewish audience was cut to the heart and asked Peter and the other apostles what they should do. Peter instructs them, "Repent and be baptized, everyone one of you, in the name of Jesus Christ for the forgiveness of sins; and you will receive the gift of the Holy Spirit . . . . Save yourselves from this corrupt generation. Those who accepted the word were baptized . . . ." (Acts 2:38.40-41a; cf. 9:14). It is against this background that one must interpret Acts 2:21 (cf. v. 47): "And it shall be that everyone will be saved who calls on the name of the Lord"; "Lord" in this verse no longer refers to the God of the OT but to Jesus. So, baptism in Jesus' name leads to the forgiveness of sins, the reception of the Spirit and salvation. A similar event occurs in the story of the Philippian jailor who asks Paul and Silas, "'Sirs, what must I do to be saved?' And they said, 'Believe in the Lord Jesus, and you and your household will be saved'" (Acts 16:30-31). They then spoke the word of the Lord to him and to his whole household, and after the jailor had washed their wounds, he and his entire family were immediately baptized (vv. 32-33). Clearly, according to this passage salvation is through faith in the Lord Jesus and actualized in baptism.

Acts 28:23-31 are a unit held together by "bearing witness to the kingdom of God and trying to convince them (the Roman Jews) about Jesus" (v. 23: διαμαρτυρόμενος τὴν βασιλείαν τοῦ θεοῦ, πείθων τε αὐτοὺς περὶ τοῦ ᾽Ιησοῦ) and "he proclaimed the kingdom of God and taught about the Lord Jesus Christ" (v. 31: κηρύσσων τὴν βασιλείαν τοῦ θεοῦ καὶ διδάσκων τὰ περὶ τοῦ κυρίου ᾽Ιησοῦ Χριστοῦ). The pericope also begins and ends with a notice of Paul's hospitality or openness (vv. 23, 30); moreover, the responsive stance of the Gentiles (v. 28) balances off the unresponsive one of the Roman Jews in vv. 24-25a[142]. What concerns us is v. 28: "Let it be known to you that this salvation of God has been sent to the Gentiles; they will listen." The verse clearly states that the salvation is God's, but is there any other indication in the pericope about the nature of this salvation? The obvious answer is that the description of this salvation must be the kingdom of God and the

---

[142] See Dupont, "Le conclusion des Actes," 359-404, for the relationship between the Jewish refusal to accept the gospel message and the mission to the Gentiles and for the references to salvation both at the beginning of Luke's Gospel and the end of Acts.

things about Jesus, both of which occur at the beginning and end of the pericope. Given Luke's preference for double expressions, these two phrasings may well be synonyms for one another; and so we can probably conclude that "the kingdom of God" is equivalent to "the things about Jesus." Be this as it may, the fact remains that the only things mentioned in the pericope, which explain "this salvation of God," are the "kingdom of God" and "the things about Jesus." Consequently, at the end of Acts, significant because of its placement, we find "the things about Jesus" as, at least, a partial description of salvation.

Up to this point we have studied Luke's programmatic passage and his declarations about Jesus as Savior, in so far as this can be determined by a review of the Greek word for "save" and its cognates. Even before Jesus' birth, the text speaks him as saving; but also at his birth and presentation in the temple and throughout the whole of the Gospel and Acts. Jesus brings universal salvation, and following Jesus challenges one to lose his life to save it. Through a strikingly powerful use of irony during Jesus' passion, Luke reaffirms that Jesus saves. Finally, for Luke belief and baptism in the name of the Lord Jesus are means of salvation. Before concluding this section, we should note that of the four verses which constitute the universal framework of Luke-Acts, three (Luke 3:6[143]; 24:47[144]; Acts 28:28) relate this universality to salvation through Jesus. A thorough analysis of the fourth verse, Acts 1:8, would show that it in no way contradicts this relationship. However, our presentation of Jesus as savior in Luke-Acts is far from complete since the word-pattern for this theme is quite extensive.

Forgiveness of Sins

Above we briefly mentioned Acts 26:18, " . . . to open their eyes that they may turn from darkness to light and from the power of Satan to God, so that they may obtain forgiveness of sins and an inheritance among those who have been consecrated by faith in me," which summarizes the ministry given by the risen Jesus to Paul. This verse proves helpful in understanding

---

[143] Bock, *Proclamation from Prophecy*, 93-99, considers the Old Testament passages which have influenced Luke 3:4-6.

[144] " . . . and that repentance, for the forgiveness of sins, would be preached in his name to all the nations beginning from Jerusalem."

Luke's notions of "forgiveness of sins" and "light." In it "light" is op-posed to "darkness" and the "power of Satan" to "God." So, "light" and "God" go together as do "darkness" and "the power of Satan," and the two phrases, "from darkness to light" and "from the power of Satan to God," are parallel to one another and say the same thing. There are two separate realms, that of God and that of Satan. The purpose of turning to the light and to God is to "receive forgiveness of sins" and "a place among those sanctified by faith in Jesus"; and again both phrases parallel one another and state a similar idea, salvation. When "by faith in me (Jesus)", which phrase should be taken with the whole verse, one turns to the light and to God, one receives forgiveness of sins and a place among those sanctified: in brief, salvation. To be sure, in the Our Father, God is asked to forgive our sins (11:4); and on the cross, if the verse be genuine([145]), Jesus asks the Father to forgive his executioners because they do not know what they are doing (23:34a; cf. 12:10). However, in Luke-Acts forgive-ness of sins is more frequently associated with Jesus.

We have already noted that in the *Benedictus* John the Baptist is to go before Jesus to give knowledge of salvation to his people in the forgiveness of their sins (Luke 1:77). The healing of the paralytic (5:17-26), an apparent combination of a miracle and a dispute story, can now best be described as a proclamation story, for the emphasis falls on vv. 22-24([146]). When Jesus saw the faith of the paralytic and those who were carrying him, he said to the former, "As for you, your sins are forgiven" (v. 20). This leads to the scribes and Pharisees' thinking, "Who is this who speaks blasphemies? Who but God alone can forgive sins" (v. 21)? Jesus knows what they are thinking and asks them, "What are you thinking in yours hearts? Which is easier to say, 'Your sins are forgiven' or to say, 'Rise and Walk'? But that you may know that the Son of Man has author-ity on earth to forgive sins—he said to the man who was paralyzed, 'I say to you, rise, pick up your stretcher, and go home'" (vv. 22b-24). The connection that Jesus draws between ill-health and sin is true to Jewish thought, but the implied charge of the scribes and Pharisees must be ironical, because Luke's readers knows that Jesus is not blaspheming but

---

[145] Radl, *Das Lukas-Evangelium*, 12-13, defends the reading.

[146] Fitzmyer, *The Gospel According to Luke I–IX*, 578-580, may well be correct when he claims that v. 24ab is the evangelist's comment.

can truly forgive sins (cf. 1:77)([147]). The question of the scribes and Pharisees about anyone else other than God being able to forgive sins could suggest a certain equality of Jesus with God; but we will see that it remains only that, a suggestion. Naturally, the miracle supports Jesus' solemn assertion that the Son of Man has authority on earth to forgive sins.

Elsewhere, Jesus likewise draws a connection between ill health and being a sinner. At the call of Levi, Jesus responds to those who criticize his eating with publicans and sinners, "Those who are healthy do not need a physician, but the sick do; I have not come to call the righteous to repentance but sinners" (5:31-32). V. 32 is a general statement of Jesus' mission, and naturally relates to the theme of forgiveness of sins which we considered in the previous pericope. "Physician" in v. 31 becomes a term of salvation.

Jesus tells the sinful woman, "Your faith has saved you; go in peace." Previously in the story Jesus proclaimed that her sins, although many, are forgiven (v. 47) because she has shown great love and then directly tells her, "Your sins are forgiven" (v. 48). Those who were around began to say to one another, "Who is this who even forgives sins?" (7:49); their question proves an important element of the story because it moves the reader to reflect on who Jesus is. As the story of the sinful woman stands in Luke's text, it is almost entirely unique to him; and the verses we are considering contain the following elements: Jesus tells the woman that her sins are forgiven and his audience wonders about his claim to this authority; Jesus also establishes a connection among forgiveness of sins, the quality of her love (this must include the concern which her actions in Jesus' regard reveal), her faith and her now being able to be at peace. Furthermore, Jesus' words and actions lead to the question of his identity; and the whole event is described as the woman being "saved."

At the end of the Gospel, the risen Jesus contends that the scriptures show that repentance and forgiveness of sins are to be proclaimed in the name of the Christ to all nations, beginning from Jerusalem (Luke 24:47; cf. Acts 10:43; 13:38). And in Acts 5:31 God exalts Jesus to his right hand as Leader and Savior that he might give repentance and

---

[147] Actually, Luke uses "blasphemy" of those who speak against Jesus or the message about him or who falsely accuse Christians (Luke 22:65; 23:39; Acts 13:45; 18:6; 26:11; cf. 6:11).

forgiveness of sins to Israel. Both of these passages attribute to Jesus the ability to achieve repentance and forgiveness of sins for the believers. As noted above, Christian baptism in the name of Jesus accomplishes the forgiveness of sins (Acts 2:38); however, it should be distinguished from the baptism of repentance for the forgiveness of sins, which John proclaimed, because God, not John, achieves these results. Finally, as Jesus prayed to the Father in the Gospel (23:34)([148]), Stephen prays to the Lord Jesus in Acts 7:60: "Lord, do not hold this sin against them" and puts Jesus on the same level with the Father. The risen Jesus forgives sins.

Luke 15, which except for vv. 4-7 is unique to Luke, should be considered under the present heading; for the concern of this chapter is to explain why Jesus welcomes sinners and tax collectors and eats with them (vv. 1-2). Each of the three parables, the lost sheep, the lost coin and the prodigal (or lost) son explains Jesus' behavior. The first two parables have very similar endings: "I tell you in just the same way there will be more joy in heaven over one sinner who repents than over ninety-nine righteous persons who have no need of repentance" (v. 7) and "In just the same way, I tell you, there will be rejoicing among the angels of God over one sinner who repents" (v. 10). The elder son in the last parable represents the Pharisees and scribes who are not happy with Jesus' openness to sinners (cf. vv. 1-2); for his father concludes his explanation as follows, "But now we must celebrate and rejoice, because your brother was dead and has come to life again; he was lost and has been found" (v. 32). We thus infer that Luke clarifies Jesus' actions in the first two verses by means of these parables of joy over even one repentant sinner who moves from being dead and lost to coming to life or being found. Jesus in welcoming sinners and tax collectors actualizes God's attitude toward sinners([149]). Before concluding this discussion of forgiveness of sins, we should reflect on the twofold appearance of ἄφεσις ("freeing") in Luke 4:18. Now "freeing" figures in the two Isaian passages cited (Is 61:1-2; 58:6), and many scholars have observed that the best explanation for Luke's insertion of Is 58:6 seems to be precisely his desire to stress this idea. However, of the ten appearances of "freeing" in Luke-Acts, all the others examples deal

---

[148] Radl, *Das Lukas-Evangelium*, 12-13, and Talbert, *Reading Luke*, 219-220, defend the genuineness of this reading.

[149] Bock, *Luke 9:51 – 24:53*, 1295, 1304-1305, 1320-1321.

with the forgiveness of sins; and except for Luke 3:3, forgiveness of sins by Jesus. Luke is using the phraseology in 4:18-19 metaphorically, but would he have gone out of his way to insert a second "freeing" if he had not had a clear purpose in mind? His use of the term elsewhere for the forgiveness of sins, especially, through Jesus, provides the most probable reason for his so doing. It is this liberating activity of Jesus, especially in terms of forgiveness of sins, that Luke wants to underline in his program-matic passage([150]).

In summary, Luke relates "forgiveness of sins" to salvation, the realm of God, "light," the quality of one's love and one's being at peace. Faith and baptism in Jesus leads to the forgiveness of sins. In addition, Luke joins some of Jesus' miracles of healing and his welcoming sinners and tax collectors with the forgiveness of sins. According to Luke, the risen Jesus can forgive sins.

Light As an Image of Salvation:
We have already seen that "light," is an image of salvation: Jesus is the dawn from on high which will break on us, to give light to those who sit in darkness and in the shadow of death, to guide our feet in the way of peace (Luke 1:78-79); and the infant Jesus is "the light for the unveiling of the Gentiles" (2:32)([151]). "Light" opposes the darkness, belongs to the realm of God and looks to the forgiveness of sins and a place among those sanctified by Christ (Acts 26:18), and the risen Christ is destined to announce this light to the people and to the Gentiles (Acts 26:23). The context of these last two pas-sages directs our attention to the appearance of the risen Jesus to Paul as "a light from heaven brighter than the sun, shining around him and his com-panions" (Acts 26:13; cf. vv. 15-16; 9:3-4; 22:6-11.14). Given the context (Acts 26:18.23; cf. Luke 2:27-32), the most probable reason why Luke chose "light" to describe the vision of the risen Christ is that Luke views him as Savior. Moreover, the uniqueness of this light "brighter than the sun would suggest the remarkable nature of this salvation([152]). Earlier Christians are

---

[150] O'Toole, "Il Giubileo," 157-158, and Talbert, *Reading Luke*, 55.

[151] Muñoz Iglesias, "Christo, luz de los gentiles," 27-44.

[152] O'Toole, *Acts 26*, 57-64, 72-78.

designated "the sons of light" as opposed to "the sons of this age" (Luke 16:8; cf. Acts 26:18).

Closely related with Acts 26:13 is Acts 13:47, "For so the Lord has commanded us, 'I have made you a light to the Gentiles, that you may be an instrument of salvation to the ends of the earth.'" The verse definitely identifies "light" with "an instrument of salvation." Paul and Barnabas are in Pisidia Antioch and have already successfully preached in the synagogue; but when on the next Saturday they again attempt to do so, some Jews oppose them. The above citation is part of their response to these opponents. "Lord" (κύριος) in Acts 13:47 could refer to God since the text speaks of "the word of God" in v. 46 and the citation is from the OT. However, most likely "Lord" looks to the risen Jesus (Acts 26:15-18; cf. 9:6.15-17) since the mission given in Acts 13:47 is very much like that which he gives to Paul in Acts 25:15-18 and like his own in v. 23. This understanding would also include Acts 22:14-15; for ὅτι in v. 15 means "because"([153]), and so God predestines Paul as a witness to the Just One but does not himself mission him. In fact, a probative argument that in Acts 13:47, Luke associates the risen Jesus with salvation and light is the nature of the mission itself. To be sure, the "us" in Acts 13:47 has to refer to Paul and Barnabas; but more problematic is the question: to whom does "you" (singular: σε) refer?([154]) Grammatically, it should not look to both Paul and Barnabas; and more probably "you" singular refers to the risen Jesus because, even if Jesus is the "Lord," he would be citing an OT passage and so the appearance of "you" singular is not that strange. In addition, Simeon identified the infant Jesus as salvation and as "light for the unveiling of the Gentiles" (Luke 2:32). Moreover, in Acts 26:23 Luke predicates of the risen Jesus the mission, "He would proclaim light both to our people and to the Gentiles"; and this passage and Acts 13:47 both depend on the Greek wording of Is 49:6 (cf. 42:6), and for Luke Jesus is the Servant of Yahweh. There is no denying that Paul actually carries out Jesus' mission in Acts 26:23 (cf. v. 18), but the same understanding would hold for Paul and Barnabas in Acts 13:47. As Paul carries out the risen

---

[153] Zerwick, *Analysis philologica*, 315.

[154] Koet, *Five Studies*, summarizes the various interpretations of σε in this verse, but his claim that the references look also to the Jewish audience conflicts with the context. For a more accurate understanding see Rese, "Die Funktion der alttestamentlichen Zitate," 76-79.

Jesus' mission in Acts 26:18, so he and Barnabas would be doing in Acts 13:47([155]).

Luke 11:33, of which only Luke has a doublet (cf. 8:16), should also be understood as a reference to Jesus as light. This verse follows the pericope of the demand for a sign (11:29-32), which contains the following clear references to Jesus, "Just as Jonah became a sign to the Ninevites, so will the Son of Man be to this generation . . . and there is something greater than Solomon here" and "there is something greater than Jonah here." There follows, without any break, v. 33, "No one who lights a lamp hides it away or places it (under a bushel basket), but on a lampstand so that those who enter might see the light." The most reasonable referents for "lamp" and "light" are those to Jesus([156]) in the previous pericope. Of course, such an understanding is supported by the fact that Luke has already spoken of Jesus as "light" and will do so later in Luke-Acts.

Luke joins "seeing" and "sight" with the "light" that Jesus brings as expressions for salvation. According to the programmatic passage, Jesus is to give sight to the blind (Luke 4:18; cf. 7:21-22). Such a healing is not only an experience of salvation but the image of "sight" means one can see the light (cf. 1:78-79; 2:32); the restoration of sight to the blind beggar (18:35-43) partially actualizes this mission because when he regains his sight, although it is not directly associated with salvation, he does follow Jesus([157]). Luke plays on the word "seeing" in the story of Zacchaeus (19:3-5): Zacchaeus seeks to see Jesus; but actually Jesus, the Son of Man who came to seek and save the lost,

---

[155] Luke does write of pairs, like Peter and John or Paul and Barnabas, in which one member of the pair actually proves to be a silent partner.

[156] Fitzmyer, *The Gospel According to Luke X–XXIV*, 939; Lagrange, *Évangile selon Saint Luc*, 339 and Schweizer, *The Good News according to Luke*, 196. In agreement with a number of other scholars, Prete, *L'opera di Luca*, 195-201, wants "lamp" and "light" to refer to Jesus' teaching and wisdom, but this is true only secondarily since the comparisons in the previous verses are between persons.

[157] Much the same has to be said about Luke 10:21-24, for the eyes of the disciples are blessed because they see and hear what many prophets and kings wanted to see. From the context, the immediate object of their vision is Jesus himself and potentially what he wishes to reveal to them about the Father.

first sees him (v. 10). The Jesus whom Zacchaeus hoped to see is identified with salvation (v. 9); in fact, he saves the lost.

Consequently, Jesus and his saving action can be compared to the dawn, light, a lamp and sight. "Light" characterizes the realm of God and salvation and opposes the realm of Satan or darkness. "Light" can designate the salvation announced to the Gentiles; "eyes" and "sight," too, can look to salvation and to the revelation that Jesus is able to give about the Father.

Grace[158]

We have already viewed the confessional statement in Acts 15:11: "On the contrary, we believe that we are saved through the *grace* of the Lord Jesus, in the same way as they" and the assertion in the programmatic passage about Jesus that all were amazed at "the words of grace that came out of his mouth" (Luke 4:22). Similar to both of these passages is Acts 14:3 where Paul and Barnabas remained a long time in Iconium, "Speaking out boldly for the Lord, who confirmed the word about his grace by granting signs and wonders to occur through their hands." "Lord" in this passage must refer to the risen Jesus because, if Paul and Barnabas were speaking out boldly for God (the Father), no Jew would have had any reason to stir up the Gentiles and poison their minds against them (v. 2)([159]). Consequently, in Acts 14:3 "his" with "grace" is a subjective genitive, and Jesus gives grace and with miracles supports Paul and Barnabas' bold proclamation of him.

At other times, God gives the grace, but the grace is belief in Jesus or the message about him. According to Acts 11:23 (cf. 14:26) Barnabas arrives in Antioch and when he sees the grace of God he rejoiced and exhorted them all to remain faithful to the Lord with steadfast devotion. "Lord" in this verse must again refer to Jesus since earlier we learn that certain Christians from Cyprus and Cyrene came to Antioch and proclaimed to the Hellenists the Lord Jesus and that a great number turned to the Lord (vv. 21-22). The grace of God, which Barnabas saw, was precisely that a great number had turned to Jesus. So, faith in Jesus is the grace of God. Another passage also speaks of the grace of God in terms of Jesus. After Paul's speech at Pisidian Antioch, many Jews and devout

---

[158] See Bossuyt – Radermakers, *Jésus: Parole de la Grâce selon Saint Luc.*

[159] However, Haenchen, *The Acts*, 420, n. 7, is not sure; for he writes, "We cannot tell whether κύριος here means God or Christ."

converts to Judaism follow Paul and Barnabas who urge them to continue in the grace of God (Acts 13:43; cf. 20:21-24). However, "the grace of God" must refer to the contents of the speech which centers on Jesus as savior (13:23; cf. vv. 26, 38-39) and the one whose resurrection realizes God's promise and our eternal life([160]). In summary, grace can mean what Jesus says and what he does to save us; the grace of God, on the other hand, can designate the gift of faith in Jesus or of the message about him.

Ἔλεος, *"Loving Mercy" or "Compassion"*
Loving mercy or compassion most appropriately is an attribute of God (Luke 1:50.54; cf. v. 58) and flows from his fidelity to the covenant and to his promises. For Luke it often relates to Jesus (but see 1:58; 16:24). In the *Magnificat* the "loving mercy" ultimately pertains to Mary's being the mother of Jesus; but others, especially the disadvantaged, benefit from this divine activity. Earlier, we saw in the *Benedictus* that God's "loving mercy" relates to his raising up a mighty Savior in the house of his servant David and to giving his people knowledge of this salvation in the forgiveness of their sins. In v. 78 "Because of the tender mercy of our God, the dawn (Jesus) from on high will visit those in darkness and the shadow of death, to direct their steps on the way of peace (cf. v. 79). Luke also predicates this "loving mercy" or "compassion" of Jesus. The ten lepers call to Jesus, "Jesus, Master! Have mercy on us" (17:13). Jesus instructs them to go and show themselves to the priests, and as they go, they are made clean. In this instance, Jesus exercises his loving mercy through a miracle. A similar story appears in Jesus' healing of the blind beggar near Jericho. Luke surely underlines the determination of the beggar for, despite objections, he twice pleads, "Jesus, Son of David, have mercy pity on me" (18:38; cf. v. 39). Jesus responds, "Receive your sight; your faith has saved you," and immediately the blind beggar receives his sight, follows Jesus and glorifies God (vv. 42-43). Awe seizes the crowd, which identifies Jesus as a "great prophet" and concludes that God has visited his people.

Σπλαγχνίζω ("be compassionate") belongs to Luke's theme of Jesus' mercy. The heart-rending situation of the widow of Nain moves

---

[160] For support of this interpretation, see my "Christ's Resurrection in Acts 13, 13-52," 361-372.

Jesus to compassion (Luke 7:13; cf. 1:78). He tells her not to weep and touches the litter and says, "Young man, I bid you get up," and gives him back to his mother (vv. 14-15).

Consequently, "loving mercy" or "compassion" reveals God's fidelity to his covenant and promises and can be an attribute both of God and of Jesus. They are concerned to save. God works his loving mercy through Jesus, or Jesus' own compassion brings someone salvation.

Jesus As Miracle Worker[161]

In the Pentecost speech, Peter describes Jesus of Nazareth as "a man commended to you by God with mighty deeds, wonders and signs which God worked through him in your midst, as you yourselves know" (Acts 2:22). And later, in the prayer of the persecuted early Christians, we find, ". . . as you stretch forth (your) hand to heal, and signs and wonders are done through the name of your holy servant Jesus" (Acts 4:30; cf. 7:36). These general statements about Jesus' miracles, as each of his miracles, belong to the area of salvation, for they liberate human beings from physical and sometimes moral evils[162]. The programmatic passage speaks of miracles (Luke 4:18.25-27; cf. 7:21-22); and above it was noted that faith in Jesus leads to cures (7:1-10; 8:50; Acts 3:16f; 14:9; cf. 9:34). Several times, according to Luke, after Jesus has worked a miracle, he says, "Your faith has saved you" (8:48; 17:19; 18:42). He cures Peter's mother-in-law and many other sick persons (4:38-40; 5:12-15; 6:18-19; 8:2; 9:11), and the power of the Lord was upon him to heal the paralytic (5:17; cf. 6:19; 7:8-9; 8:46). In the story about the man with the withered hand, Jesus questions the scribes and Pharisees who are looking for an excuse to accuse him, "I ask you, is it lawful to do good on the Sabbath rather than to do evil, to save life rather than to destroy it" (6:9)? Then, after looking around at all of them, he instructs the man to stretch out his hand; when he does so, his hand is restored (cf. vv. 6-11). Jesus raises the son of the Widow of Nain from the dead (7:11-17) and encourages Jairus about his daughter with the words, "Do not be afraid; just have faith and she will be

---

161 For general considerations of this topic, confer Achtemeier, "The Lukan Perspective," 547-562, and Busse, *Die Wunder der Propheten Jesus.*

162 George, *Études,* 71-73, 84; Rigaux, *Témoignage,* 387-390. This is not to deny that Luke also utilizes Jesus' miracles to develop other aspects of his theology.

saved" (8:50). The feeding of the five thousand (9:13-17) reveals that Jesus' miraculous activity proves more than sufficient to meet given needs. If I am correct in my interpretation of healing of the badly stooped woman in 13:10-17([163]), these verses are an image for the kingdom of God (cf. vv. 18-21); and a comparison of 13,10-17 with 14:1-6, the healing of the man with dropsy, leaves no doubt that the badly stooped woman plays a major role in the former pericope.   The woman (and those in the story who imitate her) experiences the kingdom.   She experiences salvation ("set free," cf. vv. 12, 15-16; cf. 4:18), shares in the promises made to Abraham and responds correctly with praise of God.   It may even be that her "standing up straight" (13:13; cf. 21:27-28) should be understood as being in anticipation of the final redemption.

Jesus commands evil spirits to leave people and they do so (Luke 4:35-36; cf. v. 41; 6:18b; 7:21; 8:2). Jesus drives out the evil spirits of the Gerasene demoniac, and those who had seen the cure tell the townspeople how he had been healed (8:36: πῶς ἐσώθη). Jesus tells the cured man to announce to others what God had done for him, and the man goes through the whole city recounting everything that Jesus had done for him (v. 39). Luke in the healing of the boy with the unclean spirit (9:37-43) adds the human touch that Jesus gave him back to his father and that everyone was astounded "by the majesty of God." In Luke 11:14-23, Jesus makes the point that if he cast out demons by the finger of God, then has the kingdom of God come upon them.

Jesus gives the Twelve and the disciples power over demons and to heal (9:1.34.47; 10:19), and they perform miracles in the name of the risen Lord. In Jesus' name, Peter and John cure the man born lame (esp. Acts 3:6-13.16; 4:7-12.14-16.21-22); and this miracle helps to unify Acts 3–4 and serves as the basis for Luke's forceful statement of Jesus as the only savior. Peter on his own initiative (cf. Luke 7:13-15; 13:12) at Lydda tells the paralytic, "Aeneas, Jesus Christ heals you. Get up and make your bed" (Acts 9:34)([164]), and Aeneas immediately stands up. At Philippi Paul orders the spirit of divination in the name of Jesus Christ to come out of the slave-girl who earns a great deal of money for her owners by fortune-telling, and it comes out at that very moment (Acts 16:16-18).

---

[163] "Some Exegetical Reflections," 84-107.

[164] Polhill, *Acts*, 245.

Miracles characterize both the earthly and risen life of Jesus. Faith leads to miracles; and whether one speaks of saving, healing or doing good, miracles belong to Luke's theme of "salvation," the kingdom of God and of Jesus as savior. Jesus gives this power to his disciples who in his name both perform miracles and have power over evil spirits.

"Leader" and "Salvation"

The Lucan title "leader" (ἀρχηγός) should be associated with "savior," for Acts 5:31 reads, "God exalted him (Jesus) at his right hand as leader and savior to grant Israel repentance and forgiveness of sins." In this verse, we again see Luke's propensity for double expressions, and the risen Jesus as savior is also the leader who achieves salvation for Israel, here expressed as "repentance" and "forgiveness of sins." Thus, the other Lucan use of "leader" in the phrasing, "the leader of life" (Acts 3:15)([165]), would mean that Jesus leads the Christians to life, i.e., to the resurrection since Luke uses "I live" of the risen Jesus([166]). Perhaps, "way"([167]) should also be included under this title since it implies a leader, and surely this is how Luke represents Jesus on his journey to Jerusalem. Moreover, a way leads somewhere; and Jesus leads us to salvation and the resurrection.

Peace([168])

The basic meaning of "peace" in the LXX is "totality" or "wholeness"; and it can mean prosperity, a paradisiacal existence in which all forms of strife

---

[165] Bruce, *The Acts*, 140, observes that the Aramaic of this phrase would be the same as τὸν ἀρχηγὸν τῆς σωτηρίας (Heb 2:10). Polhill, *Acts*, 132, also allows for the meaning, "the author, the originator and source of life"; however, this is not an idea that occurs elsewhere in Luke-Acts.

[166] Luke 24:5.23; Acts 1:3; 25:19; cf. Luke 20:38; Acts 9:41; 20:12.

[167] For general treatments of Luke's use of "way," see Edwards, *Luke's Story of Jesus*, 55-77; Geiger, "Der Weg als roter Faden durch Lk-Apg," 673; Lyonnet, "'La voie,'" 149-164; Repo, "Christianity as a 'Way,'" 533-539; W.C. Robinson, *Der Weg des Herren* and Repo, *Der 'Weg' als Selbstbezeichnung des Urchristentums.*

[168] See Comblin, "La paix," 439-460; Kilgallen, "Peace," 55-79; O'Toole, "Εἰρήνη, an Underlying Theme in Acts 10,34-43," 461-476; Riesenfeld, "The Text of Acts 10,36," 191-194; Swartley, "Politics and Peace (*Eirene*) in Luke's Gospel," 18-37; Foerster and von Rad, εἰρήνη, 400-420.

have been removed, or happiness and untrammeled growth in a harmonious community (Is 2:2-4; Ez 34:25-31). As an eschatological term it can express the conditions under the rule of the future ideal king (cf. Is 9:2-7; 11:1 – 12:6; Zech 9:9-10; Mic 5:2-5)([169]). These explanations of Evans are well taken; but as he himself would agree, for Luke peace is now somehow achieved by or through Christ.

In our consideration of "light" as an image of salvation, we saw in the *Benedictus* Jesus as "the dawn" who is "to shine on those who sit in darkness and death's shadow, to guide our feet into the path of peace" (1:79). Since the *Benedictus* is a prayer of thanksgiving for the salvation that God is achieving in Jesus, and since "the dawn" refers directly to Jesus, "peace" must express part of Jesus' saving activity. The context allows us to go a step further because the guiding of our feet into the path of peace implies moving away from sitting in "darkness and the shadow of death," images of the realm of Satan (cf. Acts 26:18), and "path" looks to Luke's later development of Jesus' journey to Jerusalem and its saving results and to Christianity as the "Way."

At the birth of Jesus, an angel proclaims, "For today in the city of David a savior has been born for you who is the Messiah (the Christ) and Lord" (Luke 2:11)! Then, after the indication of the sign that the child will be wrapped in bands of cloth and lying in a manger, we read of the angels who praise God and say, "Glory to God in the highest and on earth peace to those on whom his favor rests" (2:14)! This "peace" must have to do with the Savior, who is Christ the Lord, born in the city of David; for, although God is the ultimate agent, somehow he is working with or through Jesus. A verse from the triumphal entry of Jesus into Jerusalem (19:38), which is partially unique to Luke, parallels 2:14 and reads, "Blessed is the king who comes in the name of the Lord. Peace in heaven and glory in the highest!" In contrast to what is said in 2:14 "peace" is now heavenly, and there are no parallels in Jewish sources for the expressions, "Peace in heaven and glory in the highest." In 19:38 Jesus is clearly designated as "king," but the placing of "peace" and "glory" in heaven probably makes the point that his kingdom is not of this world: it is from God and so is spiritual and heavenly([170]). However this may be, the phras-

---

[169] Evans, *Saint Luke*, 207.

[170] Evans, *Saint Luke*, 680-681.

ing still points to the salvation that follows on Jesus' kingship; and in the context the disciples are praising him because of all the miracles they have seen (cf. 19:37).

At the beginning of the *Nunc Dimittis* (Luke 2:29-32) we read, "Now, Master, you may let your servant go in peace, according to your word . . . ." The rest of the pericope reveals why Simeon can now depart in peace. The phrase "according to your word" suggests a partial solution inasmuch as these words must refer to v. 26: "It had been revealed to him by the Holy Spirit that he should not see death before he had seen the Messiah of the Lord." The implication is that Simeon now has peace because God has been faithful to his word that Simeon would see His Messiah. However, good grammar tells us more. The sentence in which Simeon speaks of his departure in peace, continues with a ὅτι causal clause: "for my eyes have seen your salvation which you prepared in the sight of all the peoples, a light for unveiling (of the darkness over) the Gentiles, and glory for your people Israel" (v. 32). Simeon can depart in peace because he has seen God's Messiah, the infant Jesus, who is God's universal salvation(171).

From what has been said thus far, we can gain some insight into another Lucan passage that speaks of peace in relationship to Jesus. In Luke 10:1-12 the missionaries make two "entries," one into individual homes (v. 5) and the other into cities (v. 8); in vv. 5-6 Jesus sends out the Seventy(-two) with the words, "Into whatever house you enter, first say, 'Peace to this household.' If a peaceful person lives there, your peace will rest on him; but if not, it will return to you." At first, one might be tempted to think that "peace" in these verses is only a greeting. But does such an interpretation square well with "peaceful person" or, especially, with the idea that the peace rests on that person or returns to the missionaries? Evans gives three reasons why "peace" has a salvific meaning in these verses(172): 1) peace here is an objective force which can rest on someone or be recalled, 2) in the context the disciples are announcing the arrival or proximity of the kingdom and 3), the Hebraism, "son of peace," can also

---

171 For this conclusion and a thorough study of the passage, confer Prete, *L'opera di Luca*, 167-185.

172 Evans, *Saint Luke*, 447-448.

mean one destined for peace, i.e., salvation. Thus, "peace" in these verses most likely looks to salvation.

When Jesus sees Jerusalem, he weeps over her and says, "If this day you only knew what makes for peace—but now it is hidden from your eyes" (Luke 19:42; cf. vv. 41, 43-44). This scene immediately follows Jesus' triumphal entry into Jerusalem, and so we have some idea of to what "on this day" particularly refers. Jesus explains this further in v. 44 when he states that Jerusalem will fall, "because you did not recognize the time of your visitation." "What makes for peace" must be Jesus' triumphal entrance into Jerusalem, the proclamation that he is the king who comes in the name of the Lord and the recognition of the time of Jerusalem's visitation in the person of Jesus (cf. 1:68.78; 7:16; cf. 1:69-79). Although Jerusalem's failure to recognize the significance of Jesus for her is explained by the majestic passive in "but now it is hidden from your eyes," this failure and the prophetic prediction of Jerusalem's fall remains and stands in sad contrast to "what makes for peace"([173]).

In his speech to Cornelius and his household (Acts 10:34-43), Peter asserts, "You know the word (that) he (God) sent to the Israelites as he proclaimed peace through Jesus Christ, who is Lord of all" (v. 36). The Greek of vv. 36-38 does not flow smoothly. Nonetheless, "the word" that God sent, is best explained in the context by "proclaimed peace through Jesus Christ." "The word" is universal since anyone who fears God and does justice is acceptable to him; and of course, the Cornelius-event is a key passage for universality in Luke-Acts. "Who is Lord of all" must be Jesus and corresponds well with this universality. "The word," "the peace through Jesus Christ" and "What has happened all over Judea beginning in Galilee after the baptism that John preached . . . . how God anointed Jesus of Nazareth with the Holy Spirit and power. He went about doing good and healing . . ."(vv. 37-38), all point to Jesus. In fact, the rest of the speech likewise speaks of Jesus, and the whole speech more or less constitutes a summary of what "peace" and "the word" mean and, incidentally, also a summary of the Gospel of Mark. However, "peace" is more specific than "word" and expresses more an end-result of Jesus'

---

[173] Plummer, *St. Luke*, 450, notes the parallel in Luke 14:32 and observes, "There is a possible allusion to the name Jerusalem, which perhaps means 'inheritance of peace.'"

salvific activity; salvation is now universal, divisions are broken down and so Jesus can be called "Lord of all"([174]).

The latter part of Luke 24:36, "He stood in their midst and said to them, 'Peace be with you,'" is not textually certain. If it is genuine and our above interpretation of 10:5-6 is correct, "Peace be with you" may very well be not only a greeting but also carry a salvific nuance. The scene is of the risen Jesus whom Luke has earlier connected with peace, and the greeting does remind us of the one used by Jesus' messengers in 10:5-6. Moreover, although it is true that "Go in peace" can be just a polite farewell (cf. Acts 16:36), nevertheless, when it is used after the forgiveness of the sinful woman (Luke 7:50) or after the cure of the woman suffering from hemorrhages (8:48), it more probably carries the salvific nuance of wholeness, i.e., made whole. In fact, in both passages each woman is likewise told, "Your faith has saved you." Consequently, Luke's account of the risen Jesus' greeting, "Peace be with you" (24:36), may well carry such a salvific nuance([175]).

The Lucan understanding of "peace" depends mainly on the LXX. The peace, which those favored by God receive, can mean the message about Jesus, his salvific activity of doing good and healing those oppressed by evil spirits, an encounter with Christ the Savior or the wholeness which results from his activity. Peace looks to universal salvation and is associated by Luke with Jesus as king (Christ) and with his kingdom, but not as these were usually understood in that historical period. "Peace" stands in opposition to sitting in darkness and the shadow of death and to the fall of Jerusalem.

Redemption([176])

In the *Benedictus*, the God of Israel is blessed because he has visited and worked the redemption (Luke 1:68: λύτρωσιν) for his people, and the next verse explains that he did this by raising up "a mighty Savior" in the

---

[174] For further reflections on this pericope see my "Εἰρήνη, an Underlying Theme in Acts 10,34-43," 461-476, and Riesenfeld, "The Text of Acts 10,36," 191-194.

[175] Lenski, *St. Luke's Gospel*, 1197, is also of this opinion and explains that normally responses were made to greetings such as Jesus' here, and comments, "We see why none was made in this instance."

[176] Marshall, *Jesus the Savior*, 239-241, 244-245.

house of David, his servant. As noted above, the reference in v. 69 must
be to Jesus (cf. 1:32-33; 2:11); and this verse is in Hebrew parallelism to v.
68b, that is, with different words they both communicate the same idea.
Later, in the temple, the prophetess Anna praises God and speaks about
Jesus to all those who were looking for the redemption of Jerusalem
(2:38). In both of these passages, the redemption through Jesus appears in
a context of prophecy, relates to the Jewish people and leads to praise of
God. The former passage sees this as an expression of God's faithfulness
to his covenant and promises; the latter as a fulfillment of the expectations
of the people of Jerusalem, which supposedly also rely on these promises.

In Luke 21 Jesus speaks of the coming of the Son of Man and
indicates some of the signs, which will accompany this event; in vv. 27-28
(cf. Dan 7:13), he makes the prediction, "And then they will see the 'Son
of Man coming in a cloud' with power and great glory. But when these
signs begin to happen, stand erect and raise your heads because your
redemption is at hand"([177]). The context is clearly eschatological, and vv.
31 and 36 relate this event to the kingdom of God and judgment; but Luke
likewise unites the drawing near of redemption with the coming of the Son
of Man (v. 28). This last verse is unique to Luke and naturally proves en-
couraging to disciples as opposed to others.

Two other passages should be considered here: Luke 24:21 and
Acts 7:35. On the way to Emmaus, the risen Jesus joins Cleopas and his
companion, but they do not recognize him. He asks them what they were
discussing, and they begin to tell him about Jesus and to lament, "But we
were hoping that he would be the one to redeem Israel" (Luke 24:21).
The reader knows that Cleopas and his companion are on the "way," a
Lukan designation for Christianity. Since their eyes are kept from recog-
nizing Jesus, the two disciples are in the dark and rather moving toward
salvation, where there is light and one sees. After the above citation, Jesus
explains that what happened to him was exactly what the scriptures
predicted. Thus, Luke is working on two levels: that of Cleopas and his
companion and that of the reader. Although for the moment Cleopas and
his companion appear to have lost their hope in Jesus as the redeemer of
Israel, this is hardly the case with Luke's reader who knows that through

---

[177] Bock, *Luke 9:51 – 24:53*, 1687, approvingly cites Büchsel (ἀπολύτρωσις, 352),
who interprets "redemption" in the verse in a broad sense: "not deliverance from the
penalty of sin but deliverance from a fallen world."

Jesus God redeems Israel (cf. 1:68-69; 2:38) and that, therefore, the hope of the disciples was and is well founded.

In Acts 7:35, we read of Moses, "God sent as (both) ruler and redeemer through the angel who appeared to him in the bush." We noted in our consideration of Jesus as a prophet an extensive comparison between him and Moses and concluded that Luke predicates "redeemer" of Moses because he views him an archetype of Jesus, who truly is the redeemer[178]. With wonders and sign, Moses did lead the Hebrews out of Egypt (Acts 7:36).

Luke takes over the tradition of the Passover Meal and so Jesus' words, "This is my body given for you . . . . This cup is the new covenant in my blood, which will be shed for you" (Luke 22:19b-20[179]). Some of this redemptive terminology occurs again in the enigmatic passage in Paul's speech to the Ephesian elders at Miletus, when he instructs them to watch over themselves and over all the flock of which the Holy Spirit has made them overseers, "to shepherd the church of God that he obtained with the blood of his own Son"[180]. Surely, in this passage God is the primary agent of redemption, but that redemption is achieved through the blood of Jesus; and since Paul is giving this speech, Luke may have wanted to imitate his vocabulary. More importantly, Luke accepts these traditional phrasings about Jesus' redemptive death; but he has not integrated them into his own theological thinking[181]. Nonetheless, since he has taken over this terminology, Luke has accepted this description of Jesus' death and includes it in his two volumes. In that sense, these phrasings form part of Luke's own overall Christology.

In summary, redemption is primarily God's activity, but for Luke it designates what God has done through Jesus for Israel or the Church. Jesus himself can redeem, and the concept relates to him as the eschato-

---

[178] See Henchen, *The Acts*, 282, 289; L.T. Johnson, *The Acts*, 129, 136-137; Kürzinger, *The Acts*, I, 127-129 and Polhill, *Acts*, 199.

[179] The textual evidence in favor of including vv. 19b-20 is very strong; and, in fact, they constitute the *lectio difficilior*.

[180] This translation offered by the NRSV:CE is the most reasonable one.

· [181] Of course, Luke thought that Jesus' death was salvific; but he viewed the whole of Jesus' life, of which his death was surely a part, as salvific.

logical Son of Man. Luke is willing to take over the Pauline phrasing, "obtained thorough the blood of his own Son"; and probably Luke names Moses "redeemer" because he is an archetype of Jesus, who truly is redeemer.

Blessing

"Blessing" can mean salvation. At the end of his speech in Solomon's Portico, Peter tells his audience (Acts 3:25-26), "You are the children of the prophets and of the covenant that God made with your ancestors when he said to Abraham, 'In your offspring all the families of the earth shall be blessed.' For you first, God raised up his servant and sent him to bless you by turning each of you from your evil ways." Elsewhere[182] I have proposed that ἀνίστημι, "I raise" in v. 26 refers to Jesus' resurrection. Whether that be true or not, Jesus in this verse is identified as the Lord's "servant" (παῖς, cf. Acts 3:13; 4:27.30) whom, in loyalty to the covenant made with Abraham, God sent to bless the Jews. This "blessing" (cf. Luke 24:50-51) can actualize itself for every Jew (and Luke's reader) in rescuing them "from their wicked ways"and so bringing them to salvation.

Various beatitudes provide other examples of blessing as a Christological and salvific expression. A clear example of this is the beatitude, "Blessed are you when people hate you, and when they exclude and insult you, and denounce your name as evil on account of the Son of Man. Rejoice and leap for joy on that day! Behold, your reward will be great in heaven. For their ancestors treated the prophets in the same way" (Luke 6:22-23; cf. 9:24.26; 12:8-9; 21:12-19). One is blessed when he is persecuted because of Jesus; he is like the prophets and his reward in heaven will be great. The blessing is a present experience, in view of a final reward in heaven. This passage and its parallels help us understand another parallel in Luke 7:23, "And blessed is the one who takes no offense at me." If one responds properly to Jesus, he already begins to experience salvation.

Privately, Jesus assures the disciples, "Blessed are the eyes that see what you see. For I say to you, many prophets and kings desired to see what you see, but did not see it, and to hear what you hear, but did not hear it" (Luke 10:23-24). From the context, the particular blessing that

---

[182] "Some Observations on *Anistêmi*," 85-92.

the disciples are receiving consists in the Son's (Jesus') revelation of the Father[183].

Luke ends the parable of the watchful slaves (Luke 12:35-40) with the exhortation to be ready because the Son of Man is coming at an unexpected hour. Hence, "Lord" in vv. 36-37 of the parable represents the Son of Man, and Jesus is speaking of himself. By means of the parable Luke portrays the Parusia and what Christians should do until it comes. Only Luke writes of those servants who are waiting when Jesus comes, "Blessed are those servants whom the master finds vigilant on his arrival. Amen, I say to you, he will gird himself, have them recline at table, and proceed to wait on them . . . blessed are those servants" (vv. 37-38). So, those servants who are alert when Jesus comes at the Parusia will be rewarded. There follows immediately the instruction about the faithful or unfaithful servant (12:41-48). Of the faithful servant, it is said, "Blessed is that servant whom his master on arrival finds doing so. Truly, I say to you, he will put him in charge of all his property" (vv. 43-44). Luke is still thinking of the Parusia and developing the thought of how one should behave until Jesus comes again. If the servant, who now most likely represents a Church official, remains faithful, he will be rewarded most generously and called "blessed." "Reward" is a salvific term, and "blessed" indicates participation in the benefits that Jesus brings to the Christians who do their duty and respond appropriately[184].

In the introduction to the parable of the great dinner (Luke 14:15-24), which despite the parallel in Matt 22:1-14 appears to have been considerably reworked by Luke, one of the guests said to Jesus, "Blessed is the one who will dine in the kingdom of God" (v. 15). Although he answers with a parable, Jesus does not reject the man's statement. Rather the parable serves to correct a possible misperception about who will be in the kingdom of God. Surprisingly, those originally invited will not participate in the banquet, but rather the poor, the crippled, the blind, the lame and those from the roadways and the lanes. The guest's "blessed" should properly not designate those who are invited but do not come but rather

---

183 Feldkämper, *Der betende Jesus*, 172-177.

184 Fitzmyer, *The Gospel According to Luke X–XXIV*, 985-987, while conceding this salvific aspect, contends that the emphasis is rather on watchfulness, faithfulness and prudence; for the concept "blessed" see his *The Gospel According to Luke I–IX*, 632-633.

those who are invited and have the good sense to accept the Lord's invitation. These latter are those who dine in the kingdom of God.

A final but different type of example regarding the salvific meaning of "blessing" occurs when the woman from the crowd raised her voice and said to Jesus, "Blessed is the womb that carried you and the breasts at which you nursed" (Luke 11:27b; cf. 1:42.45.48). True, Jesus does answer her, "Rather blessed are those who hear the word of God and obey it" (11:28). Nonetheless, Jesus clearly does not intend to reject the thought that his Mother was blessed because she carried him in her womb and nursed him. More probably, that thought is assumed as a fact, and thus allows Jesus to stress how important it is to hear and obey the word of God, which would be radically true of Mary (cf. 1:38). Obviously, Mary's womb and her nursing of Jesus do not bless him; but she is blessed because of her being the mother of the Son of God. On the other hand, "blessed" in 11:27 is associated with Jesus but not directly with his salvific activity.

In summary, "blessing" can point to Jesus' salvific activity or anyone's reception of it. Once, it clearly refers to the promise to Abraham. Various beatitudes provide examples of participation in the blessings that Jesus brings to those who suffer on his account, remain loyal to him and live diligently in expectation of his coming. Being blessed is a present experience, although it primarily looks to a future reward.

Resurrection

Luke views our resurrection as part of salvation and sometimes clarifies that the disciples' association with Jesus brings about their resurrection. We have already seen that Jesus is the leader of life (Acts 3:15) who guides his followers to eternal life and that Jesus assures those who have suffered on his account of a great reward in heaven (Luke 6:22-23)([185]). However, other passages connect the resurrection of individuals with the following of Jesus.

The story of the rich ruler (Luke 18:18-30) relates the following of Jesus to eternal life. Perhaps we should start with the end of the story. Peter expresses his concern about the destiny of the disciples: "Look we have given up our possessions and followed you." And Jesus responds:

---

[185] Luke 9:24 and 17:33 probably likewise imply the resurrection since they speak of salvation, and "living" can carry a resurrectional meaning; certainly, these verses deal with salvation in this life.

"Amen, I say to you, there is no one who has given up house or wife or brothers or parents or children for the sake of the kingdom of God who will not receive (back) an overabundant return in this present age and eternal life in the age to come" (18:28-30). In these verses, "and followed you (Jesus)" has to mean the same as "for the sake of the kingdom of God" since both ideas are immediately subsequent to leaving of home or the equivalent, and Jesus is responding to Peter's concern. So, those who leave these things to follow Jesus will not only get very much more back in this age but in the one to come, eternal life. Unfortunately, the rich ruler has something he will not leave, his wealth (vv. 22-23). An initial answer to the rich ruler's question about what he must do to inherit eternal life is found in the listing of the commandments in v. 20, which in the next verse he states that he has observed. However, Jesus still sees a lacuna in the stance of the rich ruler, connects his question about inheriting eternal life with having treasure in heaven and challenges him to sell all of his property and give it to the poor and then to follow Jesus[186]. To be sure, the rich ruler stands in contrast to the blind beggar who when he can see follows Jesus (v. 42) and to Zacchaeus' correct attitude toward his wealth (19:7-10).

Luke 10:17-20, unique to Luke, is related to 18:18-30. Both of these passages treat the following of Jesus. In the former the seventy (-two) joyfully return to Jesus and relate how in his name demons were subject to them. However, Jesus tells them how he saw Satan fall from heaven and recalls some of the powers he has given them. He then advises them, "Nevertheless, do not rejoice because the spirits are subject to you, but rejoice because your names are written in heaven" (v. 20). Lagrange points out that the metaphor of God writing the names of the elect in a book was well known (cf. Ex 32:32; Is 4:3; Dan 12:1; Ps. 69:28-29)[187]. However, the reason that their names appear in this book is that they are Jesus' disciples and are carrying out the mission assigned them.   .

Since Jesus is the leader of life (Acts 3:15) and Luke uses ζάω, "I live," of the risen Jesus and of other risen persons[188], Acts 11:18b, "God

---

[186] Evans, *Saint Luke*, 649-650.

[187] Lagrange, *Évangile selon Saint Luc*, 304. Lenski, *St. Luke's Gospel*, 585, provides additional references for the book of life, namely, Phil 4:3; Rev 3:5; 13:8; 20:12; 21:27.

has then granted life-giving repentance to the Gentiles too," should be included in our consideration. This gift should be viewed Christologically because in the previous verse the text speaks of the Gentile Christians as receiving the same gift as the Jewish Christians when they believed in the *Lord Jesus* (cf. Acts 15:11).

When in the Transfiguration scene Moses and Elijah speak of Jesus' "exodus" (τὴν ἔξοδον αὐτοῦ), Luke cannot be thinking only of Jesus' passion but must also have in mind his resurrection([189]). As Moses' Exodus also related to all of Israel, so, Jesus' exodus and its results also embrace all of his followers. Furthermore, since in Acts 7 Luke has developed an extensive comparison between Moses and Jesus, it is possible that the "living" of v. 38c, "And he received living utterances to hand on to us" may well look to the resurrection, i.e., words which give life, because Luke portrays Moses as a type of Jesus, the leader of life.

The story of the good thief (Luke 23:39-43) occurs only in Luke. Although the one thief blasphemes Jesus with the words, "Are you not the Messiah? Save yourself and us," the good thief admonishes him and admits their guilt and defends Jesus' innocence. He then asks Jesus to remember him when he comes into his kingdom. Jesus assures him, "Amen, I say to you, today you will be with me in Paradise" (v. 43). The blasphemy of the one thief continues the irony that Luke has interwoven into his Passion Narrative. The truth is that Jesus does save and so can assure the good thief of his salvation with Jesus in Paradise([190]), which must relate to both of their resurrections since they will die that very day.

In two pericopes that discuss the Parusia or the messianic banquet we find a connection between Jesus and the resurrection. At the beginning of the pericope of the narrow door (Luke 13:22-30), someone asks Jesus if few will be saved. Jesus then urges his audience to strive to enter through the narrow door because, once the owner closes the door, they could be left outside. Although they will then plead with the owner and recall shared meals and his teaching them (v. 26), he will not recognize

---

[188] George, *Études sur l'œuvre de Luc*, 329.

[189] Feuillet, "'L'exode' de Jésus," 181-192; Nolland, *Luke 9:21 – 18:34*, 499-500 and Mánek, "The New Exodus," 8-23.

[190] For a discussion of the meaning of "Paradise," see Talbert, *Reading Luke*, 221.

them; and they will have bitter grief since they will be excluded from the banquet in the kingdom of God where the Patriarchs and prophets sit with others from around the world. Surely, the pericope is an exhortation to Jesus' Jewish listeners to accept him while there is still time. Salvation and participation in the banquet of the kingdom of God depend on one's response to Jesus imaged as the owner of a house[191].

We have already reflected on the parable of the great banquet (Luke 14:15-24) under the heading of "'Blessings' Can Mean Salvation." Eating bread in the kingdom of God is a way of expressing the resurrection[192], and the host of the banquet stands for Jesus. So, this parable has a message similar to that of the narrow door[193]: Jews are exhorted not to be indifferent to Jesus' invitation, and others, especially the disadvantaged, are informed that this invitation and blessing of being at the banquet can include them.

Luke in Acts 13:13-52 establishes a clear connection between Jesus' resurrection and our own, but a detailed exegesis of this passage is required to show this[194]. Several factors indicate the unity of this pericope. It follows a set pattern (Acts 13:13-52; 14:1-6; 17:1-11; 18:4-18; 19:8-10; 28:17-32), which can be modified, of how Paul enters a village and is treated by the Jews[195]:

1. Paul and his companions go to the synagogue and preach to the Jews first.

2. Some Jews reject the message.

3. The preaching then turns to the Gentiles.

4. Some Jews become upset and cause a disturbance.

---

191 Schweizer, *The Good News according to Luke*, 227.

192 For instance, Plummer, *St. Luke*, 360, writes of v. 15, "'The resurrection of the just' (v. 14) suggests the thought of the Kingdom, and this guest complacently assumes that he will be among those who will enjoy it."

193 Nolland, *Luke 9:21 – 18:34*, 736, holds that these are parallel.

194 For a more thorough consideration of this topic, see my "Christ's Resurrection in Acts 13,13-52," 361-372.

195 Trocmé, *Le "Livre des Actes"*, 109-110.

5. Paul (or another Christian preacher) leaves or is thrown out of the city.

Λόγος ("word": Acts 13:15.26.44.46.48-49), ἀκούω ("to hear": Acts 13:16b.44.48), and σωτήρ and cognates ("savior": Acts 13:23.26.47; cf. vv. 38-39) support this unity. Moreover, Acts 13:42 (cf. v. 43) connects the speech with its aftermath through the phrase, "As they were leaving, they invited them to speak on these subjects the following Sabbath." Things are not yet settled, and the difference in the makeup of the audiences does not contradict the unity of Acts 13:13-52 since the real audience of these verses consists in Luke's readers. On the other hand, the speech does not begin to speak of Jesus' resurrection until Acts 13:30; but, if one accepts that vv. 32-33 deals with Jesus' resurrection, then the major portion (vv. 30-37) of the remainder of the speech has to do with this topic.

But the question arises: should one see Jesus' resurrection in Acts 13:32-33, "We ourselves are proclaiming this good news to you that what God promised our ancestors he has brought to fulfillment for us, (their) children, by raising up Jesus, as it is written in the second psalm, 'You are my Son, this day I have begotten you?'" The data favor a resurrectional interpretation of "raising up," instead of understanding it of Jesus' entry into this earthly life. If vv. 32-33 do not report Jesus' resurrection, then the train of thought is broken because Acts 13:30-31.34-37 speak of the resurrection of Jesus([196]). True, "promise" could refer back to Acts 13:23 where it deals with Jesus' earthly ministry; but, more probably, one should relate it to Acts 26:6-8.22-23 which, in accord with the Scriptures, describe a promise of a resurrection of the dead realized first in Jesus. Acts 26:4-23 forms a diptych: the first panel of the diptych tells us of Paul's life (Acts 26:4-5), and the promise made to Israel's ancestors of the resurrection of the dead (Acts 26:6-8); and the second panel continues the first with further information about Paul's life (Acts 26:9-21) and introduces Jesus' resurrection (Acts 26:22-23). So, the second part of each panel treats the resurrection. Initially, we are told that the promise made to Israel's ancestors consists in the resurrection of the dead and then that the Christ must suffer and, by being first to rise from the dead, proclaim light both to the people and to the Gentiles. Luke does not understand "first" in

---

[196] See Haenchen, *The Acts*, 411, ft. 3; Lövestam, *Son and Saviour*, 8-11.

v. 23 primarily chronologically; rather Christ's resurrection is first because his resurrection begins that of the Christians (cf. Acts 3:26)([197]).

Certainly, Luke intends to quote Ps 2 in Acts 13:33. This quote, however, is best understood in relationship to Heb 1:5; 5:5, which according to the majority of scholars treat Jesus' exaltation; and probably Luke and the author of Hebrews rely on a common tradition. In fact, Luke quotes Ps 2 in Acts 13:33 with the exact same Greek words as found in these verses from the Letter to the Hebrews. Finally, Luke in Acts 2:25-36; 13:34-37 (cf. Ps 15LXX) relates Jesus' resurrection to his descent from David; and upon careful reflection, one must admit that Luke 1:32-33 interrelate Jesus' sonship, the throne of David his father, and a kingdom which will last forever. However, such a statement implies that Jesus will be raised from the dead; otherwise, he cannot reign forever, nor could his kingdom last forever. Further, in Acts 13:33 Luke writes of Jesus as "Son" with the words of the Davidic Ps 2. Consequently, Acts 13:32-33 speaks of Jesus the Son of God and descendant of David whose resurrection fulfills God's promise to our forbearers.

How does this theme of Jesus' resurrection fit with Acts 13:44-52? "Eternal life" in Acts 13:46-48 certainly embraces more than Jesus' resurrection; we are dealing with the resurrection of those who believe (cf. v. 48). So, in Acts 13:32-33 Luke sees a connection between Jesus' resurrection and our own; for God fulfills the promise to our forbearers for us, (their) children, by raising Jesus from the dead. Consequently, Luke has Paul speak of the salvation that Jesus brings (Acts 13:23.26); but a large portion of the speech (vv. 30-37; cf. vv. 46-48) considers a major aspect of that salvation: Jesus' resurrection and its effect on our own.

Acts 13:13-52 provides an insight into other passages, other than those considered above, in which Luke connects Jesus' resurrection with ours. Two passages that very probably draw a connection between our resurrection and Jesus' are Acts 4:2 and 17:30-31. As Peter and John were speaking to the people, the priests and the captain of the temple and the Sadducees came upon them, "disturbed that they were teaching the people and proclaiming in Jesus the resurrection from the dead" (Acts 4:2: καταγγέλλειν ἐν τῷ ʾΙησοῦ τὴν ἀνάστασιν τὴν ἐκ νεκρῶν). The Greek of Acts 4:2 is compressed, but well

---

[197] For detailed argumentation for this position, see my *Acts 26*, 86-122.

represented by the above translation([198]).   Naturally, the Sadducees would
have been offended by any proclamation of Jesus' resurrection. However, if
Peter and John are not claiming a connection between Jesus' resurrection and
that of others, it is more difficult to see how their Jewish opponents could
bring a convincing charge against them since most Jews of the time accepted a
general resurrection (cf. Acts 23:6-9). Would other Jews even be offended by
the claim that Jesus is raised? Luke himself reports the popular convictions
that certain people were raised or viewed as active after their death (Luke 9:7-
8,19). Thus, more probably, Peter and John were proclaiming a connection
between Jesus' resurrection and that of others.

Acts 17:30-31 reads, "God has overlooked the times of ignorance,
but now he demands that all people everywhere repent because he has
established a day on which he will judge the world with justice through a
man he has appointed, and he has provided confirmation for all by raising
him from the dead." How has God kept faith by raising Jesus from the
dead? If this is only in terms of Jesus' resurrection, why speak of a confirmation for everyone? Is it only that everyone will be assured of Jesus as
his or her just judge? However, does this not imply a resurrection of the
dead, for without it what significance would any judgment have; there
would be no one to be judged? Rather the thought of Acts 17:30-31 also
includes the thought that we found in Acts 13:32-33: through Jesus'
resurrection God demonstrates fidelity to his promise of our own resurrection. This interpretation would make better sense of the strange accusation of some of the Athenians during the introduction to the speech,
"'He sounds like a promoter of foreign deities', because of Paul's
preaching about 'Jesus' and 'Resurrection'" (v. 18: τὸν Ἰσοῦν καὶ τὴν
ἀνάστασιν εὐηγγελίζετο) and of the beginning of v. 32 in the aftermath
of the speech, "When they heard about the resurrection of the dead"
(plural). These Athenians could not accept any dead person's resurrection.

Three other passages call for brief consideration. At the presentation of Jesus in the temple, Simeon blesses Jesus' parents and says to
Mary, "Behold, this child is destined for the fall and rise (ἀνάστασις) of
many in Israel, and to be a sign that will be contradicted" (Luke 2:34).

---

[198] Bruce, *The Acts*, 148, notes that the disciples seem to be arguing from Jesus' resurrection to a general principle of resurrection; Polhill, *Acts*, 140, holds that Jesus'
opponents were upset because the idea of a general resurrection had messianic over-
tones and could mean revolt and so would not be politically acceptable to the Romans.

The most natural interpretation of "fall and rise" in this verse would be in terms of Acts 3:22-23, where if one does not listen to the prophet like Moses, Jesus, one will be cut off from the people. In this case, "rising" (Luke 2:34) means, "bringing into (the people of Israel)"; however, there is the outside possibility that Luke wants to play on the Greek word, and also suggests a resurrectional nuance.

The two other passages are Luke 7:11-17 and 8:40-56 in which Jesus resuscitates someone from the dead. Surely, we do not have in these two miracles stories the actual resurrection. However, Luke uses ἐγείρω ("I raise": 7:14; 8:54) for each resuscitation; and his general description of this activity in 7:22, "the dead are raised" corresponds to one phrasing that he has for the resurrection of the dead (Luke 9:7; 20:37; Acts 3:15; 4:10; 13:30; 26:8)([199]).

Therefore, although one does not find in Luke-Acts the lucidity of Paul or John on the topic of the extent to which Jesus' resurrection affects ours, Luke does view our resurrection as part of salvation and holds for a connection between Jesus' resurrection and that of the Christians([200]). Jesus' resurrection affects ours and is the fulfillment of the promise made to the fathers, and God has been faithful to what he has said in the scriptures. Other expressions for the resurrection of the dead are "life," "eternal life" and participation in the messianic banquet, all of which the Christians receive through belief in Jesus and discipleship

"Consolation" As an Expression of Salvation

At the presentation of Jesus in the temple, Luke describes Simeon as "awaiting the consolation of Israel" (Luke 2:25). This phrase stands at the beginning of its pericope and parallels the description of Anna, the prophetess, at the end of the story, "spoke about the child to all who were awaiting the redemption of Jerusalem" (v. 38). The natural conclusion is that "consolation" is a synonym for "redemption"; for, like "redemption," it looks to the salvation that Jesus brings([201]). This understanding is

---

[199] George, *Études,* 79-80.

[200] George, *Études,* 325-331; Glöckner, *Die Verkündigung des Heils,* 206, 216-218;

[201] Lenski, *St. Luke's Gospel,* 144; Plummer, *St. Luke,* 66 and Prete, *L'opera di Luca,* 44, 169-173, 181.

confirmed by the rest of the story about Simeon, who holds the child Jesus in his arms and proclaims that his eyes have seen the Lord's salvation, which as shown above is probably in apposition to both "light" and "glory" (vv. 29-32). Moreover, since Simeon prays to God who is now dismissing him, he must have found the consolation of Israel (cf. Is 40:1; 49:13; 51:3; 61:3; 66:13) in the infant Jesus; for there is nothing else in the pericope which would justify his contentment about God's action in his regard.

Luke in another passage writes of "consolation," although the Greek word is frequently translated as "encouragement." In Antioch of Pisidia after the reading of the law and the prophets, the officials of the synagogue address Paul and Barnabas, "My brothers, if one of you has a word of consolation for the people, please speak" (Acts 13:15). As the phrase stands, "consolation" serves as a description of the speech that Paul is about to give. After a very brief summary of Jewish history and of Jesus' life and identification as savior (v. 23), Paul again offers a summary description of the speech, "My brothers, children of the family of Abraham and those others among you who are God-fearing, to us this word of salvation has been sent" (v. 26). There is an obvious parallel between "a word of consolation" (v. 15) and "this word of salvation" (v. 26; cf. vv. 23, 44, 46, 48, 49), and both phrases serve as a summary description of the speech. Finally, above we demonstrated that the latter half of the speech describes how God through Jesus' resurrection fulfills his promise to the Jewish ancestors of eternal life for us. So, there is little doubt that "consolation" (v. 15), or, if one prefers, "encouragement" constitutes another way of expressing the salvation that God achieves through Jesus

Other Lucan Expressions of Salvation

There are a number of other Lucan Christological expressions of salvation. Some of these we have already seen in connection with other salvific concepts: "visitation" (1:68,78; 19:44; cf. 7:16), "I rescue" (1:74; cf. Acts 7:34; 26:17), "physician" (Luke 5:31; cf. 4:23), "harvest" (10:2, 2x), "cornerstone" (Acts 4:11; cf. Luke 20:17), "justify" (Acts 13:38-39) and "an inheritance among those who have been sanctified by faith in me" (Acts 26:18). In this last verse both "inheritance" and "sanctified" are expressions of salvation realized by faith in Christ. "Repentance" should be included here since according to Acts 5:31 (cf. Luke 5:32) Jesus, whom God has raised to his right hand as leader and savior, has the task of giving repentance to Israel and forgiveness of sins. In this verse repentance is something the risen Jesus gives as he does forgiveness of sins; it is not something a human being, on his or her own, can achieve. This interpretation is confirmed by Luke 24:46-47, which assert that the Scriptures show that "repentance for the forgiveness of sins is to be proclaimed in his (the Messiah's) name to all nations." So, the name of the risen Jesus is instrumental in there being repentance for the forgiveness of sins([202]). Finally, one of the summaries of the earthly Jesus' life reads: "How God anointed Jesus of Nazareth with the Holy Spirit and power. He went about doing good and healing all those oppressed by the devil, for God was with him" (Acts 10:38; cf. Luke 4:18-19; 6:9) and is a general statement of his salvific activity.

Luke's use of "word" (λόγος or ῥῆμα) becomes a little more complicated. At times, it definitely seems to have salvific power. Jesus' word was in power (Luke 4:32; cf. v. 36; 24:19); and the centurion begs Jesus, "But say the word and let my servant be healed" (7:7). At Jesus' word, Peter is willing to let down the fishing nets, which became so full that they began to break (5:5-6). Earlier Luke spoke of the words of grace that came out of Jesus' mouth (4:22), and repeats the idea in Acts 14:3. Apparently, not only Jesus' words, but the word about him are in themselves means of salvation. We have seen that "the word" can be in apposition to "peace" (Acts 10:36-37) and that in a context of Jesus as savior, whose resurrection effects ours, "consolation," "salvation" and "eternal life" explain "word" (Acts 13:15.26.46-48; cf. 5:20).

Although "word" and other expressions for the gospel message naturally proclaim and to some extent actualize the salvation that Jesus brings; most often this is not stated. However, when later reference is made to "to proclaim good news to the poor" (Luke 4:18) in the programmatic passage, the reference stands in the midst of various statements of salvation (7:22: "The blind regain their sight, the lame walk, lepers are cleansed, the deaf hear, the dead are raised, the poor have the good news proclaimed to them)." Apparently, Luke views this phrase, too, as a statement of salvation. Something should likewise be said about the kingdom (of God). "Kingdom (of God)" is not a univocal term in Luke-Acts; it can mean an award (Luke 9:62), something for which to strive (12:31), a gift (12:32; cf. 18:17) and a different type of existence, not of

---

[202] For a thorough consideration of repentance in Luke-Acts, see Nave, *The Role and Function of Repentance.*

this world([203]).   The kingdom of God begins the destruction of Satan's reign and brings salvation to the Christians. Jesus' miracles, and power and authority over demons are evidence of this salvation([204]).   At times, the concept of the kingdom definitely deals with the salvation Jesus brings. In answer to the opponents who charge him with acting in the power of Beelzebub, Jesus responds, "But if it is by the finger of God that I drive out demons, then the kingdom of God has come upon you" (11:20)([205]). In the previous verses we notice that toward the end of the story of the rich young ruler, Peter is concerned about what those who have left their possessions and followed Jesus will receive in recompense. Jesus assures him that there will be no one who has left his home and near and dear ones for the sake of the kingdom who will not have a hundredfold in this life and in the age to come eternal life (18:28-30). Therefore, Jesus interprets following him as acting for the sake of the kingdom and promises a reward for this both in the present life and in eternal life. Also, we noted that the good thief asks Jesus to remember him when the latter comes into his kingdom and Jesus replies, "Amen, I say to you, today you will be with me in paradise" (23:43). Jesus identifies his kingdom with paradise. Finally, if I am correct in my interpretation of 13:10-17([206]), Luke first reports Jesus' marvelous healing of the badly stooped woman and then, without any break, expands on this miracle and its effects in the parables of the mustard seed and of the leaven as images of the kingdom. Thus, the cure of the badly stooped woman functions as a springboard and an initial image of the kingdom of God.

Summary of Luke's Presentation of Jesus As Savior
The main source for Luke's notion of salvation is the LXX, and Jesus acts as savior during the course of each person's life by liberating from physical and moral evil. Some passages play a larger role in Luke's presentation of

---

[203] E.g., Luke 7:28; 13:28-29; 14:15; 18:16; 19:11; 22:16-18.29-30; Acts 1:3.6.

[204] See my "The Kingdom of God in Luke-Acts," 147-162, esp., 155-157.

[205] For a thorough redactional study of this verse, see George, *Études sur l'œuvre de Luc*, 127-132.

[206] See my "Reflections on Luke 13:10-17," 84-107.

Jesus as savior than others(^{207}). Even before Jesus is born, Luke's reader knows that through him God is now going to save his people, and this holds true for the whole of the Gospel and Acts where Jesus is the risen savior. Jesus' salvation is universal, and belief and baptism in his name effect this salvation. Jesus can forgive sins, and some of his miracles and his welcome of sinners and tax collectors pertain to this theme. Light characterizes the realm of God and salvation and under various forms (e.g., dawn, lamp and sight) serves to depict Jesus' salvific activity. "Grace" too can signify what Jesus says and does to save or "the grace of God," the message about Jesus or faith in him.   "Loving mercy" flows from God's fidelity to his covenant and promises and can be predicated both of God and of Jesus who express this attribute by their concern to save. However, generally Luke links "loving mercy" with Jesus. During his earthly existence and as risen Savior, Jesus performs miracles. Faith in Jesus leads to these miracles, which manifest the kingdom of God. Jesus communicates to his disciples the ability to hear and have authority over evil spirits. He leads people to repentance, forgiveness of sins and life; and probably, Chrisitianity as the "way" bears on the heading of "Jesus as leader." Luke's concept of "peace" can mean the message about Jesus, his doing good and healing those oppressed by evil spirits or the wholeness that results from this salvific activity. It is universal and associated by Luke with the Christian understanding of Jesus as king (Messiah) and his kingdom. Redemption likewise designates what God has done through Jesus for Israel or the Church. Jesus himself can redeem, and the concept is associated with him as the eschatological Son of Man. Luke is willing to use the Pauline phrasing "obtained through the blood of his own Son" and to name Moses redeemer or liberator because he is an archetype of Jesus. "Blessing" can point to Jesus' salvific activity or one's participation in it. "Being blessed" is a present experience, although it looks to a future reward. Luke sees a salvific connection between Jesus' resurrection and that of the Christians, and this connection fulfills the promise made in the OT to the fathers. Other expressions for our resurrection are "life," "eternal life" and participation in (the eschatological banquet of) the kingdom

---

^{207} E.g., *Benedictus*, Luke: 2:11-14.25-38; 4:14-44; 5:17-26.31-32; 6,20-23; 7:47-50; 10:21-24; 14:21-24; 13:10-17; 15; 18:18-30.38-43; 19:10; 23:35.37.39; Acts 2:21.37-41.47; 4:11-12; 5:31; 10:36; 13:13-48; 15:10-11; 26:18.23; 28:23-31.

of God. In addition, "consolation," or, if one prefers, "encouragement," expresses the salvation that God achieves through Jesus.

There are a number of other Lucan Christological expressions of salvation which we only listed above but which definitely bear on Luke's presentation of Jesus as savior. Jesus is God's instrument in his salvific visitations of the house of David and in the healing of the son of the widow of Nain; God also rescues through Jesus. "Physician" has to look to salvation, for a physician heals. Jesus as the cornerstone must support those imaged as the building, and he clearly justifies individuals from what the law could not. An "inheritance" means that someone receives something, and the context reveals that this is eternal life, and those who are sanctified by faith in Jesus now belong to the realm of God. Repentance, too, bears on the salvation that Jesus brings; for it leads to the forgiveness of sins. At times Jesus' very word saves or moves someone toward salvation. Apparently this statement can also be made about any expression of the gospel message and of the kingdom. Whoever belongs to the kingdom of God is in his realm and not in that of the Satan (Acts 26:18).

Elsewhere I have argued that according to Luke Jesus is the savior of the disadvantaged, especially sinners, women, the sick, the poor and the persecuted[208].

---

[208] *The Unity*, 109-148.

Chapter Four

Jesus As Servant of Yahweh([209])

Scholars are far from agreement in their understanding of Luke's treatment of Jesus as Servant of Yahweh in Luke-Act([210]). Some even doubt that there is enough data to say that the theme belongs to Luke's Christology. Here a case will be made for the opposite opinion, and an explanation given about Luke's meaning for this title. Naturally, a study of the topic must address a number of questions. Although most of Luke's references to Jesus as this servant do refer to one of the hymns about the Servant of Yahweh([211]), how many of the other Isaian passages predicated of Jesus did Luke regard as falling under this theme([212])? Furthermore, how many of these references are unique to Luke? In addition, although some of Luke's references to Jesus as Servant of Yahweh are obvious, others are subtler; and it must be demonstrated that each of these passages is in fact probably such a reference. For instance, this last observation is relevant as regards what interpretation should be given to παραδίδωμι, "I hand over," and ἄγω, "I lead," and the cognates of the latter. Do these

---

[209] This chapter is a reworking of my article, "Jesus as Servant of Yahweh," 328-346. See also Jeremias, παῖς θεοῦ, 700-707.

[210] The title "Servant of Yahweh," seems to be more prevalent than "Suffering Servant," although either expression applies to Jesus.

[211] Is 42:1-7; 49:1-9a; 50:4-11; 52:13 – 53:12; not all scholars would agree on the verses belonging to the first two hymns. Of course, neither the NT nor Luke limits use of the Servant of Yahweh hymns to Jesus. Paul sees himself as the servant (Gal 1,15-16 [cf. Is 42:6; 49:1.6]; 2 Cor 6:1-2 [cf. Is 49:8]; Rom 15:20-21 [Is 52:15]); and Luke portrays Christians as carrying out Jesus' ministry as the Servant, e.g., Paul and Barnabas (Acts 13:46-47; cf. Is 49:6) and Paul himself (Acts 26:18; cf. Is 42:7; 61:1).

[212] Other passages from Isaiah which Luke uses and probably were attributed by him to the theme of Servant of Yahweh would be Is 35:5; 40:5LXX; 50:7LXX?; 58:6; 60:1-3; 61:1-2.

verbs also serve Luke to picture Jesus as the Servant of Yahweh? More-over, what is Luke's word pattern for his presentation of Jesus as the Servant of Yahweh? According to the present interpretation, this pattern would have to include the following vocabulary: "I lead"; ἐκλεκτός, "elect" and cognates; παῖς, "servant"; "I hand over"; "salvation"; and "light of the Gentiles." Nonetheless, our best approach to the question expressed in the title of this chapter is to begin with a study of those passages in which Luke most probably views Jesus as the Servant of Yahweh or as acting as the Servant acted.

The Lucan View of Jesus' Death As That of the Servant of Yahweh([213])
Let us begin our consideration here with Acts 8:32-33 (cf. Is 53:7-8LXX)([214]). That passage leaves no doubt that Luke uses this description of the Servant to summarize how he presents Jesus in his passion narrative([215]): "This was the scripture passage he was reading: 'Like a sheep he was led to the slaughter, and as a lamb before its shearer is silent, so he opened not his mouth. In (his) humiliation justice was denied him. Who will tell of his posterity? For his life is taken from earth.'" The Ethiopian eunuch is reading this passage and asks Philip about whom the prophet was speaking. As a result, beginning with this passage, Philip proclaims to him Jesus. We find in Acts 8:32-33 clear references to Jesus' passion, "Like a sheep he was led to the slaughter," "justice was denied him" and "his life was taken from the earth." In citing these verses from Isaiah it is reasonable to assume that Luke wanted to identify Jesus as the Servant who carried out the mission assigned to

---

[213] On this point see George, "Le sens de la mort de Jésus," 186-217; Green, "The Death of Jesus, God's Servant," 18-28 and Lampe, "The Lucan Portrait of Jesus," 163, cf. 169-170. Green's article is particularly relevant.

[214] Up to the present, no one has convincingly demonstrated that Luke knew Hebrew; and his OT references are to the LXX. However, the possibility remains that some Lucan texts were formed by earlier church tradition and based on the MT. Of course, some references to the Servant of Yahweh could be Luke's own phrasing.

[215] Korn, *Die Geschichte Jesu*, 254-257 and Marshall, *Luke, Historian and Theologian*, 171-173.

him([216]). We know that elsewhere Luke calls Jesus "servant" (Acts 3,13.26; 4:27.30)([217]); and, as we shall see, he makes other references to Is 52:13 – 53:12. The citation of the scripture passage in Acts 8:32-33 locates these happenings within God's providence and also comments on Jesus' comportment during the passion: he is meek and humble and does not speak. Nevertheless, he still did not get a fair trial, nor was there any reason to think that someone would care enough to record his memory.

This understanding of Acts 8:32-33 as bearing on Jesus' passion is confirmed by one of the passion predictions and by four Servant of Yahweh references that occur during Luke's passion narrative. The third passion prediction (Luke 18:32-33, "He will be handed over to the Gentiles and he will be mocked and insulted and spat upon; after they have scourged him they will kill him") contains two expressions similar to those found about the Servant's suffering in Is 50:6, "I gave my back to those who scourged me . . . . My face I did not shield from the buffets and spitting," and so suggests that Luke sees Jesus' suffering as similar to that of the Servant's([218]). During the Last Supper discourse, Jesus claims, "That this scripture must be fulfilled in me, namely, 'He was counted among the wicked'; and indeed what is written about me is coming to fulfillment" (Luke 22:37; Is 53:12). Again we have a reference to the Servant passage, Is 53; and the citation, "it is necessary" and the predicted fulfillment all point to Jesus' being associated with criminals as being God's will([219]). Later in the garden this association is confirmed; for Jesus says to the high priests, elders and temple soldiers that they came out armed with swords and clubs as against a thief (Luke 22:52). Actually, Jesus is crucified with two criminals (23:32-33; cf. vv. 39-43)([220]). The

---

[216] Polhill, *Acts*, 225, points out the aspects of the citation that relate to Jesus' passion.

[217] Jeremias, παῖς θεοῦ, 700-701, 707 is convinced of the archaic character of these verses as well as of Acts 8:32-33.

[218] Fitzmyer, *The Gospel According to Luke X–XXIV*, 1210, raises the question: whether Luke understood these allusions to Is 50:6 or not; but offers no answer.

[219] See Nolland, *Luke 18:35 – 24:53*, 1076-1078.

[220] For a consideration of the influence of Luke 22:37 on the context of the latter passage, see Rese, *Alttestamentliche Motive*, 155-160.

officials' mockery, noted above, includes the designation of Jesus as "the chosen one" (23:35; cf. Is 42:1) and marks the second Servant of Yahweh reference during the passion. A further reference to Jesus as the Servant of Yahweh lies in Jesus' not answering a word to Herod's questions (Luke 23:9; cf. Acts 8:32 [Is 53:7]: "As a lamb before its shearer is silent, so he opened not his mouth.")

A final reference to Jesus as the Servant of Yahweh occurs a number of times during Luke's passion narrative. A number of scholars contend that Luke presents Jesus' passion as the martyrdom of a just man([221]). This statement is true, but is the more generic identification of a literary form. Luke is more specific than this. His own explanation of what he has done occurs in Acts 8:32-35 and is particularly evident in his many declarations of Jesus' innocence which should be linked with the Lucan portrayal of him as Servant of Yahweh. Is 53:9 reads "Though he had done no wrong nor spoken any falsehood"; the Hebrew of Is 50:9 makes the same point: הן אדני יהוה יעזר־לי מי־הוא ירשיעני ("See, the Lord God is my help; who will prove me wrong"). The previous verse, Is 53:8 (cf. Acts 8:33) had already begun to introduce the notion of innocence; for it states, "Oppressed and condemned, he was taken away, and who would have thought any more of his destiny?" Furthermore, Is 53:11 asserts that God will, "justify the just one who serves many well." Luke has definitely portrayed Jesus as innocent during the passion([222]). Pilate says that he finds no guilt in Jesus (Luke 23:4) and in a threefold manner repeats this conviction when he reports that neither has Herod found any charge worthy of death in him (vv. 14-15). Pilate then again states Jesus' innocence (v. 22). The good thief also affirms that Jesus has done nothing

---

[221] E.g., Karris, *Luke: Artist and Theologian, passim*. During his account of the passion, Luke has likewise either explicitly or implicitly, and through irony, identified Jesus as the Christ (Luke 22:67-69; 23:2.35), king (23:2-3.37-38; cf. 22:16.18.29-30.69) and Son of God (22:70-71; cf. 23:34.46). No one title or statement suffices to express fully who Jesus is; but the Servant of Yahweh tradition helps Luke explain the reality and shock of Jesus' passion.

[222] Nolland, *Luke 18:35 – 24:53*, 1118, writes, "The failure here to find any cause of culpability in Jesus is of a piece with Luke's stress elsewhere on the politically innocuous nature of the Christian faith (Acts 3:13; 18:14-16; 19:40; 25:18-20.25; 26:32; etc.). It is part of Luke's concern with the public image of the Christian movement in the larger Greco-Roman world."

amiss (v. 41). In more solemn fashion, the centurion glorifies God and asserts of Jesus, "Truly this was a just man" (v. 47) while the other Synoptics have "Truly, this man was Son of God" (cf. Mk 15:39; Mt 27:54); and if the beating of one's breast means an individual knows that he has participated in an evil action, we would have still another statement of Jesus' innocence when the crowd leaves the crucifixion beating their breasts (cf. Luke 23:48)([223]).

The theme of Jesus' innocence also appears in Acts. In his speech in Solomon's Portico, Peter claims that his audience had demanded that a murderer be freed and denied the holy and just one and so killed the author of life, even though Pilate had judged he should be freed (Acts 3:13-15). Subsequently, Stephen concludes his speech with the accusation that the members of his audience are the betrayers and murders of the just one (cf. 7:52). These latter expressions are similar to the words of the centurion at the crucifixion who proclaimed Jesus' innocence with the words, "Surely this was an innocent man" (Luke 23:47). Finally, Paul at Antioch of Pisidia explains that the inhabitants of Jerusalem and their rulers, ignorant of the message of the prophets, even though they found no crime in Jesus worthy of death, still demanded his execution and so fulfilled what the scriptures said (13:27-29). This extensive theme of Jesus' innocence is later matched by that of Paul in Acts([224]), and both portrayals relate to the Lukan presentation of Jesus as Servant of Yahweh.

Acts 4:27

There is reason to think that Luke also intends to refer to Jesus as the Servant of Yahweh in Acts 4:27([225]). It is true that 4:25 (cf. Luke 1:69) speaks of David as "your servant," and this fact would naturally lead one to conclude that "servant" is used two verses later of Jesus because he is David's descendant. Moreover, v. 27 also says of Jesus, "whom you anointed"; and thus identifies him with the Christ of the Lord of v.26. However, the context (vv. 25-27; cf. Ps 2:1-2) also speaks of the

---

[223] Fitzmyer, *The Gospel According to Luke X–XXIV*, 1520, observes, "In Luke 18:13 the gesture is a clear sign of guilt and contrition . . . ." The parable of the Pharisee and the tax collector (Luke 18:9-14) is unique to Luke among the Synoptics.

[224] See Acts 23:9.29; 24:18-20; 25:7-11.18.25a; 26:31-32; 28:17-19.

[225] See Kilgallen, "Your Servant Jesus," 185-201.

opposition to the Lord and his Christ and so well agrees with Luke's use of the figure of the Servant of Yahweh to explain Jesus' passion.

Moreover, few authors doubt that in the previous chapter (Acts 3:13.26) Luke writes of Jesus as the Servant of Yahweh. We have already seen that in the programmatic passage (Luke 4:14-44), which parallels the thought of Acts 4:26-27, Jesus implicitly identifies himself as a prophet, but we will see that in Luke 4:14-44 Luke likewise views Jesus as the Servant of Yahweh and the Christ. So, Luke may well have joined these last two identifications of Jesus when he composed Acts 4:26-30 (cf. vv. 23-31).

Acts 3:13-15 supports the above understanding of 8:32-33 (and of 4:27); for as we shall see below, the sentence, "The God . . . has glorified his servant Jesus" (3:13), looks to Is 52:13 and to Jesus' resurrection[226]. First I note that immediately following this phrase in Acts 3:13 we find in vv. 13b-15, "Whom you handed over and denied in Pilate's presence, when he has decided to release him. You denied the Holy and Righteous One . . . . The author of life you put to death." These verses support this article's interpretation of Acts 8:32-33. There is the obvious reference to the Servant of Yahweh hymn and the designation of Jesus as servant. Moreover, we will contend below that "I hand over," belongs to the word-pattern of this title. Also, the adjective "just"appears in Is 53:11, "to justify the just one who serves many well," and so this idea is found in the context which speaks of the servant's glorification. In addition, it was demonstrated above that "the just one" is associated with Jesus' innocence, another aspect of Jesus as Servant of Yahweh theme. Since the contents of Acts 3:13-15 resembles that of 8:32-33, the former passage supports the interpretation that the latter provides a summary of Luke's portrayal of Jesus as Servant of Yahweh during the passion[227].

Παραδίδωμι, "I Hand Over"

We are now ready to look at other data in or associated with the passion narrative, namely, "I hand over," and "I lead" and its cognates, which support the argument that Luke in these scenes intends to present Jesus as

---

[226] See O'Toole, *Acts 26*, 87; (*pace*) Haenchen, *The Acts*, 205.

[227] Coming at things from a different angle, Fitzmyer, *The Gospel According to Luke I–IX*, 212, contends that the suffering predicated of the Son of Man comes from the Servant of Yahweh tradition.

the Servant of Yahweh. M.D. Hooker, in agreement with F.J. Foakes Jackson and K. Lake, writes, "It is hard to see what other word the writers could naturally have used. It seems far more likely that παραδίδωμι was used as the most natural word, though probably it afterwards did much to strengthen the Christian interpretation of Isaiah when the coincidence in language was noted"(228). Nevertheless, "to hand over" does appear to belong to the word pattern of Luke's presentation of Jesus as Servant of Yahweh(229). This conclusion flows from Luke's own statement in his presentation of the passion that he so views Jesus. It also flows from two passages from Isaiah: Is 53:6 ("We had all gone astray like sheep, each one going astray in his own way; but the Lord handed him over for our sins"); and Is 53:12, where "to hand over" occurs twice ("Therefore, he will inherit many people and divide the spoils of the strong, because he was handed over to death and counted among criminals. He bore the sins of many, and for their sins was handed over)." Of course, we have already seen that only Luke applied this last verse to Jesus in the sense that he was to be numbered with criminals (cf. Luke 22:37).

In fact, "to hand over" actually appears often in reference to Jesus' passion. According to the second passion prediction, the Son of Man is to be "handed over" into the hands of men (Luke 9:44); in the third, he is to be "handed over" into the hands of the Gentiles (18:32). Later the scribes and high priests send some self-righteous individuals to trap Jesus in what he says so that they can "hand him over" to the procurator (20:20). Judas plots to "hand him over" and seeks an opportune moment to do so (22:4,6), and at the Last Supper Jesus shows that he is aware of who will "hand him over" and predicts that man's future (vv. 21-22). Later in the garden, Jesus asks Judas if he is "handing him over" with a kiss (v. 48). Pilate "hands Jesus over" to the will of his opponents (23:25). The two men at the tomb tell the women to remember what Jesus had predicted while he was with them in Galilee that the Son of Man had to be "handed over" into the hands of sinful men, be crucified and rise on the third day (24:6-7; cf. Acts 2:23). The two disciples on the road to

---

228 Hooker, *Jesus and the Servant*, 80. Unlike the present one, Hooker's approach is historical.

229 Cf. Hahn, *The Titles of Jesus*, 59-61, who sees Isaiah as the source for Luke's use of παραδίδωμι.

Emmaus explain how the high priests and rulers had "handed Jesus over" to death (24:20); and above we noted that Acts 3:13 speaks of Jesus as servant but also accuses the Jewish audience of "handing him over." Hence, although παραδίδωμι is the natural word to use for the "handing over" of Jesus, there is solid evidence that it belongs to the Lucan word pattern of Jesus as Servant of Yahweh. Isaiah uses this verb about the Servant of Yahweh. Moreover, Luke applies Servant terminology to Jesus during his presentation of the passion, and "to hand over" is part of this terminology. This verb pictures Jesus' rejection and, given the references to Isaiah, helps to reveal that what happened was foreseen in God's providence. One might object that in Isaiah the Lord hands over the servant while in Luke human agents do this; but in the latter situation it is ultimately God's providence which permits this human act.

Here we should address the question of what weight to attribute to Luke 22:19 (cf. 1 Cor 11:24), "This is my body, which is given (διδό-μενον) for you." The underlined words were added by Luke himself, probably in imitation of "which will be shed for you" (v. 20) predicated of the cup. The latter phrasing finds a parallel in both of the other Synoptics (cf. Mk 14:24; Mt 26:28) and according to a number of authors represents the vicarious suffering of the Servant of Yahweh (cf. Is 53:4-6.11-12). Surely, Luke has taken over this traditional expression of vicarious suffering and expanded on it with "which is given for you." Nonetheless, he does not integrate the Pauline understanding of Jesus' death as redemptive into his own Christology[230]; and, probably, for Luke the Greek word for "which is given" also carries the nuance of "to be handed over," of which the Greek actually occurs twice in two verses almost immediately following (Luke 22:21-22). It was God's will (permissive) that Jesus be handed over to his suffering. Consequently, "which is given"

---

[230] Lohse, *Märtyrer und Gottesknecht*, 187-191. In his citation of Is 53:7-8 (cf. Acts 8:32-33) Luke leaves off the end, ἀπὸ τῶν ἀνομιῶν τοῦ λαοῦ μου ἤχθη εἰς θάνατον, which could be rendered "because of the iniquities of my people he was led to death." And at the Last Supper the citation of Is 53:12 (cf. Luke 22:37), does not include what immediately follows in the LXX, "He bore the sins of many, and for their sins was handed over." Nor does Luke cite any other Isaian passage, which speaks of vicarious suffering (e.g., 53:4-6.11). See also Rese, *Alttestamentliche Motive*, 98-99. For Luke, the whole of Jesus' life, including his death, was salvific; but he does not have the Pauline understanding or emphasis on Jesus' death. Still Luke wants his reader to know that Jesus' death was on their behalf (Luke 22:19-20; Acts 20:28).

would constitute part of Luke's portrayal of Jesus as the Servant of Yahweh and make the additional point that Jesus himself accepted his Father's will.

The only other passage in Luke-Acts where Jesus' redemptive death occurs is Acts 20:28 when Paul in his farewell speech to the Ephesian elders speaks of God's church "acquired through the blood of his own son." Apparently, Luke in Paul's farewell speech and in the traditional material of the Last Supper (Luke 22:19-20) was willing to take over these statements of vicarious suffering and redemptive death. However, we find no clear additional evidence that Luke wanted to integrate vicarious suffering or Paul's understanding of Jesus' redemptive death into his own Christology.

Ἄγω, "I Lead" and Its Cognates

"I lead" and its cognates very likely belong to the word pattern of Luke's portrayal of Jesus as Servant of Yahweh. In Acts 8:32 (cf. Is 53:7), Jesus is led as a lamb to the slaughter; and although not cited in its entirety in Acts 8:33, Is 53:8 concludes with the words, "That he was cut off from the land of the living, led to death for the sins of my people." Naturally, one could again bring up the consideration of M.D. Hooker and ask what other word would Luke have been able to use, and our response would have to be much like the one given for "to hand over." In fact, during the passion, Jesus' captors led him into the house of the high priest (Luke 22:54) and later before the Sanhedrin (v. 66). Then the whole crowd leads him before Pilate (23:1), and finally they led him away to crucify him (23:26). These examples apparently flow from Luke's desire to picture Jesus as the Servant of Yahweh. It may be that the hostile action of the Jewish audience at Nazareth, leading Jesus to the brow of the hill in order to throw him off (Luke 4:29), should be included here since it stands in the programmatic passage which probably portrays Jesus as Servant of Yahweh and so would be a foreshadowing of his passion.

Luke 22:24-27

What we have said thus far about Luke's passion story leads us to ask whether Luke 22:24-27 (cf. 9:45; Mk 10:42-45) should be considered part of Luke's portrayal of Jesus as the Servant of Yahweh. Of the Synoptics, only Luke has introduced into the Last Supper scene the argument over who of the disciples is the greatest. Although we find no verbal connection between Jesus' response to this argument and Acts 8:32-33, Luke probably viewed the two descriptions as similar. In Luke 22:24-27 Jesus warns against being like the kings of the Gentiles who lord it over their subjects and make their power felt and who like being called benefactors. This is not to be the conduct of the Christian disciple; for the greatest among them should act as the younger, and the leader as the servant. In fact, διακονῶν, "serving," occurs three times in these verses; and is developed by the reflection that it is true that the one who reclines at table is greater than the one who serves, but Jesus is among them as the one who serves. Jesus' humility and attitude of service resemble the thought of Acts 8:32-33, his being led as a sheep to the slaughter, a lamb to be sheared, silent and not opening his mouth, humble. Yet there is no fair trial. Nor will he be remembered in history. The possible resemblance between Luke 22:24-27 and Acts 8:32-33 finds further support in the context of the former, the Last Supper scene. More specifically, these verses stand between two statements about Jesus' suffering and are preceded by the woe pronounced for him by whom Jesus is "handed over" (cf. Luke 22:21-23.28). Therefore, Jesus' service includes his suffering. We also read in the context, "This is my body given for you" and of the cup "poured out for you" (cf. Luke 22:19-20). These words likewise look to Jesus' passion and would describe Jesus' service. To be sure, the evidence is not strong; but it appears that by inserting the argument about who is greatest, Luke has introduced into his Last Supper scene a reflection similar to that found in Acts 8:32-33. And in this sense, Luke 22:24-27 would belong to Luke's portrayal of Jesus as Servant of Yahweh.

Some Servant of Yahweh Passages Describe Jesus' Whole Ministry
The passages of interest here are Luke 2:29-32; 4:18-19; Acts 13:47; 26:23 (cf. Luke 2:25-35; 3:22; 4:14-44; 7:21-23; Acts 26:16-18; 28:28[?]). In the *Nunc Dimittis*, Jesus is not identified as the Servant of Yahweh. But a general description of his mission is provided which is based on that of the servant, who is to bring salvation, which is presented under the image of "light"([231]) to the Gentiles. (Cf. Is 42:6-7a: "I, the Lord, have called you for the victory of justice, I will grasp you by the

---

[231] *Contra*: Korn, *Die Geschichte Jesu*, 51-52, 159, and Voss, *Die Christologie der lukanischen Schriften*, 167-168. "Light" for Luke does not refer primarily to preaching, but to the salvation that Jesus brings.

hand; I will strengthen you, and I set you as a covenant of the people, a light for the Gentiles, To open the eyes of the blind . . . ." [see also 60:1-3][232].) The thought of Luke 2:30-32, that Jesus brings salvation, imaged as "light," to both Jews and Gentiles, is partially repeated in Acts 13:47, "I have made you a light to the Gentiles, that you may bring salvation to the ends of the earth"(233). Here Luke explicitly cites a similar passage, Is 49:6, where the word "you" in the singular does not refer to either Paul or Barnabas but to Jesus whose agents they are(234). Of course, the last fours words of this citation from Acts 13:47 played a part in the description of the mission in the programmatic Acts 1:8. Luke returns to the theme of "light" but also asserts that Jesus must suffer in Acts 26:23 (cf. v. 18) where he quotes Paul as proclaiming "that the Christ must suffer and that, as the first to rise from the dead, he would proclaim light to our people and to the Gentiles." Thus, according to Luke, Jesus through Paul (cf. v. 18) actualizes the mission of the Servant of Yahweh who brings salvation, "light," to the Gentiles, but will be rejected and must suffer. In this way, Luke can justify Jesus' Gentile mission and his passion; yet contend that this mission is universal, for both Gentiles and Jews.

Elsewhere I have indicated why a number of scholars contend that Luke is also presenting Jesus as the Servant of Yahweh in Luke 4:18-19 (cf. vv. 16-30)(235). There are four main arguments for this contention: 1) The citations in these verses are taken from Isaiah (61:1-2 and 58:6), and the phrase "The Spirit of the Lord is upon me" is quite similar to that found in the first Servant Hymn (Is 42:1: "Upon whom I put my spirit"). Further, the idea of Is 42:7, "To open the eyes of the blind, to bring out prisoners from confinement, and from the dungeon, those who live in

---

232 Rese, *Alttestamentliche Motive*, 184, discusses the probable OT influence.

233 See Grelot, "Note sur Actes XIII 47," 368-372, on this verse.

234 Koet, *Five Studies*, 110-114, provides a summary of the various interpretations of the Greek word σε in this verse. However, Koet's claim that the reference is to the Jewish audience conflicts with the actual context that speaks of Jesus' mission and, subse-quently, that of Paul and Barnabas. At the moment portrayed, the latter mission is not being accepted by their Jewish audience.

235 "Does Luke Also Portray Jesus as the Christ," 498-522; see also Koet, *Five Studies*, 32 and 51, and Marshall, *Luke: Historian and Theologian*, 119 and 127-128.

darkness" (cf. 49:9), resembles the idea of Luke 4:18. 2) Luke 2:25-35 constitutes a parallel to 4:16-30 and both passages speak of the salvation ("light" in 2:32 corresponds well with "sight to the blind" in 4:19) which Jesus will bring; but we have demonstrated that the former passage describes Jesus' mission like that of the Servant. 3) Jesus' baptism (3:21-22) likewise constitutes a parallel to 4:18-19([236]), and the phrase, "with you I am well pleased" (3:22) is a reference to the servant (Cf. Is 42:1: "Jacob my servant I will uphold; Israel my elect my soul longed for." The MT, "Here is my servant whom I uphold, my chosen one with whom I am pleased," brings this connection out better.) 4) The mission to the Gentiles and, as we will see below, the rejection and attempt to kill Jesus found in Luke 4:16-30, would square well with the contention that Luke wants to present Jesus as the Servant of Yahweh. Furthermore, Luke 7:21-22 take up the thought of 4:18-19, and again specific reference is made to the "blind seeing." Probably, Acts 28:28 (cf. 3:6; Is 40:5) should be mentioned here since it speaks of salvation to the Gentiles. We have claimed that Luke links this salvation with Jesus as Servant of Yahweh.

The Relevance of Certain Phrases for Jesus As the Servant of Yahweh
Luke has predicated certain phrases of Jesus, which show that he views him as the Servant of Yahweh whom God has specially chosen and with whom he is pleased. We have already seen this in the scene of Jesus' baptism; for the voice from heaven says, "You are my beloved son, with you I am well pleased" (Luke 3:22). This last clause accurately represents the sense of the Hebrew of Is 42:1. Later, at the Transfiguration, the voice from the cloud says of Jesus, "This is my chosen son; listen to him" (Luke 9:35); this is a clear reference to the Hebrew text of Is 42:1([237]). Very probably, in the Transfiguration scene Mark's (9:7) "the beloved" has been changed to "my chosen" (Luke 9:35) so as to identify Jesus with the Servant([238]). Another reference to Is 42:1 is found during the scene of

---

[236] Korn's (*Die Geschichte Jesu*, 66) contention that "anointed me" (Luke 4:18) is best clarified by Luke 1:32-35 fails to appreciate that v. 35 of the latter passage is speaking about the unique relationship between God and the child Jesus, not about Jesus' mission.

[237] Confer Bovon, *L'Évangile selon Saint Luc 1–9*, 488-489.

[238] Fitzmyer, *The Gospel According to Luke I–IX*, 803, grants the possibility of an allusion to Is 42:1LXX.

Jesus' passion when the leaders mock Jesus with the words, "He saved others, let him save himself, if he is the Christ, the elect of God" (Luke 23:35). Thus, we have three clear references to Is 42:1 and to Jesus as the Servant of Yahweh with whom God is pleased or whom he has chosen for a special task. Of course, the last passage stands in Luke's passion narrative; and so helps to clarify the Servant nature of this task.

The phrasing of Is 50:7LXX, "The Lord God is my help; therefore, I am not disgraced, I have set my face like flint (ἀλλὰ ἔθηκα τὸ πρόσωπόν μου ὡς στερεὰν πέτραν), knowing that I will not be put to shame," leads us to ask the question whether Luke sees Jesus as the Servant of Yahweh when he writes of him, "When the days of his being taking up were fulfilled, he resolutely determined (καὶ αὐτὸς τὸ πρόσωπον ἐστήρισεν) to journey to Jerusalem" (Luke 9:51). In the Greek, the phrasing "I have set my face like flint" certainly seems to resemble "he set his face." Moreover, Luke particularly portrays Jesus as the Servant of Yahweh during his passion; and the journey to Jerusalem leads precisely to the passion (and resurrection). The reference to the OT and "fulfilled" would imply that this is God's will; and the Servant did receive his mission from the Lord. Finally, Is 50:7LXX itself stands in a context of persecution and opposition (cf. vv. 6, 8-9). Therefore it is probable that in Luke 9:51 Luke wants us to view Jesus as the Servant who is determined to do what God asks of him.

Another possible reference to the Servant of Yahweh tradition may be found in Luke 11:21-22 where Jesus is compared to the stronger warrior who takes away the armor of his opponent and divides the plunder (τὰ σκῦλα), for it reminds us of the words "He will divide the spoils of the strong" (Is 53:12; cf. Luke 3,16: καὶ τῶν ἰσχυρῶν μεριεῖ σκῦλα). However, the citation of Is 53:12 in Luke 11:21-22 is not obvious; for instance, M.D. Hooker feels that the reference is actually to Is 49:24-25: "Can someone take spoils (σκῦλα) from a giant? If he unjustly takes a prisoner, will he be rescued? Thus says the Lord, 'If one imprisons a giant, he will take the spoils (λήμψεται σκῦλα); and the one who takes from the strong will be saved. I will give you (just) judgment, and I will rescue your sons'"([239]).

---

[239] Hooker, *Jesus and the Servant*, 73.

Jesus' Resurrection Associated with His Being the Servant of Yahweh
Luke has associated Jesus' resurrection with his being the Servant of
Yahweh. In Acts 3:13-15, "The God of Abraham, (the God) of Isaac, and
(the God) of Jacob, the God of our ancestors, has glorified his servant
Jesus . . . . The author of life you put to death, but God raised him from
the dead." The immediate context itself suffices to justify the claim that
"has glorified" refers not only to the miracle which Jesus has just performed but also to his resurrection[240]. True, the miracle could be the
source of this glory. However, between the two statements of Jesus'
resurrection in Acts 3:13-15, Peter speaks of his audience's handing over,
rejecting, and executing the holy and just one; and so we have a kind of
chiasmus, which emphasizes Jesus' suffering and resurrection ("glorified ...
handed over and denied . . . you denied . . . you killed whom God raised
from the dead"). This claim is supported by the Emmaus story, where
Jesus chides the two disciples because they do not believe what the
prophets said, namely, that the Christ must suffer and enter his glory
(24:26), for in this passage "glory" must be a reference to Jesus' resurrection.

Another passage which probably likewise refers to Jesus'
resurrection is the citation of Is 53:8 in Acts 8:33, "That his life was taken
from the earth"[241]. It appears that Luke has intentionally not cited the
entire LXX text: the rest of the verse reads, "And he was led to death for
the sins of my people." This allows Luke to do two things. As noted
above, he apparently wanted not to speak of Jesus' death as redemptive in
the Pauline sense. But in addition, the wording of the other part of Is 53:8
found in Acts 8:33, "That his life was taken from earth," could mean that
Jesus' life was moved from earth and so carry the nuance of Jesus'
resurrection. This interpretation finds support in Luke's almost universal
practice of not mentioning Jesus' death without referring to his resurrection[242]. Besides, it is not easy to imagine how the Ethiopian eunuch

---

[240] Voss, *Die Christologie der lukanischen Schriften*, 133, cites other authors who hold
this position. See also Rese, *Alttestamentliche Motive*, 1112-1113. *Contra*: Haenchen,
The Acts, 205.

[241] See Loisy, *Les Actes des Apôtres*, 379-380 and Schütz, *Der leidende Christus*, 103-104.

[242] Perhaps the only example where Luke writes of Jesus' death without reference to his
resurrection would be Luke 9:44. In all the other instances, the mention of Jesus' death

would have been that impressed by a gospel message, which related only Jesus' meek, silent and humble death.

The Activity of Jesus As Servant of Yahweh after His Resurrection
At both the beginning (Acts 3:13; cf. Is 52:13) and the end of Peter's discourse in the Portico of Solomon, Jesus is identified as παῖς. According to v. 13, God glorified his Servant; at the end of the discourse Peter asserts that God has raised up his servant (τὸν παῖδα αὐτοῦ) and sent him to bless the Jews in turning each of them from their evil (v. 26). Elsewhere, I have argued that "raise" in both vv. 22 and 26 refers to Jesus' resurrection([243]). Thus, after his resurrection, Jesus, the Servant of Yahweh, is imaged as a priest sent to bless the Jews; this post-resurrectional blessing consists in turning each of them from their evil. The other passage in which Jesus would obviously be active after his resurrection as the Servant of Yahweh is Acts 4:30. Above, we argued that in 4:27, Jesus, the holy servant whom God anointed, should not only be understood as Messiah because of the mention of God's servant David in v. 25, but also as Servant of Yahweh. If this interpretation is accurate, then in 4:30, the persecuted Christians would be praying that God work signs, wonders and marvels through Jesus who is likewise the Servant of Yahweh. However, the miracles spoken about in this verse must now clearly occur after Jesus' resurrection, so the Christians' petition must look to a post-resurrectional activity on the risen Jesus' part.

Two other passages that we have already studied indirectly view Jesus, the Servant, as active after his resurrection, namely, Acts 13:47 and 26:23. Each of these passages attributes to Jesus, with Servant-of-Yahweh terminology, an activity which is actually being carried out by his followers. In Acts 13:46-47, Paul and Barnabas tell their Jewish audience that it was first necessary to speak the word of God to them; but since they rejected it and did not judge themselves worthy of eternal life, Peter and Barnabas were going to turn to the Gentiles since the Lord had commanded them, "I made you (σε) a light to the Gentiles, that you (σε) may bring salvation to the ends of the earth." Since the word σε surely

---

is accompanied by the message of his resurrection. See Glockner, *Die Verkündigung des Heils*, 211-212, and Haenchen, *The Acts*, 312.

[243] "Some observations on *Anistêmi*," 85-92.

does not refer to Barnabas and Paul, they must be carrying out a mission that is attributed to Jesus. This interpretation is confirmed by Acts 26:23, which speaks of the Christ who must suffer and be first to rise from the dead to proclaim light to the people and to the Gentiles; for during his earthly life Jesus did not proclaim light to the Gentiles. On the contrary, this task is part of the mission given by the risen Jesus to Paul (cf. vv. 17-18) but which Luke also identifies as the mission of Jesus([244]).

Conclusion

Not all of the above Lucan references to Jesus as the Servant of Yahweh are equally convincing. Further, our investigation has not been limited only to Isaian hymns that today are associated with this theme. Moreover, the word pattern for this theme is not always as clear as would be desirable. On the other hand, many of the above Servant of Yahweh references are unique to Luke (e.g., Luke 2:29-32; 4:18-19; 7:21; 9:51; 11:21-22?; 20:20; 22:19.37.48; 23:9.35; 24:7.20; Acts 3:13-14.26; 4:27.30; 8:32-33; 13:47; 26:23; 28:28?). This is not to deny that a few of these citations may be questionable, or that Luke got some of these citations or terminology from his sources, e.g., the use of παραδίδωμι from Mark. So, although some authors have questioned whether the tradition of Servant of Yahweh enters into Luke's Christology, the evidence shows that it does: some aspects of the tradition about the Servant form a not insignificant aspect of Luke's Christology. To be sure, for Luke no one Jewish tradition or title was able to express fully who Jesus was. However, a few passages (cf. Luke 2:29-34; 4:18-19; Acts 13:47; 26:23) provide a general summary of Jesus' ministry in terms of Servant of Yahweh terminology. These passages particularly look to Jesus' saving activity, universal mission and suffering. In fact, although the concept "prophet" provided Luke with a means of explaining Jesus' suffering (e.g., Luke 4:24-30; 13:33-35), that of "Servant of Yahweh" was more suited for this purpose. In addition, Luke's use of "light" for salvation very likely depends on the Servant of Yahweh tradition, and this tradition likewise provided him with his best argument for Jesus' universal mission.

Other Lucan passages use Servant-of-Yahweh terminology to bring out given characteristics of Jesus. He, as Servant, is specially chosen and pleasing to God and determined to do God's will as is seen by his

---

[244] See my *Acts 26*, 118-122.

setting his face firmly for Jerusalem; probably he, as Servant, is the stronger warrior who carries off the plunder of his opponents.

For Luke, Acts 8:32-33 provide a summary of Jesus' passion. Obviously, as a OT citation, the passage underlines that these events somehow fit into God's providence. It is true that during the passion Luke also names Jesus the Christ, King and Son of God; but granted that the Christ must suffer, none of these designations serves to provide a broad summary of Jesus' passion. Nor is it sufficient to assign Luke's passion story to the genre of the martyrdom of a just man. Rather, Luke is more specific and presents Jesus as the Servant of Yahweh who is humble and silent, but who is nevertheless deprived of a fair trial and will not even be remembered. Gentiles, Jews, king and procurator unite against him; he is handed over and led before both Jewish and Roman authorities. However, the fact is that, as the theme of Servant of Yahweh confirms, he is innocent. Probably, "to be given" in Luke 22:19 should be taken in the sense of handed over, and Jesus' willingness to follow his Father's will is also clearly present in the context. The correct interpretation of what is said about Jesus as "the one who serves" in Luke 22:24-27, is not easy to establish. However, given the correspondence of these verses to their immediate context and their similarity to the thought of Acts 8:32-33, it is reasonable to conclude that they identify Jesus' passion as "service" and constitute part of the Lucan portrayal of Jesus as the Servant of Yahweh.

The portrayal of Jesus as Servant of Yahweh likewise relates to his resurrection, because God glorifies his servant; and probably the words of Acts 8:33, "That his life was taken from the earth," are a reference to the resurrection. Surely, as the Servant of Yahweh, Jesus remains active after his resurrection; for he blesses the Jews in turning each of them from their evil, and the persecuted Christians pray that God work signs and wonders for them through the name of his holy servant. Through his followers, he also carries on his mission.

If one asks what specifically Luke achieves through his presentation of Jesus as the Servant of Yahweh, the followings points should be noted:

1) This presentation does belong to Luke's Christology and can function as a summary of Jesus' mission. He is God's chosen one.

2) The Servant Tradition particularly served Luke to explain Jesus' suffering and passion and to underline his innocence.

3) Finally, the theme of Jesus as Servant of Yahweh expands Lucan "salvation" with special reference to the image of "light" and justifies Jesus' mission to the Gentiles.

CHAPTER FIVE

Jesus As the Christ (the Messiah)([245])

It is a commonplace in scholarly circles that Luke among the Synoptics favors the title, "The Christ" or "The Messiah" (ὁ Χριστός)([246]) for Jesus, and, later in the Gospel and in Acts, "the Christ who must suffer([247])." Likewise in Acts after his resurrection "Christ" becomes part of Jesus' name([248]). These last passages will concern our discussion only when they

---

[245] See on this topic: Bousset, *Kyrios Christos*, 69-118; Byrne, "Jesus as Messiah," 80-95, who, despite his awareness that "Messiah" in Luke means more than merely "the anointed", does not want to distinguish it from "Son of God"; Cadbury, "The Titles of Jesus in Acts," 357-359, 362-363; Fitzmyer, *The Gospel According to Luke I–IX*, 197-200; Foakes Jackson and Lake, "Christology," 346-368; Grundmann, Χριστός, 532-537; Hahn, *The Titles of Jesus*, 136-222, 240-278; Jacquier, *Les Actes des Apôtres*, ccx-ccxv; O'Toole, "The Kingdom of God in Luke-Acts," 147-162; van Iersel, *'Der Sohn'*, 66-89 and Voss, *Die Christologie*, 61-97. Jones, "The Title *Christos* in Luke-Acts," 69-76, contends that Luke's presentation is dominated by his own theological emphasis and suggests solutions to pressing problems of the late first century A.D. (76); Resseguie, "The Lukan Portrait of Christ," 5-20, seeks to describe the correct redactional approach and stresses more the parenetic aspect of Luke's Christology. Bock, *Luke 1:1 – 9:50*, 30, contends that in Luke's Christology Messiahship is the fundamental category around which the other concepts revolve.

[246] Luke 2:26; 4:41; 9:20; 22:67; 23:35.39; 24:26.46; Acts 2:31; 3:18; 5:42; 8:5; 9:22; 17:3[2x]; 18:5.28; 26:23; cf. Luke 3:15; 20:41; Acts 4:26-27.

[247] Lohfink, *Die Himmelfahrt Jesu*, 237-239 points to the following pattern common to Luke 24:26.46; Acts 3:18; 17:3; 26:23, the title ὁ Χριστός a passion saying with πάσχειν, a resurrection saying with ἀνίστημι (exceptions: Luke 24:26, εἰσελθεῖν εἰς τὴν δόξαν αὐτοῦ; Acts 3:18, but Jesus' resurrection appears in v. 15). However, he does not believe that this scheme is a Lucan creation. Wilckens, *Die Missionsreden*, 116, contends that the formulations of Acts 17:3 and of 26:23 are Lucan but the vocabulary reminds one of the passion predictions. Confer Luke 9:20-22.

[248] E.g., Acts 2:38; 3:6.20; 4:10.33; 5:42; 8:12.37; 9:34; 10:36.48; 11:17; 15:26; 16:18; 20:21; 24:24; 28:31.

actually communicate something about Jesus as "the Christ." On the other hand, any study of "Christ" in Luke-Acts has also to reckon with the reality that this title should be studied in association with: Jesus' Davidic lineage([249]), his being "king," and with "kingdom," "reign," "seated on the throne," "Son of Man," "Son of God," and even "Lord." As our investigation proceeds, it is hoped that the exact nature of these associations will become clear.

The present chapter will consider Jesus as the Christ in the Infancy Narrative and in parallel passages and then cover the other gospel passages, which speak of our topic. At the end of these considerations, any remaining material in the Gospel about Jesus as king or descendant of David will be studied. Lastly, attention will be given to the data in Acts about Jesus as the Christ or about other designations which belong to this word-pattern.

Jesus As the Christ in the Infancy Narrative and Parallel Passages
Already in the Infancy Narrative Luke introduces Jesus as the Christ. In the annunciation to Mary, the angel Gabriel tells her that she will bear a son whom she should name, "Jesus," and that he will be great and called, "Son of the Most High, and the Lord God will give him the throne of David his father, and he will rule over the house of Jacob forever and of his kingdom there will be no end" (Luke 1:32-33). This prediction and promise are an obvious reference to Nathan's prophecy of God's covenant with David (2 Sm 7:11-17; cf. 4QFlor 10-13)([250]). So, Jesus will occupy David's throne; but his rule will be forever, not like that of other Davidic descendents who ruled only for a comparatively brief period of time. Upon reflection, one realizes that this statement implies Jesus' resurrection; for if he did not in some way endure forever, he could hardly reign forever. In vv. 32-33 Luke assumes an identification of Jesus as the descendent of David with "He will be great"([251]) and "Son of the Most

---

[249] For a discussion of this topic, see Burger, *Jesus als Davidssohn*, 107-152. See also M. de Jonge, *Christology in Context*, 104.

[250] Confer Laurentin, *Luc I–II*, 71-73, 122-123, 140-141.

[251] When μέγας is used absolutely in the LXX it is an attribute of God himself (cf. Pss. 47:2[=144:3]; 85:10; 134:5); see also Acts 8:10; 19:27-28.34-35 and Fitzmyer, *The Gospel According to Luke I–IX*, 325.

High"(^{252}). Luke again brings up Jesus' descent from David in his gene-alogy (3:31)(^{253}) and as in the annunciation (1:34) clarifies that Joseph is not his father (3:23).

Luke employs "Most High" of God in both vv. 32 and 35 and also speaks of Jesus as "Son of God" (v. 35). This has led many exegetes to conclude that Luke views Jesus as the Christ or Messiah also in v. 35. However, we will see that with the title, "Son of God" (v. 35) Luke wanted to communicate a unique relationship between Jesus and God, which is not conveyed by "Christ." Actually, in his Gospel, Luke, with step-parallelism, three times (1:32-33.35; 9:7-8.18-20.35; 22:66-71) estab-lishes a separation between the assertions that Jesus is "the Christ" and that he is "Son (of God)." Earlier, we demonstrated that in Luke 9:1-50 Herod's question (v. 9) centers the chapter on the question of the identity of Jesus, who is first regarded by the ordinary people as a prophet; then Peter identifies him as "the Messiah (Christ) of God" (v. 20) and then the voice from the cloud identifies him as "This is my chosen Son, listen to him" (v. 35). A similar separation and thus an implied difference in mean-ing between these two titles occurs in the scene of Jesus before the Coun-cil where only Luke divides the interrogation into two separate questions: "If you are the Christ (the Messiah), tell us" (22:67) and "They all asked, 'Are you then the Son of God?'" (v. 70; cf. Mark 14:61-62).

Another important parallel to Luke 1:26-38 appears in Acts 2:23-36 because what the angel says about Jesus in the former passage is realized in the latter. Peter in the Pentecost speech argues that Ps 15:8-11LXX could not have been realized in David since his tomb is there in Jerusalem. Then, in v. 30, Peter refers to 2 Sam 7:12-13 and so to the promise made to David and claims that it has been realized in Jesus who has been exalted at the right hand of God (Acts 2:33)(^{254}). He continues his argument with the statement that David, who did not ascend to heaven, proclaimed, "The Lord said to my Lord, 'Sit at my right hand, until I make

---

[252] Elsewhere, too, Luke uses ὕψιστος almost exclusively in reference to God (cf. Luke 1:76; 6:35; 8:28; Acts 7:48; 16:17).

[253] Böhler, "Jesus als Davidssohn," 538, holds that Luke traces Jesus' being a descent of David through Nathan to avoid the sinful line of Solomon.

[254] For the arguments in support of this interpretation see O'Toole, "Acts 2:30 and the Davidic Covenant," 245-258.

your enemies your footstool'" (vv. 34-35; cf. Luke 22:67-69; Ps 109:1LXX). Peter immediately concludes with the solemn statement (Acts 2:36), "Therefore, let the whole house of Israel know for certain that God has made him both Lord and Messiah, this Jesus whom you crucified." So, as the Angel Gabriel predicted of Jesus in the annunciation story, in accord with the covenant God made with David, Jesus has been raised to God's right hand, i.e., he has been enthroned. Moreover, still in comparison with the annunciation account, Peter's solemn proclamation reports that the ultimate agent of Jesus' enthronement is God, mentions "the whole house of Israel" and explicitly speaks of Jesus as "Christ."

A little later in the Infancy Narrative, Zechariah in the *Benedictus* (Luke 1:67-79) prophesies that the God of Israel should be blessed because he has visited and worked redemption for his people and, "has raised up a horn for our salvation within the house of David his servant" (v. 69). Given what we know from the annunciation story (vv. 26-38), the most obvious referent for "a horn for our salvation within the house of David his servant" would be Jesus who here([255]), too, is viewed as the descendent of David, that is, as the Christ but now seen as an instrument of God's salvation for Israel. The fact that Zechariah is prophesying points to the truth of the statement. An association of the Christ with salvation also occurs in the scene of the shepherds, for an angel proclaims in Luke 2:11, "For today in the city of David a savior has been born for you who is Christ (Messiah) and Lord." The fact that an angel delivers this message, which the shepherds later explain as "this thing that has taken place, which the Lord has made known to us" (v. 15) not only reveals its importance but leaves the reader in no doubt as to its truth. Luke 2:11 likewise justifies our earlier claim that Luke's concept of "the Christ" should be associated with being a descendent from David and with Jesus being savior (cf. 1:69).

Jesus, the Christ, is again connected with salvation in the presentation of Jesus in the temple (Luke 2:25-38). Three times (vv. 25, 26, 28), Luke clarifies that Simeon is acting under the influence of the Holy Spirit; and Luke directs his reader's attention to the realization of the Spirit's revelation to Simeon, "that he should not see death before he had seen the Christ of the Lord" (v. 26b). The baby Jesus in Simeon's arms must be the

---

[255] Lenski, *St. Luke's Gospel*, 163; Loisy, *L'Évangle selon Luc*, 105 and Plummer, *St. Luke*, 40.

Christ; and Simeon in his prayer recognizes this and further identifies Jesus as God's salvation for all humankind (v. 31). In apposition to "your salvation," (v. 30) are "light" and "glory," in the two phrases, "a light for revelation to the Gentiles, and glory for our people Israel" (v. 32)([256]), which, therefore, are other expressions for salvation. Moreover, we saw in the chapter of Jesus as savior that "the consolation of Israel" (v. 25), "peace" (v. 29), the "rising" in the prediction, "this child is destined for the fall and rise of many in Israel" (v. 34) and "the redemption of Jerusalem" (v. 38) are all expressions of salvation and so Luke has underlined his presentation of Jesus as the Christ who saves. A significant parallel to Jesus' presentation in the temple is found in Acts 26:23, "that the Christ must suffer" and that, as the first to rise from the dead, he would proclaim light both to the people and to the Gentiles. In this verse, too, the Christ brings light, which we have just seen is an image of salvation, to both Jews and the Gentiles. Finally, Simeon in Luke 2:34-35 tells Mary that not everyone will accept Jesus, "Behold, this child is destined . . ., and to be a sign that will be opposed—and you yourself a sword will pierce—so that the thoughts of many hearts may be revealed." Jesus, the Christ, will be a challenge to all of Israel; everyone will have to take a stand in his regard, either for him or against; and his own mother, Mary, will share in this rejection.

John the Baptist's Comments on the Christ
When Luke portrays the Jewish people as wondering whether John the Baptist might be "the Christ" (Luke 3:15), Luke clarifies through John's response that someone more powerful than he is coming, the thongs of whose sandals John does not feel worthy to loose. Of this one John says, "He will baptize you with the Holy Spirit and fire. His winnowing fan is in his hand to clear his threshing floor and to gather the wheat into his barn, but the chaff he will burn with unquenchable fire" (vv. 16c-17; cf. Mt 3:11c-12). Therefore, John refuses the title, "the Christ" because that individual is more important than he. He associates this more powerful one, "the Christ," with baptism in the Holy Spirit and with fire and judgment.

---

[256] Lagrange rightly sees this grammatical interpretation as preferable to taking "glory" in apposition to "revelation." Grogan, "The Light and the Stone," 151-167, contends that Luke 2:25-35 can only be understood when seen against the background of the book of Isaiah.

This association of "the Christ" with baptism proves useful in our analysis of Luke 4:18.

Jesus As Christ in the Programmatic Passage (Luke 4:14[16]-[30]44)

Luke 4:18 reads, "The Spirit of the Lord is upon me, because he has anointed me (οὗ εἵνεκεν ἔχρισέν με) to bring good news to the poor." A few exegetes interpret this verse as an identification of Jesus as Suffering Servant. However, the majority of authors interpret this "anointing" as a reference to Jesus being appointed a prophet([257]). They reason that the OT citations used in vv. 18-19 are taken from a prophet (Is 61:1-2; 58:6) who is explicitly named in v. 17. Also, in this passage Jesus implicitly identifies himself as a prophet (v. 24); and later in the passage he is compared to two other OT prophets, Elijah and Elisha (vv. 25-27). Moreover, what evidence other than "anointed" is there in the programmatic passage that Jesus is seen as the Christ or descendent of David? On the other hand, there are reasons to conclude that Luke does want to depict Jesus in Luke 4:18 as the Christ([258]). Luke's reader already knows that Jesus is the Christ, the descendant of David, who will bring salvation to all humankind and who is associated with baptism in the Spirit, yet will be rejected by some of his own people (cf. 1:31-35; 2:11.25-35; 3:15-17.21-22). Some of this information corresponds to the contents of the programmatic passage; and Jesus, Son of David, heals the blind beggar near Jericho (18:35-43; cf. 7:21) and thus fulfills another prediction of 4:18. Elsewhere, Luke not infrequently cites Sacred Scripture to show that Jesus is the Christ or the Christ who has to suffer ([259]); so since the Scriptures are used as proof in 4:18-19, Luke probably views Jesus in these verses as the Christ. Also, "has anointed" is a translation of the verb, χρίω, from which also derives the title, "Christ," and so it could easily be pointing to Jesus as the Christ.

There are two other arguments which support an understanding of "has anointed" in Luke 4:18 as a reference to Jesus as Christ. Earlier we claimed that Luke 4:14(16)-(30)44 constituted a strong unity; this conten-

---

[257] E.g., Fitzmyer, *The Gospel According to Luke I–IX*, 529-530, 532.

[258] See O'Toole, "Jesus as the Christ in Luke 4,16-30," 498-522; for the possible Old Testament influence on Luke 4:17-19, confer Bock, *Proclamation from Prophecy*, 105-111.

[259] Luke 24:26.46; Acts 2:34-36; 3:18-21; 9:22(?); 17:3; 18:5(?).28; 26:23.

tion was based on the occurrence of the same vocabulary at both the beginning and end of the pericope: "to preach the good news" (vv. 18,43: εὐαγγελίσασθαι), "it is necessary" (v. 43: δεῖ corresponds to the divine will expressed in the scripture citation, vv. 18-19), "I send" (vv. 19,43: ἀποστέλλω), "to proclaim" (vv. 18-19,44: κηρύσσω) and "synagogue" (vv. 16,44; cf. 15, 20, 28, 33, 38: συναγωγή). Apparently, in the synagogue of Nazareth Luke wanted to present first a description of Jesus' mission (vv. 16-30) and then to portray Jesus actualizing it. Within the unit of 4:14-44, we find the summary statement of vv. 40-41 in the latter of which Luke writes of Jesus, "He laid his hands on each of them and cured them. And demons also came out from many, shouting 'You are the Son of God.' But he rebuked them and did not allow them to speak because they knew that he was the Christ." In v. 41 "the Son of God" may have the same meaning as "the Messiah (Christ)", and Jesus is realizing his mission, "to let the oppressed go free" (v. 18). So, in the very unit where we are contending that "has anointed" (v. 18) points to Jesus as the Christ (Messiah), Luke later so pictures him.

The second, and perhaps the strongest argument for our interpretation of "has anointed" in Luke 4:18 stands in Acts 4:27: "Indeed they gathered in this city against your holy servant Jesus whom you anointed (ὃν ἔχρισας), Herod and Pontius Pilate, together with the Gentiles and the peoples of Israel." In this passage Luke uses "you anointed" of God who anoints Jesus as the Christ because "Jesus" likewise refers to "against his Christ (anointed)" (v. 26). The Davidic and messianic Ps 2:1-2 (cf. Acts 4:25-26) is fulfilled in the opposition of both Jews and Romans to Jesus during his passion(260). Since this is the only time Luke clarifies how he is using "I anoint" of Jesus, it does not seem unreasonable to claim that in Luke 4:18 through his use of "has anointed" he also wants to identify Jesus as the Christ.

This whole consideration leads to the conclusion that in Luke 4:18 of his programmatic passage Luke with the words, "The Spirit of the Lord is upon me, because he has anointed me to bring good news to the poor," wants to portray Jesus as "the Christ"(261). Since vv. 18-19 form a unified citation which describes a definite mission, Jesus as the Christ is to bring

---

260 See Bruce, *The Acts*, 157-158; Haenchen, *The Acts*, 226-227 and Polhill, *Acts*, 149.

261 See Bock, *Luke 1:1 – 9:50*, 407,420.

good news to the poor, to proclaim release to captives and recovery of sight to the blind, to let the oppressed go free and to proclaim the year of the Lord's favor. Moreover, since the flow of thought in vv. 16-30 really follows from the scriptural citation, four elements can reasonably be claimed as belonging to Luke's portrayal of Jesus as the Christ: his activity will be prophetic in nature, he will work miracles and have a universal mission, but be rejected by his own people.

Luke 7:18-35

If we consider Luke's Gospel up to Luke 7:18-35, there are two possible referents for "Are you the one who is to come, or should we expect another?" (v. 19; cf. v. 20). Zechariah says of his son John that he will go before the Lord to prepare a straight path for him (1:76; cf. Mal 3:1-2.23-24); and, indeed, the citation of Mal 3:1 about John the Baptist in Luke 7:27, "See, I am sending my messenger ahead of you, who will prepare your way before you" demonstrates that Luke is thinking of this passage. However, the problem remains since we would still have the question of how Luke is referring to Jesus with "Are you the one who is to come." If we remain loyal to the thought of Luke 1:76 (cf. 3:4-6), the answer would be to Jesus as Lord; and this interpretation finds support in the text. Although in 7:18-35 the reading of "the Lord" in 7:19 with reference to Jesus is questionable, nonetheless it is preferred by textual experts ([262]).

The referent for "Are you the one who is to come, or should we expect another" appears in John the Baptist's own response to the people who are full of expectation (Luke 3:15) and wondering if he might be the Messiah. John responds to this expectation, "I am baptizing you with water; but one mightier than I is coming; I am not worthy to loosen the thongs of his sandals. He will baptize you with the Holy Spirit and fire" (3:16). John's words quoted in Acts 13:25b, "Behold, one is coming after me. I am not worthy to unfasten the sandals of his feet," constitute a strong parallel to these verses. However, the previous vv. 22-23 have clarified that Jesus is a descendant of David; and so we have the word pattern of Jesus as "the Christ." In Ephesus, Paul finds "disciples" and asks them if they had received the Holy Spirit; they reply that they have not even heard of the existence of the Holy Spirit and were baptized with John's baptism. Paul says to them "John baptized with the baptism of

---

[262] See Metzger, *A Textual Commentary*, 119.

repentance, telling the people to believe in the one who was to come after him, that is, in Jesus" (Acts 19:4). These "disciples" are then baptized in the name of Lord Jesus, and Paul lays hands on them and they receive the Holy Spirit([263]). The reference to Luke 3:16 and to the difference between the baptism of John and that of the Christ is quite clear (Acts 19:2-6). Consequently, since John the Baptist sent his two apostles to ask Jesus if he is "He who is to come" and since we find in Luke 3:15 the people both full of expectation (cf. 7:19-20) and wondering if John might be the Christ, more probably "Are you the one who is to come, or should we expect another" refers to Jesus as the Christ([264]). The fact that Jesus in the parallel programmatic passage is "anointed" (4:18; cf. v. 41; Acts 4:26-27) and so identified as Christ would support this interpretation, as likewise would Luke 19:38 (cf. 13:35), "Blessed is the king who comes in the name of the Lord" because "king" belongs to the word pattern of "Christ."

Luke 9:1-50([265])

Above in our consideration of Jesus as a prophet we discussed the structure of Luke 9:1-50 and how Herod's question in v. 9b about Jesus' identity introduces the various answers given. Twice we are informed that the ordinary people associate him with the prophets (vv.7b-8, 19), but Jesus' further question indicates the inadequacy of this identification([266]). Luke with this question introduces step-parallelism and Peter's answer, "The Christ of God." To be sure, Peter's answer is acceptable, but not totally so because a few verses later the voice from the cloud further specifies Jesus' identity and proclaims of him, "This is my chosen Son; listen to him!" (v. 35). Furthermore, Jesus corrects Peter's answer. Jesus does not

---

[263] The fact that these "disciples" are baptized in the name of the Lord Jesus (Acts 19:5) could favor interpreting "Are you the one who is to come" as a reference to Jesus as "Lord", but to give a baptismal formula such weight appears a weaker argument.

[264] Bock, *Luke 1:1 – 9:50*, 657, 665-666; Green, *The Gospel of Luke*, 295-296; Schweizer, *The Good News according to Luke*, 135; *pace* Fitzmyer, *The Gospel According to Luke I–IX*, 666.

[265] For a brief consideration of Luke's Christology in these verses, see Ellis, "La composition de Luc 9," 193-200.

[266] Marshall, *The Gospel of Luke*, 366.

say that Peter's answer is wrong([267]); in fact, he orders the disciples to tell no one about it. This command, which probably originally hinted at the confusion and political misunderstanding which would result from such an identification, in Luke's time more highlights the truth of Peter's insightful identification and not unreasonably leads to the claim of some authors that the messianic secret in Luke consists in the *suffering* Messiah([268]). More precisely, Peter's answer does not totally embrace how Jesus is the Christ (the Messiah); for in accord with God's plan Jesus, now named "the Son of Man," must suffer much, be rejected by the Jewish authorities and killed, yet be raised on the third day (v. 22). There follows a reflection on how one is to be a disciple, and then Jesus makes the puzzling assertion, "Truly, I say to you, there are some standing here who will not taste death until they see the kingdom of God (v. 27; cf. vv. 23-26). "The kingdom of God" belongs to the word pattern of Jesus as the Christ, and Luke in this verse drops Mark's statement that the kingdom of God, "has come in power"(9:1). So, Luke is not speaking of the ultimate establishment of the kingdom, but of the experience of its presence in Jesus himself. Consequently, Peter's identification of Jesus as the Christ of God is acceptable but not complete nor precise enough: Jesus must first suffer and then rise. This brings us to the presentation of Jesus as "the Christ" in the last three chapters of Luke's Gospel. Luke 22:1 – 23:56a report Jesus' passion, and Luke 23:56b-24:53, his resurrection and subsequent appearances.

Luke 22:1 – 23:56a([269])
At the Last Supper, Jesus says that he will not eat of the Passover (again?) until it is fulfilled in the kingdom of God (Luke 22:16); two verses later he repeats the idea, but this time in terms of not drinking of the vine until the kingdom of God comes (v. 18). These verses should be considered with vv. 29-30, "And I confer a kingdom on you, just as my Father has conferred one on me, that you may eat and drink at my table in my kingdom; and you will sit on thrones judging the twelve tribes of Israel." This banquet spoken of in vv. 29-30 is messianic; for in these verses the scene is

---

[267] Hare, *The Son of Man Tradition*, 56-57.

[268] Cf. Fitzmyer, *The Gospel According to Luke I–IX*, 200.

[269] M. de Jonge, "The Use of ὁ Χριστός," 184-186, provides a summary of Luke's treatment of Jesus during his passion.

heavenly since there is reference to a final judgment, "kingdom" belongs to the word-pattern of "the Christ" and the eating and drinking occur at Jesus' table. The Last Supper looks to the messianic banquet. So, on either side of the Institution Narrative itself, Jesus speaks of the kingdom. Before the institution, he speaks of "the kingdom of God", but afterwards he clarifies that it is his kingdom, too. Jesus speaks of the kingdom of God as a future reality at which he will eat of the Passover and drink of the fruit of the vine. Those authors who understand these verses (vv. 16, 18) as saying that Jesus did not partake of the Last Supper are mistaken: such an interpretation does not square well with "took his place" (v. 14), with his expressed intention, "I have eagerly desired to eat this Passover with you before I suffer (v. 15)," or with "from this time on (v. 18)." Moreover, would not the image of unity conveyed by a meal or by the kingdom be vitiated, should Jesus not have participated in the Last Supper? Consequently, Jesus views the Last Supper as radically connected to the messianic banquet; and the participation of the Christians, which Luke explicitly states is to be repeated in Jesus' memory (v. 19b; cf. 1 Cor 11:24-25), looks to this banquet. Furthermore, the phrasing of Luke 22:29-30 recalls the prophecy of Nathan to David (2 Sm 7:12-16; cf. Luke 1:32-33); and now, just as God covenanted with Jesus a kingdom, Jesus covenants that kingdom with the apostles. This promise, as the covenant of old, gives hope and assurance, and eating and drinking at Jesus' table express its unity and fellowship.

Luke's theme of the "kingdom" at the Last Supper is even more extensive. Of the Synoptics only Luke has introduced into this scene the dispute over greatness (Luke 22:24-27). In his reaction to this inappropriate attitude, Jesus says, "The kings of the Gentiles lord it over them and those in authority over them are addressed as 'benefactors.'" Nonetheless, among the apostles, the most important should become like the youngest, and the leader like one who serves, for this is the way that Jesus has acted in their midst. Given the fact that these verses are located in the Last Supper scene between Jesus' various statements about the kingdom of God, one naturally concludes that unlike pagan kings and others in authority, Jesus, the king, does not lord it over his subjects nor insist on titles like "benefactor"([270]); rather he benefits and serves his followers.

---

[270] For a discussion of this topic, confer Danker, *Benefactor*. However, Luke rejects this title (Luke 22:25-26), but terminology associated with "benefactor" in other

Jesus' kingdom is one of service, and it is no mere chance that the last words in this Lukan reflection are, "the one who serves" (v. 27) ([271]).

In the appearance before the Council (Luke 22:66-71), Luke has eliminated the false witnesses and the charge about the destruction of the temple, the dialogue between Jesus and the High Priest, the rending of the latter's garments, the charge of blasphemy and the accusation that Jesus deserves death. Thus, Luke both safeguards the personhood of Jesus and at the same time centers the scene on him. In our discussion of Jesus as the Son of Man, we noted that Luke in this scene separates the question about Jesus being the Christ from that of his being the Son of God. When asked if he is the Christ, Jesus does not respond directly but observes, "If I tell you, you will not believe, and if I question you, you will not respond" (Luke 22:67b-68a). He then predicts the Son of Man's being seated at the right hand of the power of God, which looks to Jesus' exaltation and enthronement (cf. Acts 2:33-35; 7:55-56). This prediction further separates the Sanhedrin's two questions and provides additional information. So, we have step-parallelism in the two questions: first question, Jesus' observations, Jesus' prediction, and then the second question. Although Jesus does not directly answer the first question, Jesus' observations are far from a denial; rather they show his awareness of the unbelieving and prejudiced stance of the Sanhedrin in his regard. The second question of the Sanhedrin and Jesus' response reveal that the former have understood his answer to the first question as positive but likewise perceive that his prediction and response to their second question about his being Son of God claim considerably more. For our present purpose, it is sufficient to note that Jesus does not deny that he is the Christ, and that his prediction about the Son of Man and the Sanhedrin's understanding of it do not permit an identification of the two titles of Jesus, the Christ and Son of God.

At the first appearance before Pilate, only in Luke do the members of the Sanhedrin accuse Jesus of perverting their nation, forbidding payment of taxes to the emperor, and saying that he is the Christ, a king (Luke 23:2). Pilate then asks Jesus if he is the king of the Jews; and Jesus replies, "You say so" (v. 3). Pilate's response to all this is to tell the chief priests and the crowds that he sees no basis for a case against Jesus (v. 4;

---

literature could have influenced Luke's soteriology, although he primarily depends on the OT to express his theme of salvation.

[271] Διακονεῖν (cf. ὁ νεώτερος) occurs three times in Luke 22:26-27.

cf. vv. 1-3); and, in fact, during the passion Luke stresses Jesus' innocence([272]). Naturally, Luke's reader shares Pilate's opinion, but really knows a great deal more than he. For the reader, Jesus has not been perverting the people but calling them to share in God's salvation now made particularly manifest in himself. Moreover, in the story about paying taxes to Caesar (20:20-26), Jesus does not forbid paying taxes to Caesar but rather says, "Then pay to Caesar what belongs to Caesar and to God what belongs to God (v. 25)([273])." Also in the Gospel, although others identify Jesus as Messiah (Luke 4:41; 9:20; cf. 18:35-43), Jesus himself does this only indirectly (cf. 22:67-68). The reader has this information on the reliable testimony of an angel (1:31-33; 2:11) and of Simeon under the influence of the Holy Spirit (2:25-35). Although he modifies it, Jesus does not reject Peter's identification of him as "the Christ" (9:20) or the joyful proclamation of the multitude of the disciples that he is the king who comes in the name of the Lord (19:38; cf. 19:11-27; 22:15-16.18.29-30). Furthermore, Jesus knew that he was no political personage or a military liberator, but someone who had to suffer and that his kingdom, although present, was religious and heavenly in nature. So, Pilate's statement of Jesus' innocence is accurate. The charges against him are false, even that of claiming to be the Messiah; for Jesus himself did not explicitly claim it. Moreover, what he did claim had little or nothing to do with being a "king" like Caesar.

During Jesus' crucifixion, a number of times reference is made to his being "the Christ" and "king of the Jews([274])." In contrast to the people, who just stand there watching, the leaders scoff at Jesus, "He saved others, let him save himself if he is the chosen one, the Christ of God" (Luke 23:35). Their lack of faith stands in direct contrast to Peter's earlier confession, "the Christ of God" (9:20) and partially to that of the

---

[272] Confer Luke 23:14-15.22.41.47-48; cf. Acts 3:13-14; 7:52; 13:28.

[273] See Lagrange, *Évangile selon Saint Luc*, 577; Lenski, *St. Luke's Gospel*, 1103; Loisy, *L'Évangile selon Luc*, 543.

[274] Nolland, *Luke 18:35 – 24:53*, 1149, rightly joins Luke 23:33(*sic*)-38 to 39-43 because the criminals are at the beginning and end of these verses; and the people, now separated from their leaders' behavior, and the penitent thief frame the threefold scene of mockery, that of the leaders, the soldiers and the non-believing thief. Nolland probably intended that the first section begin with v. 32.

voice from heaven, "This is my chosen Son; listen to him." The leaders grant that Jesus has saved others, but they seek a further sign before they will accept him as the Christ. This kind of behavior resembles that of Herod Antiphas, which merits only Jesus' silence (23:8-9; cf. 11:16.29-32). Luke's reader recognizes the irony of the situation([275]), for the scoffing of the leaders is expressed in confessional language: Jesus is the Savior, the Christ and the elect of God. The double mention of "saving" in the scoffing of the leaders recalls the fact that Jesus, the Christ, saves (e.g., 2:11.26-34). However, God wants him to be the suffering Christ who will be "mocked, insulted and spat upon" (18:32). The soldiers imitate the leaders, as soldiers are wont to do, and likewise mocked Jesus, "If you are the king of the Jews, save yourself" (23:37). They also take their clue from the inscription over Jesus, "This is the king of the Jews" (v. 38). Luke again phrases their ironic mockery in confessional language, for the reader knows that Jesus is the king of the Jews (e.g., 1:30-33; 18:38) and savior.

Another mockery occurs, very similar to the two just seen. "Now one of the criminals hanging there blasphemed Jesus([276]), saying, 'Are you not the Christ? Save yourself and us'" (Luke 23:39). The sign above Jesus' head, "This is the King of the Jews" (v. 38) may well have also motivated his words. Again, we have irony and confessional terminology about Jesus, "the Christ," and his ability to save. The other criminal rebukes his accomplice's lack of fear of God and grants that they have been justly condemned; he likewise recognizes Jesus' innocence and asks him, "Jesus, remember me when you come into your kingdom" (23:42). This criminal has better sense and perception than the Jewish leaders and Roman soldiers; he realizes that Jesus is king and can save. From Jesus, he receives the reassuring response, "Amen, I say to you, today you will be with me in paradise" (v. 43). Given the various references to Jesus as the Christ in the crucifixion scene, Luke's description of Joseph of Aremathea proves of interest. Luke predicates of Joseph, "was awaiting the kingdom of God" (v 51) which recalls the same phrasing, "awaiting," used of Simeon (2:25) and Anna (v. 38) in the *Nunc Dimittis* where Jesus as the Christ of God is a dominant theme. So, during the whole Passion Scene, Luke stresses through irony that Jesus is the Christ, the King of the

---

[275] Bock, *Luke 9:51 – 24:53*, 1836, 1840-1841, 1854.

[276] During the passion and elsewhere Luke uses "blasphemy" of Jesus' opponents who do not recognize Jesus for who he truly is (Luke 22:65; cf. Acts 18:6; 26:11).

Jews, God's elect, who saves; and the good thief and Joseph of Arimathea realize this and act accordingly. If 23:34a, "Father, forgiven them, they know not what they do," be genuine, it along with Jesus' promise of paradise to the good thief demonstrate that in the very passage where he is mocked as saving, Jesus is saving. His seeming control of the situation has led some scholars to speak of a Lukan glorification of Jesus during his passion comparable to that found in John.

Luke 24

Only Luke at the end of his Gospel twice explains that what happened to Jesus, the Christ, was in accordance with the Sacred Scriptures. Luke 24:26 reads, "Was it not necessary that the Christ should suffer these things and enter into this glory?" In vv. 46-48, Jesus claims, "Thus it is written that the Messiah would suffer and rise from the dead on the third day and that repentance, for the forgiveness of sins, would be preached in his name to all the nations, beginning from Jerusalem. You are witnesses of these things([277])." These affirmations find further confirmation in Jesus's words, "That everything written about me in the law of Moses and in the prophets and psalms must be fulfilled" (v. 44). Probably, responding to a concern of the churches he knew, Luke explains that the Scriptures show that it was God's will that the Christ must suffer and rise from the dead and that in his name repentance for the forgiveness of sins be proclaimed to everyone (cf. 2:30-32; 3:6; Acts 28:28). The reference to the earlier passion predictions is obvious; these predictions have been fulfilled.

This raises the question of forgiveness of sins in "the Christ's" name. Attention has already been called to the connection between the Christ and salvation (e.g., 2:11.25-35; 23:35.37.39), and forgiveness of sins is an alternative Lucan expression for salvation (e.g., Luke 1:77; 5:20-24; 7:47-50; 11:3). In the present context one might be tempted to conclude that, since Luke 24:47 literally speaks of "repentance for the forgiveness of sins," what is achieved in "the Christ's" name is repentance that leads to forgiveness of sins. However, there are a number of passages in Acts, which call such an interpretation into question. In the aftermath

---

[277] Schweizer, *The Good News according to Luke*, 377, calls attention to Acts 2:32-33.38; 3:15-16.19; 5:28-32; 10:3.43 in which passages the name of Jesus, forgiveness of sins and the witness of the apostles are joined.

to the Pentecost speech, Peter, in answer to the question of what his audience is to do, says, "Repent and be baptized, every one of you, in the name of Jesus Christ for the forgiveness of your sins; and you will receive the gift of the Holy Spirit" (Acts 2:38). Again, there is mention of "repentance", but clearly one purpose of "baptism in the name of Jesus Christ" is the forgiveness of sins; another, the gift of the Holy Spirit. Luke in Acts 2:38 speaks of no other agent of the forgiveness of sins. Although the connection between "the Christ" and the forgiveness of sins is surely less clear, nevertheless, much the same idea appears in Acts 3:18-19, for God has brought to fulfillment what he had announced beforehand through all the prophets, that his Christ must suffer. "Repent, therefore, and be converted, that you sins may be wiped away" (v. 19).

Another passage bears on this question, for the context speaks of Jesus as the descendent of David. In his speech in the synagogue at Antioch of Pisidia, Paul refers to the messianic Ps 2:7 (Acts 13:33), to "the benefits assured to David" (v. 34; cf. Is 55:3LXX) and, as is done in the Pentecost speech, interprets God's word to David that he would not see "corruption" in terms of Jesus' resurrection (Acts 13:35-37; cf. Ps 15:10LXX). He then solemnly concludes (Acts 13:38-39), "You must know, my brothers, that through him forgiveness of sins is being proclaimed to you and in regard to everything from which you could not be justified under the law of Moses, in him every believer is justified"[278]. Through Jesus the forgiveness of sins can be obtained; and this forgiveness the Law of Moses could not achieve. The double mention of "justify" (vv. 38-39) confirms the salvific nature of the passage. This connection between Jesus and the forgiveness of sins finds considerably additional support in Acts (5:31; 7:60; 10:43; 22:16; 26:18), although in the contexts there are no references to him as the Christ.

An accurate understanding of "the Christ's" ability to forgive sins depends on a correct interpretation of questions like that of the scribes and Pharisees, "Who is this who speaks blasphemies? Who but God alone can forgive sins" (Luke 5:21). This question will be addressed in a subsequent chapter, "Luke Is Willing to Predicate the Same Things about Jesus as He Does of God," below.

---

[278] Polhill, *Acts*, 305, claims, "The next statement, which is a fuller explication of the forgiveness of sins, could hardly be more Pauline." However, did Paul hold that the Law in any way whatever was able to justify one? For further discussion, see Bruce, *The Acts*, 311-312, and Kilgallen, "Acts 13,38-39," 480-506.

Other Passages about Jesus As Descendent of David, As King or about His Kingdom([279])

Some Lucan passages link the "kingdom of God" to Jesus' presence and actions. When accused of casting out devils in the name of Beelzebub, Jesus answers, "But if it is by the finger of God that I drive out demons, then the kingdom of God has come upon you" (Luke 11:20). Jesus' presence and actions explain why he can say to the Pharisees who asked him when the kingdom of God is coming, "The coming of the kingdom of God cannot be observed and no one will announce, 'Look, here it is' or 'There it is.' For behold, the kingdom of God is among you" (Luke 17:20-21)([280]). Luke unites Jesus with the coming of God in the blessing of the little children. The disciples are trying to prevent people from bring children to Jesus. But Jesus calls for them and says, "Let the children come to me and do not prevent them; for the kingdom of God belongs to such as these" (Luke 18:16). Coming to Jesus relates to belonging to the kingdom.

Luke certainly identifies the following of Jesus with the kingdom of God. In the narrative about the claims of discipleship, which occurs at the beginning of the journey to Jerusalem (Luke 9:57-62), we read, "But you, go and proclaim the kingdom of God" (v. 60). When another would-be disciple expresses his willingness to follow Jesus but first wants to say farewell to those at his house, Jesus challenges him with the words, "No one who sets a hand to the plow and looks to what was left behind is fit for the kingdom of God" (v. 62)([281]).

Jesus' comment about the rich ruler's unwillingness to follow him (Luke 18:18-30) is, "How hard it is for those who have wealth to enter the kingdom of God" (v. 24), and so he associates following him with entry into the kingdom. Toward the end of the pericope, Luke repeats this idea. When Peter wants to know about himself and the other disciples who have left everything and followed, Jesus responds that there is no one who has left all his family members "for the sake of the kingdom of God," who will not receive much more in this life and eternal life in the age to come (vv. 28-29; cf. 14:26).

---

[279] For a more extensive consideration of this topic, see O'Toole, "The Kingdom of God," 147-162, esp. 149-151; confer also Ernst, *Herr der Geschichte*, 55-63.

[280] Plummer, *St. Luke*, 406, defends the translation, "among you," "For the Kingdom of God was not in the hearts of the Pharisees, who are the persons addressed."

[281] See Bock, *Luke 9:51 – 24:53*, 983-985.

For "following Jesus" Luke has substituted "for the sake of the kingdom of God." Only Luke of the Synoptics speaks of "the kingdom of God" in v. 29; and in comparing this verse with Mk 10:29, one notes that Luke has substituted "for the sake of the kingdom of God" for Mark's "for my sake and for the sake of the gospel." For Luke, the two phrases convey the same idea.

The blind man twice calls on "Jesus, son of David" to have mercy on him (Luke 18:38-39; cf. vv. 35-43). Jesus orders that the blind man be brought to him, grants his request and restores his sight and commends his faith. This miracle occurs during the journey to Jerusalem where the kingdom of God plays a larger role and not much before the parable of the king who entrusts ten pounds to his servants (19:11-27) and Jesus' triumphal entry into Jerusalem where only Luke inserts the identification of him as "king" (v. 38). Luke 8:35-43 recalls Jesus' explanation in the programmatic passage of his own mission as including the gift of sight to the blind; and above we argued that in the passage Luke also presents Jesus as the Christ. Once the blind man's sight is restored, he uses it as he should: he follows Jesus and praises God. So, the blind man's identification of Jesus as "son of David" has its role in Luke's presentation of Jesus as the Christ([282]).

When Jesus enters Jerusalem, the whole multitude of the disciples began to praise God joyfully because of all the marvelous miracles they had seen and to shout, "Blessed is the king who comes in the name of the Lord" (Luke 19:38; cf. v. 37; Ps 117:26LXX; Zec 9:9). Only Luke speaks of a king in this passage, which tells us a number of things about Jesus, the Christ([283]). Jesus has worked a number of impressive miracles, is favored by God ("Blessed"), and comes in his name. The phrases, "Peace in heaven, and glory in the highest," reveal the heavenly dimensions of this event and proclamation and recall the words of another multitude, those of angels at Jesus' birth, "Glory to God in the highest and on earth peace to those on whom his favor rests" (2:14). Since in 2:11 Jesus is designated "Christ and Lord in the city of David," we rightly conclude that as king he brings both earthly and heavenly peace; and his arrival calls for praise of God and joy. So significant is Jesus' kingly arrival in Jerusalem that, when the Pharisees tell Jesus to order his disciples to stop their joyful shouts, he responds that should they do so the

---

[282] Loisy, *L'Évangile selon Luc*, 452-453; Plummer, *St. Luke*, 431 and Schweizer, *The Good News according to Luke*, 289; *pace* Burger, *Jesus als Davidssohn*, 111.

[283] Loisy, *L'Évangile selon Luc*, 469-470.

very stones would shout out (19:39-40). Nature itself could not allow this
event to pass without an appropriate response.

Luke 19:11-28
If Luke's reader has not already realized it, once the proclamation of Jesus
as king during his triumphal entry into Jerusalem has occurred, he now
perceives that the parable of the ten pounds (Luke 19:11-27), much of
which is unique to Luke (cf. Mt 25:14-30)([284]), also relates to the portrayal of Jesus as king and so as "the Christ." Of particular interest to us is
that those aspects of the parable, which deal with royal rule, are found
only in Luke. To be sure, the "parable," as it presently stands, is a complex
unit made up of a number of diverse elements, but we will continue to follow our methodology of taking the text as it presently exists. Only Luke
speaks of a king and a kingdom in this scene. Moreover, for Luke the pericope is strategically located, particularly should one accept that it occurs
at the end of Jesus' journey to Jerusalem. It is during the journey that
Luke speaks most of the kingdom of God; and the journey itself falls into
three sections, each of which opens with a general notice about the movement toward Jerusalem (9:51; 13:22; 17:11); and the first and the last sections end with parables on the kingdom of God (13:18-21; 19:11-27)([285]).
Therefore, the following of Jesus and the instructions given during the
journey on how one is to live relate to the understanding of the parable of
the ten pounds. Moreover, according to v. 11, Jesus tells the parable because some thought that the kingdom of God was to appear immediately.
Luke wants to correct this supposition, at least as regards the fullness of
the kingdom, as Acts 1:6-8 and the whole of Acts confirm. Often parables
make one main point; nevertheless, Luke in the present one directs our attention to a number of aspects and so it is probably more accurate to speak
of an allegory in 19:11-27. The aspects addressed are: the association of
Jerusalem and the kingdom of God; the question of when the kingdom will
come; the responsible manner in which the king's servants are to comport

---

[284] For the relationship between the parable in Matthew and the one in Luke, see
Fitzmyer, *The Gospel According to Luke X–XXIV*, 1228-1231. Confer also: Bock,
Luke 9:51 – 24:52, 1526-1529; Lagrange, *Évangile selon Saint Luc*, 490-492; and
Plummer, *St. Luke*, 437.

[285] George, *Études sur l'œuvre de Luc*, 298, n. 2 and Grundmann, "Komposition des
lukanischen 'Reiseberichts,'" 259, 264-270.

themselves until his return (v. 13); the identification, unique to Luke, of another group, called "the citizens," who hate the king and do not want him to rule over them and send a delegation to accomplish this aim (v. 14); a twofold judgment scene: that of the servants (vv. 15-26) and another of those who did not want the king to rule over them (v. 27).

No definite answer is given as to when the kingdom is to come; but the reader is in no doubt that according to the parable it *will* come and, perhaps, quite suddenly because the return of the king with royal power in v. 15 occurs rather abruptly and no mention is made of any considerable passage of time. On the other hand, the disciples proclaim Jesus as king during his triumphal entry into Jerusalem. The challenge, until the fullness of the kingdom comes, is to responsible behavior, concretized in the nobleman's giving each of his servants a pound (a laborer's wages for three months) along with the instruction, "Engage in trade with these until I return" (v. 13). The appearance of this parable and the attention to money right after the story of Zacchaeus and his right attitude toward his wealth is not accidental (cf. v. 8). When the king returns, the responsible behavior of his servants is the first thing to which he attends. Actually, only three servants give an account of how they used the pound. The first two demonstrate remarkable diligence, and each of them is awarded with the charge of a number of cities corresponding to the pounds earned. The third servant earned nothing. He speaks of his fear of the Lord whom he judges severe, "because you are a demanding person; you take up what you did not lay down and you harvest what you did not plant" (v. 21; cf. v. 22). Although this servant is fearful and pathetic, there is no softening on the part of the newly appointed king who calls him a "wicked servant" and asks why he didn't put the money into a bank so that at his return the king could collect it with interest. The pound is taken from the wicked servant and given to the servant who has ten pounds (interestingly, the king did not take the ten pounds from him); but no more is said about the fate of the "wicked" servant. The charge that the king was "severe" is not really justified, because the wicked servant did not do what he was told; he did not do business with the pound given him. "From those who have nothing" (v. 26) would be the servants who failed to use what the king gives them in accord with his instructions. They lose even what they have. On the other hand, those who have fruitfully carried out their lord's instructions are given even more. Thus, the puzzling saying in v. 26 is a generalization of the message of the parable proper in vv. 13, 15-25. The challenging behavior of the king becomes even more manifest in v. 27 (cf. v. 14); for he orders that his "enemies," who hated him and did not want him to rule over them and even sent a delegate to achieve this, be brought in and slaughtered before him. The most obvious reference to these "citizens" of the king is those Jews who did not want to accept Jesus. The slaughter is an image(286), which stresses the tragic nature of not accepting Jesus, their king (287).

In summary, the parable of the ten pounds in cryptic fashion presents Jesus as a king whose kingdom somehow relates to Jerusalem. However, Jesus' kingdom will not be realized immediately. The main emphasis of the parable falls on the duty of the king's servants to take their pound (whatever they have received from their king) and use it to his and their advantage and on those Jews, who have not accepted Jesus as their king but should do so before it is too late. The image of the slaughter vividly communicates the futility and disastrous results of not doing so.

Luke 20:42-44

In Luke 20:42-44, Jesus begins with a reference to the commonly accepted belief that the Christ was to be David's son, that is, his descendent. He then counters, if that be true, how can David in the messianic Ps 109:1LXX speak of the Christ as his lord. The Christ is David's descendent; but since he is also David's lord, the Christ must be greater than David. This latter affirmation is unusual, for generally a descendent was viewed as inferior to his forebears, and it is all the more surprising because David played a major role in Jewish history; he was the greatest of their kings, the one who unified the tribes, enlarged the kingdom and found favor with God(288). We will see that Luke already gave his reader the answer to the riddle about how David can call the Christ Lord in Luke 1: 32-35; Act 2:34-36 provide an even more complete answer(289).

---

286 Lenski, *St. Luke's Gospel*, 959, writes of an "Oriental image," a drastic image, which fits the terrible reality.

287 Confer Luke 1:31-33; 19:38-39; 23:2-3.37-38; Acts 2:23-36; 13:22-23.

288 Howard, "David," 41-46.

289 Confer Burger, *Jesus als Davidssohn*, 115-116, who wants to see the answer to the question in Acts 2:33.

Jesus As (the) Christ in Acts

In the Acts of the Apostles, Luke continues his presentation of Jesus as "the Christ." In Acts 4:25-28 there is a specific reference to the Davidic Ps 2:1-2 which is said to have been fulfilled in Jerusalem when Herod and Pontius Pilate along with the Romans and peoples of Israel united against God's holy servant and *anointed one*, Jesus. This corresponds well with the Lucan theme that according to the Sacred Scriptures the Christ had to suf-fer (Acts 3:18) and then to rise from the dead (Luke 24:26.46; Acts 2:30-31; 17:3; 26:23;). Seemingly, also using the scriptures, Paul in Corinth bears witness to Jesus as the Christ (18:5; cf. v. 4). The simple statement, "Jesus is the Christ" (5:42), constitutes the good news; and all of these passages in a sense do precisely that, namely, summarize very briefly the Christian message. In fact, in 8:5 Luke writes of Philip that he proclaimed "the Christ" to the Samaritans.

Jesus, exalted to God's right hand, received the promise of the Holy Spirit and pours this Spirit out on those at Pentecost (Acts 2:32-33; cf. Jn 20:19-23). In Acts 2:31 Luke makes clear that David in Ps 15LXX spoke of the resurrection of the Christ; and earlier Jesus himself, identified as the Christ (Luke 24:46), says he as Son will send the promise of his Father on the Eleven and those with them and that they will be clothed with power from on high (cf. v. 47). Acts 1:4-5 (cf. v. 8) continue this thought and repeat the distinction between the baptism of John and that of Jesus; in fact, v. 5 leads to the conclusion that Pentecost is a baptism in the Spirit. So, Luke in accord with John's specification that the Christ will baptize in the Spirit (cf. Acts 19:2-6) asserts that the exalted Jesus pours out the Holy Spirit at Pentecost([290]).

In Acts 2:24-32 Peter connects the resurrection of the Christ with David's prophetic words, "That neither was he abandoned to the nether-world nor did his flesh experience corruption," in Ps 15:8-10LXX; Paul returns to this argument in Acts 13:34-37. Luke speaks of Jesus' enthrone-ment in Acts 2:33-34 (cf. 7:55-56; Luke 22:69). According to Peter's argument, David did not rise from the dead, because Peter and his audi-ence clearly know where his grave is (Acts 2:29); so the enthronement spoken of in Ps 109:1LXX cannot refer to him. Rather it refers to Jesus as the Christ who has been exalted to God's right hand (Acts 2:33). So, Jesus is the Lord, to whom the Lord (God) says, "Sit at my right hand

---

[290] Confer Haenchen, *The Acts*, 183,187.

until I make your enemies your footstool" (vv. 34-35). Peter next solemnly asserts, "Therefore let the whole house of Israel know for certain that God has made him both Lord and Christ, this Jesus whom you crucified" (v. 36)([291]). "Lord" in this verse is surely a reference to the "Lord" whom the Lord (God) instructs to sit at his right hand (cf. v. 21). However, "Christ" in v. 36 also refers to the citation in vv. 34-35 of Ps 109:1LXX; for as indicated above almost all of the Pentecost speech is dominated by the consideration of Jesus as the descendent of David, who is risen, exalted and enthroned. Moreover, the very citation of the Davidic messianic Ps 109:1LXX, likewise justifies our seeing "Christ" in v. 36 as reference to this psalm.

Luke through the mouth of Paul also states that the Christ will be the first to rise from the dead and that he has a mission to proclaim light both to the people and to the Gentiles (Acts 26:23; cf. Is 42:6; 49:6). This mission reminds us of the one we saw for the "anointed" Jesus in the programmatic passage. Above we likewise argued that Jesus' resurrection actually fulfills the promise of God to the Fathers, and so when Paul speaks of Jesus as "the first to rise from the dead" the reference is not only chronological (cf. Acts 13:32-33.46-48). The mission that Paul attributes to the risen Christ in Acts 26:23 is one that he himself actually receives from the risen Jesus (vv. 16-18; cf. Luke 2:30-32; Acts 3:26; 5:31)([292]).

Peter explicitly speaks of "the Christ" in Acts 3:18 and then, again in accord with Scriptures, relates Christ Jesus to the Parousia (Acts 3:19-21)([293]). The study of Acts 3:20-21 has created considerable scholarly interest. Whatever meaning these verses may have had in the earlier tradition([294]), Peter now definitely relates them to the Parousia([295]). He ex-

---

[291] L.T. Johnson, *The Acts*, 52-53, correctly observes that Luke has used both of these titles of Jesus prior to his resurrection ("Christ": Luke 2:11.26; 4:41; 9:20; 20:41; "Lord": Luke 2:11; 10:1; 11:39; 12:42; 22:61).

[292] See O'Toole, *Acts 26*, 118-122.

[293] Kurz, "Acts 3:19-26," 309-323. Bayer, "Christ-Centered Eschatology," 249-250, feels that Kurz is mistaken because it is Luke's vital Christology which heavily influences and shapes his eschatology, not vice versa.

[294] On this topic, see J.A.T. Robinson, "The Most Primitive Christology of All," 177-189; for a very thorough treatment of the passage, see Barbi, *Il Cristo celeste*.

horts his Jewish audience to repent so that their sins can be forgiven and suggests that this repentance may help bring a time of spiritual regeneration and that the Lord will send Jesus Christ who must remain in heaven until the universal restoration foretold by the prophets.

Continuation of the Presentation of Jesus As David's Descendent

Also in Acts, Luke continues to present Jesus as David's descendent and so as the Christ. We have already seen that in the Pentecost speech (Acts 2:14-36), Peter through references to Ps 15:8-11LXX, the oath made to David and Ps109:1LXX, considers Jesus' resurrection (Acts 2:24-32), exaltation (v. 33) and enthronement (vv. 34-36). Again, through such Davidic OT passages as Ps 2:7([296]), Is 55:3LXX and Ps 15:10LXX Paul in Acts 13:32-39 explains Jesus' resurrection. Verses 23 and 25 recall Jesus' Davidic ancestry, designate him, "savior," and refer back to Luke 3:15a-17, where the people are wondering whether John the Baptist is the Christ, and to his answer, "I am not worthy to loosen the thong of his sandals" (v. 16b). In addition, Paul speaks of the "promise" in 13:32 (cf. v. 23) on which, I have contended, Luke expands to show the connection between Jesus' resurrection and that of all the dead ([297]). According to Luke, the resurrection of Jesus, the resurrection of the dead and so of our resurrection, are the realization of this promise.

Paul also speaks of descent from David. Jesus as David's descendent serves other purposes in Acts. According to Luke James refers to Jesus with the words of Amos 9:11-12LXX([298]), cited in Acts 15:16-17, "After this I shall return and rebuild the fallen dwelling of David; its ruins I shall rebuild and raise it up again so that the rest of humanity may seek out the Lord, even all the Gentiles on whom my name is invoked." A number

---

[295] Polhill, *Acts*, 134-135.

[296] For a thorough study of the Old Testament background, see Bock, *Proclamation from Prophecy*, 240-257; Schweizer, "The Davidic 'Son of God,'" 186-193, investigates the background in the OT and early Christianity of the idea that the begetting of the Son of God, prophesied in Ps 2:7, took place on Easter.

[297] See O'Toole, *The Unity*, 56-59.

[298] Actually, Luke does not scrupulously follow the LXX; for the details, cf. L.T. Johnson, *The Acts*, 264-265.

of scholars want to see in these verses a twofold Lucan understanding of how Christian salvation occurs. First, the house of David had to be re-established, and then the rest of humankind can participate in God's salvation. From an historical point of view, this interpretation has some validity, but it is doubtful that such a concern was of importance to Luke. Although he attends to the literary fiction that Christian universality did not occur until the Cornelius event (cf. Acts 10:1 – 11:18), Luke begins quite early in his Gospel to present the universality of salvation, e.g., Luke 2:14.30-34; 3:6.8; 4:14-44. More importantly, Luke thinks more of a continuum, which moves from the beginning of God's salvific interaction with the human race, through Jewish history, to the end times. Nonetheless, whether one wants to opt for a two stage development or not, James in Acts 15:14-17 continues Peter's message that Jewish Christians and all other Christians are saved through the grace of the Lord Jesus and envisions this as a restoration of Israel in terms of the house of David (cf. Luke 1:31-33; Acts 13:22)([299]) and all of humankind seeking the Lord.

Jesus As King and His Kingdom

In Thessalonica a mob seized Jason and some believers and dragged them before the authorities. These opponents accuse Jason of receiving Christian missionaries as houseguests (Acts 17:1-9; cf. 1 Thes 2:14-16; 3:3). More particularly, they say of these missionaries, "These people who have been creating a disturbance all over the world have now come here . . . . They all act in opposition to the decrees of Caesar and claim instead that there is another king, Jesus" (Acts 17:6b-7). These accusations remind one of the charges made against Jesus in the scene before Pilate (cf. Luke 23:2-5) and so should be understood in the same way, namely, as irony. Jesus is a king, but not in the sense the opponents of Christianity view a king; the rest of the charges are basically erroneous and reduce to a rejection of the Christian message. Interestingly, Luke depicts these opponents as summarizing Christianity as holding, "there is another king, Jesus"; and, in fact, "the kingdom of God" can summarize the gospel message for Luke. In Samaria Philip preaches the good news "about the kingdom of God and the name of Jesus Christ" (Acts 8:12). Paul entered the synagogue at Ephesus and for three months spoke out boldly and persuasively about "the kingdom of God" (Acts 19:8). Further, in his speech to the Ephesian elders at Miletus Paul tells them that he knows that

---

[299] *Pace* Burger, *Jesus als Davidssohn*, 141.

they will not see him again and then summarizes his activity among all of them as "to whom I preached the kingdom" (Acts 20:25). Luke takes up this phraseology again at the end of Acts, Paul is described as "bearing witness to the kingdom of God and trying to convince them about Jesus from the law of Moses and the prophets" (Acts 28:23) and "without hindrance he proclaimed the kingdom of God and taught about the Lord Jesus Christ" (v. 31). Of course, Luke does like to use double expression; but given his willingness to interchange one's response to Jesus and to the kingdom of God (cf. Luke 18:22.24.28-29), it is not unreasonable to conclude that in Acts 8:12; 28:23.31 "the kingdom of God" is equivalent to "the name of Jesus," "Jesus" and "the Lord Jesus Christ." Moreover, in Acts 28:23 the phrase, beginning with "trying to convince them," does appear to explain the one introduced, "by bearing witness to." Likewise worthy of note is that we find this phrasing about the proclamation of the kingdom in the very last verse of Acts, a place of emphasis.

Other Activities of the Christ in Acts

Given the connection that Luke expressed in Luke 3:16-17 (cf. Acts 1:4.5.8; 19:1-6) between the Christ and a baptism in the Holy Spirit, it seems justified to include here Acts 2:38 and 10:48 (cf. 11:17). Acts 2:38 reads, "Repent and be baptized, everyone one of you, in the name of Jesus Christ for the forgiveness of your sins; and you will receive the gift of the Holy Spirit"; and Acts 10:48, "He ordered them to be baptized in the name of Jesus Christ." In these texts, the words "Jesus Christ" carry the full force of "Christ"([300]). Perhaps, this should also be claimed for "Jesus Christ" when used for the cure of the lame man at the Beautiful Gate of the temple (3:6-7; 4:10) and the healing of Ananias (9:34). Acts 4:10-12 contain, perhaps, the most forceful NT statement of salvation only through the name of Jesus Christ of Nazareth; and above we saw that Luke does not hesitate to write of the saving activity of the Christ. Once Luke writes of Christ Jesus in a passage, which originally may have presented a different aspect of Christology but which now surely refers to the Parousia (Acts 3:20-21)([301]).

---

[300] See Bruce, *The Acts*, 129-130.

[301] Polhill, *Acts*, 134-135.

Summary of Jesus As the Messiah, "the Christ"

Luke is willing to predicate "(the) Christ" of Jesus from his birth onwards and shows a preference for the title, "the Christ," which needs to be studied in association with Jesus' being "king," "descendant of David" and related concepts. According to Luke, the Christ must suffer; and the writers of the OT foretold what he would do and what would happen to him. Although it is difficult to determine the meanings of "the Christ" and "Son of God" in Luke 4:41 (cf. Acts 9:19b-22) because the text itself provides little information, there is other solid evidence that "Son of God" conveys considerably more than "the Christ." "The Christ" is a more important Lucan Christological title than "prophet" and can likewise be associated with "Son of Man" and "Lord." Jesus, "the Christ," is surely superior to John the Baptist. At his baptism, Jesus was anointed with the Holy Spirit and with power and, consequently, is identified with baptism in the Holy Spirit. According to Luke, "the Christ" is the descendent of David who fulfills the prophecy of Nathan (2 Sam 7:11-17) and will rule over the house of David forever, but must first suffer and be rejected.

Most likely, through his use of "has anointed" in Luke 4:18 Luke also presents Jesus as the Christ in the programmatic passage and so describes his mission. This mission is prophetic: Jesus works miracles and has a universal mission. He proclaims salvation to both Jew and Gentiles, and in his name forgiveness of sins is proclaimed and actualized in baptism. During the crucifixion, Luke by means of irony stresses that Jesus is the Christ, "the King of the Jews" who saves. Through the resurrection of Jesus, the descendent of David, God fulfills his promise to our Fathers of our own resurrection. The Christ is exalted and enthroned at God's right hand and at Pentecost pours out the Holy Spirit. Presently, he must remain in heaven until the universal restoration, and then he will come again.

Jesus is "the King of the Jews" who comes in the name of the Lord; as "the Christ" he is greater than David, for the latter called the Christ, "Lord." Jesus' presence and actions related to the kingdom as does following him. The message about Jesus and the things relating to him can even be interchanged with "the kingdom of God." Jesus' kingdom relates to Jerusalem but will not be fully realized immediately.

In Acts, Luke continues to develop the themes that Jesus is the descendent of David and that as "the Christ," he had to suffer and then rise from the dead. The Davidic kingdom will be restored to Israel, and the Christ is a source of salvation for everyone. Even though "Christ" has to some extent become part of Jesus' name, baptism and miracles in the name of Jesus Christ probably should be included in the present consideration. Jesus Christ is the source of salvation for everyone (Acts 4:10-12).

Jesus himself makes the kingdom present, and his kingdom brings joy and peace both on earth and in heaven. Following Jesus can be identified with the kingdom of God, and anyone who refuses his inevitable kingship acts very foolishly. The Christ calls his followers to live in a certain way: to take up one's cross *daily* and to follow Jesus with total confidence and fidelity so as to share in the salvation he brings; they are to use what they have received from their king for his and their own good. Jesus' kingdom is one of service. The disciples now proclaim that Jesus is "the Christ", and he can work through the Christians to carry out his mission. The Christian Passover is an image of the messianic banquet, and Christians are to imitate the good thief who confesses Jesus and asks that they be remembered when he enters his kingdom. At the end of the Gospel, the Eleven and those with them received the instruction that in Christ's name, repentance for the forgiveness of sins is to be proclaimed to everyone.

In distinction to the other Synoptics, Luke uses "has anointed" of Jesus and stresses the designation of Jesus as "the Christ," who has to suffer. Luke distinguished this title from Jesus as the "Son of God." Luke develops the Christ's relationship with baptism in the Spirit, including Pentecost (cf. Acts 1:5), and expands on Jesus as the descendent of David. Jesus' kingdom will last forever. Upon his entry in Jerusalem, only the Lucan Jesus is proclaimed king. The Christian Passover is an image of the messianic kingdom. As the descendent of David, Jesus is raised from the dead and through him in faithfulness to his promise God raises the Christians. Luke, in contrast to Mark and Matthew, relates the following of Jesus more to the kingdom of God, and Jesus' kingdom is one of service and the appropriate use of talents. Luke's Christ is related to Jesus' exaltation, enthronement and second coming. According to Luke, Jesus as the Christ has a prophetic mission, and this mission continues after his resurrection.

CHAPTER SIX
Jesus, the Son of Man

Obviously, the historical origins of the title, "Son of Man," can prove useful for determining its significance; but scholars do not agree about the data or how to interpret them[302]. Not everyone even agrees that Jesus used the title of himself. A. Vögtle and others are convinced that Luke 12:8-9 should play a key role in determining whether Jesus actually so designated himself[303]. On the other hand, I.H. Marshall does not hesitate to conclude his consideration of the Son of Man with the words, "But it may be claimed that the view that Jesus spoke of himself by means of this phrase offers the least difficulties, and that here we have a valuable insight into his self-understanding[304]."

Our methodology particularly directs our attention to the meaning and nuances that Luke himself gives this expression. Some occurrences of this title are unique to Luke (6:22; 17:22; 18:8; 19:10; 21:36; 22:48; 24:7; Acts 7:55-56), and he stresses the aspects of faith and of suffering. Luke also introduces the Son of Man's enthronement and a connection between

---

[302] Confer: Black, "Der Apotheose Israels"; Bruce, "The Background," 50-70; Caragounis, *The Son of Man: Vision and Interpretation*, 9-144; Colpe, ὁ υἱὸς τοῦ ἀνθρώπου, 457-459, 461-462; on 457-458 he provides the various sources for this title in Luke; Deissler, "Der 'Menschensohn'"; Fitzmyer, *The Gospel According to Luke I–IX*, 208-211; Hahn, *The Titles of Jesus*, 15-53; Hampel, *Menschensohn und historischer Jesus*, 7-48; Higgins, *The Son of Man*, 3-28; Lindars, *Jesus Son of Man*, 1-16; K. Müller, "Der Menschensohn im Danielzyklus"; M. Müller, *Der Ausdruck "Menschensohn"* 10-88; Schweizer, "Menschensohn"; Tödt, *The Son of Man in the Synoptic Tradition*, 22-31; Tuckett, "The Son of Man in Q," 196-215; Weimar, "Daniel 7"; Voss, *Die Christologie*, 39-45. Caragounis, Hampel and Hare provide extensive bibliography.

[303] Vögtle, *Die 'Gretchenfrage' des Menschensohnproblems*, 9-13 and Tuckett, "The Son of Man in Q," 208-209.

[304] *The Origins of New Testament Christology*, 79.

the second coming and the nearness of the kingdom; he develops the Son of Man's saving mission and protective witness on behalf of his faithful followers. On the other hand, along with Mark and Matthew, Luke uses this title to refer to Jesus himself and his human activity, to his extraordinary authority and power, to his suffering and resurrection and to his Parusia and being judge. Our present consideration will follow these last four uses of "Son of Man", but the Son of Man's enthronement will be introduced at the appropriate place.

Human Aspects of the Son of Man

The title "Son of Man" differs from other titles since almost always (cf. Acts 7:55-56) Jesus, not others, so designates himself. At an historical level, M. Müller phrases it well when he writes, "'Son of Man' does not tell us who Jesus is, but Jesus tells us who the 'Son of Man' is([305])." Our investigation takes this reflection one step further since we are interested in the significance that Luke himself attributes to "Son of Man." In the last Lukan beatitude (Luke 6:22-23), Jesus blesses his audience when others hate, ostracize, revile and defame them on account of the Son of Man. In this "Q" passage only Luke has "on account of the Son of Man"; Matthew (5:11) has "on account of me([306])." Most scholars hold that Luke has the original reading, which Matthew has replaced with "me". Of interest to us is the fact that the two expressions are interchangeable. Jesus likewise identifies himself as the Son of Man when he informs a possible disciple that he has nowhere to lay his head (Luke 9:58), though we know that he spent some nights on the Mount of Olives (21:37). Implicitly, any of Jesus' disciples has to be ready to share this human condition([307]) .

---

[305] Der Ausdruck "Menschensohn," 258: "Zugespitzt ausgedrückt kann man es so formulieren, daß nicht der Ausdruck 'Menschensohn' uns erzählt, wer Jesus ist, sondern daß Jesus uns erzählt, wer der 'Menschensohn' ist."

[306] Surely, according to Luke, Jesus uses "Son of Man" to refer to himself; Rigaux, Témoignage, 164, holds that Luke has the more primitive tradition and that Matthew has changed "Son of Man" to "me" here as he also does in Mt 10:32. See also Tuckett, "The Son of Man in Q," 204. For the opposite opinion, confer Lindars, Jesus Son of Man, 134-136.

[307] Hare, The Son of Man Tradition, 60.

Some passages speak of Jesus' normal human experiences. In Luke 7:34 (cf. vv. 31-35) Jesus names himself Son of Man and grants that he eats and drinks like a normal human being; however, this behavior impresses the people no more than did John's not eating bread or drinking wine. These opponents show no consistency in their response and so reveal themselves as basically fickle. Nonetheless, wisdom's children reveal who she is. These children are probably those who have responded appropriately to John the Baptist and Jesus (cf. 7:29)[308]. As noted, in 9:58 Jesus speaks of the hardship the Son of Man must confront.

Superhuman Powers Are Attributed to the Son of Man
Those who are persecuted because of the Son of Man are blessed and should rejoice and skip for joy, for they can be compared to the prophets and have a great reward in heaven (Luke 6:23)[309]. God rewards those who suffer for their belief in the Son of Man who somehow functions as a cause of their receiving a heavenly reward.

We first encounter "Son of Man" in the healing of the paralytic (Luke 5:17-26). Prior to so identifying himself (v. 24), Jesus told the paralytic that his sins are forgiven, and the subsequent dialogue between the scribes and the Pharisees reveals that they view the forgiving of sins as a divine prerogative and that any human being who claims such authority blasphemes. In response to these doubts, Jesus asks, "Which is easier to say, 'Your sins are forgiven you,' or to say 'Get up and walk?'"[310]. He then gives the purpose of the miracle he is about to perform, "In any case, to make it clear to you that the Son of Man has authority on earth to forgive sins" and instructs the paralytic "I say to you, get up! Take your mat with you, and return to your house" (vv. 23-24). Thus, the emphasis is on the purpose of the miracle; and although we find in Luke 5:17-26 what appear to be the traces of two earlier stories, a dispute and a miracle,

---

308 Bock, *Luke 1:1 – 9:50*, 684-685; Nolland, *Luke 1 – 9:20*, 346-347 and Schweizer, *The Good News according to Luke*, 136-137. Fitzmyer, *The Gospel According to Luke I – IX*, 681, includes among the children both John the Baptist and Jesus.

309 Lenski, *St. Luke's Gospel*, 353, reflects on the nature of this reward.

310 Plummer, *St. Luke*, 155, observes, "It is easier to say, 'Thy sins are forgiven,' because no one can prove that they are not forgiven. But the claim to heal with a word can be easily and quickly tested."

the emphasis is presently on Jesus' words in vv. 23-24. Scholars are not agreed on the literary form of the story, but the most reasonable interpretation appears to be a pronouncement story[311], that is, the emphasis falls on Jesus' words in v. 23 (cf. 24). The miracle confirms Jesus' claim to be able to forgive sins; since this is so, he is surely not blaspheming. The context of 5:17-26 hints at Jesus' divinity, but the pericope does not directly address the question.

"Forgiveness of sins" is a Lukan expression for salvation, and so this is an appropriate place to consider the last verse of the story of Zacchaeus, "The Son of Man has come to search out and save what is lost" (Luke 19:10; cf. 15:32). Luke ends this story (vv. 1-10), unique to himself, with a summary statement of Jesus' whole ministry; and we have a quest story[312]. The reader has not been completely prepared for this statement, for the story is about someone who seeks to see Jesus but who is actually first seen by Jesus. In fact, Zacchaeus is sought and saved by the Son of Man who seeks the lost (cf. 15:4.6.8-9.24.32) and who previously observes about Zacchaeus, "Today salvation has come to this house, for this is what it means to be a son of Abraham." The Son of Man saves; but in this story Luke also portrays the Son of Man as actively seeking the lost who ironically may well see themselves as the ones doing the seeking.

Luke 6:1-5 concludes with the words, "The Son of Man is Lord of the Sabbath"; and so we have a pronouncement story of the controversy dialogue kind[313] rather than a dispute story. This statement flows from Jesus' defense of his apostles' doing what was not permitted on the Sabbath. Jesus defends their actions by pointing out that, when David and his men were hungry, David entered the temple and ate the bread of the Presence and gave some to his companions, even though it was only lawful for the priests to eat this bread. The suggested comparison between him and his disciples and David and his men is audacious[314], but Luke has already established that Jesus will inherit the throne of David (cf. 1:32-33; cf. v.

---

[311] Fitzmyer, *The Gospel According to Luke I–IX*, 578.

[312] O'Toole, "The Literary Form of Luke 19:1-10," 107-116.

[313] Nolland, *Luke 1 – 9:20*, 253.

[314] Of course, in the passage Jesus himself does not violate the Sabbath and, in this, differs from David.

69; 2:11). Jesus, who indirectly identifies himself as the Son of Man, claims that he has authority to interpret what can be done on the Sabbath. This claim proves all the stronger since both Luke and Matthew have dropped Mk 2:27, "Then he said, 'The Sabbath was made for man, not man for the Sabbath'"; and thus the pronouncement is a more forceful expression of Jesus' own superior authority([315]). For Jesus' audience this had to be a fantastic claim since he placed himself in opposition to the Jewish teachings of the time and claimed more authority in interpreting the Sabbath regulations than did anyone else. This claim will be discussed in our consideration of Jesus as "Lord."

The Son of Man Must Suffer
Exactly how the title "Son of Man" became associated with suffering is not easily determined. Our earlier considerations of Jesus as prophet and Servant of Yahweh are the most likely sources of this influence; and Jesus' actual experiences along with the intermingling of the meanings of the various titles very likely led to this association. Included in Jesus' normal human experiences are the suffering and rejection he as Son of Man is to endure. We have already seen that Jesus was rejected even though he ate and drank like any other human being (Luke 7:32-34), but "Son of Man" is also the designation of Jesus in the passion predictions. When Peter identifies Jesus as "The Christ ('The Messiah') of God," Jesus instructs the disciples to tell no one and explains, "The Son of Man must first endure many sufferings, be rejected by the elders, the high priests and the scribes, and be put to death, and then be raised up on the third day" (9:22). The "must" (δεῖ) reveals that in God's providence, his Messiah is to suffer([316]); and so Jesus, who is both the Messiah of God and the Son of Man has to suffer. On the other hand, the statement about Jesus' coming resurrection was traditional Pharisaic doctrine (cf. 20:27-40; Acts 23:6-8; 24:15.21; 26:4-8), although for them apparently the resurrection did not occur immediately after one's death (cf. Luke 20:33). Unique to Luke and a close parallel to Luke 9:22 are 17:24-25; although in this latter passage no mention is made of the resurrection, it does appear in "The Coming of the

---

[315] Lagrange, *Évangile selon Saint Luc*, 176.

[316] Prete, *L'Opera di Luca*, 246, n. 9, writes of the strong Christological import of δεῖ in Luke; cf. Luke 2:49; 4:43; 9:22; 13:33; 17:25; 19:5; 22:37; 24:7.26.44.

Kingdom" (vv. 20-37). According to vv. 24-25, Jesus predicts that the Son of Man must first suffer much and be rejected "by this generation" before his day comes; and Tödt points out the uniqueness of Luke's here joining together this suffering with the Parousia which joining occurs nowhere else([317]).

We find this reference to the suffering of the Son of Man repeated in Luke 9:44, but Luke makes no reference to the resurrection. He has placed 9:44 shortly after the voice from heaven instructs Peter, James and John, "hear him" (v. 35; cf. Acts 3:22-23; Dt 18:15-19) and introduced v. 44 with the words, unique to him, "Pay close attention to what I tell you . . . ." Thus, the Lucan emphasis in the verse falls on suffering.

In the third passion prediction (Luke 18:31-34; cf. Is 50:6), Luke again speaks of the suffering of the Son of Man but now again of his resurrection. True, Luke does not take over Mark's words "He began to tell them what was going to happen to him" (10:32); but he adds, "So that all that was written by the prophets concerning the Son of Man may be accomplished" (Luke 18:31). Unique to Luke, too, is v. 34 the threefold statement of the disciples not perceiving what was being said; the majestic passive, "was hidden from them," demonstrates that their lack of awareness was due to divine providence. Only Luke has introduced into the Last Supper scene itself an additional prediction of the Son of Man's passion, "The Son of Man is following out his appointed course, but woe to that man by whom he is betrayed" (22:22; cf. Mk 14:21; Mt 26:24)([318]). In another passage unique to Luke, the two men at the tomb remind the women that these passion predictions have been fulfilled, for they ask them why they are seeking the living among the dead. They proclaim Jesus' resurrection and recall Jesus' words in Galilee, "That the Son of Man must be delivered into the hands of sinful men, and be crucified, and on the third

---

[317] *The Son of Man in the Synoptic Tradition*, 107.

[318] Luke has inserted considerable information about Jesus' suffering into his Last Supper scene. Only he writes of Jesus' desire to eat this Passover with his apostles before he suffers (Luke 22:15), inserts into the traditional material the words about Jesus' body, "Given for you" (v. 19) and "You are the ones who have stood loyally by me in my temptations" (v. 28), expands on Peter's protest, "Lord at your side I am prepared to face imprisonment and death itself" (v. 33) and contends that now the apostles will need a wallet and bag and should even buy a sword since the scripture must be fulfilled about him, "He was counted among the wicked" (v. 37; cf. vv. 35-38).

day rise again" (Luke 24:7). The women do remember and return from the tomb and announce all these things to the Eleven and the others (v. 8); the wording of this latter verse suggests that the statement in v. 7 has become a summary of the gospel message (cf. Acts 3:13-15; 7:52; 13:27-30; 17:3; 1 Cor 15:3-4).

The Son of Man Is Enthroned

"Jesus before the Council" (Luke 22:67-71) occurs during the passion, but what Jesus predicts about the Son of Man relates to his enthronement reported in Acts 2:32-36 (7:55-56; cf. Luke 20:42-43). In the former passage Luke has changed details of Mark's presentation (14:55-65) which could have had a negative effect on the portrayal of Jesus, e.g., the high priest does not directly address Jesus nor tear his garments, Jesus does not blaspheme rather his opponents do (Luke 22:65), nor are there false witnesses or an explicit condemnation or mistreatment or mockery of Jesus. Moreover, Luke has separated the first question, "If you are the Christ, tell us" (22:67), from the second, "Are you then the Son of God" (22:70), and inserted between them Jesus' prediction in v. 69, "But from this time on the Son of Man will be seated at the right hand of the power of God." This prophetic prediction calls for several observations. It refers to the future, and the Son of Man is viewed as a heavenly individual. His sitting at the right hand of the power of God, the position usually reserved for the eldest son of the king, implies that he is the Son of God; at least, that is how the Sanhedrin understands it. Thus they ask their second question. Jesus' prediction likewise develops the first concern of the Sanhedrin about his being the Christ because, as noted, "sitting at the right hand," relates to being the son of the king and so to kingly rule. Naturally, "king" and cognate expressions belong to the word-pattern of Christ; moreover, the mention of "power" also looks to kingdom since in v. 69 Luke is citing Dan 7:13 and the next verse reads, "His power is an everlasting power that shall not be taken away, his kingship shall not be destroyed" (v. 14). However, what is of particular interest to us is that Luke has dropped Mark's "And coming with the clouds of heaven" (14:62; cf. Luke 21:27; Dan 7:13) and in its place inserted only "of God." This omission and addition change the meaning of the verse; Luke 22:69 no longer refers to Jesus' Parusia but to his enthronement([319]).

Stephen's vision in Acts 7:55-56 (cf. 2:33-36) is similar to the thought of Luke 22:69 and is the only place in the whole NT where "Son of Man" appears on the lips of someone other than Jesus. As in Luke 22:69([320]), the context is heavenly; and Jesus, identified as the Son of Man, stands at God's right hand; but why is he *standing*([321])? Normally he would be sitting. Surely, we are not dealing with the Parousia; most probably the standing relates to Stephen's situation and to his subsequent prayer. The Son of Man wants to fulfill his promise in Luke 12:8 to acknowledge before the angels of God those who acknowledge the Son of Man before humankind. Therefore, the Son of Man is in heaven at God's right hand and favorably disposed to Stephen in his moment of crisis.

The Son of Man and the Parousia and Judgment

Although "He who is to come" (Luke 7:19-20) may well refer to Jesus as Messiah (19:38; cf. 13:35), Luke is willing to predicate "coming" of the Son of Man (9:26; 12:40; 18:8; 21:27; cf. 19:10). Near the end of 7:18-35 Jesus contrasts himself with John the Baptist and says, "the Son of Man has come eating and drinking . . ." (v. 34). Moreover, in the closest parallel to "He who is to come," 3:15-17, in v. 17 we find judgment terminology, which typically relates to the Son of Man (9:26; 12:8-9; 21:36).

Luke associates "Son of Man" with Jesus' second coming and the final judgment. Luke 9:26 (cf. 13:23-30) reads, "If a man is ashamed of

---

[319] Tödt, *The Son of Man in the Synoptic Tradition*, 102-103; Schweizer, *The Good News according to Luke*, 348, writes of Jesus' exaltation.

[320] For a listing of the similarities and differences between Acts 7:56 and Luke 22:69, see Sabbe, "Acts 7,56," 260-267; but in my opinion Luke 22:69 is more than a messianic proclamation.

[321] Lindars, *Jesus Son of Man*, 139-144. On the other hand, Sabbe, "Acts 7,56," 267-279, reviews the various interpretations offered of "standing" and concludes that it implies no new significance different than that found in Luke 22:69. Colpe, ὁ υἱὸς τοῦ ἀνθρώπου, 462-463, suggests various reasons why the Son of Man is standing. Lampe, "The Lukan Portrait of Jesus," 172, observes, ". . . whereas in Acts vii 13ff., where especially in the LXX version with its addition of καὶ οἱ παρεστηκότες παρῆσαν αὐτῷ, the suggestion is that the Son of Man stands before the Ancient of Days." See also Focant, "Du Fils de L'Homme," 575-576 and Polhill, *Acts*, 207-208.

me and my doctrine, the Son of Man will be ashamed of him when he comes in his glory and that of his Father and his holy angels" and makes clear reference to Jesus' Parusia and the final judgment; for elsewhere Luke uses "glory" of Jesus' resurrection (24:26; cf. Acts 3:13) and of God at whose right hand the risen Jesus stands (Acts 7:55-56). So we are challenged not to deny Jesus and his message; for at the Parusia our present actions will determine the stance of the Son of Man toward us. This reflection on the judgment is repeated in 12:8-9([322]), "I tell you, whoever acknowledges me before men—the Son of Man will acknowledge before the angels of God. But the man who has disowns me in the presence of men will be disowned in the presence of the angels of God." We have first a promise and then a threat. There is likewise Hebrew parallelism since the ideas of the first verse are repeated in the second, although stated negatively. However, Luke has complicated the situation a bit with v. 10, "Anyone who speaks a word against the Son of Man will be forgiven, but whoever blasphemes the Holy Spirit will never be forgiven." At first hearing, v. 10 seems opposed to the idea in v. 9; but it does speak of a "word" and not of a more general denial. Besides, the references in vv. 8-9 are to the risen Jesus, designated as the Son of Man, who will judge in terms of people's response to him, but v. 10 looks to the earthly Jesus([323]) and underlines how important it is, after Jesus' resurrection, to be docile to the Spirit([324]). V. 10 would also introduce God's mercy, because "will be forgiven" (ἀφεθήσεται) is a majestic passive and so looks to divine forgiveness.

Luke 11:29-32 likewise envisions the last judgment; for, as we shall see below, "sign" (vv. 29-30; cf. v. 16) relates to this theme, and a number of the verbs in the pericope are in the future, "But no sign will be given it (this generation) . . . so will the Son of Man be (a sign) for the present generation . . . . The queen of the North will rise at the judgment .

---

[322] Higgins, "'Menschensohn' oder 'ich' in Q," 117-123, establishes the priority of Luke 12:8 and its reference to the Son of Man.

[323] Hare, *The Son of Man Tradition*, 63-64.

[324] The mention of blasphemy against the Spirit brings up a thought found in Mark 3:28-30; Mt 12:31-32; Heb 6:4-8; 10:26-31 and 1 John 5:16-17 that there is a sin which will not be forgiven. However, we cannot address that question here. For a discussion of the Lukan passage, see Fitzmyer, *The Gospel According to Luke X–XXIV*, 964.

. . and will condemn them . . . . At the judgment, the citizens of Nineveh will rise along with the present generation, and they will condemn it." Luke twice writes of the future judgment and condemnation. The exact referent for "this generation" spoken of in the pericope is not immediately obvious; but Jesus is present to it, and it fails to accept him. Most likely, "this generation" first refers to those who did not recognize Jesus during his earthly life, and then to the reader and any generation, which acts similarly. The surprising final verse of the parable of the widow and the judge, "But when the Son of Man comes, will he find any faith on the earth" (18:8) is likewise relevant here. This parable is unique to Luke; and the final verse appears just to be added on, although the parable encourages the reader to pray always and so the thought of 18:8 is similar to that of 21:36([325]). The mention of God's doing justice for his chosen ones who night and day call out to him definitely looks to a judgment; and we know that the Son of Man's coming is associated with the final judgment. Moreover, we have learned from Luke 9:26 and 12:8-9 that one's response in this world to Jesus and his word will determine Jesus' to him at the Parusia. An individual's faith will be what at the Parusia concerns the risen Jesus.

The first part of the parable about the watchful servants ends with the words, "Be on guard, therefore. The Son of Man will come when you least expect him" (Luke 12:40; cf. Mt 24:44). The thought is clear, and so the only solution is to be always prepared since the arrival of the Son of Man will be like that of a thief, unexpected (Luke 12:39). Moreover, vv. 35-38 and 41 are unique to Luke. Vv. 35-38 stress how prepared and watchful the servants of the master (vv. 36-37: τὸν κύριον) should be so as to be ready to open the door when he comes. If he so finds them, they are blessed; and "I tell you, he will put on an apron, seat them at table, and proceed to wait on them" (v. 37). These last words are an obvious hyperbole, for masters do not conduct themselves in this manner. Nonetheless, they make the point of how satisfied the master will be with the behavior of such servants. With v. 41, "Peter said, 'Do you intend this parable for us, Lord, or do you mean it for everyone,'" Luke now directs the instructions to church leaders. Until the Son of Man comes, church leaders are to be faithful and prudent and not mistreat their fellow servants or be

---

[325] Tödt, *The Son of Man in the Synoptic Tradition*, 97-98.

gluttons or drunks; if they do what they should, they will be rewarded, otherwise punished.

Luke has not only associated the second coming and judgment with the Son of Man but also "days" (Luke 17:22.26) or "day" (vv. 24?, 30-31). With "days" Luke lets his reader know that a period of time is involved, the last day of which will be the Parusia. Luke 17:20-37 (cf. 14:15-24)([326]), "The Coming of the Kingdom," should be considered a unit([327]), although one might want to separate vv. 20-21 from 22-37 since the former verses are addressed to the Pharisees. However, there is no change of place between vv. 21 and 22; and the Pharisees continue to be a part of Jesus' audience. Also, vv. 20-21 and vv. 22-37 both contain questions about a future event. In v. 21 we find, "They will not say, 'Look here it is' or 'There it is'" and in v. 23, "And there will be those who will say to you, 'Look there he is' or 'Look, here he is.'" Vv. 22-37 also contain four mentions of the Son of Man (vv. 22, 24, 26, 30); and much of the pericope is unique to Luke (cf. vv. 20-22, 25, 28-29, 32-34). The rest is a combination of material taken from Mark and "Q." By means of vv. 20-21 Luke in the later verses relates the kingdom of God to the Son of Man (cf. 22:69; Acts 7:55-56). Jesus in Luke 17:23 tells the disciples that, when they will want to see one of the days of the Son of Man, they will not see it. Instead, they will get conflicting reports to which they should pay no attention. The "for" of v. 24 ("For just as lightning flashes and lights up the sky from one side to the other, so will the Son of Man be ([in his day])", demonstrates that this verse explains Jesus' statement in v. 23 and clarifies that the day of the Son of Man will be as sudden and unexpected, yet as obvious as the lightening in the sky. This interpretation is confirmed by Jesus' answer to the question of the disciples, "Where, Lord", "Wherever the carcass is, there will the vultures gather" (v. 37). Vultures leave little doubt about where the carcass is. The days of the Son of Man will be like those of Noah or of Lot and occur in the midst of people's normal activity, yet in a surprising manner. There will be a judgment, for "One will be taken and the other left" (vv. 34-35), but first the Son of Man must suffer. The proper response to the day of the Son of Man is to give oneself

---

[326] For a perceptive analysis of this pericope, see Schnackenburg, "Der eschatologische Abschnitt Lk 17,20-37," 213-234.

[327] See Rigaux, *Témoignage*, 226-227.

totally to him (v. 33; cf. 9:24) and not to be concerned about one's personal safety or possessions.

Luke 21:25-36 constitutes a parallel to 17:20-37, but there are differences. One can justify considering 21:25-36 as three separate pericopes, vv. 25-28, "the coming of the Son of Man," vv. 29-33, "the lesson of the fig tree," and vv. 34-36, "the exhortation to watch." However, both v. 27 and v. 36 speak of the Son of Man. Moreover, the ideas in vv. 25-36 are related. For the statements in vv. 31 ("When you see these things happening"), v. 32 ("Until all these things take place") and v. 36 ("Pray constantly for the strength to escape all these things that are is going to happen") are definite references to v. 25 ("There will be signs in . . . ."), v. 26b ("Men will die of fright in anticipation of what is coming upon the earth") and v. 28 ("When these things begin to happen"). These latter two verses with their apocalyptic imagery set the scene, and v. 26a reports the human fear and foreboding, which characterize such scenes. In v. 27, "After that, men will see the Son of Man coming in a cloud with great power and glory," Luke cites from Dan 7:13-14. In Luke 21:25-36 no mention is made of the day of the Son of Man, although "that day" does appear in v. 34; but surely that is what Luke is describing. V. 31 identifies the event as the nearness of the kingdom of God, and only Luke of the Synoptics introduces this concept here and in 17:21-22. Moreover, the reference in 21:27 to the coming of the Son of Man, joined with the nearness of the kingdom (v. 31), relates well with Jesus' prediction in 22:69 and realized in Acts 2:32-36. The cloud in Luke 21:27 represents a heavenly aspect, and "much glory" looks to Jesus' own resurrection (24:26; cf. Acts 3:13) and to God's own existence (cf. Luke 9:26; Acts 7:55). In contrast to Luke 17:20-37 and unique to Luke is the "Exhortation to Watch" (21:34-36) against dissipation, drunkenness and worldly concerns lest that day entrap them. This alertness is to be accompanied by prayer so that they may be able to stand before the Son of Man. The phrase, "To stand before the Son of Man," portrays him as a judge; but the nuance is positive since one can escape the things destined to happen, and v. 28 speaks of the nearness of redemption and v. 31 of the kingdom of God.

Luke 21:25-36, then, forms a unit and speaks of the nearness of the kingdom and of the Son of Man who with power and glory comes on the cloud. No clear time reference is given, but fearful and foreboding cosmic events will mark the event. Luke himself inserts the instructions to avoid unacceptable behavior and to watch and pray so as to escape these fearful events and to stand confidently before the Son of Man.

Conclusion

For Luke, "Son of Man" can designate Jesus himself and his human activity, but the Son of Man also has extraordinary powers, for he can forgive sins and is lord of the Sabbath. He came to seek and save the lost. Nonetheless, in God's providence, the Son of Man will be rejected, handed over, suffer and be killed; yet raised on the third day. The Son of Man will be enthroned and sit at the right hand of God and so has an intimate relationship with him. The Sanhedrin views Jesus' prophecy in Luke 22:69 as a claim to be Son of God. Thus, "Son of Man" can be associated with "Christ" ("King") and "Son of God." The Son of Man will come a second time, in power and glory, and be judge. This day of the Lord or nearness of the kingdom is described apocalyptically and will come suddenly and unpredictably. Nonetheless, those who have been faithful to the Son of Man will find in him a defender and be able confidently to appear before him.

Luke has followed Mark and "Q" in his presentation of the "Son of Man." However, as is verified by viewing the passages unique to him([328]), Luke has underlined the need for faith in the Son of Man, expanded on the aspect of suffering, introduced his enthronement and related the Son of Man's second coming to the nearness of the kingdom. Luke has likewise developed the Son of Man's saving mission, second coming, for which his faithful followers are to watch in prayer, and his protective witness on their behalf.

---

[328] G. Schneider, "Der Menschensohn," 281-282. Colpe, ὁ υἱὸς τοῦ ἀνθρώπου, 459, overstates the situation when he writes, "One cannot find any specifically Lucan Son of Man Christology in his Gospel."

CHAPTER SEVEN
Jesus the Son (of God)([329])

We will first briefly address two problematic passages, Luke 4:41 (cf. Mk 1:34; Mt 8:16) and Acts 9:19b-22, which could leave the reader with the impression that for Luke "the Christ" and "Son of God" are synonyms. However, the context of neither of these passages provides us with enough information to decide the question. This chapter next considers those passages where Luke has been much clearer on the meaning he attributes to Jesus as the Son (of God) or an equivalent expression. Finally, we will treat a number of other passages where the meaning of Jesus as Son (of God) or as one who can address God as "his Father" is less clear but relevant to our discussion.

Luke 4:40-41: "You Are the Son of God . . . They Knew That He Was the Christ"
In Luke's Gospel no human being, on his or her own, identifies Jesus as Son of God, but the same is not true of "the Christ." In Luke 4:40-41, Jesus lays his hands on the sick and heals them, and demons come out of many of those cured and shout, "You are the Son of God." Luke, in an editorial note, then writes that Jesus rebukes them and does not let them speak, "because they knew he was 'the Christ'" ("the Messiah"). The cry of the demons that know the identity of Jesus actually sounds like a confessional statement. The passage is not surprising in that the demons get their cry out before Jesus acts to silence them. Luke wants his reader to hear their cry and, in explaining Jesus' order to be silent, adds another

---

[329] For the background of this title, confer M. de Jonge, "Messiah," 777-788; for general considerations of this topic in Luke-Acts, see Fitzmyer, *The Gospel According to Luke I–IX*, 205-208; George, *Études sur l'œuvre de Luc*, 215-236; Hahn, *The Titles of Jesus*, 279-333; Lövestam, *Son and Saviour*, 88-112; Rasco, "Jesús y el Espíritu", 322-334; Rigaux, *Témoigage*, 419-425; Schweizer, υἱός, 380-382; van Iersel, *"Der Sohn"*, 3-28.

designation of Jesus. So, Luke accepts the demons' identification of Jesus as "Son of God" in a context where he is freeing the sick from demons. Earlier in this same passage another demon exclaims (4:34), "Ha! What have you to do with us, Jesus of Nazareth? Have you come to destroy us? I know who you are—the Holy One of God." So in this programmatic passage, demons identify Jesus as both "the Holy One of God" and "Son of God." However, below we will see that these two designations of Jesus occur in 1:35, which is Luke's principle introduction to the mystery of Jesus' divinity. Nonetheless, it seems best to present the whole consideration about Luke's designation of Jesus as "Son of God" before we draw any conclusion about its meaning in 4:41.

Immediately after his conversion experience, Paul spends a few days with the disciples in Damascus; then according to Acts 9:20, he began to proclaim in the synagogues that Jesus was the Son of God. Two verses later and in the same pericope, we read, "Saul (Paul) for his part grew steadily more powerful, and reduced the Jewish community of Damascus to silence with his proofs that this Jesus was the Christ (the Messiah). After quite some time had passed, certain Jews conspired to kill Saul . . . ." (vv. 22-23). Often, Luke speaks of Jesus, as "the Christ," in terms of the fulfillment of the Sacred Scriptures, but the surest conclusion we can draw from these verses is that both titles can summarize the gospel message. So, Luke in Acts 9:19-23 could want us to take "Son of God" and "the Messiah" as synonyms; but we will see below that Luke uses both of these titles elsewhere in the same context but separates them and gives them different meanings. The present chapter should help us determine whether this is what Luke does in Acts 9:19-23, even if the order in which these two titles appear there is not the same as elsewhere. What is clear is that whatever "Son of God" and "the Messiah" meant about Jesus, such proclamations were unacceptable to certain Jews. Neither title can just mean someone who had a mission from God. Their meanings have to be more specific and of sufficient weight to explain the dangerous opposition of some Jews; but if these titles are summary statements of the Christian gospel message, Jewish opposition proves quite understandable.

Passages Where the Meaning of Jesus As the Son of God or Similar Expressions Is Clearer

<u>Luke 1:35</u>: Jesus—"<u>Will Be Called Son of God</u>"[330]
In a number of other passages (Luke 1:35; 9:35; 22:66-71; cf. 2:48-49; 10:21-22), Luke, by using the expression "Son of God," attributes to Jesus a unique and intimate relationship with God the Father. From the announcement of Jesus' birth 1:26-38, vv. 30-35 are of interest to us. The angel Gabriel assures Mary that she has found favor with God and continues, "Behold you will conceive in your womb and bear a son, and you shall name him Jesus. He will be great and will be called Son of the Most High, and the Lord God will give him the throne of David his father, and he will rule over the house of Jacob forever, and of his kingdom there will be no end" (Luke 1:31-33; cf. 2 Sm 7:11-16; 4QFlor 10-13). However, then Mary presents a difficulty to Gabriel, "How can this be, since I have no relations with a man" (v. 34); and Gabriel responds, "The Holy Spirit will come upon you and the power of the Most High will overshadow you; hence the holy offspring to be born will be called Son of God." The appropriate background for understanding the above passage is the LXX, i.e., Jewish. This is not to deny that the Judaism of the time had been significantly influenced by Hellenism[331], but rather to assert that anyone with a Jewish background would in any serious religious matter use Greek mythology about gods or stories of emperors to explain a salvific event only if such an explanation could be squared with how Jews thought about the divine.

The statement about Jesus' being David's son causes no difficulty. As we have seen, Davidic descent belongs to the theme of Jesus as "the Christ." The questions which face us are: what significance should we

---

330 Collins, "The *Son of God* Text from Qumran," 65-69, calls attention to 4Q246 which contains the following striking parallels to our present text, "will be great," "he will be called son of the Most High" (Luke 1:32) and "he will be called Son of God" (v. 35). The Qumran text also speaks of a kingdom, which will have no end (cf. Luke 1:33). Nonetheless, scholars are divided in their understanding of this text; and Collins concludes (82), "The Qumran text, however, provides a welcome illustration of the usage of the title ("Son of God") in the matrix from which Christianity emerged: the eschatological oriented Judaism of the early Roman empire."

331 For the Mediterranean background, see Talbert, *Reading Luke-Acts*, 65-90.

attribute to "great" and "Son of the Most High"; Mary's words, "How can this be since I do not know man," surely assert her virginity, but do they serve any other purpose; how are we to understand Luke 1:35; and, in summary fashion, in the announcement of Jesus' birth, does Luke write only of Jesus as "the Christ"([332]), or of Jesus as "the Christ" (vv. 32-33) and as "Son of God" (v. 35), which latter title is not identical with the former and expresses a much more intimate relationship with the Father([333])?

"He will be great" (Luke 1:32) reminds us of John the Baptist about whom the same phrase is used in 1:15; but there is a difference since according to the early chapters of Luke's Gospel (3:15-17; 7:18-28; cf. Acts 13:22-25), Jesus is definitely superior to John. The Samaritans say of Simon, "This man is the power of God which is called great" (Acts 8:10) and Artemis can be described as the great goddess (Acts 19:27-28.34-35)([334]). So, the attribute, "great," conveys Jesus' importance in God's plan; but it does not help us see if Luke in the annunciation passage wants to distinguish between Jesus as "Messiah" and as "Son of God."

A number of authors have claimed that "Son of God" (Luke 1:35) really is a repetition of "Son of the Most High" (v. 32). Obviously, it is not an exact repetition; but the authors who see in the annunciation only a designation of Jesus as Davidic Messiah are obliged to conclude to the identity of the two expressions. Luke likes repetition, but he does not seem to use it in v. 35. True, we indicated above that "Son of God" might be a synonym of Jesus as the Christ (4:41; cf. Acts 9:19b-22). However, this passage is yet to appear in the Gospel. Moreover, there are good reasons

---

[332] Although he expresses a certain openness, this is the position of Bock, *Luke 1:1 – 9:50*, 123-125 and *Proclamation from Prophecy and Pattern*, 61-69; the same is true of Nolland, *Luke 1 – 9:20*, 54-58, who observes (55), "No doubt we are meant to be left with a good measure of mystery concerning this child whose mode of origin is quite unprecedented." See also Bovon, *Luke 1*, 52 and Grundmann, *Das Evangelium nach Lukas*, 58-61. This seems also to be the understanding of Plummer, *St. Luke*, 24-25. On the other hand, Luke does supply us with information which guides our inter-pretation of what he says about Jesus.

[333] See Prete, *L'opera di Luca*, 129 and George, *Études sur l'œuvre de Luc*, 219-221.

[334] Bovon, *Luke 1*, 46, provides other examples.

to doubt that "Son of God" in Luke 1:35 only continues or repeats the identification of Jesus as Davidic Messiah.

Mary's request for an explanation in Luke 1:34, "How can this be, since I have no relations with a man" proves crucial for the correct interpretation of v. 35([335]). "This" has to look to Mary's conceiving a child since her question reveals that up to that very moment she remains a virgin, a point that Luke has already made in v. 27, "to a virgin betrothed to a man named Joseph"([336]). Surely, both "Son of the Most High" (v. 32) and "Son of God" (v. 35) are metaphors since God who is spirit does not function sexually, as does a human father; nonetheless, these two metaphors are not communicating the same idea. In v. 32, "Son of the Most High" stands in the same sentence as God's promise of the throne of David and so looks to Jesus as the Davidic Christ and to his future mission or assignment. Nothing in v. 32 leads us to connect "Son of the Most High" directly with the nature of Jesus' conception. On the other hand, Mary's question in v. 34 does direct us to interpret "Son of God" in v. 35 in terms of Jesus' conception and to conclude that God is Jesus' father([337]). About "Son of God," J.A. Fitzmyer has pointed out that "the full title is never found in the OT predicated directly of a future, expected Messiah"([338]); consequently, the title itself does not require that it be understood of Jesus as "the Christ." Indeed, in a Jewish context, would Mary's virginity have to do with establishing Jesus as the Christ (Messiah)? What we have in v. 35 is an insistence on God's fatherhood of

---

[335] Prete, *L'opera di Luca*, 163-166, cf. 125-129, 135-138, 140-141, 147-151, recognizes the importance of Luke 1:34 and provides an extensive discussion of this verse. See also Schweizer, *The Good News according to Luke*, 29.

[336] Luke records that Joseph was Jesus' supposed father (Luke 2:48-49; 3:23; cf. 1:27.34; 4:22). Is 7:14 (Mt 1:23; cf. vv. 18-22) could have been in whatever source Luke had for the annunciation, but this would not be easy to demonstrate.

[337] Brown, *The Birth of the Messiah*, 311-316. However, Brown is not totally clear on what Luke means by "Son of God." On p. 316 in n. 56, he concludes, "Luke is certainly using 'Son of God' in a proper sense in 1:35d, but he is not necessarily saying what Ignatius said twenty or thirty years later: 'Our God, Jesus Christ, was conceived of Mary' (Ephesians xviii 2; also vii 2)." See also Rossé, *Il vangelo di Luca*, 53-57, 63.

[338] Fitzmyer, *The Gospel According to Luke I–IX*, 206

Jesus in a manner that never appeared about the Christ or Messiah([339]). Other reasons support such an understanding.

Above we demonstrated that Luke 4:18 (cf. 3:22), "The Spirit of the Lord is upon me, because he has anointed me," reports the activity of the Spirit with Jesus, who is the Christ. However, the activity of the Spirit in that verse is quite different from what we find in 1:35 where the Holy Spirit will come upon Mary and the power of the Most High will overshadow her. Luke 1:35 (cf. Gn 1:2) has to do with Jesus' conception, with God's generative and creative activity in Mary([340]), not as in 4:18 with Jesus being a prophet, the Servant of Yahweh or the Christ or with his mission([341]). "The Holy Spirit will come upon you" and "The power of the Most High will overshadow you" are parallel expressions and communicate the same idea, the direct divine generative interaction with Mary for the conception of her offspring who will be called "Holy" and "Son of God"([342]).

"Holy" (Luke 1:35) designates someone or something related to God or set aside for divine service. Luke uses it most often of the Holy Spirit. At Jesus' presentation in the temple, we read "Every firstborn male shall be designated as holy to the Lord" (2:23); and "Holy" may have been an early Christological title (cf. Luke 4:34; Acts 3:14). Twice Jesus is called God's "holy servant" (Acts 4:27.30). Of particular interest to us is 1:49 (cf. 18:18-19), "holy is his name," used of God in the *Magnificat*; "holy" is an attribute of God. If our interpretation below of the activity of the Holy Spirit and of God's creative and generative power at Jesus' conception be accurate and Jesus in 1:35 is "Son of God" in an intimate and unique sense, "holy" is predicated of him in this same verse([343]), precisely because of who he is.

---

[339] Byrne, "Jesus the Messiah," 84-86, recognizes this difference but does not want to distinguish between "Messiah" and "Son of God."

[340] Radl, *Der Ursprung Jesu*, 344-346; (*pace*) Mainville, "Le messianisme de Jésus," 326-327.

[341] Kilgallen, "The Conception of Jesus (Luke 1,35)," 227, also insists on this distinction.

[342] See Brown, *The Birth of the Messiah*, 290, 313-315.

The Greek word for "overshadow" (ἐπισκιάζω) appears of the cloud of Presence, which in the OT "settled" over the tent of meeting (Ex 40:35)([344]), and of the cloud at the Transfiguration (Luke 9:34); in both passages it designates divine presence. To be sure, at the annunciation the Holy Spirit and the power of the Most High actualize the divine presence. Theories, which interpret "overshadow" as a sexual image, are misplaced in literature like the NT that depends so heavily on the sophisticated Jewish tradition of the nature of God. Other than the divine activity of the Spirit and the power of the Most High, the overshadowing of Mary's offspring could reinforce the meaning given to "Son of God" in 1:35; for the divine activity relates most directly to the conception of the offspring himself([345]).

It is common knowledge that Luke compares John the Baptist and Jesus in his Infancy Narrative, and a comparison of the identity and role of John the Baptist and of Jesus in their respective annunciation scenes proves instructive. John will be great before the Lord (Luke 1:15), but Jesus will be great and Son of the Most High (v. 32). John will prepare a people, but has a temporary role (v. 17); Jesus will rule the people and his kingdom will last forever (v. 33). John will be a prophet and from his mother's womb filled with the Holy Spirit (v. 15), but through the intercession of the Spirit and the overshadowing of the Most High Jesus is conceived Son of God (v. 35)([346]). Jesus exists because of the Holy Spirit. Furthermore, God miraculously overcame Elizabeth's barrenness to bring about John's conception; so we anticipate that God will act even more miraculously in Jesus' conception.

J.J. Kilgallen very well summarizes the data of Luke's annunciation story and its consequence when he insists that the fatherhood of God only becomes intelligible in the context of Mary's virginity, the lack of any human father for Jesus, and that Jesus' actual physical conception keeps both of these elements from being just symbolism. Together these three

---

[343] Laurentin, *Luc I–II*, 122.

[344] Lövestam, *Son and Saviour*, 93-94. Lagrange, *Évangile selon Saint Luc*, 34, calls attention to the parallel LXX passages, Ps 90:4; Nm 11:25; 1 Kgs 8:10; Is 6:4.

[345] Brown, *The Birth of the Messiah*, 327-328.

[346] L.T. Johnson, *The Gospel of Luke*, 38

elements and their effect on one another bring the message about Jesus in Luke 1:35 "into the mystery of the divine"([347]). Later Church history will explain in more theological and ontological terms this mystery of Jesus' divine sonship.

In Luke 1:26-38, the author first writes of Jesus as the descendent of David and so the Christ (vv. 32-33) and then as "Son of God" (v. 35), and Luke does this in at least two other passages (9:1-50 and 22:66-71). Before we begin our consideration of these two passages and of others in Luke-Acts that relate to Jesus as Son (of God), we need to note that 1:35 occurs in the introduction to these two volumes and so guides and alerts the reader to interpret correctly any later statements about Jesus as the Son (of God)([348]). We have already studied Luke 9:1-50 and 22:66-71 in association with other christological titles, so our present considerations will be brief and to the point.

Luke 9:35: Jesus—"My Chosen Son"
Elsewhere([349]), I have demonstrated that Luke 9:1-50 constitutes a unit and is so structured that the emphasis falls on the Transfiguration. It is only in the Transfiguration Story that a completely satisfactory answer is given to Herod's question about who Jesus is (v. 9). Up to the Transfiguration, the questions are arranged in step-parallelism and various answers given. Luke in ch. 9 actually presents three identifications of Jesus and moves from rumors, to the opinion of the crowds, to that of the disciples

---

[347] Kilgallen, "The Conception of Jesus (Luke 1,35)," 225-246, esp. 244-246. See also Voss, *Die Christologie*, 173-174 and Laurentin, *Luc I–II*, 73-79, 141, 146. Marshall, "Incarnational Christology," 15-16, concludes, "The evidence in the Synoptics not only fits an incarnational understanding of Jesus but positively cries out for it . . . . The recognition that Jesus was the Son of God was the starting-point for reflection which made use of Wisdom and Logos language." Hahn, *The Titles of Jesus*, 296-297, 305-307, can speak of the Spirit's "creative vital energy" (296) but wants to interpret "will be called Son of God" as an adoptionist formulation (297). This interpretation seems gratuitous.

[348] Kilgallen, "Jesus' First Trial," 411-415; see also his "The Conception of Jesus (Luke 1,35)," 236, 240-243.

[349] For a more thorough consideration of this question, see O'Toole, "Luke's Message in Luke 9:1-50."

(Peter) and finally to the voice from heaven([350]). In Luke 9:7b-8, the ordinary people identify Jesus with various prophets; and in v. 19 this identification is repeated. Then Luke uses step-parallelism and moves from this first designation to Peter's answer to Jesus' question about his identity, "The Christ (Messiah) of God" (v. 20)([351]). Peter's answer in part is acceptable since Jesus does not reject the identification but rather instructs the disciples to tell no one about it. However, Peter's identification of Jesus is not totally acceptable because a few verses later Luke, again with step-parallelism, feels the need to report the proclamation of the voice from the cloud about Jesus, "This is my chosen Son, listen to him" (v. 35), which parallels that of the baptism (3:22). The voice from heaven identifies Jesus as "my chosen Son" and instructs the three apostles to "listen to him" (cf. Acts 3:22), which looks to the response to Jesus' message. As in the Infancy Narrative, in Luke 9:34 we again find "overshadow," "a cloud came and cast a shadow over them," which confirms the divine presence and specifies whose voice comes from the cloud. So, God's answer to the Lucan Herod's question about Jesus' identity would be that he is "my son." Luke first reports that some think Jesus is a prophet, then Peter identifies him as the Christ of God, and finally the voice from the cloud, as "My Son"; and the dignity of the persons using these titles grows, from the ordinary people, to Peter, to the voice from the cloud (God). The disciples who know Jesus better than the ordinary people view Jesus as "the Christ (Messiah) of God," but the one who knows him best, God, calls him, "My Son." The titles are not identical but rather are reported in a climactic arrangement; and the last title, its visionary context and the one revealing it communicate more about Jesus than do "prophet" or even "the Christ of God." The statement of the voice from heaven about Jesus, is at a more exalted level, both in terms of the knowledge of the one speaking and of the significance of the title proclaimed. The most reasonable inference is that Luke wants "This is my Son" understood much as we determined for "Son of God" in 1:35. According to R.E. Brown, the descent of the Holy Spirit and the overshadowing by the divine presence are

---

[350] Coleridge, *The Birth of the Lukan Narrative*, 229, n. 1, observes that in the OT God often appears on stage and speaks a good deal; however, in later narrative texts this is not the case. "The closest he comes to it is in cases such as the baptism and transfiguration scenes in the Third Gospel where the unnamed voice from heaven sounds.

[351] By dropping Mark 6:45 – 8:26, Luke has placed 9:7-9 quite close to vv. 18a-20.

alternative ways of establishing and confirming Jesus' sonship. At the Transfiguration, the overshadowing of the cloud and the voice from heaven reveal the Christological mystery of divine sonship to the reader([352]).

Luke 22:66-71: Jesus before the Sanhedrin([353])
There are clear parallels between Luke 9:1-50 and Jesus' passion, e.g., the presence of Herod Antipas and the two passion predictions (vv. 21-22, 43b-45)([354]); but of particular interest to our present investigation is the use of both "Christ (Messiah)" and "Son of God" in the scene before the Sanhedrin (Luke 22:66-71). After he is arrested, mocked and mistreated, the next day Jesus appears before this assembly of the elders of the people, both chief priests and scribes. Luke has dropped from the scene anything, which might reflect negatively on Jesus, and he alone of the Synoptics separates the first question of the Sanhedrin, "If you are the Christ (Messiah), tell us" (v. 67) from their second question, "Are you, then, the Son of God?" (v. 70). This separation allows Luke to differentiate between the two titles([355]) and to highlight "Son of God" in relationship to "the Christ." The phrasing of the Council's first question parallels Peter's confession of Jesus as the Christ of God (9:20; cf. 1:32-33); and their question about Jesus as the Son of God, the affirmation of the voice from the cloud (9:35; cf. 1:35). Between these two questions, Luke inserts Jesus' first reply, "If I tell you, you will not believe; and if I question you, you will not respond" (vv. 67b-68) and his prediction, "But from this time on the Son of Man will be seated at the right hand of the power of God" (v. 69). The following aspects of Luke 22:66-71 bear on our present argument. The occasion is a solemn one: Jesus encounters the highest Jewish religious authority of the time; yet it is also an ironical one since Jesus is really the person whom they doubt him to be. Jesus' words about the Son of Man

---

[352] Brown, *The Birth of the Messiah*, 315; see also Byrne, "Jesus the Messiah," 88.

[353] Matera, "Jesus before the ΠΡΕΣΒΥΤΕΡΙΟΝ," 517-533 argues convincingly that Luke's version of this event does not preserve an independent tradition.

[354] For a more complete listing, see O'Toole, "Luke's Message in Luke 9:1-50," 84-87 and Talbert, "The Lukan Presentation," 492-497.

[355] See Kilgallen, "Jesus' First Trial," 401-403, and Tödt, *The Son of Man in the Synoptic Tradition*, 103.

give the background for the Council's second question. He predicts that the Son of Man (Dn 7:13), that is he himself, will be seated at the right hand of the power of God (Ps 109:1LXX; cf. Acts 2:32-36; 7:55-56). As noted above, Luke has changed Mark's phrasing so that the prediction now refers to Jesus' enthronement([356]). Luke explains "the divine sonship along the lines of an elevation to the right hand of God which is no longer apocalyptically limited and shaped by the *parousia*"([357]). Obviously, the prediction refers to the future; and the Son of Man is viewed as a heavenly being. His position at God's right hand implies that he is God's own son; and this is how the Sanhedrin understands it and so places its second question, "Are you, then, the Son of God?" They take Jesus' answer to this question, "You say that I am," as affirmative; for they conclude that they have no further need of witnesses because they heard it from his own lips([358]).

We need to pause for a moment here and consider Luke's portrayal of the thinking of the Sanhedrin. We know that he has omitted any charge against Jesus of blasphemy since that would put Jesus in a bad light. According to Lv 24:14-16.23; Ex 22:27LXX and 1 Kgs 21:10.13, anyone who curses or reviles God or a prince of the people or blasphemes God's name is guilty of blasphemy and should be put to death. From Luke 5:21 we learned that any human claim to forgive sin is blasphemy; but with a miracle and with the implication that on earth God gives the Son of Man this authority, Jesus skirts that charge. It is true that according to Mk 14:61-64 and Mt 26:63-66 Jesus is accused of blasphemy; but since they place "the Christ," "the Son of God" and Jesus' citations of Dn 7:13 and Ps 109:1LXX altogether, the reader cannot determine with what he should associate the charge. By arranging the scene as he did, Luke has quite clearly associated the Sanhedrin's negative response to Jesus with what

---

[356] Tödt, *The Son of Man in the Synoptic Tradition*, 102-103.

[357] Schweizer, υἱός, 381.

[358] Plummer, *St. Luke*, 519; Lagrange, *Évangile selon Saint Luc*, 573-574; Marshall, *The Gospel of Luke*, 850-851; Matera, "Jesus before the ΠΡΕΣΒΥΤΕΡΙΟΝ," 529-530; Bock, "The Debate over Jesus' Blasphemy," 190-191, points out that this Son of Man remark was very direct and claimed for Jesus an approach to God, allowed to no other human being. Such a remark would be particularly offensive to the Jewish religious authorities, *pace* Byrne, "Jesus as Messiah," 91.

they interpret as his positive response to their question in Luke 22:70, "Are you then the Son of God?". This claim finds support in the fact that at the time of Jesus there is no clear evidence that one could be condemned for claiming to be the Christ. In v. 71 the members of the Sanhedrin understand Jesus to be claiming a radical, intimate relationship with God([359]). The most helpful parallel to 22:70 is Jn 10:34 (cf. vv. 31-39; 5:18), "The Jews answered him, 'We are not stoning you for a good work but for blasphemy. You, a man, are making yourself God.'" So, Luke in the scene before the Council portrays Jesus as not directly answering the first question about whether he is the Christ (the Messiah) but then affirming that he is Son of God; and in the context this latter title communicates the mystery of Jesus' divinity. The last verse of the pericope is forcefully ironical since the members of the Sanhedrin are quite correct: they have no further need of testimony. As J. Heil observes([360]), Jesus' witness to who he is suffices. All one need do is believe, but this truth is perceived only by Luke's reader.

Luke 2:49: "My Father"([361])
Jesus speaks of God as "my father" in Luke 2:49; 22:29; 24:49 (cf. 10:22). Jesus at the age of twelve accompanies his parents up to the temple for the feast of the Passover. After the celebration, Mary and Joseph begin the return home but learn that Jesus is not in the group of pilgrims. They return to Jerusalem and find him in the temple brilliantly interacting with the teachers; Mary asks why he has treated them like that because she and his father were quite anxious and searching for him. Jesus replies, "Why were you looking for me? Did you not know that I must be in my Father's

---

[359] Lövestam, *Son and Saviour*, 109, writes of "a deep significance" of the affirmation. See also George, *Études sur l'œuvre de Luc*, 227 and Rossé, *Il vangelo di Luca*, 932-934. For the Old Testament background of Luke 22:69 and the conclusion that Jesus is Son in a fuller than messianic sense, see also Bock, *Proclamation from Prophecy*, 139-143.

[360] Heil, "Luke 22:66-71," 282-283.

[361] For a consideration of Jesus' own use of "Father" in the Synoptics, see van Iersel, "*Der Sohn*," 93-116. Van Iersel concludes that for Jesus, the title did not express a theological teaching but a deeply lived reality. Jesus knew that his whole being was related to the Father.

house?" "I must" tells us that what is happening is in accord with God's will. In contrast to Mary's question, Jesus distinguishes between Joseph and his true Father in whose house or in whose affairs Jesus must be occupied. This reference to Jesus' true father leads us back to the annunciation of Jesus' birth, where Luke stresses Mary's virginity and the Angel Gabriel affirms that due to the intervention of the Holy Spirit and to the power of the Most High her child will be called, "Son of God([362])." Luke 2:49 repeats that message of the intimacy and unique oneness which exists between Jesus and God([363]). On the other hand, whether ἐν τοῖς τοῦ πατρός μου be translated as "in my Father's house," "with my Father," "with my Father's associates" or "about my Father's affairs," it includes Jesus' mission. Such an interpretation is supported by the amazing manner in which Jesus listened to the teachers and asked them questions, for the story is enclosed within an inclusion which reports Jesus' wisdom and his later ministry of teaching([364]). Consequently, the parallels between Luke 2:47-49 and 1:35 and of the former passage with Jesus' many wise explanations of the scriptures justify our seeing in 2:49 the same thought as that of 1:35, a radical and intimate relationship between Jesus and the Father ([365]), and a mission of Jesus, the Father's Son, as the wise teacher.

---

[362] George, *Études sur l'œuvre de Luc*, 229; Rossé, *Il vangelo di Luca*, 109.

[363] Fitzmyer (*The Gospel According to Luke I–IX*, 444) phrases it, "his relation to his heavenly Father transcends all natural family ties." See also Brown, *The Birth of the Messiah*, 483, 492; Laurentin, *Luc I–II*, 141-146 and Plummer, *St. Luke*, 77-78.

[364] Talbert, *Reading Luke*, 36-37, also notes the importance of Luke 24 in which the risen Christ explains the scriptures for the disciples. Talbert cites passages in which Jesus wisely interprets the scriptures, Luke 4:1-13.16-21; 7:26-27; 10:25-28; 20:17-18.37-38.41-44; 24:25-27.32.44-47. See also H.J. de Jonge, "Sonship, Wisdom, Infancy," 317-354, and Kilgallen, "Luke 2:41-50: Foreshadowing of Jesus, Teacher." L. T. Johnson, *Gospel of Luke*, 61-62, sees in Luke 2:41-52 an anticipation of the Emmaus story and points to parallels between the former passage and 24:1-8, "after three days" (2:46; 24:7) and "remember his words" (2:51; 24:8; cf. 2:19).

[365] Bock, *Luke 1:1 – 9:50*, 271;

Luke 10:22: "No One Knows . . . Who the Father Is except the Son"[366]
Our author has taken over the tradition in Luke 10:21-22 (cf. vv. 23-24) and
so accepts it as part of his Gospel. In fact, Jesus' prayer of thanksgiving in
Luke 10:21-22 (cf. Mt 11:25-27) have been designated "a meteorite fallen
from the Johannine sky"[367]. The verse of greatest interest to us, Luke 10:22,
reads, "All things have been handed over to me by my Father. No one knows
who the Son is except the Father, and who the Father is except the Son and
anyone to whom the Son wishes to reveal him." Vv. 21-22 treat Jesus' filial
relationship with the Father; for "Father" occurs five times, and "Son" is used
absolutely three times. V. 22 presents a strict parallel between "No one knows
who the Son is except the Father" and "who the Father is except the Son."
This total mutual knowledge of each other implies the deepest possible
intimacy and association[368]. Other assertions in the verse are likewise truly
remarkable. Before Christianity, in the Jewish tradition, never did anyone
claim that God, the Father, had handed everything over to him, that he alone
knew the Father, and that he, therefore, could reveal the Father to whom he
choose. Moreover, who would be capable of having everything handed over
to him by the Father; and is there anyone but God or his equal who can know
Father? So in 10:21-22 Jesus is claiming for himself divine attributes; and
Luke has taken over this traditional statement and thus demonstrated that he is
not at all opposed to predicating divine attributes of Jesus[369].

---

[366] Van Iersel, "Der Sohn," 146-161, presents an analysis of this verse along with Mt
11:27.

[367] Von Hase, *Geschichte Jesu*, 422. Plummer, *St. Luke*, 282, suggests a comparison
with Jn 3:35; 6:46; 8:19; 10:15.30; 14:9; 16:15 and 17:6.10; Fitzmyer, *The Gospel of
Luke I-IX*, 866, proposes the additional comparisons of Jn 6:65; 7:29; 13:3; 14:7.9-11;
17:25.

[368] Crump, *Jesus the Intercessor*, 74-75, insists that it is precisely as Son, and because
of his unique status and intimate relationship with God, that Jesus' prayer is so
efficacious. Marshall, *The Gospel of Luke*, 435-438, writes of an exclusive relationship
with the Father and provides a fuller discussion of the pericope. See also Lagrange,
Évangile selon Saint Luc, 304-308.

[369] Christ, *Jesus Sophia*, 98-99, views Jesus as a bearer of wisdom, as wisdom itself.
The blessing in Luke 10:23-24 is Luke's comment on vv. 21-22 and explains that Jesus'
message about the mystery of the kingdom is open to the disciples. See also Bock, *Luke
9:51 – 24:53*, 1011-1012.

Jesus particularly shares in the Father's activity of revealing himself not to the learned and clever, but to the simple (Luke 10:21); and 12:32, "Do not be afraid any longer, little flock, for your Father is pleased to give you the kingdom," is unique to Luke and repeats the message of the Father's concern for individuals of less importance. Also, unlike Matthew, Luke concludes the pericope with a blessing (10:23-24), which relates what he has just said to what the Seventy(-two) have seen and heard. Up to this point they have principally seen and heard Jesus, and these experiences must form part of his revelation of the Father.

Other Passages Relevant to an Understanding of Jesus As "Son (of God)"

Jesus As "Son (of God)" in the Rest of Luke's Gospel
"Son (of God)" comes up a number of times in the rest of Luke's Gospel; however, in these passages the meaning of the title is not as clear as it has been in those treated thus far. Certainly, we have to give primary consideration to the context of the title to determine its import. However, as noted above, once Luke has established for the reader that Jesus is the unique Son of God in Luke 1:35, he can guide the reader's interpretation of any later appearance of this title. Perhaps, we also need to remind ourselves that Luke works on two levels, that of his fictional audience and that of his real audience, his reader.

Luke 3:21-22: "You Are My Beloved Son"[370]
Luke through the imprisonment of John the Baptist has completely eliminated him from the scene of Jesus' baptism (Luke 3:21-22; cf. Mk 1:9-11; Mt 3:13-17). Moreover, the grammar of the passage demonstrates that Luke has subordinated Jesus' baptism and his prayer to three other aspects of the story: the heavens opening, the descent of the Holy Spirit upon Jesus in a bodily form like a dove and the voice from heaven. Luke has arranged these three actions in climactic order; and the emphasis falls on the solemn proclamation, "You are my beloved Son, with you I am well pleased" (v. 22). The opening of the sky alerts us to a communication between a heavenly being and Jesus. The descent of the Spirit in bodily form

---

[370] For a thorough presentation of the possible Old Testament background for these verses, cf. Bock, *Proclamation from Prophecy*, 99-105.

over Jesus marks him as a central character in the story and underlines the reality of the Spirit's presence. The heavenly voice identifies Jesus, "You are my Son, the beloved" (cf. 20:13). "You" (σύ) is in a position of emphasis([371]), and "my Son" explains why the heavens were opened and clarifies that the voice is God's([372]). In Luke 3:22, "beloved" definitely modifies "son" and could be a reference to the Servant of Yahweh (Is 42:1; cf. Mt 12:18); but since Luke does write "son," the more likely source is the story of the command to Abraham to sacrifice Isaac (Gen 22:1-19) where God (or his messenger) designates Isaac as Abraham's "beloved" or "only" (vv. 2, 12, 15-16: ὁ ἀγαπητός) son. In Luke 3:22, "beloved," because of the article before it and the one before "my son," receives the emphasis and underlines the Father's affection for Jesus and may well indicate the uniqueness of his sonship.

These reflections naturally lead us back to Luke 1:35 and its message about the mystery of Jesus' divine sonship. Nonetheless, this is not to deny our earlier distinction between the nature of the divine activity there, creative and generative, and that at the baptism (e.g., Acts 10:38) in which Luke confirms this sonship and relates it to Jesus' mission. The descent of the Spirit and the voice from heaven at Jesus' baptism reveal the Christological mystery of his divine sonship to the reader([373]); for, though not conveying the same meaning, the Holy Spirit at Jesus' conception and the Holy Spirit at his baptism are closely related.

Although the Greek phrasing agrees more with the Hebrew than with the Greek text of the Old Testament, "with you, I am pleased" (Luke 3:22) very likely looks to Is 42:1 (cf. Mt 12:18) and so refers to the mission of the Servant of Yahweh, which we have seen Jesus will carry out. Obviously, in Luke 3:22 (cf. 4:18-19; Acts 10:38) this mission is associated with Jesus, as "Son."

---

[371] Danker, *Jesus and the New Age*, 51.

[372] George, *Études sur l'œuvre de Luc*, 217-218, writes, "Le Fils, ici, c'est le messie investi par le Père dans le secret de leurs relations mystérieuses." Luke may use "son" of Jesus both as Son of God and, less often, as the Christ; and the reader has to be able to determine the meaning in a given context.

[373] Bock, *Luke 1:1 – 9:50*, 344-345, is correct to speak of divine confirmation in this passage; but in view of Luke 1:35, this confirmation is not of Jesus as Messiah-Servant but as Son-Servant

Jesus' Genealogy: "Of God"

Jesus' genealogy follows immediately on the baptism scene; the genealogy ends with the phrases, "the son of Adam, the son of God" (Luke 3:38). "Of God" most directly refers to Adam as son of God; however, Adam is not the son of God as the other individuals in this genealogy are sons of their given fathers. We do not have here a Lukan presentation of Jesus as the New Adam. On the other hand, since we are dealing with Jesus' genealogy, which surprisingly is traced back to God, Luke might intend that his reader understand "of God" in terms of what he has written in Luke 1:35; 2:49 and 3:22 (cf. v. 23). The implication would be that "of God" in the genealogy reminds the reader of its import in these three passages, that is, Jesus' unique relationship with God.

Luke 4:1-13: The Devil Tempts Jesus, the "Son of God"

In the temptation scene (Luke 4:1-13), the devil twice uses "Son of God." The presence of the Holy Spirit and the title, "Son of God," connect the temptation scene with the announcement of Jesus' birth (1:26-38), with his baptism (3:21-22); the title alone, with Jesus' need to be in his Father's house (2:49). The devil says to a famished Jesus, "'If you are the Son of God, command this stone to become bread.' Jesus answered him, 'It is written, "One does not live by bread alone"'" (4:3-4; Dt 8:3). A similar situation occurs in the last temptation, when the devil places Jesus on the pinnacle of the temple and tells him, "If you are the Son of God, throw yourself down from here, for it is written, 'He will command his angels concerning you, to guard you,' and 'With their hands they will support you, lest you dash your foot against a stone'" (Luke 4:9-11; cf. Ps 90:11-12LXX). Jesus said to him in reply, "It also says, 'You shall not put the Lord, your God, to the test'" (Luke 4:12; cf. Dt 6:16). Luke's reader knows that Jesus is truly the Son of God; so the devil is either trying to find out who Jesus is, or misuses the title to try to get Jesus to do something that would directly contradict its significance. According to Luke, Jesus more than matches the devil's scheming temptation. Through his correct understanding of the Sacred Scriptures he knows that he, as Son of God, is not to perform miracles which only serve himself and his own needs. Nor is he to test God by putting himself in a situation where God will have to work a miracle or Jesus will end up killing himself. Thus, Jesus demonstrates what it really means to be Son of God: be faithful to

God's word in the scriptures and, by implication, do what God wants (cf. 2:49)([374]). To be sure, doing God's will particularly distinguishes Jesus, the Son of God.

Luke 8:28: "Jesus Son of the Most High God"

In the healing of the Gerasene demoniac (Luke 8:26-39; cf. 4:32-35) we read, "When he (the demoniac) saw Jesus, he cried out and fell down before him; in a loud voice he shouted, 'What have you to do with me, Jesus, Son of the Most High God([375])? I beg you, do not torment me'" (v. 28). The following elements of the story are of interest to us. A preternatural being identifies Jesus as "Son of the Most High God([376])" with whom the demon has nothing in common; they represent two radically separate realms (cf. Acts 26:18). The demoniac falls before Jesus and thus reveals who is the central and dominant character in the scene, and his loud shouting and begging Jesus not to torment him likewise make this point. "Most High" is a Lucan word (Mk 2x; Mt 1x; Luke-Acts 9x; Heb 1x) and always somehow relates to God. Luke in 8:28 has taken the expression over from Mark, but the closest parallels in Luke-Acts are Luke 1:32 (cf. Acts 16:17), "He . . . will be called Son of the Most High" and Luke 1:35, " . . . and the power of the Most High will overshadow you. Therefore the child to be born will be called holy, the Son of God." At first, because of the phrase, "Son of Most High," Luke 1:32 seems the closer parallel; but it deals with Jesus as the Christ and his reign over the house of Jacob; the closer parallel is probably 1:35 precisely because it also states a contrast to 8:28, "the child to be born will be called holy."

---

[374] Although Bock, *Luke 1:1 – 9:50*, 368-384, understands "Son of God" as messianic, he is certainly correct in his interpretation of Jesus' temptation scene as demonstrating that Jesus was righteous and faithful.

[375] See Plummer, *St. Luke*, 229-230, for the Old Testament evidence as well as that of Acts 16:17, that this title was usual among heathen nations and would show that the man was not a Jew. For Plummer, this title would also demonstrate the likelihood that the owners of the swine were not Jews. Nolland, *Luke 1 – 9:20*, 408 contends that at least for Luke such an assertion can hardly be true in view of his uses of "Most High" elsewhere (e.g., Luke 1:32.35.76; 6:35).

[376] Lenski, *St. Luke's Gospel*, 469-470, views this title as an affirmation of Jesus' divinity.

The predicate, "holy," merits our attention. The demon in 8:28 asks, "What have you to do with me, Jesus, Son of the Most High God" and so recognizes the tremendous distance and contrast that exist between Jesus and it. Luke also describes the demon as "unclean"; and when we come to know that the man was actually possessed by many demons, they themselves ask to be sent into the nearby herd of pigs, unclean animals according to Jewish tradition (cf. Lk 15:15-16; Lv 11:7-8; Dt 14:8). The demons then possess the herd of pigs that charge over the bluff into the lake and drown. This destructive act further establishes the distance between Jesus, who saves, and the demons that are violent to the end. The man, freed from the demons, begs to go with Jesus, but the latter instructs him to go home and to "recount what God has done for you"([377]); so he goes and proclaims throughout the whole town "what Jesus had done for him." Although this instruction and proclamation describe the same activity([378]), it would go beyond the data to claim that one can conclude from them that Jesus is somehow divine; but they do support the claim of a parallel between 8:28 and 1:35 and so point us toward such a conclusion.

Luke 20:13: "My Beloved Son"

In the expanded and allegorized parable of the vineyard and tenants (Luke 20:9-19)([379]), the owner of the vineyard finally decides to send his "beloved son" in the hopes that the tenants will respect him and hand over the just share of the produce (cf. 19:11-27). The vineyard obviously stands for Israel (cf. Is 5:1-7), and the three slaves, each of whom is successively treated more brutally, represent the prophets and messengers sent to call Israel to respond properly to God. The tenants stand for the scribes and

---

[377] There is the outside possibility that "God" could refer to Jesus, but Luke does not address the question in that manner.

[378] Confer Fitzmyer, *The Gospel According to St. Luke I–IX*, 740, who observes, "A certain parallelism is detected in the last two sentences." The man is instructed to proclaim all that God has done for him, but he goes and announces all that Jesus had done for him. Both "God" and "Jesus" are in emphatic positions.

[379] Fitzmyer, *The Gospel According to Luke X–XXIV*, 1278-1281, after a consideration of the various possibilities, concludes to this description of the literary form of the passage.

chief priests, who are identified in the additions to the parable (20:19) and who not only did not accept Jesus but were involved in his death([380]). After what his slaves had to endure, the owner of the vineyard seems almost imprudent to send his beloved (only?) son; but the intention is to show the degree of God's love for Israel. Given the thrust of the story, the tenants' reasoning about their inheriting the vineyard should probably be understood as misguided; such an interpretation accords best with their reasoning and actions up to this point in the story([381]). They throw the son out of the vineyard and kill him, and this phrasing is probably due to the terminology used of Jesus' passion (cf. Heb 13:12)? There follows the prophetic warning that the owner of the vineyard will come and destroy those tenants and give the vineyard to others. The additions to the original parable (vv. 17-19) render the warning harsher and compare Jesus to the cornerstone, which surprisingly will break in pieces those who fall on it (cf. Is 8:14-15) and crush those on whom it falls (cf. Dn 2:44). Significantly, our author himself added Luke 20:18. Moreover, the reaction of the scribes and chief priests is much stronger than that of the ordinary people at the end of v. 16, "Let it not be so"; and except for fear of the people, they would have seized Jesus that very instant (v. 19). This desire to seize Jesus begins to actualize the prediction of the allegory; for they act against him. Of course, we are interested in the meaning of the "beloved Son" in the parable. The parable does not speak only of the earthly Jesus, for the image of the rejected stone that becomes the cornerstone (v. 17; cf. Ps 117:22LXX) represents both Jesus' passion and resurrection, and the stone on which someone falls and breaks into pieces and that will pulverize anyone on whom it falls certainly portrays the judgment (cf. 9:26; 12:8-9). In Acts 4:11, Luke again cites Ps 117:22LXX of the risen Jesus in whose name alone is salvation for humankind. More importantly, "my beloved Son" finds an exact parallel in Luke 3:22, which we already argued reveals the christological mystery of Jesus' divine sonship. In the parable of the vineyard and the tenants Luke writes of the beloved Son's rejection, death and resurrection and of his role in the judgment. This

---

[380] Cf. Luke 19:47; 20:19; 22:2.66; 23:10.

[381] See Loisy, *L'Évangile selon Luc*, 479, and confer Nolland, *Luke 18:35 – 24:53*, 952.

beloved Son is the heir of the vineyard, which will have new and co-operative tenants.

Jesus Speaks of God As His Father([382])

We have already studied Luke 10:21-24 where the mutual and complete knowledge of the Father and of the Son led us to see Jesus' divinity in the passage. There are other passages where Jesus speaks of God as his Father; and although they do not have the clarity of 10:21-24 about the intimate and unique relationship of Jesus with his Father, they do reveal certain aspects of Jesus' sonship. To be sure, Luke 1:35; 2:49 and 10:21-24 continue to guide the reader's interpretations of these passages.

Luke 22:42: "Father, If You Are Willing"

In three passages of the passion narrative (Luke 22:42; 23:34.46) Jesus addresses his Father in prayer([383]). During his prayer on the Mount of Olives Jesus asks, "Father, if you are willing, take this cup away from me; still, not my will but yours be done" (22:42; cf. Heb 5:7-10). This verse relates Jesus' sonship to a total disposition to do the Father's will([384]). Surely, an intimacy between Jesus and the Father appears in the passage itself, but there is no hint of the former's divinity. Any claim for the mystery of Jesus' divinity in the passage would have to come from what the readers already knows.

Luke 23:34: "Father, Forgive Them"

Although the textual support is not strong, some authors defend the reading in which Jesus on the cross prays,

---

[382] For background information on this topic, see Hahn, *The Titles of Jesus*, 307-314.

[383] Feldkämper, *Der betende Jesus*, 333-335, notes that of the Synoptics Luke most frequently reports prayers in which Jesus addresses God as "Father" and asserts that Jesus' prayer to the Father is a unique dialogue and reciprocal recognition of something intimate and exclusive.

[384] Fitzmyer, *The Gospel According to Luke X–XXIV*, 1436-1438, after comparing Luke's account with Mark's, rightly concludes that Luke centers on Jesus' relationship with the Father much more than on the uncomprehending disciples. See also Bock, *Luke 9:5 – 24:53*, 1758-1760, 1763; Longenecker, "The Foundational Conviction," 475, 488; Feldkämper, *Der betende Jesus*, 249-250 and Lenski, *St. Luke's Gospel*, 1073-1074.

"Father, forgive them, they know not what they do" (23:34a)([385]). If the reading is correct, this verse would bring up the Lukan themes of excusing Jesus' opponents because of their ignorance (cf. Acts 3:17; 13:27; 17:30), and of forgiveness, and constitute a parallel to Luke 11:4 (cf. vv. 1-4) and to Stephen's prayer to the risen Lord Jesus (Acts 7:60). Jesus would be loving his enemies (Luke 6:27-28) and expressing his confident filial relationship with the Father([386]). None of this would allow us to conclude to any unique oneness between them. However, between 23:34 and the agony in the garden, there stand 22:66-71; and Luke in this latter scene before the Sanhedrin portrays Jesus as first conceding that he is the Christ (Messiah) and then indicating that he is Son of God; and we argued above that in the context, "Son of God" communicates the mystery of Jesus' divinity. We also know from 22:66-71 that Jesus, who in 23:34 intercedes for his persecutors, will sit at the right hand of the power of God and so will be in any ideal position to make intercession on everyone's behalf. So, it seems quite reasonable to conclude that Luke's reader, who not only has read 22:66-71 but all the other passages which up to this point have conveyed the mystery of Jesus' divinity through "Son (of God)" or "Father," would see the mystery of Jesus' divinity in Luke 23:34.

Luke 23:46: "Father, into Your Hands I Commend My Spirit"
"'Father, into your hands I commend my spirit'; and when he had said this he breathed his last" (23:46) reports Jesus' prayerful cry before his death. However, this prayerful cry of Jesus comes only a few verses after his words to the good thief, "Amen, I say to you, today you will be with me in Paradise" (23:42). According to Luke, Jesus is definitely conscious of his forthcoming resurrection([387]); and his prayer commending his spirit to the

---

[385] Bock, *Luke 9:5 – 24:53*, 1867-1868, provides a summary of the discussion and of the opinions of various authors; see also Brown, *The Death of the Messiah*, II, 975-981, Prete, *L'opera di Luca*, 273-275, and Talbert, *Reading Luke*, 219-220. Nolland, *Luke 18:35 – 24:53*, 1144, believes that this prayer "has good claim to being based upon historical reminiscence." He not only mentions what we state above but the notable boldness of the prayer, which makes no mention of repentance.

[386] Confer Feldkämper, *Der betende Jesus*, 257-267.

[387] Jesus taught a resurrection of those deemed worthy (Luke 20:35); he predicted his own resurrection (e.g., 9:22; 18:33), spoke of his future kingdom (22:29-30), of his

Father must anticipate it. The citation of Ps 30:6LXX in Luke 23:46 (cf. Acts 7:59) does not appear in the other Synoptics who rather cited Ps 21:2LXX; most probably Luke avoids this latter citation, because it could give the impression that Jesus felt abandoned by his Father. Luke, for his part, definitely wants to underline Jesus' confidence in his Father[388], but also his acceptance of what the Father has asked of him[389]. Consequently, Jesus' prayer to the Father about his spirit occurs in a context of his unique relationship with him and, as 23:34, should be understood in the whole context of Luke's Gospel and so as relating to the mystery of Jesus' divinity. Luke 23:46 provides a brief but very clear picture of Jesus' remarkable filial confidence in his Father

Luke 24:49: "And (Behold) I Am Sending the Promise of My Father"

According to Luke 24:49 (cf. Acts 1:4-5.8), Jesus directs the Eleven and those with them, "And (behold) I am sending the promise of my Father upon you; but stay in the city until you are clothed with power from on high." There are references to "the Christ" in 24:46 (cf. vv. 45-48) and to the descendent of David throughout the Pentecost speech, toward the end of which Luke writes about the sending of the Holy Spirit; and we are now aware that Luke not infrequently associates "the Christ" with Jesus as "Son (of God)." Nonetheless, we should attribute the sending of the Holy Spirit to Jesus as the Son; for Luke 24:49 speaks of "the promise of my Father", and Acts 2:33 reads, "Exalted at the right hand of God, he received the promise of the Holy Spirit from the Father and poured it forth, as you (both) see and hear." So, Jesus as Son pours out the promise of the Holy Spirit. Obviously, Luke 24:49 occurs after 23:34 and 23:46, both of which verses bear on the mystery of Jesus' divinity. Further, Acts 2:33 parallels Luke 22:69 (cf. vv. 70-71), which in terms of "Son of God" introduces this mystery, and as we shall see, stands in a context where

---

enthronement (22:69) and of the coming of the Son of Man (17:20-37; 18:8; 21:27-28.34-36). Luke himself reports Jesus' resurrection in ch. 24 and throughout the Acts.

[388] Feldkämper, *Der betende Jesus*, 274-279. G. Schneider, *Verleugnung, Verspottung und Verhör Jesu*, 186-187, writes about the deepest bond of the dying Jesus with the Father.

[389] Pretc, *L'opera di Luca*, 277-280, rightly reminds us of this other aspect of Jesus' prayer.

Luke does not hesitate to apply an OT citation about God as "Lord" to Jesus (cf. Acts 2:21).

Conclusion

"Son (of God)" and Jesus' addressing God as "(his) Father" should be understood against a LXX background. In some Lucan passages these titles clearly convey the mystery of Jesus' divinity, but generally these passages do not provide much additional information or explanation. Nonetheless, once the reader has seen these references to Jesus' being divine, these very passages, especially Luke 1:35, guide his or her interpretation of "Son of God" and related designations elsewhere in Luke-Acts. For Luke there is some flexibility in the title, "Son of God"; for instance, he is willing to let stand the Johannine understanding of the Father and Son in 10:22. Like the other NT writers Luke uses the image of the relationship between an earthly father and his son but through Mary's virginity eliminates any earthly father. Thus he underlines the mystery of Jesus' divinity[390], his radically intimate relationship with the Father, at his conception. As God himself, Jesus is holy and the beloved or unique Son; he can lay claim to divine attributes. The Holy Spirit characterizes Jesus' sonship, but differently at Jesus' conception than at his baptism or at Jesus' prayer of rejoicing (10:21-22), and likewise relates to the Son's mission. The mission of the "Son of God" is primarily to do the Father's will and to be about his business; and the Son of God proves more loyal to his mission than was Israel to hers. Jesus, as the Son, often appears in a context of his praying (3:21-22; 9:28-29; 22:39-46; 23:34.46). The Son is a wise teacher and prays to the Father for himself and others. Even his tragic death does not dull his concern for his opponents or his filial confidence in the Father. As the Father, the Son reaches out to the simple people and is a dominant personage who opposes demons and heals. According to Luke, Jesus as "Son of God" is superior to John the Baptist in every respect, and the title is much more lofty than "prophet." It is also more exalted than "the Christ," although surely associated with that title and with the promises to David; and so more probably we should also hold for a distinction between

---

[390] One can say, as does Rigaux, *Témoignage*, 425 (cf. 419-424), that Luke does not speculate on the substantial identity of the Father with the Son, but he did at times communicate to his readers the mystery of Jesus' divinity. To be sure, "substantial" is a non-biblical term.

Jesus as the Christ and as Son of God in Luke 4:41 and in Acts 9:19b-22([391]). "Son of God" can function as a confessional statement or as a summary of the gospel message. Everyone is to listen the Son, and it is radically important that he be accepted, otherwise people run the risk of being themselves rejected. Luke links the Son with the "Servant of Yahweh," with whom the Father is well pleased and whom he has chosen. Luke also associates the "Son of God" with the heavenly Son of Man who sits at God's right hand, the place where the Son should sit.

---

[391] Cf. George, *Études sur l'œuvre de Luc*, 222.

CHAPTER EIGHT

Jesus As "(the) Lord"(392)

Luke wrote both volumes against a background of the LXX tradition; and this is the setting in which we need to understand his presentation of Jesus as "Lord." Also, Luke wrote for believers(393), individuals who like Theophilus had received Christian instruction (cf. Luke 1:1-4), even if we are not able to identify the exact content of what they had been taught. Since Luke-Acts most likely dates from about fifty years after Jesus' resurrection and Luke himself believed in the risen Jesus as Lord in its fullest sense, in his Gospel Luke can and does communicate this belief in who Jesus is to his readers(394), even though he is likewise concerned to portray accurately the story about the earthly Jesus. Thus Luke can work on two levels, that of the story line and that of his reader. As we have seen with other titles or reflections about Jesus, some passages will provide us with considerably

---

392 "(The) Lord" appears in the title of this chapter since some authors hold that Luke primarily designates Jesus as "the Lord" and God as "Lord"; although at times helpful, this distinction is not always legitimate. For general considerations of "Lord," cf. Bock, *Proclamation from Prophecy*, 148-154; see also Bousset, *Kyrios Christos*, 119-152; Cadbury, "The Titles of Jesus in Acts," 359-361; de la Potterie, "Le titre κύριος," 117-146; Fitzmyer, *The Gospel According to Luke I–IX*, 200-204 and *To Advance the Gospel*, 220-223; Foakes Jackson and Lake, *The Beginnings of Christianity I*, 410-418; Foerster, κύριος, 1086-1094; Franklin, *Christ the Lord*; George, *Études sur l'œuvre de Luc*, 237-255; Jacquier, *Les Actes des Apôtres*, ccxi-ccxii; Jones, "The Title *Kyrios* in Luke-Acts"; Kilpatrick, "'Kurios' in the Gospels," 65-70; Nevius, "*Kyrios* and *Jēsous* in St. Luke," 75-77; O'Toole, "The Activity of the Risen Jesus," 473-484; Rigaux, *Témoignage*, 408-419; Voss, *Die Christologie*, 56-60. Hahn, *The Titles of Jesus*, 68-128; on pp. 103-114, Hahn traces the development of meaning of "Lord" in its applications to Jesus. On p. 114, he concludes, "for it came to imply the divine nature and the divine dignity of the exalted Lord. Finally, this was developed in such a way as to refer both to the risen and earthly Jesus."

393 See O'Toole, *The Unity*, 18-21.

394 Nevius, "*Kyrios* and *Jēsous* in St. Luke," 77.

more evidence and clarity than others about what Luke meant when he or one of his characters identifies Jesus as "(the) Lord([395])." Surely, at times, one can defend a messianic interpretation of "Lord"; but this does not mean that Luke has not likewise attributed to it an ecclesial dimension or transcendent significance([396]). Also, the fact that the majority of occurrences of "(the) Lord" in Luke-Acts designate either God the Father or Jesus is not without its implications. Finally, 1:35 and its message about Jesus as the unique Son of God and so about the mystery of his divinity function as a hermeneutical tool for the reader of Luke-Acts.

In this chapter, we consider the passages in the Infancy Narrative([397]), which speak of Jesus as "(the) Lord" and then Acts 22:14 and other passages where we argue that "Lord" implies the mystery of Jesus' divinity. These latter passages include Acts 2:21 and 7:59-60, instances when "Lord" could refer to either God or Jesus, and "Lord" in Parousia passages([398]), in visions and at baptism. Such an understanding of Jesus as Lord would likewise seem justified in any passage that deals with later community experiences like the sending out of the Seventy-(two) (Luke 10:1). Once it has been established in the Infancy Narrative and elsewhere in Luke-Acts that "Lord" can communicate the mystery of Jesus' divinity, its occurrences throughout the two volumes are open to this interpretation. We then turn to "(the) Lord," used in the same pericope of both Jesus and of God, in the good news about "(the) Lord," faith in him, and in passages where "(the) Lord" interacts with individuals, is head of the disciples or works miracles. Of course, from Luke 1:35 and certain other passages treated in the previous chapter the reader already knows of the

---

[395] Some authors contend that Luke writes "(the) Lord" of Jesus; there is some truth to this, but Foerster, κύριος, 1087, writes that "no essential distinction can be made between κύριος with and without the article."

[396] George, *Études sur l'œuvre de Luc*, 255, writes of Luke, "Pour lui, la Seigneurie de Jésus est 'd'un autre ordre.' Elle a sa source et son terme dans le Règne de Dieu. Elle participe à celle du *kurios* de l'A.T."

[397] For background information on Luke's Infancy narrative, see Minear, "Luke's Use of the Birth Stories," 111-130.

[398] Confer Luke 12:37.42-43.45-46; 14:23; 20:13.15.

mystery of Jesus' divinity; and this knowledge also guides his interpretation of all subsequent passages.

Luke 1:43: The Mother of My Lord
There are passages in the introductory chapters of the Gospel which refer to Jesus as "Lord" and continue the notion of the mystery of Jesus' divinity in Luke 1:35. When Mary visits Elizabeth, among other things the latter exclaims, "And how does this happen to me, that the mother of my Lord should come to me" (1:43)? A number of scholars feel that this is too early in Luke's Gospel to find in "Lord" any indication of the mystery of Jesus' divinity and prefer to interpret it as a reference to Jesus being the Christ([399]). However, most probably Luke added the Infancy Narrative later([400]), and this allowed him to introduce and to highlight most of the themes, which he had presented in his Gospel and Acts. Moreover, v. 43 occurs shortly after v. 35; and if our understanding of that verse be correct, "Lord" in the former verse certainly means more than "the Christ." V. 43 speaks of Mary as the mother of the Lord and so looks back to vv. 31-35; to be sure, this could point to vv. 32-33 and so indicate that "of my Lord" signifies that Jesus is the Christ. However, the more significant aspect of Mary's motherhood in these verses appears in v. 35 and in its expression of the unique sonship of Jesus. In v. 45, Elizabeth names God "Lord." Although "Lord" with the article may well be Luke's preferred way of speaking of Jesus([401]), "of the Lord" in v. 43 is definitely influenced by the use of "Lord" (κύριος) in the LXX. And, more likely than not, it

---

[399] Bock, *Luke 1:1 – 9:50*, 137, names some of these scholars. Such an interpretation does not really come to terms with the possibility that Luke has read back into his Gospel the later insights into the risen Lord. Moule, "The Christology of Acts," 172, asks whether in the type of Aramaic used by Elizabeth there would have been a distinct difference between "my Lord" and "the Lord," the latter of which might have been more like a title of divine exaltation.

[400] This seems the more reasonable interpretation since the themes are not only very well coordinated with those of the Gospel and Acts but are affected by the later insights into who Jesus is. *Pace* Talbert, *Reading Luke-Acts*, 66-67.

[401] E.g., see George, *Études sur l'œuvre de Luc*, 240-241.

continues the thought of the mystery of Jesus' divinity introduced in v. 35([402]).

Luke 2:11
Much the same should probably be said about the unique NT expression "Christ and Lord" in the angel's proclaiming the good news of great joy, "For today in the city of David a savior has been born for you who is Christ and Lord" (Luke 2:11)([403]). In this verse, we have a parallel to 1:32-35 since "in the city of David and "Christ" would refer to the David Messiah in vv. 32-33 and "Lord" to "Son of God" in v. 35. Below we will study another parallel to "Christ and Lord" in 2:11, Acts 2:36, and argue that it conveys to the reader the mystery of Jesus' divinity. Moreover, the close association of the description of God in Luke 2:9, "The angel of the Lord appeared to them and the glory of the Lord shone around them" with "Lord" in v. 11 also supports the above interpretation of the latter. Naturally, the message of v. 35 and "Lord," used of Jesus, in the Infancy Narrative (1:43; 2:11; cf. 1:76) assist the reader's understanding of subsequent passages.

Acts 21:14: "The Lord's Will Be Done"
When in Caesarea the prophet Agabus predicts that Paul will be seized by certain Jews in Jerusalem and handed over to the Gentiles and those present hear this, they try to persuade Paul not to go up to Jerusalem; however, Paul responds that he is ready not only to be bound but even to die in Jerusalem for the name of the Lord Jesus. Since Paul will not be persuaded, those present can only say, "The Lord's will be done" (Acts 21:14). "Lord" in this passage more probably refers to Jesus([404]), for in the previous verse, Paul speaks about his being prepared to endure imprisonment and even death "for the name of the Lord Jesus." Acts 20:24 ("Yet I consider life of no importance to me, if only I may finish my course and

---

[402] De la Potterie, "Le titre κύριος," 120; Rigaux, *Témoignage*, 416-417.

[403] De la Potterie, "Le titre κύριος," 120-121; George, *Études sur l'œuvre de Luc*, 246-247.

[404] See Bousset, *Kyrios Christos*, 288, n. 144. On the other hand, I am aware that a number of scholars would not agree with this interpretation, e.g., L.T. Johnson, *The Acts*, 371, and Polhill, *Acts*, 436.

the ministry that I received from the Lord Jesus to bear witness to the gospel of God's grace"—cf. 9:16; 26:19-20), confirms this interpretation; for it appears in a context of Paul's future suffering (cf. vv. 22-23) and identifies the Lord Jesus as the one who assigned him his mission. Given that Acts 21:14 is itself in a context of doing Christ's will in the midst of opposition and suffering, one naturally thinks of the agony in the garden and Jesus' words when faced with the reality of his passion, "Father, if you are willing, take this cup away from me; still, not my will but yours be done" (Luke 22:42; cf. Acts 18:21). Granted that Luke does not have in the Lord's Prayer, "Your will be done, on earth as in heaven" (cf. Mt 6:10bc), nonetheless, in his speech at Pisidia Antioch, Paul says of David, "he will carry out my (God) very wish" (Acts 13:22). Also, in the second account of Paul's conversion experience, Ananias tells Paul, "The God of our ancestors designated you to know his will, to see the Righteous one and to hear the sound of his own voice (Acts 22:14). In summary, Luke has apparently put Jesus on the same level as the Father; for, when Luke writes in Acts 21:14, "The Lord's will be done" of what Jesus asks of Paul, one is reminded of Jesus' own words to the Father in the agony in the garden.

Luke 1:76: "For You Will Go Before the Lord to Prepare His Ways"([405])
There is some question about who the "Lord" in Luke 1:76 is([406]). In this verse, Zechariah says of his son John, "And you, child will be called prophet of the Most High, for you will go before the Lord to prepare his ways." Some scholars point to vv. 16-17 (cf. Mal 3:1.22-23LXX) and the clear statement that John the Baptist will go before God in the spirit and power of Elijah to get ready a people properly disposed. So, they also point to the presence of "people" in v. 77, "To give his people knowledge of salvation through the forgiveness of their sins" and conclude that "Lord" in v. 76 is God. The difficulty with this interpretation is that according to Luke John the Baptist actually goes before Jesus([407]). In 7:27

---

[405] See Brown, *The Birth of the Messiah*, 373, 379-381, 389-391, 491 and Laurentin, *Luc I–II*, 38-42, 127-130.

[406] Fitzmyer, *The Gospel According to Luke I–IX*, 385-386, contends that it is far from obvious that "Lord" in this verse refers to Yahweh.

[407] Confer Luke 3:4.15-17; 7:28 [cf. vv. 18-35]; 13:23-25.

Jesus in part cites Mal 3:1 about John the Baptist in the scene where the disciples of the latter come to ask if Jesus is the one coming or should they wait for another. Also in Luke 3:4-5 (cf. vv. 15-17; Acts 13:23-25) the preparation of the ways of the Lord is John the Baptist's task before Jesus' coming. So those who interpret "Lord" in v. 76 as God have to explain this claim by saying that, although the reference is to God, he does this through Jesus.

On the other hand, Luke has already written of Jesus as "Lord" in Luke 1:43, and the same could be true in v. 76. Moreover, in the annunciation of Jesus' birth, the angel Gabriel already foretold that Jesus will sit on the throne of David his father, and v. 69 introduces Jesus into the *Benedictus* because it speaks of the mighty savior in the house of God's servant David, who must be Jesus. Also Jesus is the "dawn" in v. 78, and the source of this expression may well be Mal 3:20 and in the same chapter as vv. 1 and 23, mentioned above. So, Nolland's comment about v. 76 "And there may, therefore, be a happy ambiguity about the reference of "Lord" here([408])," surely seems justified. Seeing ambiguity in v. 76 finds further support in Acts 13:10-12, where Paul threatens Elymas because he continues to try to make crooked the straight paths of the Lord (cf. Luke 1:76 and 3:4-5: "Make ready the way of the Lord, clear him a straight path . . . and the windings will be made straight and the rough ways smooth") and tells him that the hand of the Lord opposes him and so he will temporarily be blind. When he sees this, the proconsul believes because he is astonished by the teaching of the Lord. In Acts 13:12 the teaching about which the proconsul is amazed is more probably that of or about Jesus because Luke 4:32 contains much the same wording about his teaching. In Acts 13:11, the word "Lord" in the expression "hand of the Lord" is more reasonably God's (cf. Luke 1:66; Acts 4:28; 7:50; 11:21?)([409]); but the straight paths of the Lord in v. 10 (cf. Luke 1:76; 3:4-5) appear ambiguous. This ambiguity finds support in the alternate scribal reading, "the τοῦ which generally modifies "Lord" when the reference is to Jesus. So, our question in Luke 1:76 and in other passages where we find this ambiguity becomes: what weight are we to attribute to Luke's not feeling

---

[408] See Nolland, *Luke 1 – 9:20*, 89.

[409] L.T. Johnson, *The Acts*, 224, indicates that the expression echoes passages like Jgs 2:15LXX and 1 Sam 12:15.

obliged to specify with care whether with "Lord" he means God or Jesus? This is where Luke's extensive use of the LXX proves important, because it demonstrates that the Jewish tradition and its emphasis on God and what can and cannot be said of him, has deeply influenced his thinking. Luke is willing to modify that tradition only in terms of what the Christians believe about Jesus. When Luke leaves "Lord" vague, he reveals the intimate and unique relationship he sees between God and Jesus and implies the mystery of Jesus' divinity.

Acts 2:21: Everyone Shall Be Saved Who Calls on the Name of the Lord
In Acts 2:21 (cf. Joel 3:1-5LXX; Rm 10:13) we find as part of the citation from Joel the words, "And it shall be that everyone shall be saved who calls on the name of the Lord." Originally, "Lord" in this verse referred to the God of the Old Testament; but in its present context the reference is to Jesus([410]). The context of Ananias' words to Paul in Acts 22:16, "Now, why delay? Get up and have yourself baptized and your sins washed away, calling upon his name" reveals that the reference is to Jesus and that "calling upon his name" occurs at Christian baptism (cf. 9:14.21; Rm 10:8-13). When at the end of his speech at Pentecost, Peter's audience asks him what they should do, he instructs them, "Repent and be baptized, every one of you, in the name of Jesus Christ for the forgiveness of your sins; and you will received the gift of the Spirit" (Acts 2:38). Clearly, Peter is referring to the OT citation in v. 21, "Everyone shall be saved who calls on the name of the Lord." We likewise find the same Greek word for "salvation" in Peter's exhortation, a few verses later, "Save yourselves from this corrupt generation" (v. 40), after which his audience receive the word and are baptized. So, the citation from Joel, which assures the reader that whoever calls on the name of the Lord will be saved, originally referred to the God of the OT; but now it refers to Jesus, on whom the Christians call when they are baptized and so participate in salvation and receive forgiveness of sins. This cultic worship of Jesus and calling on the Lord "blurred the boundaries between Jesus and God, and Jesus was increasing regarded

---

[410] Polhill, *Acts*, 109-110, calls attention to this fact and to the importance of this verse for Peter and his speech; Kürzinger, *The Acts*, I, writes that the entire Pentecostal sermon is oriented to the message of Acts 2:21. Bruce, *The Acts*, 122, lists other applications to Jesus as Lord of OT references to Yahweh. See also Haenchen, *The Acts*, 179, 186.

as exalted to the height of divinity([411])." Luke's willingness to apply "Lord" in Acts 2:21 to Jesus shows that he feels he can put him on the same level as the Father; the fact that he does this in a Jewish context weakens the argument of anyone who does not see the uniqueness of such an application. The early Christians were very careful about whom they were willing to call "Lord," in the way they used it of God. Obviously, Luke's application of "Lord" in the OT citation in Acts 2:21 to Jesus also clarifies his source for the use of this title and is extremely important for the interpretation of it in other passages.

Acts 2:36: God Has Made Him Both Lord and Christ

At the end of the same Pentecost speech Peter solemnly proclaims, "Therefore, let the whole house of Israel know for certain that God has made him both Lord and Christ (Acts 2:36([412]), this Jesus whom you crucified." Since in v. 21 Luke has already put Jesus on the same level as his Father, there is little reason for not maintaining that he does the same in this verse([413]). Moreover, in the previous chapter we argued that the Sanhedrin interpreted Jesus' predictions in Luke 22:69 as a claim to his being "Son of God" (v. 70); and 22:69 does not speak of the Parousia but of Jesus' enthronement. Thus, its prediction is fulfilled in Acts 2:33-36, which also cities Ps 109:1LXX; and this citation speaks of both God and Jesus as "(the) Lord," "the Lord said to my Lord." Luke in Luke 22:69-

---

[411] Hahn, The Titles of Jesus, 108.

[412] Haenchen, The Acts, 187, claims that that this formula is at odds with Luke's own Christology since he assumed that Jesus during his earthly life already possessed his dignity as Son of God. This claim has its validity, but Luke could and did both express his own faith and portray how the early Christians gradually came to this belief. On the other hand, Grundmann, χριστός, 535, writes, "Since from the very first Jesus is for Luke καὶ κύριος καὶ χριστός the statement cannot be taken to imply adoptionist christology."

[413] Confer Hahn, The Titles of Jesus, 107, who writes of "Lord" in Acts 2:36 as an "adoptionist" statement, on the same page contends that, although the Hellenistic Judaic Christian Church avoided understanding the person and work of Jesus in a divine sense, a tendency in this direction was now present and could not be eliminated. Bruce, The Acts, 128, recognizes in "Lord" of the passage the mystery of Jesus' divinity and, in addition, points out the creedal nature of the phrasing. See also Bock, Proclamation from Prophecy, 187; Polhill, Acts, 115-116.

70 and Acts 2:21 has introduced the mystery of Jesus' divinity, and one should conclude the same about Acts 2:36 (cf. vv. 33-35). Sitting at the right hand of implies divine dignity as would sitting in his presence([414]). The question about David's son (Luke 20:41-44), in which Ps 109:1LXX is cited, likewise conveys the message of Jesus' divinity, although this might well be clear only for Luke reader and not for Jesus' audience in the story line([415]).

Acts 7:59-60: "Lord Jesus, Receive My Spirit . . . Lord, Do Not Hold This Sin against Them"

Another example of Jesus being addressed as the "Lord" as the God of the OT occurs in the aftermath of Stephen's speech; when the Jewish opponents are stoning Stephen, he prays (Acts 7:59-60), "Lord Jesus, receive my spirit . . . Lord, do not hold this sin against them." "Lord" in v. 60 must also refer to Jesus since in the previous verse it clearly does([416]); and it is only reasonable that, if a writer wants to change whom he means by "Lord," somehow he has to communicate this change to his reader. This Luke does not do. Acts 7:59-60 remind the reader of two passages from Jesus' passion in Luke's Gospel([417]), 23:34a.46. Luke 23:34a, which is textually questionable([418]), reads, "Then Jesus said, 'Father, forgive them, they know not what they do'" and v. 46, "Jesus cried out in a loud voice, 'Father, into your hands I commend my spirit'; and when he had said this he breathed his last." If v. 34a be genuine, it surely recalls Stephen's prayer, "Lord, do not hold this sin against them"; and Jesus prayed to his Father, as Stephen now prays to Jesus. Consequently, Luke would have placed Jesus on a level with the Father. Moreover, Jesus' entrusting his spirit to the Father in Luke 23:46 constitutes a sure parallel to Stephen's

---

[414] Foerster, κύριος, 1089; Jacquier, *Les Actes des Apôtres*, 75.

[415] See Bock, *Proclamation from Prophecy*, 132. Marshall, *The Gospel of Luke*, 743-749, surveys various interpretations of Luke 20:41-44.

[416] Bruce, *The Acts*, 212-213 and L.T. Johnson, *The Acts*, 140-141.

[417] For these parallels and the many others that Luke draws between Jesus and Stephen, see O'Toole, *The Unity*, 63-67.

[418] However, the majority of scholars accept the reading as genuine.

doing the same to him, and we have a definite example of the Father and Jesus being placed on the same level and so of the mystery of Jesus' divinity.

Passages Where "Lord" Could Refer to Either God or Jesus[419]

The importance of these passages depends on what the early Christians, and particularly Luke, were willing to predicate both of God and of others. We have already considered Luke 1:76 and Acts 13:10-12. When the early Christians want to decide whether Joseph or Matthias should succeed Judas, Luke writes (Acts 1:24), "Then they prayed, 'You, Lord, who knows the hearts of all, show which one of these two you have chosen'[420]." Scholars have identified Lord in this passage as either God[421] or Jesus[422]. Jesus may appear the less likely referent, but he is designated "the Lord Jesus" in v. 21 and constitutes a truly possible reference for "Lord" in v. 24. Moreover, Jesus did choose the Twelve (Luke 6:12-15; cf. Acts 1:2)[423]; and Acts 1:26 reminds us that Matthias thus becomes one of the apostles. Also, the tradition does know of Jesus' knowledge of what others are thinking in their hearts (Luke 5:22; 9:47; cf. 6:8; Jn 2:24-

---

[419] To be sure, one can much more easily make this distinction in Luke's Gospel; but this is not always easy in Acts. George, *Études sur l'œuvre de Luc*, 242, lists the following problematic passages, Acts 2:20.47; 8:22.24; 9:31; 10:33; 13:2; 14:3.23; 15:40; 16:14-15; 20:19. The various interpretations or silence of scholars regarding these passages invites one to cautious prudence.

[420] Foerster, κύριος, 1088, observes about Acts 1:24 that κύριε can also carry an emphatic stress vhen it stands in a prayer.

[421] Haenchen, *The Acts*, 162, provides several references to "Who knows all hearts" as a favorite expression of post-apostolic Christendom and L.T. Johnson, *The Acts*, 37, points out that καρδιογνώστης is often used of God (see Dt 8:2; Pss 7:9LXX; 43:21; 64:6; 139:23; 1 Cor 4:5; 14:25; Heb 4:12; 1 Jn 3:20; Rev 2:23). Although he grants that the literal meaning of the words permit both interpretations, Kürzinger, *The Acts*, I, 27-28, calls attention to the phrasing of Acts 15:8 and concludes that as in the prayers of the OT God is the likely referent. See also Polhill, *Acts*, 94.

[422] Bruce, *The Acts*, 112, points to ἐξελέξατο in v. 2, which is used of Jesus' choosing the original apostles.

[423] George, *Études sur l'œuvre de Luc*, 253.

25). Nonetheless, the lack of clarity about who is the "Lord" in Acts 1:24 remains and so the verse belongs to our present discussion.

Acts 13:44-49, part of the aftermath of Paul's speech at Antioch of Pisidia, proves of interest. Vv. 44, 48 and 49 (cf. 8:25) speak of "the word of the Lord", while v. 46 speaks of "the word of God." Apparently, a scribe or scribes felt the need for some clarification because an alternate reading for "the word of the Lord" in both vv. 44 and 48 is "the word of God." Why this was not done for the phrase in v. 49 is puzzling. More-over, who is "Lord" in v. 47, "For so the Lord has commanded us, 'I have made you (singular) a light to the Gentiles, that you may be an instrument of salvation to the ends of the earth.'" Some scholars rightly detect a par-allel to Luke 2:30-32 and Simeon's words about the child Jesus, and conclude that "Lord" in Acts 13:47 is God. However, in Acts 26:17-18 we find another parallel in the risen Jesus' mission to Paul, which in v. 23 is likewise attributed to Jesus himself. There is the additional problem about the "you" (singular) in Acts 13:47 because it does not logically agree with both Paul and Barnabas. In view of Acts 26:16-18.23, it probably looks to Jesus whose mission Paul and Barnabas are carrying out; but this would not justify the conclusion that "Lord" in Acts 13:47 must be God since we know Jesus shares his mission with Paul([424]).

There are other passages in which we cannot really determine whether "Lord" means God or Jesus. For instance, we read in Acts 14:3, "So they stayed for a considerable period, speaking out boldly for the Lord, who confirmed the word about his grace by granting signs and won-ders to occur through their hand([425])." Nothing in Acts 14:1-7 compels us to decide either for God or Jesus. The same has to be said about Acts 15:40, "But Paul chose Silas and departed after being commended by the brothers to the grace of the Lord"; the fact that some manuscripts provide the alternate reading, "God," for "Lord" demonstrates that scribes realized the need for clarification([426]). Perhaps, this was done under the influence

---

[424] L.T. Johnson, *The Acts*, 241-242, holds that "Lord" in Acts 13:47 is Jesus and alerts us to the use of ἐντέλλομαι in Jesus' comand to the Twelve in Acts 1:2, which continues in that of v. 8, "to the ends of the earth." Moreover, the citation in Acts 13:47 gives content to Jesus' command to Paul in Acts 22:26 and expressed in 26:18.

[425] Haenchen, *The Acts*, 420, n. 7.

[426] See the textual apparatus in *The Greek New Testament*, ed. K. Aland et alii, 469.

of the phrase in 14:26, "From where they sailed to Antioch, where they had been commended to the grace of God for the work they had now accomplished"; but it was deemed necessary.

The phrase, "word of God," is very common in Luke-Acts ([427]); but "Lord" in "word of the Lord" in one instance may well refer to the risen Lord Jesus. When after the earthquake Paul assures the jailor that he and Silas remain safely in prison, the jailor falls at their feet and asks what he must do to be saved. They advise him, "'Believe in the Lord Jesus and you and your household will be saved.' So they spoke the word of the Lord to him and to everyone in his house" (Acts 16:31-32). The nearest referent to "the word of the Lord" is "the Lord Jesus." Since some manuscripts substitute "of God" for "of the Lord," at least one scribe saw the need for clarification. The message about Jesus and baptism in his name (v. 33) do dominate the passage; and if "Lord" in "the word of the Lord" designates Jesus, he is placed on a level similar to that of God in "the word of God."

In Ephesus (Acts 19:11-20) the sons of Sceva attempt to cast out evil spirits by calling on the name of the Lord Jesus, just as Paul was doing. However, an evil spirit not only does not recognize their ability to do this but also jumps on them and sends them away naked and wounded. Their unhappy experience becomes known to all of Ephesus. Fear seizes everyone, and they glorify the name of the Lord Jesus. Many of those who believed confess their magical practices and burn their costly books. Luke concludes the pericope, "Thus did the word of the Lord continue to spread with influence and power" (v. 20). One could argue about the exact translation of this verse, but the only power we see in the pericope is that of the risen Jesus, and by placing the phrase, "of the Lord" between "power" and "the word," Luke allows that it can be taken with both([428]). To be sure, one could argue that "of the Lord" means "God"; but he would have to grant that such a conclusion is not obvious.

---

[427] See Luke 5:1; 8:11.21; 11:28; Acts 4:29.31; 6:2,7; 8:14; 11:1; 12:24; 13:5.7.46; 18:11.

[428] Bruce, *The Acts*, 413, grants this but thinks, "the latter is in every way more probable."

"Lord" in Passages about the Parousia

Our treatment of the topic Son of Man has shown that the risen Jesus' second coming and judgment (cf. Acts 10:42; 17:31) will occur at the end of the eschatological times, which began with Jesus' birth. Moreover, we argued above that, when used of the risen Christ, "Lord" can convey the mystery of Jesus' divinity (e.g., Acts 2:21.33-36; 7:59-60) and that Luke communicates this belief to the readers of his Gospel. It is true that in the parables, which we will be considering below, sometimes "lord" at one level just means the master of the house; but since these parables deal with Jesus' Parousia and the judgment, "lord" takes on the nuance of "Lord," applied to the risen Jesus.

In the parable of the watchful servants (Luke 12:35-48), the master (vv. 36-37) of the house goes to a wedding celebration, and his servants do not know when he will return. The servants are to be watchful and prepare for his return. In v. 40, it becomes clear that the parable relates to the Son of Man and to the hour of his coming([429]), and Peter addresses Jesus as "Lord" (v. 41: κύριε; cf. v. 42; 18:8) and asks whether this parable relates to the disciples or to everyone. Jesus then introduces the faithful and wise manager, probably representative of Church leaders, whom the lord (vv. 42-43, 45-47) places over his other servants. If the manager does well and treats the other servants fairly, he will surely be rewarded. If he does not, he will be punished in accord with the degree of his disobedience and of his failure to response to his responsibilities. There can be little doubt that Luke intends his readers to understand Jesus as the "lord" of the household and so to interpret this word, as would be "Lord," used of the risen Jesus

With the parable of the narrow door (Luke 13:22-30), Jesus, addressed as "Lord," answers the question about how many will be saved. The householder, who is also called "Lord" (v. 25) represents Jesus because those who will not manage to get through the door will plead, "We ate and drank in your company and you taught in our streets." However, the householder will continue to assert that he does not know them and to call them evildoers. The passage is eschatological([430]), and the judgment is also present since there will be weeping and gnashing of teeth. Those

---

[429] Confer Lagrange, *Évangile selon Saint Luc*, 366-371.

[430] Rigaux, *Témoignage*, 415.

excluded will see others from around the world in the kingdom of God with Abraham, Isaac and Jacob and all the prophets.

"Lord" in Luke 16:8 more probably refers to the risen Jesus. The wording of 16:8-9 parallels the sequence in 18:6-8, "Lord" and "I say to you"; for 16:8-9 read, "And the Lord commended that dishonest steward for acting prudently . . . . I tell you . . . ." So, the reference in 16:8 would be the Lord at the end of time. The instructions (vv. 9-13), which follow, have parenetic and eschatological import; and 16:1.9 introduces an ecclesial aspect similar to that found in 12:42-46([431]).

Much the same has to be said for our final example, the parable of the ten pounds (Luke 19:11-27)([432]). Luke writes of a nobleman, who entrusts ten of his servants with a pound each with which to do business, and goes off to a foreign land to receive his kingdom. However, his citizens hate him and send a delegation to keep him from receiving royal power. Nonetheless, the nobleman returns as king and from then on is addressed as "Lord" (vv. 16, 18, 20, 25), and the parable now represents the Parousia and the final judgment. Only three of the ten servants report on how they used the pound. The first has done exceptionally well, the second quite well, and both are abundantly rewarded. The third has actually done nothing but buried the pound and lived in fear of his master; he loses the pound, but nothing further is said of his lot. The judgment of the citizens who did not want the nobleman to become king and reign over them is much more severe; the king orders them to be slaughtered before him. This surprising and frightening slaughter of the king's enemies forcefully brings home the need to accept Jesus as our king and to accept his rule over us. As in the other parables considered here, Luke is communicating to his readers the post-resurrectional and theological import of "Lord"; the scenes he depicts look to the future and Jesus' second coming and the judgment([433]). However, his coming will not occur immediately.

---

[431] De la Potterie, "Le titre κύριος," 143, argues for this more reasonable interpretation of "Lord" in Luke 16:8, although many scholars take it as a reference to the householder.

[432] Plummer, *St. Luke*, 437, views this parable as distinct from Matthew's parable of the talents and lists the various differences between them.

[433] Lenski, *St. Luke's Gospel*, 945-959; Fitzmyer, *The Gospel According to Luke X–XXIV*, 1228, 1233.

"Lord," Used of Jesus in Visions

A few times, Luke identifies the risen Jesus in an appearance or in a vision as the "Lord" and so suggests his divinity. Luke at the end of the Emmaus story wants first to highlight the risen Jesus' appearance to Peter, and so he reports that the Eleven and those with them tell the two disciples, "The Lord has truly been raised and has appeared to Simon" (Luke 24:34)([434]). This sounds like a credal statement (cf. 1 Cor 15:3-5a). In Acts three times Luke reports the risen Jesus' appearance to Paul; in these reports Jesus is designated as "the Lord" (Acts 9:5; 22:8.10[2x]; 26:15[2x]). In the next chapter, we will see that the risen Christ in this appearance acts like God; of course, the appearance in itself would not communicate the mystery of Jesus' divinity, but the possibility of this understanding for "Lord," used of the risen Christ, remains a constant. In the first account of Paul's conversion, Luke designates the risen Jesus in his vision to Ananias, as "Lord" (Acts 9:10-11.13.15; cf. v. 17). There follows immediately on the second account of the risen Jesus' appearance to Paul, a separate appearance (Acts 22:17-21)([435]). Paul has returned to Jerusalem and is praying in the temple area; he becomes ecstatic and sees the "Lord," who instructs him to leave Jerusalem because they will not receive his message. Paul retorts that they know about his persecution of Christians and his approval of Stephen's murder, but the Lord sends him away to the Gentile mission. Later during Paul's imprisonment in Jerusalem, the Lord appears to him and says, "Take courage. For just as you have borne witness to my cause in Jerusalem, so you must also bear witness in Rome" (Acts 23:11).

"Lord" at Christian Baptisms

Above we argued that Luke applies the citation in Acts 2:21 about the Lord of the OT to Jesus and so puts them on the same level and that according to Luke Christians call on the name of the Lord (Jesus) at their baptism. Thus, there is good reason to see in the baptismal confessional statement a reference to the mystery of Jesus' divinity. In Samaria (Acts

---

[434] Fitzmyer, *The Gospel According to Luke X–XXIV*, 1569, identifies the first part of this verse as "a kerygmatic formula" and suggests that Luke himself may have inserted it, although it could have been part of the original phrasing.

[435] Kürzinger, *The Acts*, II, 121, rightly points out that the "Lord" in Acts 22:19 is the risen Jesus and writes, "But the words as they stand can refer to the Lord God in the Jewish sense."

8:14-17) Luke writes of a contrast between baptism in the name of the Lord Jesus and reception of the Holy Spirit to point out the significance of the apostles in Jerusalem and to establish the continuity of the spread of Christianity([436]). In fact, v. 16 reads, "They had only been baptized in the name of the Lord Jesus"; but we do have baptism in the name of the Lord Jesus. In Acts 19:1-7, Paul encounters "disciples" who have been baptized with John's Baptism; he informs them that John said to believe in the one coming after him, namely, in Jesus. "When they heard this, they were baptized in the name of the Lord Jesus," and Paul lays hands on them and they receive the Holy Spirit and speak in tongues and prophecy.

"The Lord" in Acts 16:14-15 very likely refers to the risen Jesus; and given their context, these verses are best treated under the present heading. The Lord opens Lydia's heart to accept Paul's words; and baptized along with her household, she begs Paul and his companions to be her houseguests, if they judge that she is faithful to the Lord. Earlier Luke used similar phrasings of the risen Jesus when he opened the eyes and the scriptures for the two disciples on the road to Emmaus (Luke 24:31-32) and when later he opened the minds of the Eleven and those with them to understand the scriptures (v. 45; cf. 2 Mc 1:4)([437]). Moreover, since in baptism one expressed her faith in Jesus, when the texts speaks of Lydia's faithfulness to the Lord, we naturally think of her faithfulness to the risen Jesus. "The Lord," then, in Acts 16:13-15 probably looks to the risen Jesus and occurs in the context of Lydia's baptism; so quite likely it implies the mystery of Jesus' divinity.

"Lord," Used in the Same Pericope of both Jesus and of God
We have already reflected on Luke 1:43-45, 2:9-11 and Acts 2:34, passages in which "(the) Lord" appears of both God and Jesus. One other pericope merits our attention. In Luke 10:1-2 Jesus, named "the Lord," selects the Seventy(-two) and sends them to every place he intends to go. He tells them that the harvest is abundant but the laborers are few and exhorts them, "So, ask the master of the harvest to send out laborers for his harvest." Scholars interpret "the Lord" in v. 2 to mean God([438]). This

---

[436] For a thorough discussion of Luke's understanding of Christian Baptism, see O'Toole, "Christian Baptism in Luke," 855-866.

[437] Bruce, *The Acts*, 359; L.T. Johnson, *The Acts*, 293.

interpretation seems justified since Jesus is instructing the disciples; and for the reference to be personal, he would have had to be speaking in the third person of himself. Nonetheless, we are not compelled to conclude to a subordination of Jesus, who sends out the Seventy(-two), to the Lord of the harvest. Rather "the Lord," with the article, is used of both God and Jesus. No other evangelist mentions the sending out of the Seventy(-two), and such a mission corresponds very well with the post-resurrectional community when there was real need to begin thinking about replacing the Twelve. Neither in the selection (6:13) nor in the sending out of the Twelve (9:1) does Luke use "Lord" of Jesus; and in 10:1 Luke prefigures the mission to the Gentiles([439]). This post-resurrectional use of "the Lord" in the Christian community is surely open to the mystery of Jesus' divinity.

The Good News or Word of "the Lord"
Four passages speak of the preaching about the Lord or of his word. After Barnabas introduces Paul to the apostles and explains how Paul saw the Lord and in Damascus boldly proclaimed his name, Paul in Jerusalem, "spoke out boldly in the name of the Lord" (Acts 9:28). The post-resurrectional context clarifies that "the Lord" in this verse is the risen Jesus. During his report about the reception of the Gentiles into the Church to the Christians in Jerusalem, Peter explains, "I remembered the word of the Lord, how he said, 'John baptized with water but you will be baptized with the Holy Spirit'" (Acts 11:16)([440]). Peter must have in mind Jesus' words in Acts 1:5 (cf. Luke 3:16), and so "the Lord" must again be the risen Jesus. According to the next pericope, certain Cypriots and Cyrenians traveled to Antioch of Syria and began to speak also to the Greeks, "proclaiming the Lord Jesus. The hand of the Lord was with them and a great number who believed turned to the Lord" (Acts 11:20-21). "Lord" in the phrase, "The hand of the Lord," is more probably God([441]); however

---

[438] E.g., Fitzmyer, *The Gospel According to Luke X–XXIV*, 846; Lenski, *St. Luke's Gospel*, 567-568.

[439] George, *Études sur l'œuvre de Luc*, 249-250.

[440] L.T. Johnson, *The Acts*, 198.

[441] See Luke 1:66; Acts 4:28.30; 7:50; 13:11; but confer Luke 3:17; 5:13. Bruce, *The Acts*, 272, cites a number of OT passages, which use the phrase of God.

"the Lord" to whom the Greeks turn is the risen Jesus, the center of the proclamation. So, in these verses, Luke uses "(the) Lord" of both the risen Jesus and of God; the Lord Jesus is proclaimed, and it is to him that the Greeks turn in belief. Finally, in the very last verse of Luke's two volumes and so in an emphatic position, we read, "He (Paul) proclaimed the kingdom of God and taught about the Lord Jesus Christ, with complete assurance and without hindrance" (Acts 28:31; cf. v. 23). All four of the passages in this paragraph relate to Jesus as the risen Lord and so possibly to his mystery of his divinity.

Turning to and Faith in "the Lord"
Luke connects the expression, "turning to" (ἐπιστρέφειν ἐπί) with God([442]); however, there are two passages where Luke more probably uses the phrasing of the risen Jesus as "the Lord." In the story of the healing of the paralytic Aeneas, Peter proclaims, "Aeneas, Jesus Christ heals you (Acts 9:34). Get up and make your bed". When they see Ananias carrying out this instruction, all the inhabitants of Lydda and Sharon "turned to the Lord" (v. 35). Peter clearly states that Jesus Christ does the healing, and in the next verse Luke reports that all the inhabitants turn to the Lord. Most reasonably, "the Lord" in v. 35 is the risen Jesus; and since Luke elsewhere joins "turning to" with God, his use of it with Jesus as "the Lord" reveals his conviction of their intimate relationship. Much the same has to be said of Acts 11:21. The Cypriots and the Cyrenians have come to Antioch of Syria and "spoke also to the Greeks the good news of the Lord Jesus" (v. 20). The hand of the Lord was with them and "a great number who believed turned to the Lord" (v. 21). The Lord to whom the Greeks turned could be God since "the hand of the Lord" at the beginning of the verse very likely refers to him. However, the proclamation is in terms of "the Lord Jesus"; and he appears to be the more likely referent. So, we have a lack of clarity in the use of "the Lord" and more probably the Greeks turn to the Lord Jesus, even though Luke more often writes about turning to God. The consideration in the next paragraph suggests that Luke's phrasing could have been influenced by his general practice in Acts of speaking of "faith" in the risen Jesus.

---

[442] See Acts 14:15; 15:19; 26:18.20; cf. 28:27.

"Belief in" (πιστεύειν ἐπί) in Acts regularly looks to the risen Jesus([443]). This makes good sense; for if the given Christian missionary is speaking to a Jewish audience, their "believing" could not be belief in God since that was already a reality and would indicate no change in their faith stance. Some passages are very clear about who the Lord is:

"If then God gave them the same gift he gave to us when we came to believe in the Lord Jesus Christ, who was I to be able to hinder God?" (Acts 11:17). "Believe in the Lord Jesus and your and your household will be saved" (Acts 16:31; cf. v. 15).

In speaking to the elders of Miletus, Paul says of himself, "I earnestly bore witness for both Jews and Greeks to repentance before God and to faith in the Lord Jesus" (Acts 20:21).

Other passages lack clarity but leave the reader with the impression that "the Lord" is the risen Jesus. When Luke writes of the many signs and wonders that the apostles performed (Acts 5:12-16), he includes a notice about the growth of the community, "Yet more than ever, believers in the Lord, great numbers of men and women, were added to them." In the raising of Dorcas to life, we have a similar conclusion to that of the healing of Aeneas, "This became known all over Joppa, and many came to believe in the Lord" (Acts 9:42). Since Luke provides us with no information to the contrary, most probably we should also understand "the Lord" as the risen Jesus. The same conclusion may hold for Acts 14:3([444]). In Acts 18:8 "believing in the Lord" very likely also refers to the risen Jesus([445]); for Paul was bearing witness to Christ Jesus (v. 5), and after Crispus and many other Corinthians had believed, they are baptized. In summary, there is evidence that one can turn to the Lord Jesus as one turns toward God; on the other hand, belief in the Lord seems to be only in the risen Jesus. However, in the OT it would be in God.

---

[443] See Acts 3:16 (cf. vv. 13-15); 10:43 (cf. vv. 38-42); 13:39 (cf. vv. 32-38); 19:4; 22:19; 24:24; 26:18 (cf. vv. 15-17; cf.16:15). Confer Bousset, *Kyrios Christos*, 288, n. 145.

[444] Jacquier, *Les Actes des Apôtres*, 417-418, contends the "Lord" in this verse can refer to either God or to the risen Jesus and offers arguments in defense of both interpretations.

[445] Bousset, *Kyrios Christos*, 288-289, n. 145.

"The Lord" Interacts with Individuals or Is Head of the Disciples

In Luke-Acts Jesus as "the Lord" interacts with individuals or functions as the head of the disciples. Some passages related to individuals. When he sees the marvelous catch of fish, Peter falls at Jesus' feet and testifies to the tremendous distance he recognizes between Jesus and himself, "Depart from me, Lord, for I am a sinful man" (Luke 5:8)([446]). Two chapters later, John the Baptist sends his disciples to the Lord (Luke 7:19; cf. v. 27) to ask whether he is the one who is to come or should they look for another. This passage surely demonstrates that John sees Jesus as superior to himself and whose coming is of supreme importance. The chief tax collector Zacchaeus assures "the Lord" that he gives half of his wealth to the poor and, if he has defrauded anyone, he will repay them fourfold (19:8). Luke balances off Peter's overconfident assertion, "Lord (κύριε), I am prepared to go to prison and to die with you" (22:33) with the poignant scene, "The Lord turned and looked at Peter, and Peter remembered the prediction of the Lord" (22:61)([447]). Paul speaks of his "serving the Lord" (Acts 20:19; cf. v. 24); and in Caesarea he reacts strongly to his fellow Christians who are very concerned about the danger of his going to Jerusalem, "I am prepared not only to be bound but even to die in Jerusalem for the name of the Lord Jesus" (Acts 21:13; cf. v. 14). The last two examples deal with the risen Jesus as "(the) Lord," and this understanding is possible in the other passages.

In other passages, Jesus as "the Lord" is leader of the disciples. In Luke 6:5, Jesus says to some of the Pharisees, "The Son of Man is Lord of the Sabbath." D.L. Bock writes, "With the remark, Jesus argues that he is the authoritative representative of the new way (as David was in the old era?) and that he has authority over the understanding and administration of the Sabbath"([448]). However, does this interpretation really explain precisely why the Son of Man can be "Lord of the Sabbath"; and can this "title" be lightly given anyone but God? Jesus' question in Luke 6:46, "Why do you call me, 'Lord, Lord,' but not do what I command" implies

---

[446] Fletcher-Louis, *Luke-Acts: Angels*, 37 (cf. 36-38), suggests that the characterization of Jesus in this episode may most helpfully be understood in terms of an angelophany.

[447] See Fitzmyer, *The Gospel According to Luke I–IX*, 202-203, for some reflections on Luke's reading "the Lord" frequently back into Jesus' earthly ministry.

[448] *Luke 1:1 – 9:50*, 527. Compare de la Potterie, "Le titre κύριος," 134.

that the hearers know what he commands but do not do it. The recognition of Jesus as "Lord" and his question would fit well in the parenetic reflections of the later Christian community. When the Samaritan village will not receive Jesus because he was headed to Jerusalem, James and John ask, "Lord, do you want us to call down fire from heaven to consume them?" (Luke 9:54). Jesus' answer not only serves to correct their understanding of who he is, but later generations will also realize that their Lord is not vengeful. At the beginning of the journey to Jerusalem, an individual says (Luke 9:61; cf. 59; Acts 18:25-26), "I will follow you, Lord," but asks first to be allowed to say farewell to his family. Jesus' answer reminds the Lord's disciples of the total dedication required in following him. When the Seventy(-two) return rejoicing from their mission, they exclaim, "Lord, even the demons are subject to us because of your name" (Luke 10:17). Above, we noted that this passage was most likely post-resurrectional and directed to the later Church when the apostles would have been advanced in years or already dead. We also see in this passage the Lord's authority over demons. Mary in the story of Jesus' visit to her and her sister represents the ideal disciple who realizes that the most important thing to do is to sit at the Lord's feet and to listen to his word (10:39)([449]). Martha in her dialogue with the Lord (cf. vv. 41-42) constitutes a foil, which permits the Lord to clarify that Mary has chosen the better part. In 11:39 the Lord admonishes the Pharisees because they clean the outside of cup and dish, but inside they are full of greed and wickedness([450]). When the apostles ask Jesus as "Lord" to increase their faith, the "Lord" replies, "If you have faith the size of a mustard seed, you would say to (this) mulberry tree, 'Be uprooted and planted in the sea' and it would obey you" (17:5-6). To be sure faith was relevant for the apostles prior to Jesus' resurrection but even more so afterwards; it would be particularly important for later Christians. As regards the day of the Lord, the disciples ask Jesus, "'Where, Lord?' He said to them, 'Where the body

---

[449] De la Potterie, "Le titre κύριος," 129-132, notes this and the ecclesial aspect of the passage; however, even though he can point to a parallel to 1 Cor 7:32-35, I do not believe that he is correct to conclude that Mary is a model for the contemplative life.

[450] De la Potterie, "Le titre κύριος," 132-134, associates this passage with Luke 13:15 and draws an interesting and convincing conclusion: given 6:5 and Acts 15:11, it is not an exaggeration to see "the Lord" in Luke's Gospel passages where Jesus so forcefully reproaches the rigid legalism of the Jews as the Lord of believers.

is, there also the vultures will gather'" (17:37). Of course, the Parousia is a post-resurrectional event; and although the Lord's answer at first appears enigmatic, the presence of vultures will hardly escape notice. Jesus tells his disciples who are going to get the colt for him to answer anyone who questions their taking the animal, "The Lord has need of it" (19:31; cf. v. 34). "The Lord" here appears ecclesial; Jesus is "the Lord" of the disciples and([451]), perhaps, even of the person with whom they are speaking. When in the discourse after the Passover meal, Jesus predicts that he will be seen as a criminal, the well-meaning apostles assure him, "Lord, look, there are two swords here" (22:38). Their lack of understanding continues when one of them during the betrayal and arrest of Jesus in the garden asks, "Lord, shall we strike with a sword" (v. 49)? Nonetheless, they are addressing him as their leader; and this is how Luke's readers would have interpreted "Lord" in the passages.

In the last chapter of the Gospel and in Acts, the risen Lord Jesus continues as leader of the disciples. The women who from Galilee have followed with Jesus come to the tomb but do not find the body of the Lord Jesus (Luke 24:3). When the apostles are discussing the successor to Judas, they determine the person must have been with them the whole time "the Lord Jesus came and went among us" (Acts 1:21), from the baptism of John until the Ascension so that he can be a witness of Jesus' resurrection. Later Luke writes of Saul's persecuting the Christians, "still breathing murderous threats against the disciples of the Lord (Acts 9:1)." "Lord of all" in Acts 10:36, "You know the word (that) he sent to the Israelites as he proclaimed peace through Jesus Christ, who is Lord of all," surely refers to the risen Jesus. Probably, "Lord of all" is to be taken personally: Jesus is Lord of both Jews and Gentiles([452]). The Apostles and the elders in Jerusalem describe Barnabas and Paul as men "who have dedicated their lives to the name of our Lord Jesus Christ" (Acts 15:26). Finally, Paul's reference to the saying of "the Lord Jesus" that it is more blessed to give than to receive (Acts 20:35b) appears in a post-resurrectional context and provides believers with a fundamental directive

---

[451] Nolland, *Luke 18:35 – 24:52*, 925, "To Luke and to his readers 'the Lord' here is the "lord of the full Christian affirmation (cf. at 7:13) . . . ."

[452] Haenchen, *The Acts*, 352, n. 4; for a general discussion of this title, see Cadbury, "The Titles of Jesus in Acts," 361-362.

about generosity. Except for Luke 10:17 (cf. vv. 12); Acts 1:21 (cf. vv. 22-24) and 21:13-14, we have not argued for the presence of the mystery of Jesus' divinity in any of these passages. However, all of the examples in this section, particularly those, which clearly speak of the risen Jesus, are definitely open to such an interpretation of "(the) Lord." Moreover, the kinds of interactions, which the Lord has with individuals, and the various expressions of his leadership of the disciples fit the post-apostolic church well and so do not argue against such an understanding.

The Lord and Miracles
Both in the Gospel and Acts, Jesus as "the Lord" works miracles. Understanding what "(the) Lord" means in these passages can prove challenging. For instance, if the person has confidence in the Lord's ability to cure but cannot be classified as a believer, it seems less likely that Luke wants to mean anything more with "(the) Lord" than "(the) master." Nonetheless, there remains the possibility that Luke uses "(the) Lord" rather for his Christian reader who would perceive its fuller meaning. For example, in Luke 5:12 a leper falls on his face before Jesus and begs him, "Lord, if you wish, you can make me clean." After the cure, the leper carries out Jesus' instructions, but in the rest of the pericope nothing further is said about his faith. Only a Christian reader could interpret "the Lord" as meaning more than just "the master"; however, that is very likely Luke's intention, to communicate this belief to his reader. After all, that is what Luke himself believes. In two passages, the Lord acts without any notice about the faith of the recipients, although they do glorify God. At the raising of the son of the widow of Nain (7:11-17)([453]), "When the Lord saw her, he was moved with pity for her (v. 13) and said to her, 'Do not weep.'" He raises her son and gently gives him back to her. Everyone glorifies God and sees in Jesus a great prophet and God's visitation of his people. Similarly, in healing of the crippled woman on the Sabbath (13:10-17), Jesus on his own initiative called her and freed her from her illness. Then, the head of the synagogue admonished the people not to come to be healed on the Sabbath; but "The Lord said to him in reply, 'Hypocrites'" (v. 15) and pointed out the hypocrisy of his opponents. After her cure the woman had glorified God, and at the end of the pericope the whole crowd rejoiced at

---

[453] Bock, *Luke 1:1 – 9:50*, 650, points out that this is the first use of "Lord" in Luke's narrative comments with regard to Jesus.

all of Jesus' marvelous deeds. In both case, Luke's reader can easily
perceive the fuller meaning for "the Lord."

Two other passages speak of the faith of one who asked for or
experienced the miracle (Luke 7:1-10; 18:35-43). As Jesus travels along
to the house of the centurion to cure his servant, the latter sends friends to
say on his behalf, "Lord, do not trouble yourself (7:13), for I am not
worthy to have you enter under my roof." The centurion further explains
his stance, and Jesus is amazed and tells those who are following that he
has not found such faith in Israel. Such faith suggests a deeper meaning of
"Lord" than just "master." The blind beggar near Jericho, who insistently
calls on Jesus as the Son of David for mercy and ultimately overcomes the
opposition of those around him, requests of Jesus, "Lord, please let me
see" (18:41). Jesus restores his sight and tells him, "Your faith has saved
you." Like a disciple, the man restored to sight follows Jesus and glorifies
God, and all the people praise God (vv. 42-43). Consequently, "the Lord"
in these passages works miracles and shows a true concern for the plight
of two women. In none of the pericopes are we obliged to understand
"the Lord" of the risen Jesus and so to see a possible reference to the
mystery of his divinity, but for a Christian reader such an understanding
remains a definite possibility.

Conclusion[454]

Luke's presentation of Jesus as "(the) Lord" is best understood within the
LXX tradition and with an eye to Luke's readers who were Christians and
steeped in this tradition. There are three keys to a correct understanding
of Luke's use of "(the) Lord": 1) his introduction of the mystery of Jesus'
divinity in Luke 1:35, which guides the reader's understanding of subsequent passages; 2) his association of this title with that found of God in
the OT (Acts 2:21.36; cf. 7:59-60; 21:14); 3) his own belief in Jesus as
"Lord" in the fullest sense of this title. When I write that Luke reads back
into his Gospel the title "(the) Lord" of the risen Jesus, which can connote
the mystery of Jesus' divinity, I am referring to Luke's own belief in Jesus
as Lord. Significantly, in his two volumes, Luke in the majority of instances identifies either God or Jesus as "(the) Lord"; when this identification
is not clear, most reasonably this vagueness results from Luke's own
intimate association of them. When writing of either of them, he does not

---

[454] Acts 15:11 was considered in the chapter "Jesus as Savior."

always feel obligated to specify to whom he is referring. When applied to Jesus in Acts or in scenes of the Parousia, in visions or in baptism stories, "(the) Lord" is surely the risen Jesus and more likely also carries the connotation of the mystery of Jesus' divinity. This possibility becomes more certain, if the context is ecclesial. In other passages, although the story line might not indicate that "Lord" implies the mystery of Jesus' divinity; nonetheless, on another level Luke can convey to his reader his own faith in the risen Jesus as Lord. In these last cases, it is not always easy to demonstrate Luke's precise intention; but it certainly does not follow that we should conclude that "(the) Lord" in all of these passages cannot refer to the risen Jesus and is not open to the mystery of Jesus' divinity.

CHAPTER NINE

Luke Predicates the Same or Similar Things of Jesus and of God([455])

Luke does predicate similar or the same things of both God and Jesus. This chapter addresses these data and falls into three parts, the third of which is by far the most extensive: relevant previous discussions, some similar statements about God and Jesus and expressions which indicate an intimate relationship between them and so suggest or communicate the mystery of his divinity.

Relevant Previous Discussions
Relevant to this topic are our previous discussions about the title "Lord" applied to Jesus, especially insofar as there is any suggestion of the mystery of his divinity. This suggestion can be found in the mutual knowledge that the Father and Son have of each other (Luke 10:22), the doing of Jesus' will as God's should be done (Acts 21:14 [cf. 20:24; Luke 22:42]) and Stephen's praying to the risen Jesus (Act 7:59-60) as Jesus prayed to the Father (cf. Luke 23:34.46). Also, God knows the hearts of human being (Acts 15:8), and Jesus (Luke 5:22; 9:47; cf. 6:8), what others are thinking in their hearts([456]).

Some Similar Statements about God and Jesus
Seeking (ζητέω) Jesus (Luke 2:48-49; 6:19; 9:9; 19:3; 24:5) is a Lucan theme, and once he definitely praises the same attitude toward God (Acts 17:27; cf. Luke 11:9-11). "The word" (ὁ λόγος) is almost always "the

---

[455] See Buckwalter, *Luke's Christology*, 184-193, 210-213, 280-284; Fletcher-Louis, *Luke-Acts: Angels*, 21-27; Jacquier, *Les Actes des Apôtres*, ccix-ccx, ccxiii. Confer also Dunn, "The Making of Christology," 451-452; Ellingworth, "Christology: Synchronic or Diachronic," 496-499; Thiselton, "Christology in Luke," 470-472.

[456] Cf. Bovon, *Luke 1*, 394.

word of God"; however, Jesus' word is in power (4:32; cf. 4:22), and as noted above, when Paul and Barnabas proclaim "the Lord" boldly in Iconium, the reference may well be to Jesus who through miracles witnesses to the word of his grace (Acts 14:3). God selects (ἐκλέγομαι) the Fathers (Acts 13:17), Jesus (Luke 9:35) and Peter (Acts 15:7); and Jesus, the Twelve (Luke 6:13; cf. Acts 1:2.24). At Jerusalem, James quotes Peter that God has "first concerned himself with acquiring from among the Gentiles a people for his name" (Acts 15:14); and in Corinth, the risen Jesus appears to Paul and encourage him because "I have many people in this city" (Acts 18:10). Paul and Barnabas entrust the newly appointed elders of Lystra, Iconium and Antioch to the Lord in whom they believe (Acts 14:23) seemingly Jesus; and later Paul alone those of Ephesus to God and the word of his grace (Acts 20:32). Luke ultimately associates all but one instance of "loving mercy" with God, but in Luke 1:72.78 this mercy is actualized through Jesus. Twice Jesus exercises loving mercy, with the ten lepers (Luke 17:13) and the blind beggar near Jericho (18:38-39). This loving mercy is not limited to him (16:24; cf. 10:37), but clearly that of Jesus is much more similar to God's.

Some Expressions Indicate an Intimate Relationship between God and Jesus

Glory

Glory (δόξα) is a characteristic of God (Luke 2:9; Acts 7:2.55), and we human beings are to give him glory (Luke 17:18; cf. Acts 12:23). However, Luke writes also of Jesus' glory[457]. The Son of Man will come in his glory (Luke 9:26; cf. 21:27), and Peter, John and James at the Transfiguration see Jesus' glory, which apparently is distinguished from that of Moses and Elijah (vv. 30-32). We note something of a parallel between what is said about God in 2:9, "The angel of the Lord appeared to them and the glory of the Lord shone around them" and Jesus' appearance to Paul, "Since I could see nothing because of the brightness (ἀπὸ τῆς δόξης) of that light (Acts 22:11; cf. 6), I was led by hand by my companions and entered Damascus" and "At midday, along the way, O king, I saw a light from the sky, brighter than the sun, shining around me and my traveling companions" (Acts 26:13). One could object that Acts 22:6.11 and 26:13 do not explicit state that what Paul saw was Christ; however,

---

[457] "To enter his glory," said of Jesus in Luke 24:26, refers to his resurrection.

26:16, "Get up now, and stand on your feet, I have appeared to you for this purpose, to appoint you as servant and witness of what you have seen (of me) and what you will see (ὧν τε εἰδές [με] ὧν τε ὀφθήσομαί σοι)," answers this difficulty. So, Luke writes of both God's glory and Jesus'.

Name

E. Haenchen observes, "The ὄνομα (proper name) is no chance attribute of the person, but expresses his very essence. Hence the power of the person named, be he human or divine is itself present and available in the ὄνομα"([458]). In his two volumes, Luke employs "name" in regard to both God and Jesus([459]). Luke connects the name of Jesus with the casting out of demons, the persecution of Christians, salvation, repentance, miracles, baptism and preaching. Key to understanding Luke's use of "name" both of God and Jesus is "Everyone who calls on the name of the Lord" which in some passages (Acts 2:21; cf. 7:59-60; 9:14.21; 22:16) surely looks to Jesus and recalls the invoking the name of Yahweh in the OT and so the invocation of the divine([460]). If in the OT citation in Acts 2:21 "Lord" originally referred to Yahweh, is not the same necessarily true of "name"? Yet both now relate to Jesus. Thus, since Christians call on the name of the Lord (Jesus) at baptism([461]), we should regard "the name of the Lord" as including the mystery of Jesus' divinity. The emphasis is on "Lord"; but "name" does not become meaningless but is rather defined by "Lord." Of course, "to call on the name of the Lord" also appertains to prayer and

---

[458] Haenchen, *The Acts*, 200; Ruck-Schröder, *Der Name*, 11-63, summarizes the history of the research on "name" and on 160-202 its use in Luke-Acts. However, Ruck-Schröder contends that Luke supposes a subordinationism in the phrase, "name of Jesus."

[459] Bousset, *Kyrios Christos*, 288, n. 145, maintains that in Acts all the appearances of "name" are always connected with Jesus except for Acts 15:14; cf. v. 17. For a thorough consideration of this topic, see O'Toole, "Activity of the Risen Jesus," 487-491.

[460] Moule, "The Christology of Acts," 161; see also Bock, *Proclamation from Prophecy*, 201; Bruce, *The Acts*, 60.

[461] Acts 2:38; 8:16; 9:14.21; 10:48; 19:5; 22:16.

liturgy. Below we will address Acts 4:12 and its universal salvation in the name of Jesus.

Power
Both ἐξουσία and δύναμις (and cognates) communicate the concept, "power," in Luke-Acts. Both God and Jesus exercise power([462]). However, in a negative sense, Satan also has power (Luke 4:6; Acts 26:18).

The Kingdom
Luke usually writes of "the kingdom of God." However, Jesus is the king (Luke 1:32-33; 19:38; cf. vv. 11-27); and of his kingdom there will be no end. With the words, "for the sake of the kingdom of God," in 18:29 Luke replaces the "followed you" of v. 28 and "for my sake and for the sake of the gospel" in Mk 10:29. When he is addressing Pharisees, Jesus' presence seems the correct explanation for his somewhat puzzling words, "For behold, the kingdom of God is among you (17:21; cf. 11:20)." Once Luke writes of Jesus, "And I confer a kingdom on you, just as my Father has conferred one on me, that you may eat and drink at my table in my kingdom; and you will sit on thrones judging the twelve tribe of Israel" (22:29-30, cf. vv. 16, 18). Jesus' conferral imitates that of his Father; he can likewise speak of the eschatological kingdom as *his* kingdom, which reaches out to the whole of Israel, reinterpreted by Luke as embracing all believers (Acts 3:22-23). The plea of the good thief, "Jesus, remember me when you come into your kingdom," repeats the theme that the kingdom is also Jesus'. When in Acts 1:6, the apostles ask Jesus, "Lord, are you at this time going to restore the kingdom to Israel," he responds that it is not for them to know the moment that the Father has chosen for this event; but he does not deny the implication that he has the ability to restore the kingdom to Israel.

---

[462] For examples of God's power, see Luke 1:35; 3:8; 5:17.21; Acts 1:7; of Jesus', Luke 4:14.32.36; 5:12-13.24; 6:19; 8:46; 20:2.8; Acts 4:7; cf. 3:12.

<u>Visit</u>
God visits his people to save or, in some way, to benefit them([463]). In Luke 1:68 (cf. Acts 15:14), Zechariah praises the God of Israel, "for he has visited and brought redemption to his people." In the next verse we learn that he does this through a mighty savior in the house of David, namely, Jesus (cf. 1:32-33). Again in the *Benedictus,* because of the loving mercy of God, "the Dawn from on high will visit us" (Luke 1:78). The "Dawn" more probably refers to Jesus, who is described as light in Luke-Acts; and this understanding holds, even if one wants to interpret "Lord" in v. 76 of God since we noted above that he acts particularly through Jesus. A similar situation occurs when Jesus raises the son of the widow of Nain from the dead, and the people recognize that a great prophet has appeared in their midst and so declare, "God has visited his people" (7:16). Once (19:44), without any reference to God, Luke in the scene of Jesus' weeping over Jerusalem cites Jesus' explanation of the negative response of Jerusalem to himself and of its coming fall, "because you did not recognize the time of your visitation." God visits his people through Jesus; and once Jesus' visit seems to be a true parallel to that of God.

<u>Grace</u>
According to Luke, χάρις can mean just being in favor with someone. However, when used of God or Jesus, it signifies their marvelous activity in the lives of others. Most often the "grace," in the latter sense, is God's, and Jesus himself grows in this grace (Luke 2:40.52). However, Luke writes of Jesus' grace, which carries much the same meaning as that of the God. At Jerusalem Peter tells his Jewish audience (Acts 15:11), "We believe that we are saved through the grace of the Lord Jesus, in the same way as they." This passage resembles two other passages in which the positive acceptance of the gospel message is attributed to the grace of God (Acts 11:23; 13:43). Since "Lord" in Acts 14:3 ("Speaking out boldly [παρρησιαζόμενοι([464])] for the Lord, who confirmed the word of his

---

[463] Denaux, "The Theme of Divine Visits," 263-268, 278-279, defends the position that Luke in his description of Jesus' mission, made use of the pattern of "divine visits on earth" which was widespread in Graeco-Roman literature and present in the Septuagint.

[464] Luke uses "speaking out boldly" (παρρησιάζω) in relationship to God (Acts 4:29-30; 19:8; cf. 13:46; 18:26?) and of Jesus (Luke 9:27-28; Acts 2:29; 28:31; cf. Acts

grace by granting signs and wonders to occur through their hand") more likely designates the risen Jesus who is the heart of Paul and Barnabas' message, we would have a good parallel to "the word of his grace" which Luke writes of God in Acts 20:32 (cf. v. 24) ("And now I commend you to God and to the word of his grace that can build you up . . . ."). These words call to mind those of Jesus in the synagogue of Nazareth (Luke 4:22), "And all spoke highly of him and were amazed at the words of grace that came from his mouth." Consequently, Luke predicates "grace" both of God and Jesus.

<u>Salvation</u>
Luke employs "saving power" and "Savior" only of God (1:47; 3:6) and of Jesus (2:11.30; Acts 5:31; 13:23; 28:28). The same is generally true of "saving" and "salvation" but for a few apparent exceptions which are easily explained. In Luke 9:25, Luke makes the point that, if someone tries to save himself, he will fail; but should he dedicate himself totally to following Christ he will save his life. That is, human beings cannot save themselves; but if they give themselves totally to Christ, he will save them. According to Acts 13:47, Paul and Barnabas react to the Jewish zealous rejection of their message with the words, "For so the Lord has commanded us (plural), 'I have made you (singular) a light to the Gentiles, that you (singular) may be an instrument of salvation to the ends of the earth.'" The lack of correspondence between "us" and "you" singular of the citation alerts us to the complexity of Luke's thought here. In fact, "Lord" probably refers to Jesus because he gives Paul his mission (Acts 9:6.15-16; cf. 26:15-18); and as we have already seen, the salvific concept of "light" primarily looks to Jesus([465]). Thus, the correct understanding of Acts 13:47 is that Paul and Barnabas are a light to the Gentiles and salvation up to the ends of the earth since they are the messengers of Jesus, the "light," and of the salvation he brings. Acts 15:1 simply reports a misunderstanding, for some who have come down from Judea erroneously want to subordinate Christian salvation to circumcision according to the custom of Moses. In Luke's account of Paul's sea voyage to Rome it first appears

---

4:13?). Moreover, it is doubtful that Luke would use παρρησιάζω ἐπί, directly of "the Lord" in reference to God since this expression generally refers to Jesus.

[465] Luke 2:32; 11:33; Acts 9:3; 22:6.9.11; 26:13; cf. Luke 1:78-79; Acts 26:18.23.

that all hope of being saved is lost (Acts 27:20; cf. v. 31); but Paul receives a vision of an angel who assured him that he is to appear before Caesar and that God has granted safety to all those traveling with him (vv. 23-24; cf. v. 34). In summary, Luke's use of "salvation" almost exclusively of God and of Jesus does not necessarily lead to a conclusion of equality between them, but it does reveal a radical union between them which leads to Jesus' being able to act as normally only God can act. This assertion should be understood against the background of the main influence on Luke, the LXX, where it is God who saves. For instance, Is 43:11 reads, "It is I, I the Lord; there is no savior but me" and reveals just how radical is the statement about Jesus in Acts 4:12, "There is no salvation through anyone else, nor is there any other name under heaven given to the human race by which we are to be saved." In fact, Luke writes mostly of Jesus who saves and can identify his actions with those of God. For instance, in the healing of the Gerasene Demoniac (Luke 8:26-39), Jesus commands the unclean spirit to come out of him and lets the "legion" of evil spirits enter the herd of swine. Later those who had seen the event describe for the townspeople how the demoniac was "saved," and at the end of the story Jesus instructs the healed man to return home and to declare "how much *God* has done for you" (v. 39; cf. Mark 5:19). What Jesus did is predicated of God. Clearly, Luke is willing to predicate of Jesus and of him alone the salvific activity traditionally affirmed of only God.

Blessing can belong to the area of salvation. Twice God is ultimately the source of the blessing (Luke 1:42; cf. Acts 3:25-26); and in one scene, Jesus (Luke 24:50-51) blesses his audience.

Forgiveness of Sins
Both the Father (Luke 11:4; 23:34[?]; cf. 3:3; 12:10; Acts 3:19; 8:22) and Jesus (5:20-26; 7:48-79; Acts 5:31; 7:60; cf. Luke 4:18) forgive sins. At other times, Jesus is not directly said to forgive sins; but forgiveness of sins is achieved by faith in him or through him or in his name. In the name of the Messiah repentance and forgiveness of sins are to be proclaimed to all nations, beginning from Jerusalem (Luke 24:47). The prophets testify that everyone who believes in the risen Jesus of Nazareth receives forgiveness of sins through his name (Acts 10:43; cf. 2:38; 22:16; 26:18); and through Jesus Paul proclaims forgiveness of sins to his Jewish audience who can now be justified from every sin from which the Law of Moses could not free them (Acts 13:38; cf. v. 39).

We need to consider in more detail the stories of the healing of the paralytic and of the sinful woman forgiven. The story of the healing of the paralytic (Luke 5:17-26) proves most helpful for appreciating Luke's understanding of Jesus' ability to forgive sins. When Jesus sees the faith of those who have let the paralytic's bed down through a hole in the roof, he says to the paralytic, "As for you, your sins are forgiven" (v. 20). Then the scribes and Pharisees begin to question, "Who is this who speaks blasphemies? Who but God alone can forgive sins?" Jesus reads their thought and asks what is easier to say, "'Your sins are forgiven,' or to say 'Stand up and walk'" (v. 23)? Then to show that the Son of Man has authority on earth to forgive sins, he orders the paralytic, "Rise, pick up your stretcher, and go home" (v. 24). The paralytic immediately does just that and goes home glorifying God. Jesus in the story draws a connection between the miracle and his ability to forgive sins. The miracle itself witnesses to this capacity, and his opponents should now know that the Son of Man has authority on earth to forgive sins. This authority likewise answers the second question of the scribes and Pharisees, "Who can forgive sins but God alone." So, Jesus is not blaspheming. J.A. Fitzmyer[466] summarizes the import of the story well when he writes, "The general sense of the conflated story presents Jesus as the Son of Man, a heaven-sent agent, able to do what people normally ascribe to Yahweh alone. This implied equality is heightened in this Lucan form of the episode by the addition of the adjective μόνος, 'alone'."

When Jesus tells the sinful woman, "Your sins are forgiven," his companions at table begin to say among themselves, "Who is this who even forgives sins?" Jesus does not answer their question but simply tells the woman, "Your faith has saved you; go in peace" (Luke 7:48-50). Jesus' final words underline his ability to forgive the woman's sins. The Lucan emphasis in the question of Jesus' table companions does not so much suggest that they doubt Jesus' ability to forgive sins as highlight query about his identity. Luke places the question of Jesus' identity precisely in terms of his forgiving of sins. By means of his treatment in Luke-Acts of Jesus' forgiving sins, Luke provides an answer to Jesus' identify; he portrays Jesus as doing what normally people ascribe to God alone.

---

[466] *The Gospel According to Luke I–IX*, 580.

Jesus' forgiveness of those who crucified him belongs to our present discussion. We have already observed that many scholars accept Luke 23:34 as genuine (cf. Acts 7:60). In this act of forgiveness Jesus demonstrates his intimate closeness to the Father in his love for his enemies and in his willingness to do good to those who hate him called for in Luke 6:27-35([467]); thus, he proves himself a son of God. Although Luke 23:34 itself is no proof of Jesus' divinity; Luke in his general treatment of Jesus' ability to forgive sins definitely predicates of him an activity reserved to God.

Redemption

Luke 1:68 reads, "Blessed be the Lord, the God of Israel, for he has visited and brought redemption to his people"; and in the next verse we learn that he does this by raising up a mighty savior in the house of David. In view of 1:32-33, the mighty savior in the house of David must be Jesus. Later in the temple area, the prophetess Anna repeats the ideas of 1:68-69, for she thanks God and speaks about Jesus to all who "were awaiting the redemption of Jerusalem" (2:38). However, in this verse, "redemption" is more directly connected with Jesus. So, we should probably understand ironically the words of the disciples on the road to Emmaus, "But we were hoping that he would be the one to redeem Israel" (24:21). Their hope was and is justified because Jesus does redeem Israel; and according to Luke both God and Jesus redeem([468]).

Repentance

Luke likewise predicates repentance of both God and the risen Jesus. After Paul explains to the apostles and other Christians in Jerusalem why he acted in Caesarea as he did, they no longer complain but rather exclaim, "God has then granted life-giving repentance to the Gentiles too" (Acts 11:18). About the Christ, the risen Jesus proclaims to the Eleven and those with them, "That repentance, for the forgiveness of sins, is to be

---

[467] See Owczarek, *Sons of the Most High*, 232-243; confer Topel, *Children of a Compassionate God*, 250-253, 274-285.

[468] Above we argued that Luke writes "redeemer" (λυτρωτής) of Moses because he is drawing a parallel between him and Jesus and, in view of Jesus being redeemer, the same is said of Moses to develop this parallel.

preached in his name to all the nations, beginning from Jerusalem" (Luke 24:47). Later the risen Jesus also gives repentance as we read in Acts 5:31, "God exalted him at his right hand as leader and savior to grant Israel repentance and forgiveness of sins." Surely, one can argue that God exalted Jesus and gave him the power to grant repentance and that "is to be proclaimed" in Luke 24:47 is a majestic passive and so God is the principle agent. Nonetheless, Luke associates repentance only with God and with Jesus; and in Acts 5:31 the exalted Jesus grants repentance.

Peace

"Peace" when used of God or of Jesus carries a different nuance than when it appears of others; for it is to be associated with salvation. Twice, peace may well be related to both God and Jesus (Luke 1:79; 2:14). However, "peace" in Luke 19:28 (cf. Acts 9:31?) should be associated with God, and this is certainly true of Jesus in Acts 10:36([469]). Furthermore, both God (Luke 2:29) and Jesus can send someone away in peace (Luke 7:50; 8:48).

Inheritance

Luke places Jesus on a level very similar to that of God when he writes of inheritance among the consecrated. Toward the end of his speech to the Ephesian elders at Miletus, Paul entrusts them "to God and to that gracious word of his that can build you up and give you the inheritance among all who are consecrated (Acts 20:32: τὴν κληρονομίαν ἐν τοῖς ἡγιασμένοις πᾶσιν). Luke repeats some of this phrasing in his description of the risen Jesus' mission to Paul. The latter part of this mission is to turn from darkness to light and from the power of Satan to God, so that they may obtain forgiveness of sins and "an inheritance among those who have been consecrated by faith in me" (Acts 26:18: κλῆρον ἐν τοῖς ἡγιασμένοις πίστει τῇ εἰς ἐμέ). God's word gives the Ephesian elders inheritance among the consecrated, and faith in Jesus consecrates Paul's future audiences. However, faith in Jesus does not only go with "those who have been consecrated"; for their very being made holy is what their forgiveness of sins means and what entitles them to the inheri-

---

[469] For a more thorough study of "peace" in this passage, see O'Toole, "Εἰρήνη," 461-476.

tance(470). If this be the case, then what is achieved by faith in Jesus in Acts 26:18 ("an inheritance among those who have been consecrated"), in 20:32 is achieved by the word of God's grace ("the inheritance among all who are consecrated"); and we have an example of what God achieves and of what Jesus can also achieve.

At Paul's Conversion Jesus Speaks and Acts As the God of the OT
Both God (Acts 22:14-15) and the risen Jesus (Acts 9:15-17; 26:16-18; cf. 20:14; 21:13) give Paul his mission. As in the case of Christ Jesus whom "he has already appointed for you" (Acts 3:20), God selected Paul "to know his will, to see the Righteous One, and to hear the sound of his voice" (Acts 22:14). In the only other occurrence of this verb (προχειρίζ-ομαι) the risen Jesus explains to Paul, "I have appeared to you for this purpose, to appoint you (σε) as a servant and witness of what you have seen (of me) and of what you will see of me" (Acts 26:16).

All of the reports about Paul's conversion experience contain variations, yet all of them have as their core the dialogue between Christ and Paul (Acts 9:4-6; 22:7-10; 26:14-16). G. Lohfink has pointed to the literary form of an *Erscheinungsgespräch* which can be found in Gn 31:11-13; 46:2-3; Ex 3:2-10. If one compares Gn 46:2-3 with Acts 9:4-6 and Gn 31:11-13 with Acts 26:14-16, the structure of this literary form can be detected: double vocative, the question of the one having the experience, the self-presentation of the one appearing, and the giving of a mission. One also finds in the OT a shorter form of this literary genre which does not have the self-presentation of the one appearing (cf. Gn 22:1-2.11-12; 1 Sm 3:4-14); but this shorter form, as the longer one, stands only in Acts (cf. 9:10-16; 10:3-6) in the NT. Acts 10:3-6 reports Cornelius' vision of an angel of God, and 9:10-16 relate Jesus' appearance to Ananias. Actually, Gn 22:1-2 corresponds with Acts 9:10-11 almost word for word. The fact that the *Erscheinungsgespräch* occurs in Acts other than in the conversion stories of Paul betrays the hand of Luke. This is all the truer since these stories about Paul originally had nothing to do with the conversion experience of Cornelius(471). Without entering into the histori-

---

470 O'Toole, *Acts 26*, 79-80. Without "faith in me" Acts 26:18 could theoretically be acceptable to any Jew; so this phrase determines the meaning of the whole verse.

471 Lohfink, *Paulus vor Damaskus* , 53-60; see also O'Toole, *Acts 26*, 6-7.

cal question, which is not our task here, we can draw some conclusions. Except for Gn 22:11-12 (which, however, does stand in the same pericope as Gn 22:1-2), every one of the OT examples of this literary form deals explicitly with an interaction between God and a human being. Consequently, although Acts 10:3-6 does report Cornelius' vision of an angel of God, Luke has chosen a literary form for Paul's conversion experience and for the appearance to Ananias, which describes Jesus as is God in the OT and so suggests an equality between Jesus and God.

More needs to be said about Paul's conversion experience. The risen Jesus in Luke's third account of Paul's conversion speaks as does God of the OT when he gave various prophets their vocations (Acts 26:16-18)([472]): Jesus instructs Paul, "stand on your feet" (v. 16), as did God, Ezekiel (2:1; cf. 2:2; 3:24). Above we reflected on "to appoint"; it is the word Moses uses in his effort to get God to choose someone other than himself to go to the Pharoah and to bring the Israelites out of Egypt (Ex 4:13). The best OT source for "I shall deliver you from this people and from the Gentiles to whom I am sending you" (Acts 26:17) is the vocational experience of Jeremiah, "To whomever I send you, you shall go; whatever I command you, you shall speak. Have no fear of them, because I am with you to deliver you, says the Lord" (Jer 1:7-8; cf. 1 Chr 16:35). The phrase, "to open their eyes" of Acts 26:18 (cf. v. 23; Luke 4:18; 7:22) corresponds to the task of the Suffering Servant (Is 42:7; cf. 35:5; 61:1), and "that they may turn from darkness to light" to Is 42:16 (cf. 49:6). Not all of these parallels carry the same weight, but enough evidence exists to assert that Luke in Acts 26:16-18 has portrayed Jesus like the God of the OT and this portrayal suggests an equality between Jesus and God.

When Paul in Acts 9 asks the Lord who has appeared to him who he is, Jesus identifies himself and then directs Paul, "Now get up and go into the city and you will be told what you must do" (v. 6). This verse reminds one of Ez 3:22-23, when the God speaks to the prophet, "The hand of the Lord came upon me, and he said to me: 'Get up and go into the plain, where I will speak with you.' So I got up and went out into the plain, and I saw that the glory of the Lord was in that place, like the glory I had seen by the river Chebar."

---

[472] O'Toole, *Acts 26*, 66-80.

Acts 22:10, "I asked, 'What shall I do, Lord?' The Lord answered me, 'Get up and go into Damascus, and there you will be told about everything appointed for you to do'"; this resembles the phrasing of God's directions to Jonah (3:1-2; cf. 2:1; 1 Kgs 17:9-10; Mic 2:10): "Get up and go to the great city of Nineveh, and announce to it the message that I told you." Consequently, although these parallels are of varying similarity, in his accounts of Paul's conversion experience Luke pictures Jesus speaking as the God of the OT who gives to various prophets their mission. Hence, Luke is suggesting equality between God and Jesus.

Both God and Jesus Protect Their Own

When his brothers became jealous of Joseph and sold him to the Egyptians, "God was with him" (Acts 7:9). In his appearance before Festus and Agrippa II, Paul concludes his final defense speech with the words, "But I have enjoyed God's help to this very day" (Acts 26:22). Paul then continues with a summary of his universal missionary activity, proclaiming nothing other than what the prophets and Moses said. In Acts 10:38 we find a summary of Jesus' earthly ministry: how God anointed him with the Holy Spirit and power and how he went about doing good and healing all who were oppressed by evil spirits, "for God was with him." Similarly, in Corinth the risen Jesus in Acts 18:9-10 says to Paul in a vision that he should not be afraid but speak and not be silent, "for I am with you" and that no one will lay a hand on him to harm him since many in the city are Christ's people. To be sure, these words fulfill Jesus' promise of protection to his persecuted followers in Luke 21:14-19. However, as God is efficaciously present and protects his own, so is Jesus; and we again have a suggestion of their equality.

Way

"Way" (ὁδός), which can mean "teaching," also designates Christianity itself ([473]) or describes how Christians live (Luke 24:32.35; Acts 8:26.36.39). Jesus must travel the way to Jerusalem (Luke 9:51; cf. 13:22; 17:11; 19:28); and the "way(s)" can be God's (Luke 20:21; Acts 2:28; 16:17). However, as we noted above about Luke 1:76([474]), in some pas-

---

[473] E.g., Acts 9:2; 19:9.23; 22:4; 24:14.22.

[474] Cf. above, 185-187.

sages there is an ambiguity about "way(s)" and about whether it should be attributed to God or Jesus([475]). These last passages are relevant to our present topic.

Prayer and Worship

All but one example of prayer, προσεύχομαι and its cognates, are predicated of God; however, if our interpretation of "Lord" as the risen Jesus in Acts 1:24 be correct, the apostles would be praying to him as normally was done only to God. Prayer belongs to the area of worship. Jesus' reply to the devil defines who should be worshipped, "It is written, 'You shall worship the Lord, your God, and him alone shall you serve'" (Luke 4:8) establishes a clear principle([476]). This understanding is re-inforced when Peter enters the house of Cornelius, for the latter meets him and "falling at his feet, paid him homage" (Acts 10:25). However, in the next verse Peter helps him up and explains that he, too, is just a man. Thus, we can appreciate the significance of the Eleven and the other disciples doing the risen Jesus homage and then returning to Jerusalem (Luke 24:52; cf. Sir 50:20-21)([477]). Jesus receives the prayers of others (Acts 1:24; 7:59-60; cf. 1:21), his name is called upon in baptism (Acts 2:21.38; 9:14.21; 10:48; 19:4; 22:16)([478]). Praising (μεγαλύνω) is mostly a Lukan word and can be used of one human being paying honor to another (e.g., Acts 5:13). On the other hand, Mary praises God (Luke 1:46) and the Jewish Christians hear the Gentiles speaking in tongues and praising God (Acts 10:46). It is at this level that we should understand the praise which the Jewish and Gentile Ephesians give the Lord Jesus, after they have seen

---

[475] Luke 1:79; 3:4-5; 7:27; cf. Acts 13:10?; 18:25-26?

[476] Examples of correct worship would be Acts 8:27 and 24:11; Luke 4:7 and Acts 7:43 portray false worship.

[477] Nolland, *Luke 18:35 – 24:53*, 1228, observes that Luke has not used "worship" earlier of a response to Jesus, and this and the link with Sir 50:21 suggests that at this point Luke hints that Jesus is the object of religious reverence which previously was not the case. See also Bock, *Luke 9:51 – 24:53*, 1925, 1930-1931, 1945-1947, 1950; Rossé, *Il vangelo di Luca*, 1049.

[478] Confer Fletcher-Louis, *Luke-Acts: Angels*, 22-23, 254 and Bousset, *Kyrios Christos*, 292-293, 330.

what happened to the sons of Sceva (Acts 19:17), "Every-one was awestruck; and the name of the Lord Jesus was praised" (Acts 19:17). Moreover, this same passage introduces the concept, "fear." Probably, "fear" or "awe" (φοβέομαι) and its cognates, do go best with "worship," and these expressions in Luke-Acts often enough occur regarding the fear or awe of God or of an angel. However, there is a striking parallel to what Luke writes in Acts 19:17 about the reaction of those in Ephesus to what happens to the sons of Sceva in Luke 7:16 (cf. 5:26), "Fear seized them all and they glorified God exclaiming . . . ." This parallel leaves the reader with the impression that Luke is willing to write equivalent expressions of both God and Jesus.

"The breaking of bread" belongs to the area of worship since the reference is to the practice of repeating the Christian Passover([479]). To be sure, Luke does not precisely identify the recognition of the risen Christ in the breaking of bread as participation in a *sacrament* as does the later Church. But the stories of the disciples on the road to Emmaus and of the Ethiopian eunuch suggest a parallelism between the "the breaking of bread" and baptism([480]) and so manifest the beginning of such a conviction.

Both God and Jesus Send the Spirit

M. Turner provides a very useful summary statement of the relationship between God and the Spirit in the whole of Jewish tradition, which bear on this topic. He writes: "God's 'Spirit' is virtually always synecdoche for God himself, and is usually a way of speaking of God's *presence* while preserving his transcendence"([481]). This statement reveals the importance of establishing in Luke-Acts a parallel between God's and Jesus' relationships with the Spirit. According to Luke, God gives the Holy Spirit (Luke 11:13; Acts 5:32; 15:8); and Jesus sends (Luke 24:49) or pours out

---

[479] Jacquier, *Les Actes des Apôtres*, ccxvii.

[480] O'Toole, "Philip and the Ethiopian Eunuch," 25-34.

[481] Turner, "The Spirit of Jesus," 422. This article has an historical approach but contains much data relevant to our present discussion. See also his, "The Spirit of Christ and Christology," 168-190 and Buckwalter, *The Character and Purpose*, 188, 193. For a brief summary of Luke's presentation of the Spirit see O'Toole, *The Unity*, 28-30, 47-49.

(Acts 2:33) the Spirit. Also, we should attribute to God the sending of the Spirit at Jesus' baptism since the Spirit comes from heaven (Luke 3:21-22; cf. 4:18; Acts 10:38). Acts 2:17-21 (cf. Jl 3:1-5LXX) proves quite significant in demonstrating that both God and Jesus send the Spirit in the same way. Of course, the citation in these verses originally refers to God; and Luke himself has made this explicit. In both vv. 17-18, God says, "I will pour out of my Spirit"; of course, this phrasing reminds us of Jesus' activity when he "received the promise of the Holy Spirit from the Father and poured it forth, as you (both) see and hear" (Acts 2:33). So, Luke has not only identified Jesus with the "Lord" on whose name everyone should call to be saved (v. 21), but also regards Jesus' pouring out of the Holy Spirit as the actualization of God's promise to do so in this OT citation[482]. Earlier Luke identifies Pentecost as a baptism (Acts 1:5; cf. 11:16); but in view of what we have just said, one cannot understand the majestic passive, "in a few days you will be baptized with the Holy Spirit" as pointing only to the Father. In fact, although Luke for theological reasons describes Christian baptism differently, calling on Jesus' name brings about the reception of the Spirit (Acts 2:38; 9:17; cf. Luke 3:16; Acts 10:45). In Acts 2:38 we find the phrasing, "you will receive the gift of the Holy Spirit," which reminds us of God who "gives" the Spirit.

The Spirit constitutes one of the ways that the risen Jesus is present to believers. In his predictions about future persecution Luke alone has interchanged the Holy Spirit and Jesus. In Luke 12:12, the disciples are told not to worry about how they will defend themselves at times of persecution or what they are to say because the Holy Spirit will teach them. But in 21:15, in a very similar context, Jesus assures his disciples "I myself shall give you a wisdom in speaking that all your adversaries will be powerless to resist or refute"[483]. There is a similar interchange between the Spirit and the Lord Jesus in Acts 20:22-24. Paul first explains his present situation as "bound by the Spirit" (v. 22) to go up to Jerusalem to face the imprisonment and hardships that await him there. He then contends that he does not value his own life, "if only I may finish my course and the ministry that I received from the Lord Jesus" to bear witness to the

---

[482] This statement is certainly true, but *pace* Bock, *Proclamation from Prophecy*, 169, we should not lose sight of the fact that "promise" is also a reference to Luke 24:49.

[483] Confer Buckwalter, *The Character and Purpose*, 211-213.

good news of the grace of God. Actually, the Holy Spirit is one way that the risen Jesus is present and acts among his followers. We see this in the scene when the Holy Spirit prevents Paul and his com-panions from speaking the word in Asia, modern day Turkey (Acts 16:6). In the next verse it is the "Spirit of Jesus" that keeps them from going into Bithynia. Consequently, both God and the risen Jesus send the Spirit; and this action particularly bears on Christian baptism. The Spirit relates to the risen Jesus in a manner very similar to how the Spirit relates to the God of the Old Testament(484).

Conclusion

Luke predicates similar or the same things of both God and Jesus. Some of this information is less helpful in determining exactly how they relate to one another, but other data prove quite significant. God and Jesus share a complete knowledge of each other, and "glory" and power characterize both. They can both be addressed as "(the) Lord" and can act through their "name." They likewise send and have a similar relationship to the Holy Spirit through whom they are present and act in this world. "Loving mercy" typifies their stance toward their followers. Both of them visit their people, and theirs is the kingdom. They save through grace, forgiving of sins, redemption and repentance. They bless and bring peace to their fol-lowers who are to accept and to pursue the way(s) determined by both God and Jesus. Luke describes Jesus' actions at Paul's conversion as the authors of the OT describe God in similar circumstances. An example of this is the literary form, *Erscheinungsgespräch*, used almost exclusively of God in the OT, and of Jesus in Paul's conversion experience. As God was with Jesus (Acts 10:38) and Paul (Acts 26:22), so Jesus is with Paul (Acts 18:9-10), and both God and Jesus can give the Christians a place among those sanctified. Their followers stand in awe and worship them. One might want to claim that Luke just wants to call attention to the close association, which exists between Jesus and the Father, as he does in 10:16. Nonetheless, in most of the examples reviewed in this section, an equality is suggested. H.D. Buckwalter states it well, when he writes, "He (Jesus) appears on an equal footing with God by virtue of what he does

---

[484] Turner, "The Spirit of Christ," 419, contends, "no convincing parallel has yet emerged to justify the claim that Judaism expected a Messiah who *bestows* the Spirit (whether individually or corporately)."

and says in working alongside the Father in decreeing, preserving, and leading the church([485])." Naturally, this equality is not stated in the sophisticated terms which later Christian generations will develop.

---

[485] Buckwalter, *The Character and Purpose*, 192.

General Conclusion

Each chapter has its own conclusion, and in these conclusions the reader can find additional information on the various topics. This "General Conclusion" attempts to summarize as briefly as possible the results of our consideration of Luke's description of Jesus. There is no denying that Luke was significantly influenced by the LXX tradition. His presentation of Jesus was no easy task; for the latter was no ordinary person. Surely, he was a human being, but his followers soon realized that he had an extraordinary relationship with God that could not easily be explained. Luke was loyal to his sources; yet he was a believer who wished to pen for his believing readers a unified story of Jesus and of the early Church. So, although at times there is some unevenness in his composition, still like any talented writer, Luke intended to write a unified and intelligible two-volume religious exposition and did so. However, at times he reads his belief about Jesus' identity back into his Gospel.

Composition criticism appears to be the methodology best adapted to the present task; this methodology is a specification of redaction criticism and concentrates on what the final composer, whom in the case of Luke-Acts tradition has named "Luke," wished to communicate to his readers about Jesus. Surely, one can ask what is specifically Lucan in his Christology; but to get the whole picture, serious consideration must also be given to what he was willing to take over and integrate into his overall presentation. This study endeavors to describe the whole of Luke's Christology, not what specific aspect of it he wished to stress, although Jesus' saving activity would surely be a contender for such a claim. In large part, Luke used titles from the Jewish tradition to write of Jesus; but the meanings he gave these titles and any other traditional descriptions he employed flow from what he and his fellow Christians believed about Jesus. Nonetheless, each of these titles each still carries definite nuances, which allow Luke to draw his portrait of Jesus.

According to Luke, the earthly Jesus was the same person who was raised from the dead, and so our presentation of Luke's Christology must take this into account. At his baptism Jesus is filled with the Spirit and carried out his universal mission. He was radically dedicated to doing his Father's will, and no temptation could turn him aside from that decision. This explains his frequenting the Jewish religious places and his commitment to prayer, which particularly occurred at important moments in his life. Jesus preached the good news and was an exceptionally wise and authoritative teacher who spoke with integrity. He taught about the kingdom of God, about himself, about discipleship and about how to live. His teaching method was much like that of the rabbis; as opportunity offered, he used parables, dialogue, exhortations and warnings. However, unlike the rabbis he called others to follow him, to take up their cross, and in his name to proclaim the kingdom of God. True listening to him demands corresponding action but also provides a solid foundation for living. One is either for him or against him, and faith in him leads to salvation. In a somewhat different manner than Mark, Luke also portrays Jesus as affectionate and expressive of his emotions; and Jesus is very popular with the people. To be sure, his passion and death are part of his earthly existence but fall under certain titles used of him, "prophet," "servant of Yahweh," "Son of Man" and "Christ." Some scholars associate "master" (ἐπιστάτης) with teacher; they may be correct, but "master" looks more to power over the material world.

In the programmatic passage (Luke 4:14-44) and related pericopes Jesus implies that he is a prophet. Jesus, the eschatological prophet, is particularly sent to the disadvantaged yet has a universal mission; but he will not be accepted by many of his own people. Although Luke compares Jesus to Isaiah, the Servant of Yahweh, Elijah, Elisha, Jonah, Jeremiah and especially to Moses, none of these parallels can explain his true greatness nor provide an accurate portrait of him. Jesus is a prophet, mighty in word and work, who works miracles and has an exodus to fulfill in Jerusalem. To belong to the people one must listen to him. Like some prophets of old, he is misunderstood, rejected and killed. These comparisons of Jesus to the prophets of the OT allow Luke to demonstrate the continuity of God's plan of salvation. Jesus also acts as a prophet; he works cures, knows what others are thinking and with what kind of person he is dealing, and predicts the future. His predictions are an important plot device and serve to carry the narrative forward. Jesus himself fulfills some prophecies of the OT, makes others that are fulfilled immediately or in the course of the Lucan narrative; and so the reader has every reason to believe that those not yet fulfilled will soon be. Jesus performs symbolic prophetic acts like the selection of the seventy(-two), the cleansing of the temple and the Passover celebration. Others consider Jesus to be a prophet. Nonetheless, "prophet" is too narrow a concept to serve Luke for much of what he wishes to say about Jesus.

Jesus is savior; there is under heaven no other name, which can save human beings (Acts 4:12). Luke begins this message in his Infancy Narrative and carries it through both of his volumes. He enlarges on this theme more than on almost any other in Luke-Acts([486]). Jesus' salvation reaches out to everyone, and belief and baptism in his name actualizes it. Jesus works miracles and forgives sins. Luke writes of the salvation Jesus brings as "light," "grace" and "loving mercy." The designation of Christianity as "the Way" plays a role in depicting Jesus' salvific activity. Jesus leads individuals to repentance, to peace, to consolation and to life and participation in the kingdom. Jesus redeems and blesses others. Luke sees a salvific connection between Jesus' resurrection and that of the Christians, and this connection fulfills the OT promise made to the fathers. The disciples carry on this salvific activity of Jesus and through their actions continue to make it available to all.

Our consideration of Jesus as the Servant of Yahweh had to be somewhat more technical because not all scholars are convinced of its validity as a Lucan Christological category. Even if the word-pattern for this theme is not always as clear as desirable, there are about twenty-two very probable references to this theme, most of which are unique to Luke. Four of these passages summarize Jesus' saving activity and universal mission in Servant-of-Yahweh terminology. Like "prophet," this theme was well suited to explain Jesus' suffering. In fact, Acts 8:32-33 (Is 53:7-8LXX) provide a summary of Jesus' passion, which Luke does not merely wish to describe as the martyrdom of a just man but more specifically as that of the Servant of Yahweh, who though humble and silent does not receive a fair trial. So, Servant of Yahweh forms part of Luke's Christology, and the terminology associated with this title can summarize Jesus' mission. Jesus is God's chosen one who as Servant of Yahweh is innocent yet undergoes suffering. This title allows Luke to vary his expressions for

---

[486] For the main theme of Luke-Acts, see O'Toole, *The Unity*, 17-94; confer also Navone, *Themes of St. Luke*.

salvation, now imaged as "light," and to justify the mission to the Gentiles. It also looks to Jesus' resurrection and post-resurrectional activity.

Luke has followed his sources in his presentation of Jesus as the Son of Man, but he does have several passages which are unique to him, and has underlined certain aspects of this title. "Son of Man" can look to Jesus and to his human activity; however, it can also embrace his authority and marvelous deeds. He will also be rejected, handed over, suffer and be killed; yet he will be raised and come again and be judge. Luke depicted the coming of the Son of Man apocalyptically and as sudden and unpredictable. He underlined the necessity of faith in the Son of Man, expanded on his suffering, introduced the enthronement at God's right hand (Luke 22:69) and associated the second coming with that of the kingdom. Luke has also developed the Son of Man's saving mission to seek and to save the lost, the second coming and the protective stance toward his loyal followers who are prayerful in awaiting his return.

Although associated with "Son of God," "the Christ" should not be identified with that title; for each of them has its own nuances. Because of his own faith Luke predicates "the Christ" of Jesus from his birth on. Luke prefers the title, ὁ Χριστός, and contends that in accord with the scriptures the Christ must suffer and be rejected. The word-pattern for "the Christ" includes Jesus as "king," "descendent of David" and related concepts. Jesus' presence is that of the kingdom of God; and at times the message about Jesus can be interchanged with "the kingdom of God." As descendent of David, the Christ fulfills the prophecy made to Nathan (2 Sam 7:11-17) and will rule over the house of Jacob forever. Jesus is greater than David, and his activity and following him belong to the kingdom; it is foolish not to accept his inevitable kingship. Jesus' kingdom is one of joy and peace and of service. The Christ challenges his followers to a different life-style. They must put total confidence in their king and use their talents for his kingdom and so for themselves. Through οὗ εἵνεκεν ἔχρισέν με in Luke 4:18, Luke very likely refers to Jesus as "the Christ" ("the anointed") and later uses irony during the passion to high-light this title and to expand on it in terms of "the King of the Jews." The Christian Passover is an image of the messianic banquet to come, but meanwhile repentance and forgiveness of sins is to be proclaimed in the name of Christ to everyone.

The Christ, exalted at God's right hand, at Pentecost pours out the Spirit, and God will send the Christ again at the end of time. Luke has associated the Christ with power and baptism in the Spirit. The resurrection of Jesus, the descendent of David, fulfills God's promise to our fathers of our own resurrection. In Acts, the disciples proclaim Jesus as "the Christ"; and "Christ" can be part of Jesus' name.

At the beginning of his Gospel (1:35), Luke introduces the mystery of Jesus' divinity. "Son of God" in this verse and in some others guides the reader's understanding of this title, of Jesus' later references to his Father and of passages where, taken by themselves, there is less clarity about the mystery of Jesus' divinity in the rest of Luke-Acts. To be sure, the Son's and the Father's total mutual knowledge of each other (10:22) likewise implies Jesus' divinity and helps one's interpretation of Jesus' radical and intimate relationship to the Father. He is the beloved or unique Son. Like God himself, Jesus is holy and can claim divine attributes. The Holy Spirit is linked to Jesus' sonship; but this connection in Luke 1:35 is fundamentally different from that at Jesus' baptism or related passages (Luke 3:21-22; cf. 4:18; Acts 10:38). The mission of the Son of God is to do the Father's will; as the Son, Jesus often enough appears in prayer. The Son is an extraordinarily wise teacher to whom everyone is to listen. Even during his crucifixion he does not lose confidence in his Father or even his concern for his very opponents. Luke connects "Son of God" with the "Servant of Yahweh," "(the) Christ," "the descendent of David" and "Son of Man"; but each of these titles has connotations proper to itself. "Son of God" can function as a confessional statement or as a summary of the gospel message.

One correctly perceives Luke's meaning for "(the) Lord," when predicated of Jesus, if he or she recognizes its sources in this same title found of the God in the OT (cf. Acts 2:21). Thus, at least potentially, the title communicates the mystery of Jesus' divinity. Luke's readers were Christians, and so he could and did read his own faith in Jesus as the Lord back into his Gospel. In the majority of instances in his two volumes, Luke writes "(the) Lord" either of God or of Jesus. The fact that Luke does not always bother to clarify to which of the two he is referring results most reasonably from his own intimate association of them. Jesus appears as "(the) Lord" in various contexts. When the passages speak of the Parousia, a vision or a baptism story, "(the) Lord" definitely is the risen Jesus; and Luke very likely intends the title in its fullest sense, that is, as conveying the mystery of Jesus' divinity. An ecclesial context would make this interpretation almost certain. However, would Luke not have been doing the same thing in other passages, which in themselves are less clear on the point? It surely would not be justified to maintain that in all of these passages Luke could not have been thinking of the risen Jesus as acting like the God of the Old Testament and so that these passages are not at all open to the mystery of Jesus' divinity. In fact, since he and his readers were believers, the likelihood is that in these other passages, too, Luke writes of "Lord" in the fullest sense.

Luke predicates similar or the same things both of God and of Jesus. They have total mutual knowledge of each other and are both addressed and act as "(the) Lord." They act through their "name," possess glory, have power, and yet loving mercy. Each sends the Holy Spirit, and through the Spirit is present and acts in this world. They visit their people, and theirs is the kingdom. Through grace, repentance and the forgiveness of sins they save and redeem, they bless and lead believers to peace and to a place among those sanctified. Theirs is the way to follow. As the authors of the OT describe God, so Jesus acts at Paul's conversion. God was with Jesus, and Jesus is with Paul; they protect their own. Believers stand in awe and worship God and Jesus. In short, Jesus appears equal to God. Luke could not use God of Jesus, for that title obviously looked to someone else, namely, the Father. However, Luke could and did portray Jesus as God is pictured and has him act in many ways, as does God.

In this volume, we have not considered how the disciples say and do the same things as Jesus or how Luke thus established continuity among the OT, Jesus and the Christian community and at the same time challenges Christians to imitate Jesus; these data have been considered elsewhere([487]). We have tried to consider all the other relevant data, which lead to a grasp of Luke's Christology. Given Luke's loyalty to sources, these data do not form the kind of systematic presentation that one might find today in a well-honed doctoral dissertation, but then God did not call such a doctoral student to the same task as the Evangelist Luke. Also, Luke has so composed his two volumes that he does provide his readers with a consistent and clear vision of whom he believes Jesus to be. It is my hope that the present exposition has been loyal to that vision.

---

[487] See O'Toole, *The Unity*, 62-94.

General Bibliography for the Study of Luke's Christology

Achtemeier, P.J., "The Lukan Perspective on the Miracles of Jesus," *Journal of Biblical Literature* 94 (1975) 547-562.

Aland, K., et alii (eds.), *The Greek New Testament.* Fourth, Revised Edition (Stuttgart 1998).

Aletti, J.-N., *L'Art de raconter Jésus Christ: L'écriture narrative de l'évangile de Luc* (Paris 1989).

Alexander, L. *The Preface to Luke's Gospel: Literary Convention and Social Context in Luke 1.1-4 and Acts 1.1* (Society for New Testament Studies, Monograph Series, 78; Cambridge 1993).

_____, "Reading Luke-Acts from Back to Front," in J. Verheyden (ed.), *The Unity of Luke-Acts* (Bibliotheca Ephemeridum theologicarum Lovaniensium, 142 ; Leuven 1999), 419-446.

Aune, D.E., *Prophecy in Early Christianity and the Ancient Mediterranean World* (Grand Rapids 1983).

Baarlink, H., "Die Bedeutung der Prophetenzitate in Lk 4,18-19 und Apg 2,17-21 für das Doppelwerk des Lukas," in J. Verheyden (ed.), *The Unity of Luke-Acts* (Bibliotheca Ephemeridum theologicarum Lovaniensium, 142; Leuven 1999), 483-491.

Barbi, A., *Il Cristo celeste presente nella Chiesa. Tradizione e redazione in Atti 3,19-21* (Analecta Biblica, 64; Roma 1979).

Barrett, C.K., *Acts 1-14* (International Critical Commentary; Edinburgh 1994).

Bauckham, R.J., "The Worship of Jesus in Apocalyptic Christianity," *New Testament Studies* 27 (1980-1981) 322-341.

Bayer, H.F., "Christ-Centered Eschatology in Acts 3:17-26," in J.B. Green and M. Turner (eds.), *Jesus of Nazareth: Lord and Christ. Essays on the Historical Jesus and New Testament Christology* (Grand Rapids 1994), 236-250. [NB: In the preface this work is dedicated to I.H. Marshall. But no mention of him appears in the title, as

would normally be the case for a Festschrift, nor is the work usually treated as a Festschrift in bibliographical listings.]

Beker, J.C., "The Christologies and Anthropologies of Paul, Luke-Acts and
Marcion," FS M. de Jonge: *From Jesus to John. Essays on Jesus and
New Testament Christology in Honour of Marinus de Jonge*, ed. M.C.
De Boer (Journal for the Study of the New Testament, Supplement
Series, 84; Sheffield 1993), 174-182.

Berchmans, John, "Some Aspects of Lukan Christology," *Biblebhashyam*
2 (1976) 5-22.

Betz, O., "The Kerygma of Luke," in O. Betz, *Der Messias Israels. Aufsätze zur biblischen Theologie* (Wissenschaftliche Untersuchungen
zum Neuen Testament, 42; Tübingen 1987), 257-272.

Black, M., "Die Apotheose Israels: eine neue Interpretation des danielischen
'Menschensohns'," FS A. Vögtle: *Jesus und der Menschensohn. Für
Anton Vögtle*, hrsg. R. Pesch, R. Schnackenburg, O. Kaiser (Freiburg
1975), 92-99.

Blinzler, J., "Jakobus und Joses Söhne eine von der Herrenmutter
verschiedenen Maria," in J. Blinzler, *Die Brüder und Schwestern
Jesu* (Stuttgarter Bibelstudien 21; Stuttgart 1967), 73-82.

Bock, D.L., *Proclamation from Prophecy and Pattern: Lucan Old
Testament Christology* (Journal for the Study of the New Testament, Supplement Series, 12; Sheffield 1987).

_____, "The Son of Man in Luke 5:24," *Bulletin for Biblical
Research* 1 (1991) 109-121.

_____, "The Son of Man Seated at God's Right Hand and the
Debate over Jesus' 'Blasphemy,'" in J.B. Green and M. Turner
(eds.), *Jesus of Nazareth: Lord and Christ. Essays on the Historical Jesus and New Testament Christology* (Grand Rapids 1994),
181-191. [NB: In the preface this work is dedicated to I.H.
Marshall. But no mention of him appears in the title, as would normally be the case for a Festschrift, nor is the work usually treated
as a Festschrift in bibliographical listings.]

_____, *Luke.* Volume 1: *1:1 – 9:50* (Baker Exegetical Commentary
on the New Testament 3A; Grand Rapids 1994).

_____, *Luke.* Volume 2: *9:51 – 24:53* (Baker Exegetical Commen-
tary on the New Testament 3B; Grand Rapids 1996).

_____, *Jesus according to the Scripture: Restoring the Portrait from
the Gospel* (Grand Rapids 2002).

Bode, E.L., *The First Easter Morning: The Gospel Accounts of the Women's Visit to the Tomb of Jesus* (Analecta Biblica 45; Rome 1970).

Böhler, D., "Jesus als Davidssohn bei Lukas und Micha," *Biblica* 79 (1998) 532-538.

Bossuyt, P. – Radermakers, J., *Jésus: parole de la grâce selon saint Luc*, 2 vols., deuxième édition, corrigée (Bruxelles 1981).

Bottini, G. C., *Introduzione all' opera di Luca. Aspetti teologici* (Studi Biblici Franciscani liber annuus, 35; Jerusalem 1992).

Bousset, W., *Kyrios Christos*, tr. J.E. Steely (New York 1970).

Bouttier, M. "L'humanité de Jésus selon Saint Luc," *Recherches de science religieuse* 69 (1981) 33-43.

Bouwman, G., "Die Erhöhung Jesu in der lukanischen Theologie," *Biblische Zeitschrift* 14 (1970) 257-263.

Bovon, F., "Das Heil in den Schriften des Lukas," in F. Bovon, *Lukas in neuer Sicht. Gesammelte Aufsätze*, übersetzt von E. Hartmann, A. Frey, P. Strauß (Biblisch-theologische Studien, 8; Neukirchen-Vluyn 1985), 61-74.

_____, *Luke the Theologian: Thirty-three years of Research (1953-1983)*, 2nd ed., tr. K. McKinney (Princeton Theological Monograph Series, 12; Allison Park 1987).

_____, *L'Œuvre de Luc* (Lectio Divina, 130; Paris 1987).

_____, *Luke 1*, tr. C.M. Thomas (Hermeneia; Minneapolis 2002).

Braun, H., "Zur Terminologie der Acts von der Auferstehung Jesu," *Theologische Literaturzeitung* 77 (1952) 533-536.

Brodie, T.L., "The Departure for Jerusalem (Lk 9,51-56) as a Rhetorical Imitation of Elijah's Departure for the Jordan (2 Kgs 1,1 – 2,6)," *Biblica* 70 (1989) 96-109.

Brown, R.E., "Jesus and Elisha," *Perspective* 12 (1971) 84-104.

_____, "Gospel Infancy Narrative Research from 1976 to 1986: Part II (Luke)," *Catholic Biblical Quarterly* 48 (1986) 660-680.

_____, *The Birth of the Messiah: A Commentary on the Infancy Narratives in the Gospels of Matthew and Luke, new updated.* (New York 1993).

_____, *The Death of the Messiah. From Gethsemane to the Grave. A Commentary on the Passion Narratives in the Four Gospels*, I–II (New York 1994).

Bruce, F.F., "The Davidic Messiah in Luke-Acts," FS W.S. LaSor: *Biblical and Near Eastern Studies. Essays in Honor of William Sanford La-Sor*, ed. G.A. Tuttle (Grand Rapids 1978), 7-17.

_____, "The Background to the Son of Man Sayings," FS D. Guthrie: *Christ the Lord. Studies in Christology Presented to Donald Guthrie*, ed. H.H. Rowdon (Leicester 1982), 50-70.

_____, *The Book of Acts*, 2nd ed. (New International Commentary on the New Testament; Grand Rapids 1988).

_____, *The Acts of the Apostles. The Greek Text with Introduction and Commentary*, 3rd revised and enlarged ed. (Grand Rapids 1990).

Buckwalter, H.D., *The Character and Purpose of Luke's Christology* (Society for New Testament Studies, Monograph Series, 89; Cambridge 1996).

Büchsel, F., ἀπολύτρωσις, *Theological Dictionary of the New Testament* IV, 351-356.

Bultmann, R., *The History of the Synopic Tradition*, 2nd ed., tr. J. Marsh (Oxford 1968).

Burchard, C., *Der dreizehnte Zeuge. Traditions- und kompositionsgeschichtliche Untersuchungen zu Lukas' Darstellung der Frühzeit des Paulus* (Forschungen zur Religion und Literatur des Alten und Neuen Testaments, 103; Göttingen 1970).

Burger, C., "Der Davidsohn bei Lukas," in C. Burger, *Jesus als Davidssohn. Eine traditionsgeschichtliche Untersuchung* (Forschungen zur Religion und Literatur des Alten und Neuen Testaments, 98; Göttingen 1970), 107-152.

Burkett, D., *The Son of Man Debate. A History and Evaluation* (Society for the Study of the New Testament, Monograph Series, 107; Cambridge 1999).

Busse, U., *Die Wunder der Propheten Jesus. Die Rezeption, Komposition und Interpretation der Wundertradition im Evangelium des Lukas* (Forschung zur Bibel, 24; Stuttgart 1977).

_____, *Das Nazareth-Manifest. Eine Einführung in der lukanische Jesusbild nach Lk 4,16-30* (Stuttgarter Bibelstudien, 91; Stuttgart 1978).

Byrne, B., "Jesus as Messiah in the Gospel of Luke: Discerning a Pattern of Correction," *Catholic Biblical Quarterly* 65 (2003) 80-95

Cadbury, H.J., "The Titles of Jesus in Acts," in F.J. Foakes Jackson and K. Lake (eds.), *The Beginning of Christianity. Part I. The Acts of the Apostles.* Vol. V: *Additional Notes to the Commentary* (Paperback edition, Grand Rapids 1979), 354-375.

_____, *The Making of Luke-Acts* (London 1927).

_____, *The Book of Acts in History* (London 1955).

Caragounis, C.C., *The Son of Man: Vision and Interpretation* (Wissenschaftliche Untersuchungen zum Neuen Testament, 38; Tübingen 1986).

Carroll, J.T., *Response to the End of History: Eschatology and Situation in Luke-Acts* (Society of Biblical Literature, Dissertation Series, 92; Atlanta 1988).

_____, "Jesus as Healer in Luke-Acts," in Lovering, E.H., Jr. (ed.), *Society of Biblical Literature, Seminar Papers, 1994. One Hundred Thirtieth Annual Meeting, 19-22 November 1994* (Society of Biblical Literature, Seminar Papers, 33; Atlanta 1994), 269-284.

Carruth, T.R., "The Jesus-As-Prophet Motif in Luke-Acts," Ph.D. Thesis, Baylor University, 1973. [Baylor University Library, Moody General Collection and Texas General Collection: BL 48.B.382 1973 C37.]

Casalegno, A., *Gesù e il tempio: Studio redazionale su Luca-Atti* (Brescia 1984).

Casey, P.M., "From Paul to John. 4. Matthew, Mark and Luke," in P.M. Casey, *From Jewish Prophet to Gentile God. The Origins and Development of New Testament Christology* (The Edward Cadbury Lectures at the University of Birmingham, 1985-86; Cambridge 1991), 147-156.

Catchpole, D.R., "The Angelic Son of Man in Luke 12:8," *Novum Testamentum* 24 (1982) 255-265.

_____, "The Anointed One in Nazareth," FS M. de Jonge: *From Jesus to John. Essays on Jesus and New Testament Christology in Honour of Marinus de Jonge*, ed. M.C. De Boer (Journal for the Study of the New Testament, Supplement Series, 84; Sheffield 1993), 231-251.

Chevallier, M.-A., "Luc e l'Esprit saint. A la mémoire du P. Augustin George," *Revue des sciences religieuses* 56 (1982) 1-16.

Christ, F., *Jesus Sophia: Die Sophia-Christologie bei den Synoptikern* (Abhandlungen zur Theologie des Alten und Neuen Testaments, 57; Zürich 1971).

Coleridge, M., *The Birth of the Lukan Narrative: Narrative Christology in Luke 1 – 2* (Journal for the Study of the New Testament, Supplement Series, 88; Sheffield 1993).

Collins, J.J., "The *Son of God* Text from Qumran," FS M. de Jonge: *From Jesus to John. Essays on Jesus and New Testament Christology in Honour of Marinus de Jonge*, ed. M.C. De Boer (Journal for the Study of the New Testament, Supplement Series, 84; Sheffield 1993), 65-82.

Colomenero Atienza, A., "Hechos 7,13-43 y las corrientes cristológicas dentro de la primitava comunidad cristiana," *Estudios Bíblicos* 33 (1974) 31-62.

Colpe, C., ὁ υἱὸς τοῦ ἀνθρώπου, *Theological Dictionary of the New Testament*, VIII, 457-459, 461-462.

Comblin, J., La paix dans la theologie de Saint Luc," *Ephemerides theologicae Lovanienses* 32 (1956) 439-460.

Conzelmann, H., "The Centre of History," in H. Conzelmann, *The Theology of St. Luke,* tr. G. Buswell (New York 1960), 170-206.

_____, *Acts of the Apostles*, 2nd ed., tr. J. Limburg, A.T. Kraabel and D.H. Juel (Hermeneia; Philadelphia 1987).

Cosgrove, C.H., "The Divine δεῖ in Luke-Acts: Investigations into the Lukan Understanding of God's Providence," *Novum Testamentum* 26 (1984) 168-190.

Crump, D., *Jesus the Intercessor: Prayer and Christology in Luke-Acts* (Wissenschaftliche Untersuchungen zum Neuen Testament 2, 49; Tübingen 1992).

Cullmann, O., *The Christology of the New Testament*, rev. ed. (New Testament Library; Philadelphia 1963).

Czachesz, I., "Narrative Logic and Christology in Luke-Acts," *Communio viatorum* 37 (1995) 93-106.

Dahl, N.A., "The Story of Abraham in Luke-Acts," FS Paul Schubert: *Studies in Luke-Acts. Studies in Honor of Paul Schubert*, ed. L.E. Keck and J.L. Martyn (New York 1966), 139-158.

_____, *The Crucified Messiah and Other Essays* (Minneapolis 1974).

Danker, F.W., *Benefactor: Epigraphic Study of a Graeco-Roman and New Testament Semantic Field* (St. Louis 1982).

_____, *Luke*, 2nd ed. (Philadelphia 1987).

_____, *Jesus and the New Age: A Commentary of St. Luke's Gospel*, 2nd ed. (Philadelphia 1988).

Deissler, A., "Der 'Menschensohn' und 'das Volk der Heiligen des Höchsten' in Dan 7," FS A. Vögtle: *Jesus und der Menschensohn. Für Anton Vögtle* hrsg. R. Pesch, R. Schnackenburg, O. Kaiser (Freiburg 1975), 81-91.

de Jonge, H.J., "Sonship, Wisdom, Infancy: Luke 2:41-51a," *New Testament Studies* 24 (1978) 317-354.

de Jonge, M., "The Use of the Word 'Anointed' in the Time of Jesus," *Novum Testamentum* 8 (1966) 132-148.

_____, "The Use of ὁ Χριστός in the Passion Narratives," in J. Dupont (éd.), *Jésus aux origines de la christologie* (Bibliotheca Ephemeridum theologicarum Lovaniensium, 40; Louvain 1975), 169-192.

_____, "The Christology of Luke-Acts," in M. de Jonge, *Christology in Context: The Earliest Christian Response to Jesus* (Philadelphia 1988), 97-111.

_____, "Messiah," *Anchor Bible Dictionary*, IV, 777-788.

de la Potterie, I., "Le titre *Kurios* appliqué a Jésus dans l'Évangile de Luc," FS B. Rigaux: *Mélanges Bibliques en hommage au R.P. Béda Rigaux*, éd. A. Descamps et A. de Halleux (Gembloux 1970), 117-146.

Delobel, J. (éd.), *Logia, Les Paroles de Jesus — The Sayings of Jesus* (Bibliotheca Ephemeridum theologicarum Lovaniensium, 59; Leuven 1982).

Denaux, A., "The Q-Logion Mt 11,27/Lk 10,22 and the Gospel of John," in A. Denaux (ed.), *John and the Synoptics* (Bibliotheca Ephemeridum theologicarum Lovaniensium, 101; Leuven 1992), 163-199.

_____, "The Theme of Divine Visits and Human (In)hospitality in Luke-Acts. Its Old Testament and Graeco-Roman Antecedents," in J. Verheyden (ed.), *The Unity of Luke-Acts* (Bibliotheca Ephemeridum theologicarum Lovaniensium, 142; Leuven 1999), 255-279.

Dennison, C.G., "How Is Jesus the Son of God? Luke's Baptism Narrative and Christology," *Calvin Theological Journal* 17 (1982) 6-25.

Dibelius, M., *Studies in the Acts of the Apostles*, in H. Greeven (ed.), tr. M. Ling and P. Schubert (London 1973).

Doble, P., *The Paradox of Salvation: Luke's Theology of the Cross* (Society for New Testament Studies, Monograph Series, 87; Cambridge 1996).

Dömer, M., *Das Heil Gottes. Studien zur Theologie des lukanischen Doppelwerkes* (Bonner biblische Beiträge, 51; Bonn 1978).

Donfried, K.P., "Attempts at Understanding the Purpose of Luke-Acts: Christology and the Salvation of the Gentiles," FS H.K. McArthur: *Christological Perspectives: Essays in Honor of Harvey K. McArthur*, ed. R.F. Berkeley and S.A. Edwards (New York 1982),112-122.

Dubois, J.-D., "La figure d'Elie dans la perspective lucanienne," *Revue d'histoire et de philosophie religieuses* 53 (1973) 155-176.

Dumais, M., "L'évangelisation des pauvres dans l'œuvre de Luc," *Science et esprit* 36 (1984) 297-321.

Dunn, J.D.G., *Christology in the Making* (London 1991).

_____, "The Making of Christology: Evolution or Unfolding?," in J.B. Green and M. Turner (eds.), *Jesus of Nazareth: Lord and Christ: Essays on the Historical Jesus and New Testament Christology* (Grand Rapids 1994), 437-452. [NB: In the preface this work is dedicated to I.H. Marshall. But no mention of him appears in the title, as would normally be the case for a Festschrift, nor is the work usually treated as a Festschrift in bibliographical listings.]

_____, "KURIOS in Acts Again," in J.D.G. Dunn, *The Christ and the Spirit*, Vol. 1. *Christology* (Grand Rapids 1998), 241-253.

_____, *Jesus Remembered: Christianity in the Making* (Grand Rapids 2003).

Dupont, J., "Jésus, Messie et Seigneur dans la foi des premiers chrétiens," *Vie spirituelle* 83 (1950) 385-416.

_____, "L'utilisation apologetique du VT dans les discours des Actes," *Ephemerides theologicae Lovanienses* 26 (1953) 298-327.

_____, "L'arrière-fond biblique du recit des tentations de Jesus," *New Testament Studies* 3 (1956-57) 287-304.

_____, "Ascension du Christ et don de l'Esprit d'après Actes 2:33," in FS C.F.D. Moule: *Christ and the Spirit in the New Testament. In Honour of Charles Francis Digby Moule*, ed. B. Lindars and S.S. Smalley (Cambridge 1973), 219-228.

_____, "La portée christologique de l'évangélisation des nations d'après Luc 24,47," FS R. Schnackenburg: *Neues Testament und*

Kirche. Für Rudolf Schnackenburg, hrsg. J. Gnilka (Freiburg 1974), 125-143.

_____, "Les implications christologiques de la parabole de la brebis perdue," in J. Dupont (éd.), *Jésus aux origines de la christologie* (Bibliotheca Ephemeridum theologicarum Lovaniensium, 40; Louvain 1975), 331-350.

_____, "La conclusion des Actes et son rapport à l'ensemble de l'ouvrage de Luc," in J. Kremer (éd.), *Les Actes des Apôtres: Traditions, rédaction, théologie* (Bibliotheca Ephemeridum theologicarum Lovaniensium, 48; Leuven 1979), 359-404.

_____, *The Salvation of the Gentiles: Essays in the Acts of the Apostles*, tr. J.R. Keating (New York 1979).

_____, "La mission de Paul d'apres Ac 26, 16-23 et la mission des apôtres d'apres Lc 24,44-49 et Ac 1,8," in J. Dupont, *Nouvelles Études sur les Actes des Apôtres* (Lectio Divina, 118; Paris 1984), 446-456.

Edmonds, P., "Luke's Portrait of Christ," *Biblical-Pastoral Bulletin* 4 (1981) 7-14.

Edwards, O.C., *Luke's Story of Jesus* (Philadelphia 1981).

Ellingworth, P., "Christology: Synchronic or Diachronic?," in J.B. Green and M. Turner (eds.), *Jesus of Nazareth: Lord and Christ: Essays on the Historical Jesus and New Testament Christology* (Grand Rapids 1994), 489-499. [NB: In the preface this work is dedicated to I.H. Marshall. But no mention of him appears in the title, as would normally be the case for a Festschrift, nor is the work usually treated as a Festschrift in bibliographical listings.]

Ellis, E.E., *The Gospel of Luke*, 2nd ed. (New Century Bible; London 1974).

_____, "La composition de Luc 9 et les sources de sa christologie," in J. Dupont (éd.), *Jésus aux origines de la christologie* (Bibliotheca Ephemeridum theologicarum Lovaniensium, 40; Louvain 1975), 169-192.

Ernst, J., *Das Evangelium nach Lukas* (Regensburger Neues Testament, 3; Regensburg 1977).

_____, *Herr der Geschichte. Perspektiven der lukanischen Eschatologie* (Stuttgarter Bibelstudien, 88; Stuttgart 1978).

_____, "Das Christusbild des Lukas," in J. Ernst (Hrsg.), *Lukas. Ein theologisches Portrait* (Düsseldorf 1985), 105-111.

Evans, C.F., "The Central Section of St. Luke's Gospel," FS R.H. Lightfoot: *Studies in the Gospels. Essays in Memory of R.H. Lightfoot,* ed. D.E. Nineham (Oxford 1955), 37-53.

_____, *Saint Luke* (TPI [Trinity Press International] New Testament Commentaries; Philadelphia 1990).

Feldkämper, L., *Der betende Jesus als Heilsmittler nach Lukas* (Veröffentlichungen des Missionspriesterseminars St. Augustin bei Bonn, 29: Bonn 1978).

Feuillet, A., "'L'exode' de Jésus et le déroulement du mystère rédempteur d'après S. Luc et S. Jean," *Revue Thomiste* 77 (1977) 181-206.

_____, "La signification christologique de Lc. 18,14 e les références des évangiles au Serviteur souffrant," *Nova et vetera* 55 (1980) 188-229.

_____, "Le pharisien et le publican (Lc. 18,9-14): la manifestation de la miséricorde divine en Jésus serviteur souffrant," *Esprit et vie* 91 (1981) 657-665.

Fitzmyer, J.A., "The Semitic Background of the New Testament Kyrios-Title," in J. A. Fitzmyer, *A Wandering Aramean: Collected Aramaic Essays* (Missoula 1979), 115-142.

_____, *The Gospel According to Luke (I–IX)* (Anchor Bible, 28; Garden City 1981).

_____, *The Gospel According to Luke (X–XXIV)* (Anchor Bible, 28A; Garden City 1985).

_____, "Jesus in the Early Church through the Eyes of Luke- Acts," *Scripture Bulletin* 17 (1987) 26-35.

_____, *Luke the Theologian: Aspects of His Teaching* (Oxford 1989).

_____, *To Advance the Gospel,* 2nd ed. (The Biblical Resource Series; Grand Rapids 1998).

Flender, H., *St. Luke. Theologian of Redemptive History,* tr. R.H. and I. Fuller (London 1967).

Fletcher-Louis, C.H.T., *Luke-Acts: Angels, Christology and Soteriology* (Wissenschaftliche Untersuchungen zum Neuen Testament, 2, 94; Tübingen 1997).

Foakes Jackson, F.J., and Lake, K., "Christology," in Foakes Jackson, F.J., and Lake, K. (eds.), *The Beginnings of Christianity: The Acts of the Apostles.* Vol. I, *Prolegomena I: The Jewish, Gentile, and*

Christian Backgrounds (Paperback edition, Grand Rapids 1979), 345-418.

Focant, C., "Du Fils de l'homme assis (Lc 22,69) au Fils de l'homme debout (Ac 7,56). Enjeux théologique et lettéraire d'un changement sémantique," in J. Verheyden (ed.), *The Unity of Luke-Acts* (Bibliotheca Ephemeridum theologicarum Lovaniensium, 142; Leuven 1999), 563-576.

Foerster, W., Κύριος, *Theological Dictionary of the New Testament*, III, 1086-1094.

_____, σωτήρ, *Theological Dictionary of the New Testament*, VII, 1015-1016.

Foerster, W. – G. von Rad, εἰρήνη, *Theological Dictionary of the New Testament*, II, 400-420

Fohrer, G., σωτήρ, *Theological Dictionary of the New Testament*, VII, 1012-1013.

Franklin, E., *Christ the Lord: A Study in the Purpose and Theology of Luke-Acts* (Philadelphia 1975).

Fredriksen, P., *From Jesus to Christ: The Origins of the New Testament Images of Christ*, 2nd ed. (A Nota Bene Book; New Haven 2000).

Frein, B.C., "Narrative Predictions, Old Testament Prophecies and Luke's Sense of Fulfillment," *New Testament Studies* 40 (1994) 22-37.

Friedrich, G., προφήτης, *Theological Dictionary of the New Testament*, VI, 841-848.

_____, "Lk 9,51 und die Entrückungschristologie des Lukas," FS J. Schmid: *Orientierung an Jesus. Zur Theologie der Synoptiker. Für Josef Schmid*, hrsg. P. Hoffmann, N. Brox, W. Pesch (Freiburg 1973), 48-77.

Fuller, R.H., *The Foundations of New Testament Christology* (London 1965).

Garrett, S.R., "Exodus from Bondage: Luke 9:31 and Acts 12:1-24," *Catholic Biblical Quarterly* 52 (1990) 656-680.

Gasque, W.W., *A History of the Interpretation of the Acts of the Apostles*, 2nd ed. (Peabody 1989).

Gavanta, B.R., *From Darkness to Light* (Philadelphia 1989).

Geiger, G., "Der Weg als roter Faden durch Lk-Apg," in J. Verheyden (ed.), *The Unity of Luke-Acts* (Bibliotheca Ephemeridum theologicarum Lovaniensium, 142; Leuven 1999), 663-673.

George, A., "La royauté de Jésus selon l'évangile de Luc," *Sciences ecclésiastiques* 14 (1962) 57-69.

_____, "Jésus fils de Dieu dans l'évangile selon Saint Luc," *Revue biblique* 72 (1965) 185-209.

_____, "Le sens de la mort de Jesus pour Luc," *Revue biblique* 80 (1973) 186-217.

_____, "L'emploi chez Luc du vocabulaire de salut," *New Testament Studies* 23 (1977) 308-320.

_____, *Études sur l'œuvre de Luc* (Sources bibliques; Paris 1978).

Ghidelli, C., *Gesù é vivo: Introduzione agli scritti di Luca* (Torino 1977).

Giblin, C.H., *The Destruction of Jerusalem according to Luke-Acts* (Analecta Biblica, 107; Rome 1985).

Gill, D., "Observations on the Lukan Travel Narrative and Some Related Passages," *Harvard Theological Review* 60 (1970) 199-221.

Gils, F., *Jésus prophète: d'après les évangiles synoptiques* (Louvain 1957).

Glöckner, R., *Die Verkündigung des Heils beim Evangelisten Lukas* (Mainz 1976).

Glombitza, O., "Die Titel διδάσκαλος und ἐπιστάτης für Jesus bei Lukas," *Zeitschrift für die neutestamentliche Wissenschaft* 49 (1958) 275-278.

Green, J.B., "'Salvation to the End of the Earth' (Acts 13:47): God as Saviour in the Acts of the Apostles," in I. H. Marshall and D. Peterson (eds.), *Witness to the Gospel: The Theology of Acts* (Grand Rapids 1988), 83-106.

_____, "The Death of Jesus, God's Servant," in D.D. Sylva (ed.), *Reimaging the Death of the Lukan Jesus* (Bonner Biblische Beiträge, 73; Frankfurt 1990), 1-28 [text], 170-173 [notes].

_____, *The Theology of the Gospel of Luke* (Cambridge 1995).

_____, *The Gospel of Luke* (New International Commentary on the New Testament; Grand Rapids 1997).

Greene, G.R., "The Portrayal of Jesus as Prophet in Luke-Acts," Ph.D. Thesis, Southern Baptist Theological Seminary, 1975. [Southern Baptist Theological Seminary, The James P. Boyce Centennial Library, Call Number: G832p.]

Grelot, P., "'Aujourd'hui tu seras avec moi dans le Paradis' (Luc XXIII, 43)," *Revue biblique* 74 (1967) 194-214 .

_____, "Note sur Actes XIII, 47," *Revue biblique* 88 (1981) 368-372.

_____, "Le Cantique de Siméon [Lc. II, 29-32]," *Revue biblique* 93 (1986) 481-509.

Grogan, G.W., "The Light and the Stone: A Christological Study in Luke and Isaiah," FS D. Guthrie: *Christ the Lord. Studies in Christology Presented to Donald Guthrie*, ed. H.H. Rowden (Leicester 1982), 151-167.

Grundmann, W., "Fragen der Komposition des lukanischen 'Reiseberichts,'" *Zeitschrift für die neutestamentliche Wissenschaft* 50 (1959) 252-270.

_____, *Das Evangelium nach Lukas* 2nd ed. (Theologischer Handkommentar zum Neuen Testament, III; Berlin 1961).

_____, χριστός, *Theological Dictionary of the New Testament*, IX, 532-537.

Haenchen, E., *The Acts of the Apostles: A Commentary*, tr. B. Noble and G. Shinn (Philadelphia 1971).

Hahn, F., *The Titles of Jesus in Christology*, tr. H. Knight and G. Ogg (London 1969).

_____, *Christologische Hoheitstitel*, 4th ed. (Forschungen zur Religion und Literatur des Alten und Neuen Testaments, 83; Göttingen 1974).

Hamm, D., "Sight to the Blind: Vision as Metaphor in Luke," *Biblica* 67 (1986) 457-477.

Hampel, V., *Menschensohn und historischer Jesus. Ein Rätselwort als Schüssel zum messianischen Sebstverständnis Jesu* (Neukirchen-Vluyn 1990).

Hare, D.R.A., *The Son of Man Tradition* (Minneapolis 1990).

Harrington, J.M., *The Lukan Passion Narrative. The Markan Material in Luke 22:54 – 23:25* (New Testament Tools and Studies, 30; Leiden 2000).

Harrington, W.J., *The Gospel according to Luke: A Commentary* (New York 1967).

Hastings, A., *Prophet and Witness in Jerusalem: A Study of the Teaching of Saint Luke* (New York 1958).

Hegermann, H. "Zur Theologie des Lukas," FS E. Barnikol: '. . . und fragten nach Jesus,' Beiträge aus Theologie, Kirche und Geschichte (Berlin 1964), 27-34.

Heil, J.P., "Reader-Response and the Irony of Jesus before the Sanhedrin in Luke 22:66-71," Catholic Biblical Quarterly 51 (1989) 271-284.

_____, The Meal Scenes in Luke-Acts: An Audience-Oriented Approach (Society of Biblical Literature, Monograph Series, 52; Atlanta 1999).

Higgins, A.J.B., "'Menschensohn' oder 'ich' in Q: Lk 12,8-9/Mt 10,32-33?," FS A. Vögtle: Jesus und der Menschensohn. Für Anton Vögtle hrsg. R. Pesch, R. Schnackenburg, O. Kaiser (Freiburg 1975), 117-123.

_____, "The Son of Man and Ancient Judaism," in A.J.B. Higgins, The Son of Man in the Teaching of Jesus (Society for New Testament Studies, Monograph Series, 39; Cambridge 1980), 3-28.

Hill, D., "The Rejection of Jesus at Nazareth (Luke iv 16-30)," Novum Testamentum 13 (1971) 161-180.

Hinnebusch, P., "Jesus, the New Elijah in Saint Luke," The Bible Today #31 (1967) 2175-2182; #32 (1967) 2237-2244.

Hockel, A., "Angelophanien und Christophanien in der Apostelgeschichte," FS K.H. Schelkle: Wort Gottes in der Zeit. FS Karl Hermann Schelkle zum 65. Geburtstag dargebracht von Kollegen, Freunden, Schülern, 1973, hrsg. H. Feld und J. Nolte (Düsseldorf 1973), 111-113.

Hood, R.T., "The Genealogies of Jesus," FS H.R. Willoughby: Early Christian Origins. Studies in Honor of H.R. Willoughby, ed. A.P. Wikgren (Quadrangle Books; Chicago 1961), 1-15.

Hooker, M., Jesus and the Servant. The Influence of the Servant Concept of Deutero-Isaiah in the New Testament (London 1959).

_____, "'Beginning with Moses and from all the Prophets,'" FS M. de Jonge: From Jesus to John. Essays on Jesus and New Testament Christology in Honour of Marinus de Jonge, ed. M.C. De Boer (Journal for the Study of the New Testament, Supplement Series, 84; Sheffield 1993), 216-230.

Howard, Jr., D.M., "David," Anchor Bible Dictionary, II, 41-46.

Hurtado, L.W., One God, One Lord. Early Christian Devotion and Ancient Jewish Monotheism (Philadelphia 1988).

_____, *Lord Jesus Christ: Devotion to Jesus in Earliest Christianity* (Grand Rapids 2003).

Jacquier, E., *Les Actes des Apôtres* (Paris 1926).
Jeremias, J., παῖς θεοῦ, *Theological Dictionary of the New Testament*, V, 700-707.
Johnson, L.T., *The Literary Function of Possessions in Luke-Acts* (Missoula 1977).
_____, *The Gospel of Luke* (Sacra Pagina, 3; Collegeville 1991).
_____, *The Acts of the Apostles* (Sacred Pagina, 5; Collegeville 1992).
_____, *Living Jesus: Learning the Heart of the Gospel* (San Francisco 1998).
_____, "The Christology of Luke-Acts," FS J.D. Kingsbury: *Who do you say that I am? Essays on Christology in honor of Jack Dean Kingsbury*, ed. M.A. Powell and D.R. Bauer (Louisville 1 1999), 49-65.
Johnson, W.C., "The Old Testament Basis for the Doctrine of the Deity of Christ," *Gordon Review* 6 (1961) 62-79.
Jones, D.L., "The Title *Christos* in Luke-Acts," *Catholic Biblical Quarterly* 32 (1970) 69-76.
_____, "The Title *Kyrios* in Luke-Acts," in G.W. MacRae (ed.), *Society of Biblical Literature, 1974 Seminar Papers. One Hundred Tenth Annual Meeting, 24-27 October 1974* (Society of Biblical Literature, Seminar Papers, 6; Cambridge, Massachusetts 1974), 85-101.
_____, "The Title 'Servant' in Luke-Acts," in C.H. Talbert (ed.), *Luke Acts: New Perspectives from the Society of Biblical Literature Seminar* (New York 1984), 148-165.

Karris, R.J., *Luke: Artist and Theologian. Luke's Passion Account as Literature* (New York 1985).
_____, "Luke 23:47 and the Lucan View of Jesus' Death,"in D.D. Sylva (ed.) *Reimaging the Death of the Lukan Jesus* (Bonner Biblische Beiträge, 73; Frankfurt 1990), 68-78 [text], 187-189 [notes].
Kealy, S.P., *The Gospel of Luke* (Denville 1979).
Keck, L.E. "Toward the Renewal of New Testament Christology," *New Testament Studies* 32 (1986) 362-377.

Kilgallen, J.J., *The Stephen Speech: A Literary and Redactional Study of Acts 7,2-53* (Analecta Biblica 67; Rome 1976).

_____, "Luke 2,41-50: Foreshadowing of Jesus, Teacher," *Biblica* 66 (1985) 553-559.

_____, "Acts 13,38-39: Culmination of Paul's Speech in Pisidia," *Biblica* 69 (1988) 480-506.

_____, "'Peace' in the Gospel of Luke and Acts of the Apostles," *Studia missionalia* 38 (1989) 55-79.

_____, "The Conception of Jesus (Luke 1,35)," *Biblica* 78 (1997) 225-246.

_____, "Your Servant Jesus Whom You Anointed (Acts 4,27)," *Revue biblique* 105 (1998) 185-201.

_____, "Jesus' First Trial: Messiah and Son of God (Luke 22,66-71)," *Biblica* 80 (1999) 401-414.

_____, "The Obligation to Heal," *Biblica* 82 (2001) 401-409.

Kilpatrick, G.D., "The Spirit, God and Jesus in Acts," *Journal of Theological Studies* 15 (1964) 63.

_____, "'Kurios' in the Gospels," FS F.-J. Leenhardt: *L'Évangile hier et aujourd'hui. Mélanges offerts au Professeur Franz-J. Leenhardt* (Genève 1968), 65-70.

Kimball, C.A., *Jesus' Exposition of the Old Testament in Luke's Gospel* (Journal for the Study of the New Testament, Supplement Series, 94; Sheffield 1994).

Kingsbury, J.D., "Jesus as the 'Prophet Messiah' in Luke's Gospel," FS L.E. Keck: *The Future of Christology. Essays in Honor of Leander E. Keck*, ed. A. J. Malherbe and W. A. Meeks (Minneapolis 1993), 29-42.

Kliesch, J.A., *Das heilsgeschichte Credo in den Reden der Apostelgeschichte* (Cologne 1975).

Koet, B.J., *Five Studies on Interpretation of Scriptures in Luke-Acts* (Leuven 1989).

Korn, M., *Die Geschichte Jesu in veränderter Zeit* (Wissenschaftliche Untersuchungen zum Neuen Testament 2/51; Tübingen 1993).

Kränkl, E., *Jesus der Knecht Gottes. Die heilsgeschichtliche Stellung Jesu in den Reden der Apostelgeschichte* (Biblische Untersuchungen 8; Regensburg 1972).

Kremer, J., ed., *Les Actes des Apôtres: Traditions, rédaction, théologie* (Bibliotheca Ephemeridum theologicarum Lovaniensium, 48; Leuven 1979).

Kürzinger, J., *The Acts of the Apostles*, 2 vols., tr. A. N. Fuerst (London 1969).

Kurz, W.S., "Acts 3:19-26 as a Test of the Role of Eschatology in Lukan Christology," in P.J. Achtemeier (ed.), *Society of Biblical Literature, Seminar Papers, 1977. One Hundred Thirteenth Annual Meeting, 28-31 December 1977* (Society of Biblical Literture, Seminar Papers, 11; Missoula 1977), 309-323.

_____, "Hellenistic Rhetoric in the Christological Proof of Luke-Acts," *Catholic Biblical Quarterly* 42 (1980) 171-195.

_____, "Luke 3:23-38 and Greco-Roman and Biblical Genealogies," in C.H. Talbert (ed.), *Luke-Acts: New Perspectives from the Society of Biblical Literature Seminar* (New York 1984), 169-187.

Kümmel W.G., *Jesus der Menschensohn* (Sitzungsberichte der Wissenschaftlichen Gesellschaft an der Johann W. Goethe-Universität, Frankfurt am Main, 3; Stuttgart 1984).

Ladd, G.E., "The Christology of Acts," *Found* 11 (1968) 27-41.

Lafferty, O.J., "Acts 2:14-36: A Study in Christology," *Dunwoodie Review* 6 (1966) 235-253.

Lagrange, M.-J., *Évangile selon Saint Luc*, 7th ed. (Paris 1948).

Lake, K.: cf. Foakes Jackson, F.J.

Lampe, G.W.H., "The Lucan Portrait of Jesus," *New Testament Studies* 2 (1955-1956) 160-175.

Laurentin, R, *Structure et Théologie de Luc I–II* (Études bibliques; Paris 1957).

_____, *Jésus au temple. Mystère de Pâques et foi de Marie en Luc 2,48-50* (Études bibliques; Paris 1966).

LaVerdiere, E., "Biblical Update, Acts of the Apostles: Jesus Christ, Lord of All," *The Bible Today* 24 (1986) 73-78.

Laymon, C.M., *Luke's Portrait of Christ* (Nashville 1959).

Leaney, A.R.C., *A Commentary on the Gospel according to Luke* (Black's New Testament Commentaries; Edinburgh 1958).

Legrand, L., "L'arrière plan néo-testamentaire de Lc I.35," *Revue biblique* 70 (1963) 161-192.

Lemcio, E.E., *The Past of Jesus in the Gospels* (Society for New Testament Studies, Monograph Series, 68; Cambridge 1991).

Lenski, R.C.H., *The Interpretation of St. Luke's Gospel* (Columbus 1946).

Léon-Dufour, X., éd., *Les Miracles de Jésus selon le Nouveau Testament* (Paris 1977).

Lindars, B., "The Myth of the Son of Man," in B. Lindars, *Jesus Son of Man: A Fresh Examination of the Son of Man Sayings in the Gospels in the Light of Recent Research* (Society for Promoting Christian Knowledge; London 1983), 1-16.

_____, "The Son of Man in Luke-Acts," in B. Lindars, *Jesus Son of Man: A Fresh Examination of the Son of Man Sayings in the Gospels in the Light of Recent Research* (Society for Promoting Christian Knowledge; London 1983), 132-144.

Lövestam, E., *Son and Savior: A Study of Acts 13:32-37. With an Appendix: "Son of God" in the Synoptic Gospels* (Lund 1961).

Lohfink, G., "Eine alttestamentliche Darstellungsform für Gotteserscheinungen in den Damaskusberichten (Apg 9; 22; 26)," *Biblische Zeitschrift* 9 (1965) 246-257.

_____, *Paulus vor Damaskus* (Stuttgart 1965).

_____, *Die Himmelfahrt Jesu. Untersuchungen zu den Himmelfahrts- und Erhöhungstexten bei Lukas* (Studien zum Alten und Neuen Testament, 26; Munich 1971).

Lohse, E., *Märtyrer und Gottesknecht* (Forschungen zur Religion und Literatur des Alten und Neuen Testaments, N.F. 46; Göttingen 1955).

_____, *Die Auferstehung Jesu Christi im Zeugnis des Lukas-evangeliums* (Biblische Studien [N], 31; Neukirchen 1961).

_____, "Lukas al Theologie der Heilsgeschichte," in E. Lohse, *Die Einheit des Neuen Testaments. Exegetische Studien zur Theologie des Neuen Testaments* (Göttingen 1973), 145-164.

Loisy, A., *Les Actes des Apôtres* (Paris 1920).

_____, *L'Évangile selon Luc* (Paris 1924).

Longenecker, R.N., "The Fundamental Conviction of New Testament Christology: The Obedience/Faithfulness/Sonship of Christ," in J.B. Green and M. Turner (eds.), *Jesus of Nazareth: Lord and Christ: Essays on the Historical Jesus and New Testament Christology* (Grand Rapids 1994), 473-488. [NB: In the preface this work is dedicated to I.H. Marshall. But no mention of him appears in the title, as would normally be the case for a Festschrift, nor is the work usually treated as a Festschrift in bibliographical listings.]

Lyonnet, S., "Le récit de l'Annonciation et la Maternité Divine de la Sainte Vierge, " *Ami du Clergé* 90 (1956) 33-48.

_____, "La voie dans les Actes des Apôtres, " *Recherches de science religieuse* 69 (1981) 149-164.

MacRae, G.W., "'Whom Heaven Must Receive until the Time': Reflections on the Christology of Acts," *Interpretation* 27 (1973) 151-165.

Maddox, R., *The Purpose of Luke-Acts* (Forschungen zur Religion und Literatur des Alten und Neuen Testaments, 126; Göttingen 1982).

Mahoney, M., "Luke 21:14-15: Editorial Rewriting or Authenticity?," *Irish Theological Quarterly* 47 (1980) 220-238.

Maile, John F., "The Ascension in Luke-Acts," *Tyndale Bulletin* 37 (1986) 29-59.

Mainville, O., "Le messianisme de Jésus. Le rapport annonce/accomplissement entre Lc 1,35 et Ac 2,33, " in J. Verheyden (ed.), *The Unity of Luke-Acts* (Bibliotheca Ephemeridum theologicarum Lovaniensium, 142; Leuven 1999), 313-327.

Mánek, J, "The New Exodus in the Books of Luke," *Novum Testamentum* 2 (1958) 8-23.

Manson, T.W., "The Life of Jesus: A Survey of the Available Material. (3) The Work of Luke," *Bulletin of the John Rylands Library* 28 (1944) 382-403.

_____, *The Sayings of Jesus as Recorded in the Gospels according to St Matthew and St Luke* (London 1949).

Marshall, I.H., "The Resurrection of Jesus in Luke," *Tyndale Bulletin* 24 (1973) 55-98.

_____, "The Significance of Pentecost," *Scottish Journal of Theology* 30 (1977) 347-369.

_____, *I Believe in the Historical Jesus* (Grand Rapids 1977).

_____, *The Gospel of Luke: A Commentary on the Greek Text* (New International Greek Testament Commentary; Grand Rapids 1978).

_____, *The Acts of the Apostles* (Tyndale New Testament Commentaries, 5; Leicester 1980).

_____, "Incarnational Christology in the New Testament," FS D. Guthrie: *Christ the Lord. Studies in Christology Presented to Donald Guthrie*, ed. H.H. Rowdon (Leicester 1982), 1-16.

_____, *Luke: Historian and Theologian* (Grand Rapids 1989).

_____, *The Origins of New Testament Christology*, updated edition (Downers Grove 1990).

_____, *Jesus the Savior: Studies in New Testament Theology* (Downers Grove 1990).

_____, *The Acts of the Apostles* (New Testament Guides, Sheffield 1992).

_____, "The Christology of Luke-Acts and the Pastoral Epistles," FS M.D. Goulder: *Crossing the Boundaries. Essays in Biblical Interpretatioin in Honour of Michael D. Goulder*, ed. S.E. Porter, P. Joyce, D.E. Orton (Studies in Biblical Interpretation, 8; Leiden 1994), 167-182.

Martin, H., *Luke's Portrait of Jesus* (London 1949).

Martin, R.P., "Salvation and Discipleship in Luke's Gospel," *Interpretation* 30 (1976) 366-380.

Martini, C.M., "Riflessioni sulla cristologica degli Atti," *Sacra Doctrina* 16 (1971) 525-534.

Matera, F., "Luke 22,66-71: Jesus before the ΠΡΕΣΒΥΤΕΡΙΟΝ," in F. Neirynck (ed.), *The Gospel of Luke*, revised and enlarged (Bibliotheca Ephemeridum theologicarum Lovaniensium, 32; Leuven 1989), 517-533.

Mattill, A.J., *Luke and the Last Things: A Perspective for the Understanding of Lukan Thought* (Dillsboro 1979).

_____ and Mattill, M.B., *A Classified Bibliography of Literature on the Acts of the Apostles* (New Testament Tools and Studies, 7; Leiden 1966).

Mattill, M.B.: cf. Mattill, A.J.

McNicol, A.J., "Rebuilding the House of David: The Function of the Benedictus in Luke-Acts," *Restoration Quarterly* 40 (1998) 25-38.

Meeks, W.A., "Asking Back to Jesus' Identity," FS M. de Jonge: *From Jesus to John. Essays on Jesus and New Testament Christology in Honour of Marinus de Jonge*, ed. M.C. De Boer (Journal for the Study of the New Testament, Supplement Series, 84; Sheffield 1993), 38-50.

Ménard, J.E., "*Pais theou* as Messianic Title in the Book of Acts," *Catholic Biblical Quarterly* 19 (1957) 83-92.

Menzies, R.P., *The Development of Early Christian Pneumatology with Special Reference to Luke-Acts* (Journal for the Study of the New Testament, Supplement Series, 54; Sheffield 1991).

Merk, O. "Das Reich Gottes in den lukanischen Schriften," FS W.G. Kümmel: *Jesus und Paulus. Festschrift für Werner George Kümmel zum 70. Geburtstag*, hrsg. E.E. Ellis und E. Gräßer (Göttingen 1975), 201-220.

Metzger, B.M., *A Textual Commentary on the Greek New Testament*, 2nd ed. (Stuttgart 1994).

Michel, H.-J., "Heilsgegenwart und Zukunft bei Lukas," FS A. Vögtle: *Gegenwart und kommendes Reich. Schülergabe Anton Vögtle*, hrsg. P. Fiedler und D. Zeller (Stuttgarter Biblische Beiträge, 6; Stuttgart 1975), 101-115.

Miller, R.J., "Elijah, John, and Jesus in the Gospel of Luke," *New Testament Studies* 34 (1988) 611-612.

Minear, P.S., "Luke's Use of the Birth Stories," FS P. Schubert: *Studies in Luke-Act. Studies in Honor of Paul Schubert*, ed. L.E. Keck and J.L. Martyn (New York 1966), 111-130.

_____, "Dear Theo: The Kerygmatic Intention and Claim of the Book of Acts," *Interpretation* 27 (1973) 131-150.

_____, *To Heal and to Reveal: The Prophetic Vocation according to Luke* (New York 1976).

Moessner, D.P., "Luke 9:1-50: Luke's Preview of the Journey of the Prophet like Moses of Deuteronomy," *Journal of Biblical Literature* 102 (1983) 575-605.

_____, "'The Christ Must Suffer': New Light on the Jesus – Peter, Stephen, Paul Parallels in Luke-Acts," *Novum Testamentum* 28 (1986) 220-256, esp. 250-253.

_____, *Lord of the Banquet: The Literary and Theological Significance of the Lukan Travel Narrative* (Philadelphia 1989).

_____, "Two Lords 'at the right hand': the Psalms and an Intertextual Reading of Peter's Pentecost Speech (Acts 2:14-36)," FS J.B. Tyson: *Literary Studies in Luke-Acts. Essays in Honor of Joseph B. Tyson*, ed. R.P. Thompson and T.E. Phillips (Macon 1998), 215-232.

Moule, C.F.D., "The Christology of Acts," FS P. Schubert: *Studies in Luke-Act. Studies in Honor of Paul Schubert*, ed. L.E. Keck and J.L. Martyn (New York 1966), 159-185

_____, *The Origin of Christology* (Cambridge 1977).

Müller, K., "Der Menschensohn im Danielzyklus," FS A. Vögtle: *Jesus und der Menschensohn. Für Anton Vögtle* hrsg. R. Pesch, R. Schnackenburg, O. Kaiser (Freiburg 1975), 37-80.

Müller, M., *Der Ausdruck "Menschensohn" in den Evangelien* (Acta Theologica Danica, 17; Leiden 1984).

Muñoz, A.S., "Christo, luz de los gentiles. Puntualizaciones sobre Lc 2,32," *Estudios bíblicos* 46 (1988) 27-44.

Muñoz Iglesias, S., "Lucas 1,35b," *Estudios bíblicos* 27 (1968) 275-299.

_____, "La concepción virginal en Lc 1,26-38 hoy," *Ephemerides Mariologicae* 43 (1993) 175-187.

Mußner, F., "Die Idee der Apokatastasis in der Apostelgeschichte," FS H. Junker: *Lex tua veritas. Festschrift für Herbert Junker zur Vollendung des siebzigsten Lebensjahres am 8. August 1961 von Kollegen, Freunden und Schülern*, hrsg. H. Groß und F. Mußner (Trier 1961), 293-306.

_____, *Die Apostelgeschichte* (Neue Echter Bibel Kommentar zum Neuen Testament, 5; Würzburg 1984).

_____, "Wohnung Gottes und Menschensohn nach der Stephanusperikope (Apg 6,8 – 8,2)," FS Anton Vögtle: *Jesus und der Menschensohn. Für Anton Vögtle*, hrsg. R. Pesch, R. Schnackenburg, O. Kaiser (Freiburg 1975), 283-299.

Nave, G.D., *The Role and Function of Repentance in Luke-Acts* (Atlanta 2002).

Navone, J., *Themes of St. Luke* (Rome 1970).

Neagoe, Alexandru, *The Trials of the Gospel: An Apologetic Reading of Luke's Trial Narratives* (Society for New Testament Studies, Monograph Series, 116; Cambridge 2002).

Nebe, G., *Prophetische Züge im Bilde Jesu bei Lukas* (Beiträge zur Wissenschaft vom Alten und Neuen Testament, 127; Stuttgart 1989).

Neirynck, F., ed., *The Gospel of Luke*, revised and enlarged (Bibliotheca Ephemeridum theologicarum Lovaniensium, 32; Leuven 1989).

_____, "Luke 4,16-30 and the Unity of Luke-Acts," In J. Verheyden (ed.), *The Unity of Luke-Acts* (Bibliotheca Ephemeridum theologicarum Lovaniensium, 142 ; Leuven 1999), 357-395.

Nevius, R.C., "*Kyrios* and *Jēsous* in St. Luke," *Australian Theological Review* 48 (1966) 75-77.

Neyrey, J.H., "Jesus' Address to the Women of Jerusalem (Luke 23:27-31 — A Prophetic Judgment Oracle," *New Testament Studies* 29 (1983) 74-86.

_____, "The Christology of Luke-Acts," in J.H. Neyrey, *Christ is Community: The Christologies of the New Testament* (Good News Studies, 13; Collegeville 1985), 105-141.

_____, "The Trials of Jesus in Luke-Acts," in J.H. Neyrey, *The Passion according to Luke: A Redaction Study of Luke's Soteriology* (Theological Inquiries. Studies in Contemporary Biblical and Theological Problems; New York 1985), 69-107.

Nolland, J., "Luke's Use of ΧΑΡΙΣ," *New Testament Studies* 32 (1986) 614-620.

_____, *Luke 1 – 9:20* (Word Biblical Commentary, 35a; Dallas 1989).

_____, *Luke 9:21 – 18:34* (Word Biblical Commentary, 35b; Dallas 1993).

_____, *Luke 18:35 – 24:53* (Word Biblical Commentary, 35c; Dallas 1993).

Norden E., *Agnostos Theos: Untersuchungen zur Formengeschichte religiöser Rede* (Stuttgart 1956).

Normann, F., *Christos Didaskalos: Die Vorstellung von Christus als Lehrer des ersten und zweiten Jahrhunderts* (Münsterische Beiträge zur Theologie, 32; Münster in W. 1967).

Norris, R. A., ed. and tr., *The Christological Controversy* (Sources of Early Christian Thought; Philadelphia 1988).

Nützel, J.M., *Jesus als Offenbarer Gottes nach den Lukanischen Schriften* (Forschungen zur Bibel, 39; Würzburg 1980).

O'Fearghail, F., *The Introduction to Luke-Acts: A Study of the Role of Lk 1,1 – 4,44 in the Composition of Luke's Two-Volume Work* (Analecta Biblica, 126; Rome 1991).

O'Grady, J.F., *Jesus, Lord and Christ* (New York 1973).

O'Neill, J.C. "The Use of ΚΥΡΙΟΣ in the Book of Acts," *Scottish Journal of Theology* 8 (1955) 155-174.

O'Toole, R.F., "Why Did Luke Write Acts (Lk-Acts)?" *Biblical Theology Bulletin* 7 (1977) 66-76.

_____, *Acts 26: The Christological Climax of Paul's Defense (Ac 22:1 – 26:32)* (Analecta Biblica, 78; Rome 1978).

_____, "Some Observations on *Anistêmi*, 'I Raise,' in Acts 3:22.-26," *Science et esprit* 31 (1979) 85-92.

_____, "Luke's Understanding of Jesus' Resurrection-Ascension-Exaltation," *Biblical Theology Bulletin* 9 (1979) 106-114.

_____, "Christ's Resurrection in Acts 13,13-52," *Biblica* 60 (1979) 361-372.

_____, "Christian Baptism in Luke," *Review for Religious* 39 (1980) 855-866.

_____, "Activity of the Risen Christ in Luke-Acts," *Biblica* 62 (1981) 471-498.

_____, "Paul at Athens and Luke's Notion of Worship," *Revue biblique* 89 (1982) 185-197.

_____, "Parallels between Jesus and his Disciples in Luke-Acts: A Further Study," *Biblische Zeitschrift* 27 (1983) 195-212. [For a bibliography of other authors who have written on this topic see pp. 195-196, nn. 1-6.]

_____, "Philip and the Ethiopian Eunuch (Acts VIII 25-40)," *Journal for the Study of the New Testament* 17 (1983) 25-34.

_____, "Acts 2:30 and the Davidic Covenant of Pentecost," *Journal of Biblical Literature* 102 (1983) 245-258.

_____, *The Unity of Luke's Theology. An Analysis of Luke-Acts* (Good News Studies, 9; Wilmington 1984).

_____, "Luke's Message in Luke 9:1-50," *Catholic Biblical Quarterly* 49 (1987) 74-89.

_____, "The Kingdom of God in Luke-Acts," in W. Willis (ed.), *The Kingdom of God in 20th-Century Interpretation* (Peabody 1987), 147-162.

_____, "Parallels between Jesus and Moses," *Biblical Theology Bulletin* 20 [1990] 22-29.

_____, "The Literary Form of Luke 19:1-10," *Journal of Biblical Literature* 110 (1991) 107-116.

_____, "Some Exegetical Reflections on Luke 13,10-17," *Biblica* 73 (1992) 84-107.

_____, "Reflections on Luke's Treatment of Jews in Luke-Acts," *Biblica* 74 (1993) 529-555.

_____, Does Luke Also Portray Jesus as the Christ in Luke 4:16-30?" *Biblica* 76 (1995) 498-522.

_____, "Εἰρήνη, an Underlying Theme in Acts 10,34-43," *Biblica* 77 (1996) 461-476.

_____, "How Does Luke Portray Jesus as Servant of YHWH?," *Biblica* 81 (2000) 328-346.

_____, "Il Giubileo, la 'buona notizia' (Lc 4,18-19) in Luca-Atti oggi: È per tutti, specie per i poveri e gli ultimi," in G. Leonardi, e F.G.B. Trolese (red.), *San Luca Evangelista Testimone della Fede che unisce: Atti del congresso internazionale: Padova, 16-21 Ottobre 2000*. Vol. I: *L'unità letteraria e teologica dell'opera di Luca* (Fonti e ricerche di Storia Ecclesiastica Padovana, 28; Padova 2002), 151-163.

Ott, W., *Gebet und Heil. Die Bedeutung der Gebetsparänese in der lukanischen Theologie* (Munich 1965).

Owczarek, K., *Sons of the Most High: Love of Enemies in Luke-Acts: Teaching and Practice* (Nairobi 2002).

Owen, H.P., "Stephen's Vision in Acts VII.55-6," *New Testament Studies* 1 (1954-1955) 224-226.

Paffenroth, K., *The Story of Jesus according to L* (Journal for the Study of the New Testament, Supplement Series, 147; Sheffield 1997).

Paglia, V., *Colloqui su Gesù. Letture del Vangelo secondo Luca* (Supersaggi, 15; Milan 1989).

Panier, L., *La naissance du Fils de Dieu: Sémiotique et théologie discursive Lecture de Luc 1–2* (Paris 1991).

Parsons, M.C., *The Departure of Jesus in Luke-Acts: The Ascension Narrative in Context* (Journal for the Study of the New Testament, Supplement Series, 21; Sheffield 1987).

_____, "The Unity of the Lukan Writings: Rethinking the *opinio communis*," FS H.J. Flanders: *With Steadfast Purpose: Essays on Acts in Honor of Henry Jackson Flanders, Jr.*, ed. N. H. Keathley (Waco 1990), 29-53.

Pathrapankal, J., "Christianity as a 'Way' according to the Acts of the Apostles," in J. Kremer (ed.), *Les Actes des Apôtres: Traditions, rédaction, théologie* (Bibliotheca Ephemeridum theologicarum Lovaniensium, 48; Leuven 1979), 533-539.

Penna, R., "Lo 'Spirito di Gesù' in Atti 16,7. Analisi letteraria e teologica," *Rivista Biblica* 20 (1972) 241-261.

Perrin, N., *A Modern Pilgrimage in New Testament Christology* (Philadelphia 1974).

Pesch, R., "Die Vision des Stephanus Apg. 7,55ff., im Rahmen der Apostelgeschichte," *Bibel und Leben* 6 (1965) 92-107, 170-183.

_____, *Der reiche Fischfang: Lk 5,1-11/Jo 21,1-14: Wundergeschichte – Berufungserzählung – Erscheinungsbericht* (Kommentare und Beiträge zum Alten und Neuen Testament; Düsseldorf 1969).

_____, *Die Apostelgeschichte* (Evangelisch-katholischer Kommentar zum Neuen Testament, 5/1-2; Zurich 1986).

Philipose, J. "*Kurios* in Luke: a Diagnosis," *The Bible Translator* 43 (1992) 325-333.

Plevnik, J., "The Eyewitnesses of the Risen Jesus in Luke 24," *Catholic Biblical Quarterly* 49 (1987) 90-103.

_____, "The Son of Man Seated at the Right Hand of God: Luke 22,69 in Lucan Christology," *Biblica* 72 (1991) 331-347.

Plummer, A. *Gospel according to S. Luke*, 5th ed., 7th impression (International Critical Commentary; Edinburgh 1960).

Polhill, J.B., *Acts* (The New American Commentary, 26; Nashville 1992).

Powell, M. A., *What Are They Saying About Luke?* (New York 1989).

Prete, B., *L'opera di Luca: Contenuti e prospettive* (Torino 1986).

Prior, M., *Jesus, The Liberator: Nazareth Liberation Theology (Luke 4.16-30)* (The Biblical Seminar, 26; Sheffield 1995).

Radermakers, J.: cf. Bossuyt, P., *Jésus: Parole de la grâce selon saint Luc.*

Radl, W., *Das Lukas-Evangelium* (Erträge der Forschung, 261; Darmstadt 1988).

_____, *Der Ursprung Jesu: Traditionsgeschichtliche Untersuchungen zu Lukas 1-2* (Herders Biblische Studien, 7; Freiburg 1996).

Ramsey, A.M., *The Glory of God and the Transfiguration of Christ* (London 1949).

Rasco, E., "Hans Conzelmann y la 'Historia Salutis,'" *Gregorianum* 46 (1965) 286-319.

_____, "Jesús y el Espíritu, Iglesia e 'Historia': Elementos para una lectura de Lucas," *Gregorianum* 56 (1975) 321-368.

_____, *La teologia de Lucas: origen, desarrollo, orientaciones* (Analecta Gregoriana, 201; Rome 1976).

Ravens, D.A.S., "Luke 9.7-62 and the Prophetic Role of Jesus," *New Testament Studies* 36 (1990) 119-129.

Recker, R.R., "The Lordship of Christ and Mission in the Book of Acts," *Reformed Review* [Holland, Michigan] 37 (1984) 177-186.

Reicke, B., "The Risen Lord and His Church: The Theology of Acts," *Interpretation* 13 (1959) 157-169.

_____, "Jesus in Nazareth — Lk 4,14-30," FS G. Friedrich: *Das Wort und die Wörter. Festschrift Gerhard Friedrich zum 65. Geburtstag*, hrsg. H. Balz und S. Schulz (Stuttgart 1973), 47-55.

Reid, B.O., "Voices and Angels: What Are They Talking about at the Transfiguration? A Redactional-Critical Study of Lk 9:28-36," *Biblical Research* 34 (1989) 19-31.

Rengstorf, K.H., διδάσκαλος, *Theological Dictionary of the New Testament*, II, 152-157.

Repo, E., *Der 'Weg' als Selbstbezeichnung des Urchristentums* (Helsinki 1964)

Rese, M., *Alttestamentliche Motive in der Christologie des Lukas* (Studien zum Neuen Testament, 1; Gütersloh 1969).

_____, "Einige Uberlegungen zu Lukas, XIII, 31-33," in J. Dupont (éd.), *Jésus aux origines de la christologie* (Bibliotheca Ephemeridum theologicarum Lovaniensium, 40; Louvain 1975), 201-225.

_____, "Die Funktion der altestamentlichen Zitate," in J. Kremer (Hrsg.), *Les Actes des Apôtres: Traditions, rédaction, théologie* (Bibliotheca Ephemeridum theologicarum Lovaniensium, 48; Leuven 1979), 61-79.

Resseguie, J.L., "The Lukan Portrait of Christ," *Studies in Biblical Theology* 4 (1974) 5-20.

Richard, E., *Acts 6:1 – 8:4. The Author's Method of Composition* (Society of Biblical Literature, Dissertation Series, 41: Missoula 1978).

_____, *Jesus, One and Many: The Christological Concept of New Testament Authors* (Michael Glazier Books; Collegeville 1988).

Riesenfeld, H., "The Text of Acts 10,36," FS M. Black: *Text and Interpretation: Studies in the New Testament presented to Matthew Black*, ed. E. Best and R.McL. Wilson (Cambridge 1979), 191-194.

Rieser, R., *Jesus als Lehre. Eine Untersuchung zum Ursprung der Evangelien-Überlieferung* (Wissenschaftliche Untersuchungen zum Neuen Testament, 2.7; Tübingen 1981).

Rigaux, B., *Témoignage de l'évangile de Luc* (Pour une histoire de Jésus, IV; Bruges–Paris 1970).

_____, "La petite apocalypse de Luc (XVII, 22-37)," FS G. Philips: *Ecclesia a Spirito Sancto edocta, Lumen gentium, 53* (Bibliotheca Ephemeridum theologicarum Lovaniensium, 27; Gembloux 1970), 407-438.

Robinson, J.A.T., "The Most Primitive Christology of All," *Journal of Theological Studies* 7 (1956) 177-189.

_____, "Elijah, John and Jesus: An Essay in Detection," *New Testament Studies* 4 (1957-1958) 263-281.

Robinson, Jr., W.C., "The Theological Context for Interpreting Luke's Travel Narrative (Luke 9:51ff.)," *Journal of Biblical Literature* 79 (1960) 20-31.

_____, *Der Weg des Herren. Studien zur Geschichte und Eschatologie in Lukas-Evangelium. Ein Gespräch mit Hans Conzelmann*, übersetzt von Gisela und Georg Strecker (Theologische Forschung, 36; Hamburg–Bergstedt 1964).

Roloff, J., *Die Apostelgeschichte* (Das Neue Testament Deutsch, 5; Göttingen 1981).

Rossé, G, *Il vangelo di Luca, commento esegetico e teologico* (Roma 1992).

Ruck-Schröder, A., *Der Name Gottes und der Name Jesu: Eine neutestamentliche Studie* (Wissenschaftliche Monographien zum Alten und Neuen Testament 80; Neukirchener 1999).

Russ, R., "Das Vermächtnis des gekreuzigten Herrn. Jesu letzte Worte in Evangelium nach Lukas," *Bible und Kirche* 50 (1995) 128-135.

Sabbe, M., "The Son of Man Saying in Acts 7,56," in J. Kremer (éd.), *Les Actes des Apôtres. Traditions, rédaction, théologie* (Bibliotheca Ephemeridum theologicarum Lovaniensium, 48; Leuven 1979), 241-279.

Sabourin, L., *La christologie à partir de textes cleés* (Recherches. Nouvelle série, 9; Montreal 1986).

_____, *Il Vangelo di Luca* (Roma 1989).

Saito, T., *Die Mosevorstellungen im Neuen Testament* (Bern 1977).

Sanders, J.A., "Isaiah in Luke," *Interpretatiion* 36 (1982) 144-155.

Schille, G., *Die Apostelgeschichte des Lukas*, 2. Ausg. (Theologischer Handkommentar zum Neuen Testament, 5; Berlin 1983).

Schmidt, D., "Luke's 'Innocent' Jesus: A Scriptural Apologetic," in R.J. Cassidy and P.J. Sharper (eds.) *Political Issues in Luke-Acts*, (Maryknoll 1983), 111-121.

Schnackenburg, R., "Der eschatologische Abschnitt Lk 17,20-37," FS B. Rigaux: *Mélanges Bibliques en hommage au R.P. Béda Rigaux*, éd. A. Descamps et A. de Halleux (Gemboux 1970), 213-234.

Schneider, G., *Verleugnung, Verspottung und Verhör Jesu nach Lukas 22,54-71. Studien zur lukanischen Darstellung der Passion* (Studien zum Alten und Neuen Testament, 22; Munich 1969).

_____, "'Der Menschensohn' in der lukanischen Christologie," FS A. Vögtle: *Jesus und der Menschensohn. Für Anton Vögtle*, hrsg. R. Pesch, R. Schnackenburg, O. Kaiser (Freiburg 1975), 267-282.

_____, *Parusiegleichnisse in Lukas-Evangelium* (Stuttgarter Bibel Studien, 74; Stuttgart 1975).

_____, *Die Apostelgeschichte* (Herders theologische Kommentar zum Neuen Testament, 5/1; Freiburg 1980).

_____, *Die Apostelgeschichte* (Herders theologische Kommentar zum Neuen Testament, 5/2; Freiburg 1982).

_____, "Gott und Christus als ΚΥΡΙΟΣ nach der Apostelgeschichte," FS H. Zimmermann: *Begegnung mit dem Wort. Festschrift für Heinrich Zimmermann*, hrsg. J. Zmijewski und E. Nellessen (Bonner Biblische Beiträge, 53; Bonn 1980), 161-174.

_____, *Das Evangelium nach Lukas*, 2. ed. (Ökumenischer Taschenbuchkommentar zum Neuen Testament, 3/1-2; Götersloh 1984).

_____, *Lukas. Theologie der Heilgeschichte. Aufsätze zum lukanischen Doppelwerk* (Bonner Biblische Beiträge, 59; Bonn 1985).

Schneider, J., "Zur Analyze des lukanischen Reiseberichtes," FS A Wikenhauser: *Synoptische Studien. Alfred Wikenhauser zum siebzigsten*

Geburtstag am 22. Februar 1953 dargebracht von Freunden, Kollegen und Schülern (München 1953), 204-229.

Schreck, C.J., "The Nazareth Pericope: Luke 4,16-30 in Recent Study," in F. Neirynck (éd.), *The Gospel of Luke*, revised and enlarged (Bibliotheca Ephemeridum theologicarum Lovaniensium, 32; Leuven 1989), 399-471.

Schürmann, H., "Zur Traditionsgeschichte der Nazareth-Pericope Lk 4,16-30," FS B. Rigaux: *Mélange Bibliques en hommage au R.P. Béda Rigaux*, éd. A. Descamps et A. de Halleux (Gemboux 1970), 187-205.

_____, "Beobachtungen zum Menschensohn-Titel in der Redequelle. Sein Vorkommen in Abschluß- und Einleitungswendungen," FS A. Vögtle: *Jesus und der Menschensohn. Für Anton Vögtle*, hrsg. R. Pesch, R. Schnackenburg, O. Kaiser (Freiburg 1975), 124-147.

_____, *Das Lukasevangelium 1,1 – 9,50*, 2nd ed. (Herders theologische Kommentar zum Neuen Testament, 3/1; Freiburg 1982).

Schütz, F., *Der leidende Christus. Die angefochtene Gemeinde und das Christuskerygma der lukanischen Schriften* (Stuttgart 1969).

Schweizer, E., "The Concept of the Davidic 'Son of God' in Acts and Its Old Testament Background," FS P. Schubert: *Studies in Luke-Act. Studies in Honor of Paul Schubert*, ed. L.E. Keck and J.L. Martyn (New York 1966), 186-193.

_____, "Menschensohn und eschatologischer Mensch im Frühjudentum," FS A. Vögtle: *Jesus und der Menschensohn. Für Anton Vögtle*, hrsg. R. Pesch, R. Schnackenburg, O. Kaiser (Freiburg 1975), 100-116.

_____, υἱός, *Theological Dictionary of the New Testament*, VIII, 380-382.

_____, "Zur lukanischen Christologie," FS G. Ebeling: *Verifikationen. Festschrift für Gerhard Ebeling zum 70. Geburtstag*, hrsg. E. Jüngel, J. Wallmann, W. Werbeck (Tübingen 1982), 43-65.

_____, *The Good News according to Luke*, tr. D.E. Green (Atlanta 1984).

Seccombe, D.P., "Luke and Isaiah," *New Testament Studies* 27 (1981) 252-259.

_____, *Possessions and the Poor in Luke-Acts* (Studien zum Neuen Testament und seiner Umwelt, B 6; Linz 1982).

Seifrid, M.A., "Jesus and the Law in Acts," *Journal for the Study of the New Testament* 30 (1987) 39-57.

_____, "Messiah and Mission in Acts: A Brief Response to J.B. Tyson (*TS* 1987)," *Journal for the Study of the New Testament* 36 (1989) 47-50.

Shelton, J.B., *Mighty in Word and Deed. The Role of the Holy Spirit in Luke-Acts* (Peabody 1991).

Smalley, S.S., "The Christology of Acts," *Expository Times* 73 (1962) 358-362.

_____, "The Christology of Acts Again," FS C.F.D. Moule: *Christ and the Spirit in the New Testament. In Honour of Charles Francis Digby Moule*, ed. B. Lindars and S.S. Smalley (Cambridge 1973), 79-93.

Soards, M., *The Speeches in Acts: Their Content, Context and Concerns* (Louisville 1994).

Squires, J.T., *The Plan of God in Luke-Acts* (Society of New Testament Studies, Monograph Series, 76; Cambridge 1993).

Stählin, G., *Die Apostelgeschichte übersetzt und erklärt* (Das Neue Testament Deutsch, 5; Göttingen 1962).

_____, "Τὸ πνεῦμα Ἰησοῦ (Apostelgeschichte 16:7)," in FS C.F.D. Moule: *Christ and the Spirit in the New Testament. In Honour of Charles Francis Digby Moule*, ed. B. Lindars and S.S. Smalley (Cambridge 1973), 229-252.

Stock, A., *The Way in the Wilderness: Exodus, Wilderness and Moses Themes in the Old Testament and New* (Collegeville 1969).

Stonehouse, N.B., *The Witness of Luke to Christ* (Grand Rapids 1951).

Strauss, M.L., *The Davidic Messiah in Luke-Acts. The Promise and its Fulfillment in Lukan Christology* (Journal for the Study of the New Testament, Supplement Series, 110; Sheffield 1995).

Summers, R., *Jesus. The Universal Savior: A Commentary on Luke* (Waco 1972).

Swartley, W.D., "Politics and Peace (*Eirene*) in Luke's Gospel," in R.J. Cassidy and P.J. Sharper (eds.), *Political Issues in Luke-Acts* (Maryknoll 1983), 18-37.

Sylva, D.D., "The Cryptic Clause ἐν τοῖς τοῦ πατρός μου δεῖ εἶναι με in Lk. 2:49b," *Zeitschrift für die neutestamentliche Wissenschaft* 78 (1987) 132-140.

Talbert, C.H., "The Lukan Presentation of Jesus' Ministry in Galilee," *Review and Expositor* 64 (1967) 492-497.

_____, *Literary Patterns, Theological Themes, and the Genre of Luke-Acts* (Society of Biblical Literature, Monograph Series, 20; Missoula 1974).

_____, *Reading Luke: A Literary and Theological Commentary on the Third Gospel* (New York 1982).

_____, *Reading Luke-Acts in its Mediterranean Milieu* (Novum Testamentum, Supplements, 107; Boston 2003)

Tannehill, R.C., "A Study in the Theology of Luke-Acts," *Australian Theological Review* 43 (1961) 195-203.

_____, "The Mission of Jesus according to Luke IV 16-30," in E. Gräßer, A. Strobel, R.C. Tannehill, W. Eltester (Hrsg.), *Jesus in Nazareth* (Beihefte zur Zeitschrift für die neutestamentliche Wissenschaft, 40; Berlin 1972), 51-75.

_____, *The Narrative Unity of Luke-Acts: A Literary Interpretation*, Vol. 1 (Philadelphia 1986).

_____, *The Narrative Unity of Luke-Acts: A Literary Interpretation*, Vol. 2 (Philadelphia 1990).

Tatum, W.B., "The Epoch of Israel: Luke I–II and the Theological Plan of Luke-Acts," *New Testament Studies* 13 (1966-1967) 184-195.

Taylor, N.H., "Luke-Acts and the Temple," *The Unity of Luke-Acts*, ed. J. Verheyden (Bibliotheca Ephemeridum theologicarum Lovaniensium, 142 ; Leuven 1999),709-721.

Taylor, V. *The Passion Narrative of St. Luke: A Critical and Historical Investigation* (Cambridge 1972).

Teeple, H.M., *The Mosaic Eschatological Prophet* (Philadelphia 1957).

Thiselton, A.C., "Christology in Luke, Speech-Act Theory, and the Problem of Dualism in Christology after Kant," in J. B. Green and M. Turner (eds.), *Jesus of Nazareth: Lord and Christ: Essays on the Historical Jesus and New Testament Christology* (Grand Rapids 1994), 453-472. [NB: In the preface this work is dedicated to I.H. Marshall. But no mention of him appears in the title, as would normally be the case for a Festschrift, nor is the work usually treated as a Festschrift in bibliographical listings.]

Tiede, D.L., *Prophecy and History in Luke-Acts* (Philadelphia 1980).

_____, "'Glory to Thy People Israel': Luke-Acts and the Jews," in K.H. Richards (ed.), *Society of Biblical Literature, Seminar Papers, 1986*.

One Hundred Twenty-Second Annual Meeting, 22-25 November 1986 (Society of Biblical Literature, Seminar Papers, 25; Atlanta 1986), 142-151.

Tödt, H.E., *The Son of Man in the Synoptic Tradition*, tr. D.M. Barton (Philadephia 1965).

Topel, L.J., *Children of a Compassionate God: A Theological Exegesis of Luke 6:20-49* (Collegeville 2001).

Trites, A.A., "The Prayer Motif in Luke-Acts," in C. H. Talbert (ed.), *Perspectives on Luke-Acts* (National Association of Baptist Professors of Religion Special Studies Series, 5; Danville 1978), 168-186.

_____, "The Transfiguration in the Theology of Luke. Some Redactional Links," FS G.B. Caird: *The Glory of Christ in the New Testament: Studies in Christology in Memory of George Bradford Caird*, ed. L.D. Hurst and N.T. Wright (Oxford 1987), 71-82.

Trocmé, É., *Le "Livre des Actes" e l'histoire* (Paris 1957).

Tuckett, C.M., "The Son of Man in Q," FS M. de Jonge: *From Jesus to John. Essays on Jesus and New Testament Christology in Honour of Marinus de Jonge*, ed. M.C. De Boer (Journal for the Study of the New Testament, Supplement Series, 84; Sheffield 1993), 196-215.

_____, "The Lukan Son of Man," in C.M. Tuckett, *Luke's Literary Achievement. Collected Essays* (Journal for the Study of the New Testament, Supplement Series, 116; Sheffield 1995), 198-217.

_____, "The Christology of Luke-Acts," in Verheyden, J. (ed.), *The Unity of Luke-Acts* (Bibliotheca Ephemeridum theologicarum Lovaniensium, 142; Leuven 1999), 133-164.

Turner, M., "The Spirit of Christ and Christology," FS D. Guthrie: *Christ the Lord. Studies in Christology Presented to Donald Guthrie*, ed. H.H. Rowdon (Leicester 1982), 168-190.

_____, "The Spirit and the Power of Jesus' Miracles in the Lucan Conception," *Novum Testamentum* 33 (1991) 124-152.

_____, "The Spirit of Christ and 'Divine' Christology," in J.B. Green and M. Turner (eds.), *Jesus of Nazareth: Lord and Christ: Essays on the Historical Jesus and New Testament Christology* (Grand Rapids 1994), 413-436. [NB: In the preface this work is dedicated to I.H. Marshall. But no mention of him appears in the title, as would normally be the case for a Festschrift, nor is the work usually treated as a Festschrift in bibliographical listings.]

Tyson, J.B., "The Lukan Version of the Trial of Jesus," *Novum Testamentum* 3 (1959) 249-258.

_____, *The Death of Jesus in Luke-Acts* (Columbia 1986).

_____, "Further Thoughts on The Death of Jesus in Luke-Acts," *Perkins School of Theology Journal* 40 (1987) 48-50.

van Iersel, B.M.F., *"Der Sohn" in den synoptischen Jesusworten. Christusbezeichung der Gemeide oder Selbstbezeichung Jesu* (Leiden 1961).

van Segbroeck, F., *The Gospel of Luke: A Cumulative Bibliography 1973-1988* (Bibliotheca Ephemeridum theologicarum Lovaniensium, 88; Louvain 1989).

van Stempvoort, P.A., "The Interpretation of the Ascension in Luke and Acts," *New Testament Studies* 5 (1958-1959) 30-42.

van Unnik, W.C., "L'usage de σώζειν 'Sauver' et des dérivés dans les évangiles synoptiques," in W.C. Unnik, *Sparsa collecta* (Supplements to Novum Testamentum, 29; Leiden 1973), 16-34.

van Zyl, S. and van Aarde, A.-G., "Die Lukaanse Jesusbeeld: In daaloog met Wihelm Bousset se 'Kyrios Christos'," *Hervormde Teologiese Studies* 53 (1997) 185-208.

Verheyden, J., "The Unity of Luke-Acts: What Are We Up To?", in J. Verheyden (ed.), *The Unity of Luke-Acts*, (Bibliotheca Ephemeridum theologicarum Lovaniensium, 142; Leuven 1999), 3-56.

Via, E.J., "Moses and Meaning in Luke-Acts: A Redactional Critical Analysis of Acts 7:35-37," dissertation, Marquette University, 1976. [Available on 35mm microfilm and available via inter-library loan from Marquette University Library.]

Vögtle, A., *Die 'Gretchenfrage' des Menschensohnproblems. Bilanz und Perspektive* (Questiones Disputatae, 152; Freiburg 1994).

von Baer, H., "Der Heilige Geist in den Lukasschriften. Zusammenfassende Beurteilung der lukanischen Anschauung von Heiligen Geiste," in G. Braumann (Hrsg.), *Das Lukas-Evangelium* (Wege der Forschung, 280; Darmstadt 1974), 1-6.

von Hase, K.A., *Geschichte Jesu*, 2. Ausg. (Leipzig 1891).

von Rad, G.: cf. W. Foerster.

Voss, G., *Die Christologie der lukanischen Schriften in Grundzügen* (Studia neotestamentica, 2; Paris 1965).

Walasky, P. W., "The Trial and Death of Jesus in the Gospel of Luke," *Journal of Biblical Literature* 94 (1975) 81-93.

Weimar, P., "Daniel 7. Eine Textanalyse," FS A. Vögtle: *Jesus und der Menschensohn. Für Anton Vögtle*, hrsg. R. Pesch, R. Schnackenburg, O. Kaiser (Freiburg 1975), 11-36.

Weiser, A., *Die Apostelgeschichte* (Ökumenischer Taschenbuchkommentar zum Neuen Testament, 5/1; Gütersloh 1981).

_____, *Die Apostelgeschichte* (Ökumenischer Taschenbuchkommentar zum Neuen Testament, 5/2; Gütersloh 1985).

Wilckens, U., *Die Missionsreden der Apostelgeschichte* (Wissenschaftliche Untersuchungen zum Neuen Testament, 5; Neukirchen 1961).

Wilcock, M., *The Savior of the World: The Message of Luke's Gospel* (The Bible Speaks Today; Downers Grove 1979).

Wilson, S.G, *The Gentiles and the Gentile Mission in Luke-Acts* (Society of New Testament Studies, Monograph Series, 23; Cambridge 1973).

Windisch, H., "Die Christusepiphanie vor Damascus (Acts 9, 22 und 26) und ihre religionsgeschichtliche Parallelen," *Zeitschrift für die neutestamentliche Wissenschaft* 31 (1932) 1-23.

Witherington, III, B., *The Christology of Jesus* (Minneapolis 1990).

_____, "Salvation and Health in Christian Antiquity: The Soteriology of Luke-Acts in Its First Century Setting," in I.H. Marshall and D. Peterson (eds.), *Witness to the Gospel: The Theology of Acts* (Peabody 1987), 145-166.

Wren, M., "Sonship in Luke: The Advantage of a Literary Approach," *Scottish Journal of Theology* 37 (1984) 301-311.

Zahl, P.F.M., *The First Christian: Universal Truth in the Teachings of Jesus* (Grand Rapids 2003).

Zedda, S., "Spirito Santo e missione profetica di Gesù in Lc 4:18," *Ricerche Storico-bibliche* 2 (1990) 71-79.

_____, *Teologia della salvezza nel Vangelo di Luca* (Studi Biblici, 18; Bologna 1991).

Zerwick, M., *Analysis philologica Novi Testamenti graeci* (Scripta Pontificii Instituti Biblici, 107; Romae 1953).

_____ and Grosvenor, M., *A Grammatical Analysis of the Greek New Testament*, 5th ed. (Rome 1996).

Ziesler, J.A., "The Name of Jesus in the Acts of the Apostles," *Journal for the Study of the New Testament* 4 (1979) 28-41.

Zmijewski, J., *Die Eschatologiereden des Lukas-Evangeliums. Eine traditions- und redaktionsgeschichtliche Untersuchung zu Lk 21,5-36 und Lk 17,20-37* (Bonner Biblische Beiträge, 40; Bonn 1972).

Zwiep, A.W., *The Ascension of the Messiah in Lukan Christology* (Novum Testamentum, Supplements, 87; Leiden 1997).

Index of Modern Authors

Index of Principal Scripture Texts from Luke and Acts

Index of Topics

This index of topics does not claim to be exhaustive, but along with the Table of Contents it should prove useful to anyone who wishes to find information about Luke's Christology or other data found in this book.

Finito di stampare
nel mese di Ottobre 2004

presso la tipografia
"Giovanni Olivieri" di E. Montefoschi
00187 Roma • Via dell'Archetto, 10, 11, 12
Tel. 06 6792327 • E-mail: tip.olivieri@libero.it